MORAL
TRANSFORMATION

The Original Christian Paradigm of Salvation

A. J. Wallace   R. D. Rusk

BRIDGEHEAD PUBLISHING
NEW ZEALAND

Moral Transformation:
The Original Christian Paradigm of Salvation

Published by Bridgehead Publishing, New Zealand.

Printed by CreateSpace, Seattle, Washington, USA.

Scripture quotations are based on the New Revised Standard Version Bible, copyright © 1989 by the Division of Christian Education of the National Council of the Churches of Christ in the USA, and are used by permission. Some quotations contain different translations of certain words or phrases.

Cover image is of New Testament Papyrus 1 (Gregory-Aland numbering), housed at the University of Pennsylvania Museum (E 2746), and public domain. Cover paper texture is by FudgeGraphics.com, and used by permission.

National Library of New Zealand Cataloguing-in-Publication Data

Wallace, A. J.
Moral transformation : the original Christian paradigm of salvation
/ A.J. Wallace, R.D. Rusk.
ISBN 978-1456389802
1. Jesus Christ—Significance. 2. Salvation—Christianity—History
of doctrines. 3. Spiritual life—Christianity. I. Rusk, R. D. II. Title.
234—dc 22

Contents

Part 3: The Importance of Jesus

Part 4: Ideas throughout history

Summary and Conclusion

Introduction

Many Christians today assume that Christian doctrines have been faithfully passed down from the Apostles without change throughout history. Yet Christians at different times in history have believed different ideas. Even today, we can look and see that Roman Catholics, Pentecostals, and the Reformed churches all hold differing beliefs. Throughout the last two thousand years, many Christian groups have existed, each with varying beliefs and interpretations of the Bible. Many of their writings still survive today. By studying these writings, historians can see the ways in which their ideas have differed from previous ideas. Tracing these differences reveals that massive doctrinal changes have occurred throughout Christian history.

One famous period of change in Christianity was the Protestant Reformation of 1517 AD to 1648 AD. Many modern Protestant doctrines originated during this time. The Reformation began as an attempt to reform the Roman Catholic Church's position on certain matters of doctrine and practice. It quickly escalated, and various social and political factors resulted in 131 years of European wars and doctrinal debates. At the end of this period, the Church had fragmented into many denominations, and individuals had freedom to follow their own beliefs. Many of the modern denominations of today formed during this period. These denominations and groups differed in many of their views, but also shared many common core beliefs about salvation and the gospel. The period since the Reformation has proven far more stable, and these common core beliefs have generally flourished. Many Christians today consider these core beliefs 'historic Christianity' without understanding the changes and controversies in their earlier history. The Reformers knowingly rejected the traditional ideas of their day, and aimed to reform tradition back to the original Christian doctrines. The violent disagreements during the Reformation reflect how strongly the Christian groups at the time held their different doctrinal views.

How could so many different Christians during this period and throughout history all see themselves as faithful to the Bible, and yet believe such different things? They all *interpreted* the Bible differently, and changes in interpretation led to changes in doctrine. The New Testament indicates that people made mistakes interpreting Paul's writings even during apostolic times.[1] Studying doctrinal history reveals two main reasons why people began to misinterpret New Testament passages. Firstly, over time readers became increasingly disconnected from the original language, people, and culture of first-century Israel. This disconnection made it difficult for readers to understand what passages meant. Secondly, the passage of time gave increasing opportunity for ideas from other sources to influence interpretation of the Bible. While the biblical text has changed little, the cultural ideas and worldviews of those who read the Bible have changed markedly. We will look at both of these factors in turn.

Why doctrines changed

Language differences played a major role in the disconnection between the New Testament and its readers. When the New Testament spread to readers who did not speak Koine Greek, they needed translations. Producing a reasonable translation is an incredibly difficult task, and even the best translation never perfectly communicates the original text. Scholars today point to many mistakes made in earlier Bible translations. One of these, the Latin Vulgate, became the dominant translation for Western Christianity in around 400 AD. For over a thousand years, knowledge of the Greek language almost disappeared from the West. Scholars had very few Greek texts available, and very few retained knowledge of Greek. During the 16th century, many scholars again began to learn ancient Greek and collect Greek texts. Studying the Bible in its original Greek became possible once more, and Christians during the Reformation did so. This proved difficult, however, since at the time only a few ancient Greek documents had been discovered. To make matters worse, the dialect of Greek in the New Testament differed from that of other ancient Greek documents discovered. As a result, scholars found it hard to determine what various Greek words used in the New Testament really meant. As recently as 150 years ago, some scholars speculated that the New Testament authors had written in a 'heavenly dialect' of Greek which had come into existence for the sole purpose of writing Scripture. To guess at what unknown words meant, scholars tried to infer their meaning based on their hypothetical origins (etymology). Unfortunately, modern linguists have concluded that this method of determining the meaning of words has fatal flaws. Fortunately, in the last 150

---

[1] 2 Peter 3:15-16.

years, archaeologists have uncovered large numbers of ancient Greek documents. We now know that the New Testament authors wrote in the common (*koine*) dialect of Greek spoken widely from around 300 BC to 300 AD. Linguists can now study thousands of pages of surviving Koine Greek documents to determine the meanings of words. As a result, modern scholars have gained a much better understanding of biblical Greek than that of the Reformers.

Cultural changes have also made the task of understanding the Bible much more difficult. People's culture, language and environment influence their way of thinking and shape their worldview. These in turn influence how people interpret and understand what they read. The authors of the New Testament lived in first-century Israel. They wrote for people who shared much of their culture, language, and social context. Consequently, their early readers could readily understand. The authors often wrote with this commonality in mind, and did not waste words to explain things already understood by their readers. Everyone knew about the political, religious and economic climates. The authors and their readers shared common history, beliefs, values and aspirations. Hence, the New Testament writers used metaphors, idioms, sarcasm, dialogue, and rhetorical statements with confidence that their readers would understand their meaning. Yet, as centuries passed, readers of the New Testament writings had less and less in common with its authors. Christianity spread across social classes and geographic boundaries, and into different social, cultural and religious climates. People living in these very different times and places had a far weaker grasp of the cultural context.

As people became increasingly disconnected from the original New Testament context, they naturally drew on ideas from their own cultures. Cultural bias influences everyone, including people who read the Bible. People tend to understand the Bible in ways that correspond with how they think about the world. The huge changes in culture that have occurred since the first century have thus caused great diversity in Biblical interpretations. As we will see later in this book, some of the major theological changes in Christian history occurred because theologians drew on ideas from their culture. A series of particularly large cultural shifts preceded and accompanied the Protestant Reformation: Western Europe moved out of the feudalistic culture of the middle ages and went through the huge cultural shifts of the Renaissance. The Reformation itself involved 131 years of major cultural change. Today, Western culture differs vastly from the culture of the New Testament authors. Having now recognised the importance of cultural context, biblical scholars have made a conscious effort in the last thirty years to understand the ancient worldview. Careful studies of ancient documents, combined with contemporary studies of different cultures around the world, have revolutionised our understanding of how ancient biblical culture and thinking differs from that of today. Dozens of recent publications analyse how people in biblical times and places understood the world around them. These findings put modern scholars in a far better position than the Reformers were to understand the New Testament in its original cultural context. Recent scholarship has shed a great deal of light on many passages in the New Testament and revealed how the original writers and audiences would have understood them. This book draws heavily on these recent studies, which bring the early Christian ideas into much clearer focus.

Developments since the Reformation

The Reformers believed that the doctrines of the Roman Catholic Church had changed and strayed away from early Christian ideas over the centuries. The Reformers aimed to undo those changes and return to the original Christian doctrines which had flourished in the early church. At the time of the Reformation, scholars had not discovered enough Christian writings from throughout church history to know whether the Reformers had really achieved their aim. By the late 18th century, this situation had changed. Researchers had discovered and published enough copies of ancient Christian writings to enable scholars to trace the changes in Christian doctrines over the centuries.[2] Their studies showed that a long string of doctrinal changes had indeed occurred within the Roman Catholic Church. Unfortunately, the studies revealed that the Reformers had not successfully identified and corrected all the doctrinal changes. Far from undoing previous changes, the Reformers had uncritically accepted many of them and introduced others. Scholars realised that the Reformation had in some ways taken the church even further away from the early Christian doctrines. Shocked, these scholars called for a return to early Christian doctrines. Their argument failed to gain much traction, however, since by then people had widely accepted the post-Reformation doctrines as an accurate reading of the Bible. Nevertheless, their findings highlighted a discrepancy between what people thought the Bible said and what the early Christians had believed. Other scholars puzzled over this

---

[2] The first study of the history of doctrine was published by the German theologian G. S. Steinbart, *System of Pure Philosophy*, 1778, according to Alister McGrath, *Historical Theology*, (Oxford: Blackwell, 1998), p. 289.

mysterious discrepancy. In the last 200 years, the discrepancy has only worsened with the discovery of many further ancient Christian writings. Different scholars have published dozens more historical studies of Christian doctrine. These studies have remained largely unanimous and have confirmed the doctrinal changes, demonstrating a huge mismatch between early Christian doctrines and the post-Reformation doctrines. We will examine this discrepancy in some detail towards the end of this book.

During the 19th century, widespread interest developed in studying the life of Jesus. According to post-Reformation theology, Jesus became incarnate to achieve salvation through his atoning death. Reasonably, this led many people to imagine that, during his life, Jesus had called people to trust in his atoning death for salvation, and perhaps also preached about his divinity. People thought that anything else the Gospels happened to say would have little importance and no relevance to salvation. The first published studies of the Gospels and the life of Jesus shocked those who held to these post-Reformation views. A few sentences in the Gospel of John seemed to support such ideas, but the vast majority of the Gospels seemed to paint a very different picture of Jesus. They recorded Jesus spending most of his time dealing with social problems. They showed him campaigning to help the poor and needy in his society and criticising the rich. Many scholars who studied the Gospels came to believe that Jesus primarily aimed to help the poor. They highlighted another apparent discrepancy between the Gospel accounts and post-Reformation theology, and their ideas became known as the 'social gospel'. Some saw the social gospel as a Bible-based call to help the poor. Others viewed it as an attack on post-Reformation doctrines, which they believed the apostle Paul had clearly taught in his letters.

At the beginning of the 20th century, almost all Christian scholars agreed that post-Reformation doctrines had a firm basis in an accurate reading of Paul's letters. This gave most Bible-believing Christians enough reason to steadfastly hold to their 'traditional' post-Reformation theology. Paul's statements on sin, righteousness, grace, faith, works and justification became seen, quite literally, as gospel.[3] The studies of the Gospels and of doctrinal history, however, still seemed to point in a very different direction. They did not seem to fit with how scholars understood Paul's writings. Many scholars attempted to resolve this discrepancy at the time by simply concluding that Paul had indeed

---

[3] Ironically, as already noted, the Bible itself cautions against relying on one's understanding of Paul's letters. (2 Peter 3:15-16).

taught doctrines that differed entirely from what the rest of the early church believed.[4] In the last thirty years, however, a massive shift has occurred in how scholars interpret Paul's writings. More and more scholars are rejecting the old post-Reformation interpretations of Paul as they improve their understanding of the context in which he wrote. These scholars now believe that Paul taught ideas that differ markedly from post-Reformation views. Ironically, this movement has become known as the 'New' Perspective on Paul. In reality, the interpretations advocated by New Perspective scholars tend to agree with the way in which Christians from the first few centuries interpreted Paul's writings.[5] Their recent scholarship has shown that Paul and the other early Christian writers all held the same basic views. This New Perspective has thus brought Christianity full circle, distancing it from the post-Reformation interpretations of Paul and instead affirming the early church's views.

Let us briefly summarise these developments. In the 18th century, scholars of doctrinal history criticised the Reformation views. They argued that those views had come from accumulated changes. Defenders of post-Reformation doctrine responded by pointing to the Bible. In the 19th century, scholars of the Gospels concluded that Jesus taught a social gospel. Defenders of post-Reformation doctrine responded by appealing to Paul's writings. In the 20th century, scholars have re-examined Paul's writings in light of a far better understanding of the ancient world and Paul's place in it. They have concluded that the Reformers fundamentally misinterpreted Paul and have called for a 'New Perspective' on Paul. Finally, in the 21st century, for the first time ever, studies of Jesus, of Paul, and of the history of doctrine all point to compatible conclusions. This book aims to draw the evidence from these different lines of study together into a clear, coherent picture of the early Christian message.

Tradition and biblical interpretation

Several of the core doctrines that came from the Reformation have become the accepted tradition of many Christians today. These doctrines have become 'how it's always been' and 'what everyone

---

[4] E.g. Arthur Cushman McGiffert, *A History of Christian Thought: Volume 1, Early and Eastern* (New York: Charles Scribner's Sons, 1932), p. 68.

[5] For example, early Christian writers such as Justin Martyr (~150 AD), Irenaeus (~160 AD), Origen (~230 AD) and Ambrosiaster (~380 AD) seem to hold 'New Perspective'-type views.

agrees on'. Christians often see them as 'the gospel' – as Christianity itself. Many of us rely upon them as comprising the safe, time-tested majority view. They form part of our creed. We may have grown up with these doctrines, heard them from the pulpits for decades, and read books about them. Many of us will have a strong attachment to these ideas from the Reformation. Therefore, understandably, the difference between those ideas and the picture of the early Christian message we present in this book may cause readers some discomfort. Christians who have held Reformation ideas for a long time can easily find support for them in the New Testament. Indeed, the New Testament might seem to teach Reformation doctrines. The picture presented in this book may at first seem totally foreign to the New Testament. It is important, therefore, to understand the effect of what modern psychology calls the *confirmation bias*. Many scientific studies have shown conclusively that people tend to filter their observations in ways that reinforce their previously held views.[6] This bias affects us in all areas of our lives, from trivial matters to strong convictions. It also affects how we read the Bible. We can identify passages that fit with our existing beliefs with ease, but miss passages that might contradict our beliefs with equal ease. In unclear biblical passages, we tend unconsciously to look for interpretations that align with the views we already hold. Consequently, people can use the New Testament to reinforce whatever doctrinal views they happen to already hold. Such convictions may indeed seem compelling; throughout history, however, Christians have held different doctrinal convictions. Therefore, we should investigate more deeply. A better approach would involve understanding and considering the full range of views held by people throughout history and weighing them against all the evidence we can gather for and against those views. We used exactly this approach to ascertain the picture of the early Christian message we present in this book.

The issue of confirmation bias is compounded by the fact that many Christians today read Bible translations that originate from within the tradition of the Reformation. The original biblical texts present many challenges for translators. Translators must *interpret* what words and phrases mean, and these can sometimes be interpreted in different ways. Hence, translators often rely on their doctrinal beliefs to guide how they interpret passages. Translators naturally look for interpretations that fit within their existing ideas – 'confirmation bias' again. Mainstream Bible translations have also tended to be conserva-

---

[6] E.g. Nickerson, R. S. (1998). *Confirmation bias: A ubiquitous phenomenon in many guises.* Review of General Psychology, 2, pp. 175 – 220.

tive, unwilling to deviate significantly from previous translations without strong reason. Most English translations arise as updates of an earlier translation, and they copy previous translations in difficult passages.[7] Translators usually change to an alternative interpretation only if they deem it necessary – using the doctrines of their tradition as a guide. Most English translations use the King James Version of 1611 as a base, which in turn relied on Tyndale's 1534 translation. For example, the 1989 New Revised Standard Version states in its preface:

> The New Revised Standard Version of the Bible is an authorized revision of the Revised Standard Version, published in 1952, which was a revision of the American Standard Version, published in 1901, which, in turn, embodied earlier revisions of the King James Version, published in 1611.

The precedent set by English translations has strengthened as more and more translators have opted for the same interpretations over time. The powerful influence of doctrinal tradition and the precedents set by existing translations both reinforce existing doctrines and create strong barriers to change. Translations only change very slowly as the doctrines and lexicons of translators gradually take into account the findings of recent scholarship. It will take decades, therefore, for English translations to reflect the insights and evidence of recent scholarship. In the meantime, traditional English Bible translations will continue to reinforce traditional post-Reformation doctrines.

Given that many people still give post-Reformation doctrines much weight, it is worth reflecting on the Reformers' own views about tradition. The Reformers sought to reject incorrect doctrines and misunderstandings of the Bible which had developed over time. Their Latin catch-phrase, *sola scriptura* ('scripture alone') referred to their determination to renounce any doctrines passed down to them as tradition which did not in fact match the Bible's teachings. They recognised that if 'tradition' had deviated from the early Christian teachings, it carried little weight – even if the majority believed it. Another catch-phrase that reinforced this idea, *semper reformata*, meant 'always reforming'. This phrase helped them to remember to pursue truth without letting tradition stand in the way. They believed that

---

[7] It is laudable that translators do not want to make speculative translations of biblical passages that they have difficulty understanding. The downside of this, however, is that plausible alternative translations are hidden from the Bible-reading public.

Christians should reform their tradition to reflect new knowledge and better understanding of scripture. The Reformers' love for truth and their pursuit of accurate biblical interpretations and authentic Christianity is laudable; yet, in light of recent scholarship, that very pursuit may oblige us to move away from some of their theological conclusions. Let us keep in mind, then, that although the post-Reformation doctrines have become today's tradition, they carry little weight if they do not match the original Christian teachings.

This book

Let us broadly outline what we will cover in this book. We will begin in Part 1 by examining how the Gospels present the life and activity of Jesus. This picture will lay the groundwork for an understanding of the early Christian doctrines of salvation. To help with this, we take a brief tour through the culture and history of first-century Israel. The cultural concepts we cover will help the reader to understand Jesus and the New Testament letters. We will see that all four Gospels paint essentially the same picture of Jesus' public ministry. Jesus' teachings focussed on concern for those in need. He sought to aid those who suffered and he challenged Jewish customs and institutions that caused suffering. Jesus showed a keen interest in helping the poor and in transforming communities. He confronted the authorities of his day on a number of issues concerning the treatment of those in need. The average person in the street saw Jesus as a prophet, like the many prophets of Israel's past, and he performed miracles as those prophets had. People also saw him as a religious teacher whose teachings conflicted with those of the religious authorities. Some hoped that God had sent him to overthrow the Roman rule of Israel. He led a movement of followers dedicated to achieving his goals. He recruited followers and often encouraged them or warned them of persecutions they would face. The authorities killed Jesus because of the things he said and did. The Gospels depict him dying as a martyr for his cause. In this book we will compare his life and ministry to those of Martin Luther King Jr. to help shed light on these themes through a modern-day parallel. Unlike King, however, Jesus' unique resurrection encouraged his disheartened followers and re-ignited his movement.

From the Gospels, we will turn in Part 2 to the rest of the New Testament to examine its doctrines about salvation. Together, these doctrines form the general paradigm of moral transformation. In presenting these early Christian doctrines, we will highlight the various ways in which they differ from the post-Reformation tradition. The early Christians adopted the Jewish belief that God would resurrect and judge the world. Both the early Christians and the Jewish people believed that, at the final judgment, everyone would be judged according to his or her life, character, and actions. By following Christ's teachings and imitating his actions, the early Christians believed they could obtain a positive judgment from God. Hence 'imitating Christ' features as a particularly important concept within the New Testament. The early Christians placed great emphasis on moral living, and moral exhortation to live correctly covers a large proportion of the New Testament. It underscores love for others as a central concept. We will then look at how some important (but poorly understood) theological terms fit into the basic early Christian paradigm – 'faith' and 'righteousness'. Drawing on recent research, we will attempt to address some prevalent misunderstandings of Paul's theology. The New Testament Christians did not believe that sin permanently stained all humans, but that people could meet God's standards by following Jesus' teachings. We will also see how Israel understood the concepts of 'forgiveness' and 'grace' quite differently from people today. The New Testament writers understood that forgiveness required repentance. They also used the term 'grace' to describe the generous favour that God did for humankind by sending Jesus. These various ideas form the basic picture of New Testament salvation theology: namely, that God graciously sent Jesus to teach humans to love one another and live rightly. By following his example and teachings obediently, we can gain a positive final judgment.

In Part 3, we will examine why the early Christians placed the greatest importance on Jesus. The early Christians spoke in many ways about what Jesus had achieved and done for them. They wrote of how Jesus had transformed their lives and led them to live rightly, using various phrases and ideas from their culture to describe this. We will study their understanding of sacrifice, since they drew on sacrificial language to explain what he had done for them. They also drew on concepts of martyrdom to write of Jesus' death. They saw the significance of his death in his goal to transform people's lives – the ministry that got him killed as a martyr. Those who had seen their own lives transformed often expressed their gratitude towards Jesus by writing of his selfless martyrdom. We will see how Jesus' resurrection provided them with crucial motivation to follow him and proved their core doctrines. The resurrection also formed a major part of their message to encourage others to also follow him.

In Part 4, we will look at how different Christians have thought about these issues throughout history. For the first few centuries after the Apostles, Christians worldwide held the views just described. Many of these early Christians learned theology from disciples of the Apostles and read the New Testament books in their native language. Their writings provide a way to confirm our interpretations of the New Testament. We will proceed to trace the ways in which Christian doctrines have changed over two millennia – slowly at some times, quickly at others. We will examine several major doctrinal changes and see that although they usually occurred because of misunderstandings and the influence of changing culture, once people accepted them, they became part of a tradition taught as truth. This brief overview will help to explain the historical origins of post-Reformation ideas about salvation. Finally, the last section of this book will critically analyse some key post-Reformation doctrines prevalent today in light of the material covered.

Throughout this book, we will attempt to show from the Gospels, New Testament letters, and other early Christian texts what early Christians believed about salvation. The Gospels present a picture of Jesus' ministry that focussed on social change and transforming the lives of individuals. In the theological paradigm of the New Testament Christians, final judgment depended upon conduct. They believed that people could attain a positive judgement by imitating and following the teachings of Jesus, and thus living a moral life. In their view, Jesus saved people by transforming their lives from sinful ways to right conduct. Early Christians worldwide held to this general view for over two centuries following the time of the Apostles. Our inquiries into the New Testament letters, the early Church writings, and history will all point to this early Christian paradigm of salvation. The agreement between these different lines of enquiry reinforces the picture of early Christianity outlined here.

Some brief caveats

We will often quote from the New Testament. We will generally use the translation given in the New Revised Standard Version. We will, however, replace some words on occasion where recent scholarship leads us to believe that the replacement better captures the intent of the original Greek text.

Not everyone today believes that God exists, that Jesus performed miracles, or that God resurrected him. Such things are matters for personal faith. This book seeks to identify the beliefs of the early Christians. It does not seek to prove or disprove the truth of their beliefs. However, it is cumbersome to write "The early Christians believed that…" in front of every statement. In the interests of simplicity and brevity, we will sometimes write statements like "God resurrected Jesus." The reader should understand all statements of this kind to refer to the beliefs of the early Christians. This simple example phrase would thus mean, "The early Christians believed that God resurrected Jesus." We will discuss and analyse what the early Christians thought, with a view to understanding their beliefs, and we will leave readers with the choice of whether or not to believe their ideas.

Part 1

How the Gospels present Jesus

The post-Reformation view of salvation often emphasises the death of Jesus to such an extent that the details of his life and activity as recorded in the Gospels are given secondary importance. In that view, Jesus atoned for the sins of the world through his death on the cross, which enables our salvation. In this book, we will argue that the early Christians did not share the post-Reformation emphasis on Jesus' death and the common interpretation of its significance. If they did not share post-Reformation beliefs on this issue, it raises the question of how they understood Jesus' life and death. In this part, we will outline the way in which the Gospel accounts depict the ministry and death of Jesus. This overview will give us a useful starting point for understanding the beliefs of the early Christians.

Chapter 1

The context of Jesus' ministry

The four New Testament Gospels present accounts of Jesus' activity, and their characteristics match well with other biographies from the ancient world.[1] In the following chapters, we will look at how the Gospels present the ministry of Jesus. We will focus on the Gospels as a whole and analyse the picture they paint of Jesus' ministry. Though the various Gospels emphasise different aspects, we will focus on the core points common to all, as the same basic story of Jesus' public ministry emerges from each of them. To understand that story, we must first understand its context: first-century Israel, a place that combined extreme cultural, religious, economic and political tension.

The Israelite culture

Every people-group has a particular culture. People around the world practise different customs, consider different behaviours acceptable and do things differently. The Maori people of New Zealand provide one example of a distinctive culture. Prior to the arrival of European settlers, Maori people spoke in their ancestral language. They wove garments out of the flax plants that grow in New Zealand to create a distinctive style of clothing. They dug down into the ground to build their houses. They built their villages on hills and fortified them with wooden walls. When greeting others, they rubbed noses. They made knives, weapons and jewellery from a green stone they called *Pounamu*. Their villages grew kumara crops and their hunters sought out the local wildlife. To cook their meals, they sometimes dug a hole and buried the food with fire-heated stones to cook for several hours. They tattooed distinctive patterns on their faces using chisels to show their status or mark important events in their lives. Their stories told of how their mythical ancestor, Maui, had fished their land of *Aotearoa* out of the sea. They had a unique way of life, a culture, which directed all aspects of how they lived. According to one famous definition, a culture

---

[1] See, for example, Richard A. Burridge, *What Are the Gospels: A Comparison with Graeco-Roman Biography*, (Grand Rapids: Eerdmans, 2004, 2nd ed.).

"includes knowledge, belief, art, law, morals, custom, and any other capabilities and habits."[2] A culture is a way of life - a shared way of thinking, behaving and understanding the world.

As Western European immigrants colonised New Zealand, two alternative cultures existed side by side. The Europeans built European-style houses and brought crops and weapons from Europe. Europeans wanted to shake hands rather than rub noses, and to pay for goods with money rather than to barter. Europeans wore wool and cotton clothing rather than flax and spoke non-Maori languages, typically English. They cooked on stoves, and held Christian religious beliefs. Over time, more and more Maori individuals learned the English language and became familiar with Western customs. Individuals and groups abandoned their traditional ways and began to live by European customs. Others adopted parts selectively from both sets of customs. Today, most people of Maori ancestry speak English and live largely by Western customs.

The process by which native peoples around the world like the Maori have dropped their ancestral customs and adopted those of Western Europe is known as *Westernisation*. Over time, communities and individuals conform increasingly to the global culture and abandon their ancestral ways of living. Such cultural change can cause strife and conflict within these societies. Some people see all the advantages of adopting the global culture - the 'new and modern way of doing things.' They want to become 'part of the wider world' and do not want to remain 'stuck in the past.' Others see their ancestral ways as better, time-tested ways of living. They do not want to abandon their traditional ways. By choosing to follow a new culture, individuals can increase their opportunities – but often at the cost of alienating themselves from their people.

The Israelites too had their own native culture, customs and practices. They had a name for it – they called it *Torah*. Torah governed their entire lifestyle. It told them what to wear, what to eat and with whom to eat. Torah told them how to sacrifice, how to plant their crops, when to celebrate their festivals and when to fast. It told them how to act on religious days. It instructed them about religious impurity, and told them how to deal with it. It included civil laws such as the punishments prescribed for theft or murder. It also told them of their history, recounting the origin of their people and telling stories of their ancestors. According to these accounts, their ancestors Moses and Abraham received the teachings of Torah from God. The Israelites also

---

[2] Edward B. Tylor, *Primitive Cultures*, 1871, p. 1.

had their own ancestral language – Hebrew. Together, these customs and practices formed the culture and self-understanding that distinguished the Israelites as a nation and a people.

The Hebrew word *Torah* literally means 'teaching', 'instruction' or 'law'. Greek writers translated it as *nomos*, and English Bibles often translate it as 'law' or 'the Law'. Such translations make it sound comparable to the laws that our modern governments create. The Torah, however, covered far more than merely political laws. It was a *culture*. One scholar describes Torah as "the constitution of the Jewish way of life, including what we would distinguish as religion, politics, custom, and morals."[3] Another scholar notes that Torah gave the ancient Jews their identity by providing them with "the distinctive characteristics, the identity markers, that define the boundary between Israel and the Gentiles."[4] One scholar succinctly summarizes Torah as "what Jews do."[5] The people of Israel saw God as their ruler who had instituted their way of life by giving them Torah.[6] This view made Torah sacred and highly treasured by the people. Most Israelites believed that those who followed Torah would receive God's blessings, but that those who abandoned it were deliberately rejecting God and his commands.

Jewish culture is not described completely into the few short written books of Scripture. Indeed, these books often reference some of the customs in passing, and assume that the reader already has some knowledge of them. The Israelites passed down their culture through oral teaching and through imitation – by hearing, seeing and doing. In around the first century, experts in the ancestral customs passed the customs carefully on to the next generation to preserve their threatened culture.

Hellenisation

In the 1st century, the 'global' culture was Greek. Greek culture had spread across the known world since Alexander the Great established a Greek Empire in around 330 BC. The Roman Empire later inherited the Greek customs. The word 'Greek' became similar in meaning to our

---

[3] Stanley Stowers, *A Rereading of Romans: Justice, Jews, and Gentiles* (Ann Arbor: Yale University Press, 1997), p. 36.

[4] Richard Hays, *The Conversion of the Imagination: Paul As Interpreter of Israel's Scripture* (Grand Rapids, Eerdmans, 2005), p. 87.

[5] Michael Winger, *By What Law? The Meaning of Nomos in the Letters of Paul* (Atlanta, GA: Scholars Press, 1992), p. 104.

[6] See Judges 8:23 for an example of such a sentiment.

word 'Western'. It came to mean following a standardised universal culture and way of doing things. Scholars call the spread of Greek culture across the world 'Hellenisation' ('Hellene' means 'Greek' in the Greek language). 'Greek' implied *civilised*, as opposed to 'barbarian'. One ancient Greek writer commented proudly: "So far has our city [Athens] distanced the rest of mankind in thought and in speech that her pupils have become teachers of the rest of the world, and she has brought it about that the name 'Hellenes' no longer suggests a race but an intelligence, and that the title Hellenes is applied rather to those who share our culture than to those who share a common blood."[7] The label 'Greek' referred to culture as much as ancestry at this time, much as 'Westerner' denotes someone from Western culture today. Someone could become a Greek by following Greek customs – even without having Greek ancestry. One scholar notes: "With the spread of Greek culture and Greek rule across the eastern Mediterranean, a 'Hellene' came to mean someone who spoke flawless Greek and embraced Greek culture and institutions, regardless of national origin."[8]

The word 'Jew' had also become a reference to a person's culture and not merely their genetic ancestry. Several books in the Old Testament make it clear that foreigners could adopt Jewish customs if they wished. 'Jew' came to denote anyone who followed Torah the way the Israelites in the province of Judea did.[9] A person could *become* a Jew by adopting their customs.[10] A Roman historian writing in 200 AD commented:

> The country has been named Judea, and the people themselves Jews. I do not know how this title came to be given to them, but it applies also to all the rest of mankind, although of alien race, who adopt their customs... They are distinguished from the rest of mankind in practically every detail of life.[11]

Similarly, Mark explained briefly in his Gospel:

---

[7] Isocrates, *Panegyricus* 50.

[8] Christopher D. Stanley, *'Neither Jew Nor Greek': Ethnic Conflict in Graeco-Roman Society*, JSNT 64 (1996), pp. 101 – 124.

[9] Bruce J. Malina and John J. Pilch, *Social Science Commentary on the Letters of Paul* (Minneapolis: Fortress, 2006), pp. 364 – 366, 371 – 374.

[10] For an example of a forced conversion in the 1st century AD see Josephus, *War* 2:454.

[11] Cassius Dio, *Roman History*, 37:16-17.

All the Jews do not eat unless they thoroughly wash their hands, thus observing the tradition of the elders; and they do not eat anything from the market unless they wash it; and there are also many other traditions that they observe, the washing of cups, pots, and bronze kettles.[12]

Great tension existed between the Greek and Jewish cultures in the 1st century AD. The New Testament writers frequently mentioned the difference between Jew and Greek ('Gentile'). We read in Acts of Timothy's Jewish mother and his Greek father.[13] This does not necessarily mean that his mother and father came from different races, since people of Israelite ancestry could be called Jews or Greeks depending on which customs they followed. Paul often wrote about this theme. He won both Jewish and Greek converts,[14] and he made the controversial claim that Jesus' followers ought to make no distinction between Jew and Greek.[15]

The pervasive influence of Greek global culture led many Israelites to abandon their ancestral culture. Many found it tempting to assimilate themselves into the global community and follow standardised universal customs. They saw opportunities for profit, progress, and power through adopting Greek culture. Israel's foreign rulers also imposed Greek political and economic regimes, and the increasing numbers of foreigners in Israel made it difficult to preserve the traditional Jewish way of life. Judaism's purity codes made business dealings with Greeks difficult. Consequently, many Israelites abandoned their native culture of Torah in favour of Greek customs. Other Israelites resisted Hellenisation. Many emphasised the God-given nature of Torah and the importance of these customs in the eyes of God. Some separated themselves from the world, living in an isolated community in order to follow pure customs. Others took part in the violent revolts that became increasingly common. These cultural tensions first climaxed almost 200 years before the time of Jesus.

A Greek king of Judea decided in 167 BC that he wanted his people to follow one culture – Greek culture. He did not want to wait for the slow process of cultural infiltration and transformation. A Jewish historian reports the event: "Then the king wrote to his whole kingdom that all should be one people; and that all should give up their

---

[12] Mark 7:3-4.
[13] Acts 16:1-3.
[14] Acts 17:11-12.
[15] Gal 3:28, Col 3:11.

particular customs... And the king sent letters by messengers to Jerusalem and the towns of Judah; he directed them to follow customs strange to the land."[16] The King wanted to change their temple and sacrificial practices, Sabbath observance, festivals, the circumcision of children, and the eating of pork.[17] He killed or tortured Israelites who insisted on following Jewish customs. As a result, many people abandoned Torah,[18] but others stood firm. The Maccabean Revolt began when a man named Mattathias refused to abandon his ancestral culture. He told the king's officials, "I and my sons and my brothers will continue to live by the covenant of our ancestors. Far be it from us to desert the Torah and the ordinances."[19] After saying this, he saw an Israelite deliberately disobeying the Torah. "When Mattathias saw it, he burned with zeal and his heart was stirred. He gave vent to righteous anger, he ran and killed him on the altar... Thus he burned with zeal for the Torah, just as Phinehas did."[20]

Traditionalists saw Phinehas, who had lived at the time of Moses, as a great hero.[21] In Phinehas' time, many Israelites abandoned their culture, through marrying foreign women and adopting their wives' cultures. Due to his commitment to God and his culture, Phinehas killed an Israelite he saw with a foreign woman. The Hebrew Scriptures praise him greatly, and say God rewarded him with "perpetual priesthood, because he was zealous for his God, and made atonement for the Israelites."[22] A later passage says his act was "reckoned to him as righteousness from generation to generation forever."[23] Phinehas had gained acclaim through killing for God and Torah, and thus would serve as a hero to later generations who fought foreign cultures.

During the Maccabean revolt, some Jews prepared themselves not only to kill for Torah, but also to die for it. The king tried to enforce cultural unity through torturing the Jews so that they would abandon their customs. Yet some heroes refused to break the Torah and instead chose torture or even death. The books of Maccabees depict them saying, "we are ready to die rather than transgress the Torah of our

---

[16] 1 Maccabees 1:41-44.
[17] 2 Maccabees 6.
[18] 1 Maccabees 1:52.
[19] 1 Maccabees 2:19-21.
[20] 1 Maccabees 2:24-26.
[21] Numbers 25; Psalm 106:31; 1 Maccabees 2:26, 54; Sirach 45:23-24; 4 Maccabees 18:12.
[22] Numbers 25:13.
[23] Psalm 106:31.

ancestors."[24] "The King of the universe will raise us up to an everlasting renewal of life, because we have died for his Torah."[25] Elsewhere one said, "I, like my brothers, give up body and life for the Torah of our ancestors."[26]

The revolt led by the Maccabees successfully reinstated a strong new self-rule of Israel. It renewed passion for following Torah throughout Israel. However, after a hundred years, their leadership disintegrated and a civil war resulted. This provided an opportunity for the expanding Roman Republic to take full control of Israel in 63 BC. The Romans appointed kings and governors in Israel, which in the first century AD comprised the provinces of Judea, Galilee, and Samaria. These Roman rulers extracted heavy taxes from the peasants. They brutally enforced political stability by killing rebellious Jews who tried to imitate the courage and success of the Maccabees. One such uprising happened in 4 BC at Sepphoris, the capital of Galilee, located only four miles from Jesus' home of Nazareth. The Roman army destroyed the entire city and sold its inhabitants as slaves. They scoured the countryside and killed everyone who had participated in the uprising.[27] Many similar slaughters occurred as the Romans brutally repressed those in Israel who opposed Roman rule. By the time of Jesus, many among the peasant classes lived in fear and helpless resignation. They could only wait and hope for God to re-establish his reign and remove these foreign rulers from power.

The Roman rulers had to extract an allocated tribute to Caesar from the populace, but often they did not stop at this. At the time of Jesus' birth, the Romans had appointed Herod 'the Great' to rule Judea. He oppressed the people greatly with his brutal rule, and undertook vast building projects that bankrupted his country. Excessive spending and taxation seem to have caused a complete economic collapse within Judea. Consequently, thousands of farming families defaulted on loans and lost their land. Herod's most famous project involved rebuilding the Temple in Greek style. It became the largest temple in the world and a monument that many flocked to see. The Gospels depict Jesus viewing the excessively opulent Temple as a representation of the oppression and suffering in Israel. In Galilee, during Jesus' lifetime, Herod's son used heavy taxes to build the city of Tiberius and to rebuild Sepphoris. The lower classes produced wealth through agriculture, but

---

[24] 2 Maccabees 7:2.
[25] 2 Maccabees 7:9.
[26] 2 Maccabees 7:37.
[27] Josephus, *Antiquities* 17.288 – 289, *War* 2.68.

heavy taxes stripped it away from them. The ruling elite exploited the peasantry, who could not overthrow them. The Temple also demanded annual tax as well as payments for sacrifices, and these added to the economic trouble of the peasantry. Jewish peasants struggled under the weight of both Roman taxes and religious financial obligations.

According to Israelite tradition, early Israel had consisted of independent tribes who saw themselves as having no common ruler except God, his priests, and the divinely appointed Judges of Israel. Eventually however, political circumstances led to the establishment of a monarchy around 1000 BC. This met with strong resistance from a small but influential minority who considered it a rejection of God's rule.[28] The populace gradually accepted rule by monarchs, but they remained the frequent target of criticism by prophets. A popular tradition developed that insisted that monarchs should be appointed in accordance with God's will by Jewish prophets, priests and the public. At the time of Jesus, the Romans appointed monarchs to their positions of power. The people generally saw these kings as oppressors rather than as God's appointed rulers.

The powerful dream of an independent kingdom of Israel lived on among the villages and communities of Israel in the 1st century AD. They looked forward to the end of the age of oppression under foreign rule, when a new age of God's reign would arise. They wanted Israel to live according to God's will as defined by Torah once again, and to return to the semi-Utopia of Israelite independence. Prophets had often reminded them of this dream when Israel struggled through trials of war, corrupt rulers, worship of other gods, and immorality. At times, the desperate situation of the few who remained faithful to God meant they could only cling on to a hope for a better future. They looked forward to a time when God would "restore the fortunes of Israel."[29] They called this future Utopia the 'Kingdom of God'. It represented a change in their social order that they hoped would bring peace, happiness, prosperity and unity under a benevolent, God-approved ruler.[30]

---

[28] 1 Samuel 8:7; 12:12; 19.

[29] For example, Jer 29 – 33; Hosea 6:11; Joel 3:1; Amos 9:14; Zeph 2:7; 3:20.

[30] See also Mary Ann Beavis, *Jesus & Utopia* (Minneapolis: Fortress, 2006).

The time of Jesus

Throughout history, people have had many ideas about what would make a Utopian society. First century Israel did not differ in this regard, and Israelites did not all agree on the precise problem nor on the solution. Many saw the problem as the encroaching of Greek culture upon their God-ordained Jewish heritage. They sought a solution by strongly maintaining their ancestral culture and separating themselves from Greek influences. Others saw rule by a pagan empire as the primary problem. They wanted to rise up in battle against the ungodly foe, in the belief that God would give them victory. Excluding Christianity, 33 revolutionary movements occurred in Israel during the period from 47 BC to 73 AD for which historical documentation survives.[31] These movements had a variety of different aims and sometimes ended up fighting one another.

By the time of Jesus, the Pharisees had become one of the most influential groups that had formed to provide a response to Israel's situation. The Pharisees were among the strongest advocates of following Torah. They believed that, above all else, Israel needed to follow Torah and resist Greek influence. They aimed to convince as many people as possible to follow Torah, and their efforts at evangelism became renowned.[32] They aimed to preserve Jewish culture through carefully learning from their elders and in turn passing on the customs themselves. They wanted to preserve and maintain their traditional Jewish way of life. From the ranks of the Pharisees came the majority of those who wanted an armed revolt against Rome, due to their patriotism and strong commitment to Israel's culture. The Pharisees firmly believed in an afterlife, and this belief distinguished them from many other Israelites. Many Jews had died as martyrs for their loyalty to Torah. The Pharisees believed that God would not allow his loyal followers to die in this way unless he rewarded them in the afterlife. They thought that God would resurrect all the dead on a day of judgment. God would publicly honour and reward those whom had remained loyal to his Torah, and punish their enemies.

The Chief Priests held considerable political power and controlled the Temple. Roman authorities appointed them from wealthy families

---

[31] A list is given by John Dominic Crossan, *The Historical Jesus: The Life of a Mediterranean Jewish Peasant* (New York, NY: HarperCollins, 1993), pp. 451 – 452. See also Horsley, *Bandits, Prophets and Messiahs* for a comprehensive discussion of these.

[32] Matt 23:15 provides a passing reference to the Pharisees' evangelistic efforts.

and not according to Torah. As a result, many saw these priests as illegitimate. The Chief Priests often exploited their power, gaining great wealth from the Temple system and living in luxury. Many Jews felt that the Chief Priests compromised the Temple and the Jewish traditions. Hence, they faced popular dissent, particularly from the Pharisees with whom they often came into conflict.

In contrast, the peasants struggled to survive. The common people in the farms and villages of Israel lived far from the mansions of the ruling elite. They suffered under the exploitation and corruption of their rulers and they longed for liberation. They hoped for men anointed by God who would save them from oppressive rule and restore the Utopian Kingdom of God. It was into this climate of foreign rule, exploitation, loss of tradition, and hope amidst powerlessness that Jesus came. Born in about 5 BC into a lowly artisan family who lived in a small village, Jesus would have seen and lived the hardship of the peasants. Though the Gospels record some miraculous events accompanying his birth[33] they skip over his youth, mentioning only his intelligence and education. He apparently debated the Torah with the local leaders from a young age and developed a good reputation for intelligence and wisdom.[34] The majority of the Gospel accounts focus on what happened after Jesus began acting more publicly in his early thirties, in about 27 AD. We will now turn to that part of his story.

---

[33] Matt 1:18-23, 2:11-22; Luke 1:26-56, 2:1-52.
[34] Luke 2:40-52.

Chapter 2

Jesus' Conflicts

The first step towards understanding the early Christians' paradigm of salvation is to understand their view of Jesus. All four Gospels tell the story of what Jesus said and did. The common threads in these accounts of his public ministry testify to the widespread view of Jesus and his activity. Over the next few chapters, we will outline the ministry of Jesus by drawing from the four Gospels. After we have established the general ways in which the early Christians thought about his ministry, we will turn to a more detailed analysis of their salvation doctrines.

Many of the Gospel scenes portray Jesus in some kind of conflict. These conflicts demonstrate what people found controversial about his position, and therefore provide insight into how the Gospels portray the public ministry of Jesus. Ultimately, we want to see how the average person living in Israel at the time might have understood Jesus' ministry.

Economics and wealth

The Gospels record Jesus clashing with those in power over the issues of poverty, wealth, and economics. Many parts of Torah concerned debt, economic stability and fairness. Despite this, most of the common people in first-century Israel struggled financially. A new law introduced to assist the poor with their debts made things worse.[1] Debt built up over time, and creditors did not remit loans as the Torah required. Huge numbers of farming families lost their ancestral land. As Jesus grew up, he would have seen many people around him losing the

---

[1] The Mosaic requirement that debts should be remitted every seven years meant that no one was prepared to loan money to those in financial need near the end of the seven year period. The *Prozbul* was introduced by Rabbis to provide a form of non-remitted loan in order to allow poor people to obtain loans. Eventually, however, all loans moved to the new form and the tradition of the seven-year remission was lost. Thus families lost their land permanently when loans were foreclosed, rather than receiving them back every seven years.

little land they owned as their wealthy creditors seized it. According to the Gospels, his message and ministry often focussed on the desperate situations of the poor.

Jesus' forerunner, John the Baptist, took a keen interest in the fair distribution of wealth. The Gospels indicate that his activity paved the way for Jesus' ministry.[2] All three examples Luke gives of John's preaching deal with economic matters. He taught, "Whoever has two coats must share with anyone who has none; and whoever has food must do likewise." He instructed tax collectors, "Collect no more than the amount prescribed for you." He encouraged Roman soldiers, "Do not extort money from anyone by threats or false accusation, and be satisfied with your wages."[3] All of these teachings focused on alleviating poverty. Following on from John's movement, Jesus too made the economic character of his vision and activity clear.

In Luke's Gospel, Jesus' first major public speech takes the form of a mission statement:

> The Spirit of the Lord is upon me, because he has anointed me to bring good news to the poor. He has sent me to proclaim release to the captives and recovery of sight to the blind, to let the oppressed go free, to proclaim the year of the Lord's favor.[4]

In this mission statement quoted from Isaiah, Jesus declared his focus on helping those who suffered economic hardship. In Jesus' time, those who could not pay their debts made up the majority of prison populations. Economic hardship also afflicted the blind, who were unable to work for wages. The "year of the Lord's favor" referred to the custom that after every fifty years, creditors would cancel all debts.[5] The whole of this mission statement concerns the alleviation of poverty. For this reason, the first sentence summarised his ministry as "good news to the poor." In Matthew, Jesus linked these ideas of helping those in need with the final judgment. He indicated the type of actions that bring people a positive judgement, and these actions concern helping those in poverty and need.[6]

In Jesus' eyes, people could not serve both God and wealth.[7] Hence, he discouraged people from trying to accumulate 'earthly' wealth.

---

[2] Matt 3:1-6; Mark 1:1-5, 1:9-11; Luke 1:5-25, 1:57-80, 3:1-6; John 1:6-8, 15, 3:28-30.
[3] Luke 3:10-14.
[4] Luke 4:16-21.
[5] Often called the "Year of Jubilee." See Lev 25:8-17 for the institution of this.
[6] Matt 25:31-45.
[7] Matt 6:24; Luke 16:13-15.

Instead, he taught that people should pursue the richness of living as a sharing community.[8] He warned against greed, for "one's life does not consist in the abundance of possessions."[9] In a parable, he reminded people that rich men who stored up wealth for themselves would still die.[10] He taught the wealthy a different approach - "sell your possessions, and give alms" freely to those in need.[11] Jesus said that God would reward them if they used their wealth to help others.[12] If the community shared among themselves, then by God's power everyone would have enough – as the Gospels depict Jesus demonstrating miraculously at shared meals involving thousands of people.[13]

When a rich ruler came to Jesus asking him how he could enter the Kingdom of God, Jesus answered that it was necessary to keep God's commandments. The rich man claimed that he had done so, yet he had probably become rich by taking from others, like most of the rich people of the time. Jesus told him that to do God's will truly, he should give his unnecessary wealth to the poor. The rich man refused. Jesus commented: "It is easier for a camel to go through the eye of a needle than for someone who is rich to enter the kingdom of God."[14] Elsewhere Jesus taught that the "deceit of riches" would indeed choke his message of the kingdom.[15] Jesus taught that God would punish and reward people in the afterlife to compensate for the injustices of this life. His story of a poor and rich man in the afterlife shows the poor beggar receiving rewards and the rich man suffering.[16] Jesus warned the rich that God would not forgive them unless they forgave people who could not pay their debts.[17]

Jesus taught the rich how much following him would cost them. He said: "None of you can become my disciple if you do not give up all your possessions."[18] Jesus also made this point using the metaphor of salt. Salt was rare and valuable in the 1st century,[19] and Jesus likened

---

[8] Matt 6:19-21.
[9] Luke 12:13-15.
[10] Luke 12:16-21.
[11] Luke 12:33-34.
[12] Luke 16:1-12.
[13] Matt 14:13-21, 15:32-39; Mark 6:30-44, 8:1-10; Luke 9:10-17; John 6:1-14.
[14] Matt 19:16-26, Mark 10:17-25, Luke 18:18-25.
[15] Matt 13:20-22.
[16] Luke 6:24-26, 16:19-31.
[17] Matt 6:12, 18:21-35; Luke 11:4.
[18] Luke 14:33.
[19] Roman soldiers were sometimes paid in salt, and that is where we get the word 'salary'. The preservative quality of salt was essential to civilised cities,

wealth to stockpiles of salt. Salt benefited people if they distributed it among those who needed it, but it became useless if hoarded since impurities degraded it over time.[20] Jesus envisioned a society in which "the last will be first, and the first will be last" because people would have equal privilege and the gap between rich and poor would not exist. He told a parable in which the employer paid equal wages regardless of how long the hired servants had worked, apparently based on a similar idea.[21] Enough wealth existed in the communities to provide easily for the poor, but the wealthy needed to share it with the poor and not hoard it greedily.

A semi-formal system of favours permeated the culture of Jesus' time. People were expected to repay the favours done for them, and they only did favours for those who would reciprocate.[22] Unfortunately, the people who most needed favours often lacked the means to repay them, so they were not helped. Jesus criticised this system while at a banquet arranged by a Pharisee. He said to invite not only rich people who could return the favour, but to invite also the poor who needed food but could not return the favour.[23] Jesus taught that the rich should do favours for the poor without expecting anything in return.[24] In another story, he said that wealth distracts the rich from the Kingdom of God, and so the kingdom is filled by the poor instead.[25] Jesus taught that God would satisfy people's basic needs like food and clothing if they focussed on his Kingdom and lived in a godly manner.[26] God would provide for those who did his will, just as he cared for the needs of birds and plants.[27]

Modern Westerners readily understand the Parable of the Talents as a good lesson in faithful stewardship. Yet scholars who have studied the culture recently think the first-century peasants who listened would

---

and therefore salt was critical for the economy and control of its distribution was a significant power. See Mark Kurlansky, *Salt: A World History* (New York, NY: Penguin, 2003) pp. 62 – 63.

[20] Luke 14:34-35. Note that the salt metaphor is used differently in the other Gospels.

[21] Matt 20:1-16.

[22] See David A. deSilva, *Honor, Patronage, Kinship & Purity: Unlocking New Testament Culture* (Downers Grove, IL: IVP Academic, 2000), for an introduction.

[23] Luke 14:12-15.

[24] Luke 6:30-36.

[25] Luke 14:16-24.

[26] Matt 6:33; Luke 12:23-32. The phrase "his righteousness" here means a godly way of living, as we will argue later in the book.

[27] Matt 6:25-34; Luke 12:22-28.

have understood it differently. For them, the events of the story echoed an all too familiar reality. Many of them had already lost their land and livelihoods to rich landowners. They would have noticed in this parable Jesus' criticism of the way the wealthy exploited others.[28] One of the servants in the story described the main character, a land-owning nobleman, as "a harsh man; you take what you did not deposit, and reap what you did not sow."[29] This described aptly many of the exploitative rich. With this history in mind, we can understand why the parable describes a delegation of concerned citizens setting out to oppose the nobleman's rule. On the nobleman's return, though, he killed them.[30] Like many rich people of the day, the ruler took from the poor and gave even more to the people who were already making wealth at their expense. Jesus summarised the net effect: "For to all those who have, more will be given, and they will have more than enough; but from those who have nothing, even what they have will be taken away."[31] This parable provides one example of how understanding the historical background of Jesus' ministry can change how we interpret the Bible. First-century listeners would probably have understood this parable not simply as a lesson to live as God's faithful stewards, but as a critique of the social problems of Jesus' society. Jesus followed this parable with a contrast, explaining the very different nature of God's rule. He taught that God would condemn those who do not help the needy, and reward those who generously share with them.[32] Jesus listed the kinds of people in need, including the poor, hungry and thirsty. He also included strangers, since they had trouble buying anything because of the way that the economic system worked in the ancient world. He included the naked, referring to people stripped of their clothing by the authorities as security for debts.[33] He also listed those in prison, who had most likely suffered imprisonment because they had failed to pay their debts.[34] Jesus had these people in mind – the people exploited by the rich elite.

Among those at the wealthy end of the economy were the tax collectors. They filled the pockets of the Roman authorities and took a

---

[28] Matt 25:14-30; Luke 19:12-28. See R. David Kaylor, *Jesus the Prophet* (Louisville, KY: Westminster John Knox Press, 1994), pp. 157 – 158 for a more detailed socio-historical explanation.

[29] Luke 19:21-22 cf e.g. Isa 65:21-23; Lev 6:2-5, 25:17.

[30] Luke 19:14, 27.

[31] Matt 25:29.

[32] Matt 25:31-46.

[33] See Matt 5:40 for an example of this.

[34] Matt 25:34-39.

generous cut for themselves, too, by collecting more than the Romans asked for. Jesus spent time with tax collectors,[35] although few people wanted to befriend them. He even recruited one into his closest group of disciples.[36] One Gospel story recounts the story of a tax collector named Zacchaeus. After talking with Jesus, he decided to no longer over-tax people. He pledged to give half of his wealth to the poor and pay back four times what he had unfairly charged in taxes. Jesus said of him: "Today salvation has come to this house, because he too is a son of Abraham."[37] The salvation that Jesus focussed on in this case concerned poverty and wealth.

The poor and disadvantaged no doubt supported Jesus' teachings, but his activity challenged and threatened the rich. Jesus repeatedly condemned the wealthy in public, dishonouring them and putting them out of favour with the common people. The rich and powerful resented the way in which Jesus challenged them to change how they lived. His challenges to their exploitation and ill-gotten wealth made him very few friends among the wealthy.

Moral purity

Much of Jesus' activity concerned economic justice, but Jesus identified and challenged other causes of poverty besides the behaviour of the wealthy. The Jewish purity code also disadvantaged some people. Many rules in the Torah dealt with ritual purity.[38] These laws identified some things as 'clean' and others as 'unclean.' People had to separate these and treat them in certain ways in order to avoid uncleanliness. The label of 'unclean' included many things, from cemeteries to pork to garments made of mixed fabrics. The purity code also deemed some people unclean. They included the sick, 'demon-possessed,'[39] prostitutes, tax-collectors and those who could not afford the necessary sacrifices for purity. Purity codes excluded these impure people from

---

[35] Matt 9:10-11, 11:19; Mark 2:15-16; Luke 5:29-30, 7:34.

[36] Mark 2:14.

[37] Luke 19:1-10.

[38] See William R. Herzog II, *Jesus, Justice, and the Reign of God: A Ministry of Liberation* (Louisville, KY: Westminster John Knox Press, 2000), pp. 156 – 158 for a brief discussion of the debt and purity codes.

[39] Ancient medicine labelled anyone with a condition that caused involuntary movement as 'demon-possessed'. They believed that spirits caused all movement, assuming any involuntary movement of the body was caused by a foreign spirit controlling the body.

society, and thus added to their economic and social hardships. Jesus challenged these religious traditions, which put him in direct conflict with the religious authorities. In particular, his teaching angered the Pharisees, since they strongly desired to maintain ritual purity.

Jesus saw that the Pharisees' emphasis on purity caused serious hardship for people. Purity regulations excluded those in need of help, rather than promoting a supportive community, as the community generally shunned those deemed unclean. The unclean suffered severe economic consequences, since they had little chance of obtaining employment, loans or favours. In their society, no social welfare system existed to support the poor, so social exclusion resulted in dire poverty. Jesus seems to have felt that the purity laws labelled many good and honest people as 'unclean', and made them suffer because society wrongfully cast them out.

In response, Jesus formed around him a group to welcome in such people. He became a "friend of tax collectors and sinners," spending much of his time with the so-called 'unclean'.[40] He welcomed people whom the rest of society had excluded, many of whom probably had no family or homes, and encouraged them to come together to help each other. Jesus gave them the support of a new kind of family (each other), and restored their social and economic privileges within the group. In various teachings, Jesus disregarded purity boundaries consistently. For example, he refused to follow the prescribed hand-washing practices[41] and deemed all foods ritually clean.[42] The Pharisees particularly valued purity during meals; yet, knowing this, Jesus welcomed a ritually unclean prostitute who came to thank him during a meal with Pharisees.[43] He even invited tax-collectors and people considered sinners to his shared meals.[44] Many Pharisees deemed non-Jewish people unclean. Yet Jesus spent time in cities of the Greeks[45] and the Samaritans, and he even talked to a Samaritan woman.[46] Jesus encouraged people not to fear contamination from unclean people, but instead to disregard their own ritual purity to help those in need.

Instead of doing away with the idea of purity entirely, Jesus taught that moral purity rather than ritual purity mattered. Showing compassion mattered, but ritual purity did not. John the Baptist had previously

---

[40] Matt 11:19; Mark 2:15-16; Luke 5:29-30, 7:34, 15:1-2.
[41] Matt 15:1-2; Mark 7:1-5; Luke 11:37-38.
[42] Mark 7:14-23.
[43] Luke 7:36-50.
[44] Matt 9:11; Luke 19:1-10.
[45] Matt 4:25; Mark 7:31.
[46] John 4:4-26.

voiced a similar idea, teaching that the purity of one's bloodline did not matter, for God preferred kind deeds.[47] Jesus taught that the moral issue of settling human disputes should take precedence over making ritual purity sacrifices to God.[48] He taught that people need not follow the fasting rituals[49] and that they could even break the ritual purity of the Sabbath day "to do good."[50] Jesus considered immoral behaviour a far greater concern than ritual impurity. He taught that eating the wrong foods did not cause impurity, but saying and doing harmful things did. Immoral behaviours like theft, murder, adultery, greed, deceit and envy made people impure.[51] Jesus emphasised that behaviour flowed out of people's hearts.[52] Thus, the manner in which they treated others demonstrated the moral purity or impurity of their hearts.[53] Jesus condemned the Pharisees because they emphasised ritual purity at the expense of right conduct.[54] He also condemned their outward displays of ritual purity, which concealed their hearts full of "greed and wickedness."[55] According to Jesus, people who followed the Torah as superficially as they did would never enjoy the Kingdom of God.[56]

Like many of the Old Testament Hebrew prophets, Jesus saw behaviour toward others and not ritual as the core of Torah. He summarised it like this: "whatever you wish that men would do to you, do so to them; for this is the Torah and the [teaching of the] Prophets."[57] Many of his teachings on ethics echoed the words of prophets like Isaiah, Amos and Micah,[58] who had challenged people on these issues just as Jesus did. Jesus sharply rebuked the Pharisees for their focus on ritual purity and their failure to follow the teachings of the Torah about caring for others. He called love and mercy the "weightier matters" of the Torah.[59] He scorned the rituals, calling them "human tradition,"[60] since they burdened people rather than helped them.[61] In contrast, Jesus

---

[47] Matt 3:7-10; Luke 3:7-9; John 8:37-47.
[48] Matt 5:21-26.
[49] Matt 9:14-15; Mark 2:18-20; Luke 5:33-35
[50] Luke 6:1-11. See also Matt 12:1-14; Mark 2:23-3:6; John 7:21-24, 9:14-16.
[51] Matt 15:10-20, Mark 7:1-23.
[52] Matt 6:22-23; Luke 11:33-36.
[53] Luke 6:43-45.
[54] Matt 15:7-9; Mark 7:6-8.
[55] Matt 23:25-28; Luke 11:37-47.
[56] Matt 5:20.
[57] Matt 7:12, see also Matt 22:34-40; Mark 12:28-34.
[58] Isaiah 1:11-17, 58:6-7; Amos 5:21-24; Micah 6:7-8.
[59] Matt 23:13-29; Luke 11:37-42.
[60] Mark 7:8-9.
[61] Matt 23:1-4; Luke 11:46.

stressed moral behaviour and helping the poor. He loosened or rejected the ritual laws to improve the lives of the poor and the others who followed him.[62] When Jesus dealt with ritually impure people, he never required them to become ritually pure, which upset the Pharisees.[63] Rather he had them repent only of moral wrongs, particularly those which caused others to suffer.[64] His interest lay not in cleansing people from ritual impurity, but in freeing them from the wrong behaviours that caused the suffering of themselves and others.[65]

While Jesus' moralisation of purity marked good news for the disadvantaged, it presented a problem for both the Pharisees and the Chief Priests. Since the Maccabean Revolt, the Pharisees had believed that Israel had to keep the Torah's purity codes in order to maintain its standing in the eyes of God. The disregard Jesus showed for the purity laws and his criticism of them seriously threatened that goal. The Chief Priests, on the other hand, acquired their wealth through the temple's sacrificial system, which focused on cleansing ritual impurity. By loosening purity laws, Jesus made much of the Temple's sacrificial system redundant and thus undermined their source of wealth. This step meant that the poor no longer had to spend what little money they had on sacrifices. As a result, Jesus' views on purity gained him enemies among both the Temple authorities and the Pharisees.

Social equality

Western society is built upon the Christian principle of equality.[66] Thus, Westerners may find it difficult to understand how radical Jesus' teaching of equality seemed in his time. Greek ideas of honour, status, and social order had permeated Israel's culture, and people lived under an enforced hierarchy of social rank. Those near the top of the order reaped the benefits, but at the expense of the lowest classes. The powerless could not attain equality, and those in power did not want equality. People short-changed by the social order included orphans, widows, women in general, and those with diseases or disabilities. Jesus spent his time with these kinds of people. He disregarded the

---

[62] Matt 11:28-30.
[63] Luke 15:1-32.
[64] Matt 9:12-13; Luke 5:29-32. See also Matt 18:11-14.
[65] John 8:31-36.
[66] E.g. Alvin J. Schmidt, *How Christianity Changed the World* (Grand Rapids, MI: Zondervan, 2001).

normal social boundaries and mixed with people seen as the dregs of society, treating them with respect and dignity.

Jesus went further, by fostering groups that lived together in equality. He founded a group in which people had equal standing no matter what their background, gender or standing in society.[67] Paul later described it: "there is no longer Jew or Greek, there is no longer slave or free, there is no longer male and female."[68] Their past world had defined family and social groups by bloodline, marriage and customs. Jesus opposed this hierarchy, however, and claimed that everyone who did God's will belonged within the same family. In this family, no one would be excluded or disadvantaged.[69]

In his teaching, Jesus challenged people's concern about social status. He praised humility and criticised efforts to gain social standing,[70] often targeting the Pharisees on this matter. He critiqued them for seeking public praise through prayers, shows of mercy, prayer, fasting, clothing, and status.[71] When attending a meal, he criticised self-seeking behaviour in the guests when he saw them choosing seats of honour for themselves.[72] He viewed good moral behaviour as more important than mixing with people of high status.[73] Jesus taught that God prefers people who do his will to the outwardly pious who do not. For this reason, he said that the tax collectors and prostitutes who had repented and followed John the Baptist had behaved better than the religious leaders.[74] His disciples sometimes competed among themselves for status. When this occurred, Jesus critiqued them and told them to behave as humble children, who had no social standing.[75] He argued that people needed to forsake concern for their own status.[76] Everyone in God's Kingdom would have equal standing. The least among them would also have the greatest status,[77] equal to everyone else. He said those "who are now first will be as the last, and the last will be as the first."[78] This radical equality turned the notion of a social hierarchy on

---

[67] James 2:1-4.
[68] Gal 3:28; Col 3:11.
[69] Matt 12:46-50; Mark 3:31-35; Luke 8:19-21.
[70] Matt 23:12; Luke 14:11, 18:14. This teaching parallels Proverbs 3:34.
[71] Luke 18:9-17; Matt 6:1-8, 16-18, 23:4-7; Mark 12:38-40; Luke 11:43.
[72] Luke 14:7-11.
[73] Luke 13:25-27.
[74] Matt 21:28-32; Luke 7:29-35. See also Luke 13:23-30.
[75] Matt 18:1-5, 19:13-15; Mark 9:32-37. See also Mark 10:13-16.
[76] Matt 19:10-12.
[77] Luke 9:46-48.
[78] Matt 19:30 our paraphrase, see also Luke 13:23-30.

its head. He rejected concern for social status and taught, "The greatest among you will be your servant."[79] He served his disciples by washing their feet, usually a task only performed by social inferiors.[80] He sacrificed his own status and life to serve others.[81] Jesus served his disciples, women, children, widows, and those who were sick or disabled without regard for social status.

Concern for social status hindered acts of compassion, and Jesus advocated extravagant compassion. His followers formed a community made distinctive by their love and compassion for each other.[82] That compassion extended past the normal social norms and boundaries. In the story of the Good Samaritan, Jesus taught that the traditional social barriers and purity laws should not limit compassion.[83] He taught people to forgive and not seek retribution,[84] and to show kindness to everyone, not only to friends.[85] His teachings did not respect the social order of society but called upon people to give kindness freely.

The Gospels record Jesus making controversial and politically subversive statements of equality. These challenges to the social structure and its hierarchy of power heralded good news again for the disadvantaged, yet threatened those whose social standing formed a part of their luxurious lifestyle. His activity sought to make worthless the very thing that the powerful elite spent their efforts to maintain and increase – high social status. They stood to lose many of their privileges if people no longer respected them as social superiors. This gave the powerful elite even more reason to oppose Jesus and his activity.

The Temple system

We can also see the concern Jesus had for economic justice in his challenge to the temple system. Temples in the ancient world operated as banks, making those who controlled them potentially very wealthy. According to Torah, the Jerusalem Temple collected revenues from a temple tax payable by all the Israelites. People had to buy pure animals for all sacrifices from the temple. On top of these sources of income, the High Priests encouraged further donations. Those who ran the temple

---

[79] Matt 20:20-27, 23:8-11; Mark 10:35-44.
[80] John 13:4-17.
[81] Matt 20:28; Mark 10:45.
[82] John 13:34-35.
[83] Luke 10:25-37.
[84] Matt 18:21-35.
[85] Matt 5:38-48.

lived in luxury at the expense of the many people they claimed to serve. Jesus criticised them for encouraging people to leave their inheritance to the temple rather than to their family.[86] One incident depicts how the temple system even exploited money from poor people who could not even afford their own food.[87] Jesus condemned such practices, admonishing the Scribes and Pharisees for teaching people to give gifts to the temple when their parents needed the money for financial support.[88]

Jesus did not believe that poor Israelites should have to pay the temple tax.[89] Instead, he taught that God desired mercy for the poor rather than the sacrifices prescribed by Torah.[90] He took the view that good character and behaviour mattered far more than the temple rituals. In a dramatic demonstration of this, he and his followers protested in the Jerusalem Temple. They stopped the ritual sacrifices required by Torah by disrupting the buying of sacrificial animals.[91] Jesus tipped over the moneychangers' tables and called the Temple "a den of robbers."[92]

The Temple authorities claimed to give exclusive access to God's forgiveness, mercy, and blessing. This claim gave them means of political and economic power. Yet Jesus challenged the idea of the Temple as sole facilitator of access to God. He announced that God had forgiven people's sins when they had not gone through sacrificial rituals prescribed by the Torah.[93] Many poor people could not afford the ritual sacrifices for forgiveness through the temple, but Jesus announced to them that God had forgiven their sins anyway.[94] A Samaritan woman discussed worship in the Jerusalem Temple with Jesus. "Our ancestors worshipped on this mountain," she said, "but you [Jews] say that the place where people must worship is in Jerusalem." Jesus told her that people could worship God without the need of any temple system.[95] He taught that they did not need to make sacrifices

---

[86] They "devour widows' houses." See Mark 12:40; Luke 20:47.

[87] Mark 12:41-44; Luke 21:1-4.

[88] Matt 15:1-6; Mark 7:9-13.

[89] Matt 17:24-27.

[90] Matt 9:13, 12:7.

[91] Matt 21:12-17; Mark 11:15-17; Luke 19:45-46; John 2:12-17.

[92] Matt 21:13; Mark 11:17; Luke 19:46.

[93] Matt 9:2-8; Luke 5:17-26. Use of the passive voice was a standard Jewish way to indicate that God was the one forgiving people in Mark 2:5, Luke 5:20, and Luke 7:48. See also his prayer for God to forgive his executors in Luke 23:34.

[94] See Herzog II, *Jesus, Justice, and the Reign of God*, pp. 124 – 132.

[95] John 4:20-24. The phrase "good character and deeds" probably best captures Jesus' reply that is often translated as the cryptic phrase, "spirit and truth."

through the temple system to gain God's help, but that God would help his followers if they asked.[96]

King Herod had rebuilt the Temple in magnificent Roman style at the expense of the local populace. Jesus announced God's judgment against the Temple, saying that God would destroy it for its corruption. "Not one stone will be left here upon another; all will be thrown down."[97] He predicted that this would happen within a generation,[98] saying that the Roman armies would destroy the Temple because Israel had not followed his teachings.[99] Jesus explained that he had not made a supernatural prophecy, but a prediction based on clearly visible circumstances. He said: "When it is evening, you say, 'It will be fair weather, for the sky is red.' And in the morning, 'It will be stormy today, for the sky is red and threatening.' You know how to interpret the appearance of the sky, but you cannot interpret the signs of the times."[100] Jesus saw that if current events continued unabated, eventually the Jews would rebel against Rome, lose, and suffer brutal retaliation. The Romans actually destroyed the Temple in 70 AD when they crushed the huge Jewish uprising that Jesus anticipated.[101] The threats Jesus made against the Temple[102] upset the authorities, and they charged him with making such threats at his eventual trial.[103] Later at his crucifixion, onlookers also mocked him for criticising the Temple.[104] Those oppressed by the temple system would have welcomed these criticisms, however, as this system had become corrupt and exploited the poor.

Physical and spiritual affliction

Physical disabilities and illnesses in the 1st century not only caused pain but also had huge implications for those affected and their families in terms of economics, purity, honour, and inclusion in society. Families and villages often excluded affected people, leaving them with little ability to earn a living and rendering them completely reliant on the

---

[96] Matt 7:7-11; Luke 11:5-13.
[97] Matt 24:1-2; Mark 13:1-2; Luke 21:5-6.
[98] Mark 13:30.
[99] Luke 19:41-44.
[100] Matt 16:2-3.
[101] Indicated by his warnings in Mark 13:7-31; Luke 12:54-13:5, 21:20-36.
[102] John 2:18-22.
[103] Matt 26:60-61; Mark 14:55-59, 15:29.
[104] Matt 27:39-40; Mark 15:29.

help of a compassionate few. Jesus' compassion for the underprivileged, marginalised, and oppressed seems to have driven his mission of social reform. Therefore, he also spent much of his time treating people with physical conditions, since recovery would benefit them hugely. A major part of his activity consisted of healings[105] and exorcisms,[106] and accounts of these take up about 20% of the Gospel texts. Crowds flocked to Jesus, the 'doctor',[107] as he crossed the boundaries of purity and honour to heal and as his fame spread. He cured fevers, leprosy, bleeding, withered hands, deafness, blindness, paralysis, and other diseases. Several accounts also tell of Jesus healing people whom others had pronounced dead. In addition, Jesus trained his followers to heal people in similar ways.[108]

Those in need of healing by Jesus welcomed his ministry. His healings, however, prompted further conflict and controversy with his opponents. Ancient societies did not understand the causes of sickness and disability as well as we do today, so they frequently attributed physical conditions to a divine punishment for sin. The disciples, for example, made this assumption when regarding a young blind man. They quizzed Jesus: "Rabbi, who sinned, this man or his parents, that he was born blind?"[109] In this sense, they saw physical conditions as 'deserved'. Furthermore, it was believed that humans did not have the right to cure sufferers of such physical conditions, since they believed that God had afflicted them for a reason. People thought that they needed to make temple sacrifices and payments in order for God to look kindly upon them and restore their health. The sick who had enough wealth for these rituals thus became a source of income for the Temple authorities. The poor who could not afford the Temple rituals, however, had little hope of God making them well.

---

[105] Matt 4:23-25, 8:1-4, 8:5-13, 8:14-15, 9:1-8, 9:18-26, 9:20-22, 9:27-35, 12:9-13, 12:15-21, 14:34-36, 15:29-31, 19:1-2, 20:29-34, 21:14; Mark 1:29-34, 1:40-45, 2:1-12, 5:21-43, 5:24-34, 3:1-6, 3:7-12, 6:53-56, 7:31-37, 8:22-26, 10:46-52; Luke 4:38-41, 5:12-16, 7:1-10, 5:17-26, 7:11-17, 8:40-56, 8:43-48, 6:6-11, 6:17-19, 13:10-17, 14:1-6, 17:11-19, 18:35-43, 22:49-51; John 4:46-54, 5:1-18, 11:1-44, 9.

[106] Matt 8:28-34, 10:1-8, 12:22-32, 15:21-28, 17:14-21; Mark 1:21-28, 1:29-34, 1:39, 9:38-40, 16:9, 5:1-20, 3:13-15, 6:7, 3:20-30, 7:24-30, 9:14-29; Luke 4:31-37, 9:49-50, 10:17, 8:2, 8:26-39, 11:14-23; 12:10, 9:37-43, 13:31-32; John 1:12-13. 2:23, 3:18, 14:13-14, 17:11-12.

[107] Luke 4:23; Mark 2:17.

[108] E.g. Matt 10:1, 10:5-8; Luke 9:1-2.

[109] John 9:1-2.

Jesus challenged that view of physical sickness and disability as God-ordained punishment.[110] In doing so, he challenged the role of the Temple as the exclusive broker of God's healing. By healing people freely, he demonstrated that people did not have to make sacrifices or payments to the Temple for God to make them well. Since people saw sickness as a punishment from God, they closely associated healing with God's forgiveness. Not surprisingly, the Gospel accounts also connect issues of healing and forgiveness. Each of Jesus' healings also demonstrated that God forgave people without the supposedly necessary sacrifices, rituals and payments to the temple. His healings thus undermined the Temple and fuelled his growing conflict with the religious authorities.

People believed some sicknesses and behaviour came not as punishments from God but as a result of unseen evil powers; particularly physically intangible afflictions that affected people in visible ways (seizures, for example). Jesus healed people suffering from such conditions, and so people saw him as also involved in a conflict with those evil powers. To his contemporaries, his exorcisms made sense as victories against evil powers or spirits. The Gospels explicitly describe several of his exorcisms of demons and healings as victories against Satan, the ruler of these evil powers.[111]

The Gospels also highlight Jesus' conflict against evil powers several times where they portray evil spirits and forces actively working against Jesus. They describe Satan tempting Jesus into an illegitimate use of his power,[112] questioning his authority,[113] and tempting him to gain power wrongly.[114] The Gospels also describe Satan trying to mislead Jesus' disciples[115] and getting Judas to betray Jesus,[116] as well as trying to hinder the effectiveness of his preaching[117] and trying to prevent Jesus from achieving his goals.[118] They present Satan as a corrupting influence on the Kingdom of God.[119] We can conclude that

---

[110] E.g. John 9:3. His freely-given healings also challenged such a view.

[111] Exorcism: Mark 3:22-26; Luke 10:17-20, 11:14-20. Healing: Luke 13:10-17. See also what is said of his disciples in Acts 10:38.

[112] Matt 4:1-4; Luke 4:1-4; see also Mark 1:12-13.

[113] Matt 4:5-7; Luke 4:5-8.

[114] Matt 4:8-11; Luke 4:9-13.

[115] Luke 22:31.

[116] Luke 22:3; John 6:70-71; John 13:2, 13:21-30.

[117] Mark 4:15; Luke 8:12.

[118] Matt 16:21-23.

[119] Matt 13:24-30, 36-43.

people also viewed Jesus' public activity as a conflict with the evil powers that opposed him and his mission.

Summary

Jesus' public ministry aimed to bring about economic, social, religious and cultural reform on both individual and community levels for the benefit of the underprivileged, marginalised, and oppressed. He taught and exemplified a new way of life that treated such people with love, equality and compassion. He crossed social boundaries and broke social norms to help the poor, the sick, and those in need; and he challenged others to do likewise. The people Jesus helped welcomed his activity, but those who stood to lose power and status from his teachings and activity opposed him. His cause brought him into conflict with opponents, especially the religious authorities. His teaching and example offered enormous hope, but his challenging message also sparked great controversy. Despite their different views, people on both sides of the conflict he generated would have seen Jesus' goal clearly. The Gospels depict Jesus working to transform people's lives.

Chapter 3

Authority

Christians today take for granted the idea that Jesus had divine authority. People in the 1st century, however, considered him a controversial teacher operating well outside the boundaries of the institutional religion. Jesus taught people to *not* follow the teachings of the accepted religious leaders. He argued that the religious leaders had an incorrect understanding of Torah,[1] and condemned them for not loving others,[2] a principle which lay right at the core of Torah.[3] He pointed out several ways in which the Pharisees broke Torah through their cunning interpretations and did not act in keeping with the spirit of love.[4] He criticised them dramatically in public, directly challenging their authority. He called them 'play actors', who pretended to provide God's teaching, forgiveness, healing and blessing while instead causing harm.[5]

Jesus wanted people to follow his message instead. For this reason, he had to convince the devout Jews who heard him that his message had divine authority and mandate. If he had failed to do this, his challenges to the economic and religious practices of his time would have had little influence. Conversely, any devout Jew who was convinced that Jesus' message came with divine mandate and authority would choose to obey his message despite its controversial nature. Hence, the paramount issue challenging Jesus' message was his authority.

Jesus claimed to have divine authority for his own teachings[6] - a very controversial claim indeed. The Gospels record him claiming to be the Messiah[7] and God's Son.[8] He claimed greater authority than John

---

[1] John 5:37-47, 7:19.
[2] John 13:34-35, 15:12-17.
[3] Matt 22:34-40; Mark 12:28-34; Luke 10:25-28.
[4] E.g. Mark 7:9-13.
[5] Matt 23:13-29; Mark 7:6-8. See William R. Herzog II, *Jesus, Justice, and the Reign of God* (Louisville, KY: Westminster John Knox Press, 2000), p. 184.
[6] Matt 7:24-29; Mark 1:21-22; Luke 4:31-32.
[7] Matt 26:62-64; Mark 14:60-62; (Luke 7:18-23); John 10:22-26.
[8] Matt 27:43; Luke 22:70.

the Baptist,[9] Abraham, Jonah, Solomon, David, and Moses. Jesus claimed controversially that God had commissioned him[10] as his appointed teacher. He came as the appointed voice of God sent to enlighten people to God's will.[11] He claimed the authority to have "twelve legions of angels" defend him against those who opposed him,[12] even "all authority in heaven and on earth."[13] Jesus portrayed himself as a prophetic teacher[14] with divine authority to reveal a clear and unique vision of what God wanted.[15] He spoke of himself as a leader of the people, like a good shepherd of sheep, leading them in a better direction.[16] Jesus taught very clearly that he had divine mandate and authority, so that people would heed his message.

His opponents sought to undermine this authority to discredit Jesus and his movement. The religious leaders questioned whether God endorsed his activity.[17] They looked for weakness in Jesus' claim to divine authority by challenging it[18] and asking "who gave you this authority?"[19] They argued that an evil spirit had given him authority, rather than God.[20]

So why did so many people believe Jesus' claims of divine authority in the face of such criticism? The answer begins with Israel's long tradition of prophets. God appointed them as his agents, who proclaimed the message of God to those living in their time. Many of the prophets had opposed the political and religious authorities of their day. Also, like Jesus, the prophets had often brought messages of social reform, critiquing current practice in areas of religion, economics, politics or foreign policy. In Israel's history prophets had often

---

[9] John the Baptist: Matt 3:11, 11:7-15; Mark 1:6-8; Luke 3:15-20, 7:24-28; John 1:19-34, 3:22-31, 5:30-36. Abraham: John 8:52-58. Jonah: Matt 12:41; Luke 11:32. Solomon: Matt 12:42; Luke 11:31, 20:41-45. David: Matt 22:41-46; Mark 12:35-37. Moses: John 6:32-35. This is also implicit in his teachings regarding the Torah.

[10] E.g. John 3:2, 6:46, 7:14-18, 7:25-29, 8:26-30, 8:42, 16:27-30.

[11] John 1:1-14, 8:12; 9:4, 12:35-36, 12:44-50, 14:6.

[12] Matt 26:53.

[13] Matt 28:18; see also John 3:35, 13:3,

[14] Prophet: Matt 13:57; Mark 6:4; Luke 4:24, 13:33-35; John 4:44. Teacher: Matt 26:18.

[15] Matt 11:25-27; Luke 10:21-24.

[16] John 10:1-18.

[17] Matt 13:53-58; Mark 6:1-6; Luke 4:22-30, 7:39; John 4:43-44, 7:40-53, 9:16, 9:15-34.

[18] John 8:13-20.

[19] Matt 21:23-27; Mark 11:27-33; Luke 20:1-19.

[20] Matt 12:24-28; Mark 3:22-26; Luke 11:15-20; John 7:20, 8:48-30, 10:19-21.

performed miracles. The Israelites understood miracles as signs of prophetic appointment. God had established a clear pattern for the prophets he sent – the miracles and wonders they performed demonstrated their divine mandate and authority. John's Gospel records someone expressing this common view that only people sent from God could do amazing miracles.[21] Because of that historical pattern, the crowds and critics looked for such signs from Jesus as proof of his divine authority.[22]

How people saw Jesus

People would have viewed Jesus' miracles and healings with the historical pattern of the prophets in mind. The Gospels tell of many miraculous healings Jesus performed, and often portray them as signs of his divine authority. They tell us that Jesus healed many people from all kinds of disease and ailment,[23] and give many accounts of specific healings.[24] We find several accounts of him curing people who could not walk[25] and even bringing to life again people who had died.[26] As well as healing physical affliction, the Gospels also tell of Jesus freeing many people from evil spirits that afflicted them.[27]

In addition to these, the Gospels record other miracles surrounding Jesus that all indicate his divine mandate and authority. We read of the miraculous accounts of the virgin birth[28] and the celestial omen of the star at his birth.[29] They record God audibly attesting to Jesus' divine authority several times.[30] The Gospels record him turning water into wine,[31] catching miraculous hauls of fish both near the start[32] and end[33]

---

[21] John 9:33.

[22] Matt 12:38-40, 16:1-4; Mark 8:11-12; Luke 11:16, 11:29-30, 23:8; John 2:18, 6:30.

[23] Matt 9:27-35,15:29-31, 19:1-2, 12:15-21; Mark 1:39, 3:7-12; Luke 6:17-19.

[24] Matt 8:1-17, 9:20-22, 12:9-13, 12:22-32, 14:34-36, 20:29-34; Mark 1:29-34, 1:40-45, 3:1-6, 3:20-30, 5:24-34, 6:53-56, 7:31-37, 8:22-26, 10:46-52; Luke 4:38-41, 5:12-16, 6:6-11, 7:1-10, 8:43-48, 11:14-23, 12:10, 13:10-17, 14:1-6, 17:11-19, 18:35-43, 22:49-51; John 4:46-54, 9.

[25] Matt 9:1-8, 21:14; Mark 2:1-12; Luke 5:17-26; John 5:1-18.

[26] Matt 9:18-26; Mark 5:21-43; Luke 7:11-17, 8:40-56; John 11:1-44.

[27] Matt 7:22, 8:14-17, 8:28-34, 15:21-28, 17:14-21; Mark 1:21-34, 5:1-20, 7:24-30, 9:14-29, 9:38-40, 16:9, 16:17; Luke 4:31-41, 8:2, 8:26-39, 9:37-43, 9:49-50, 10:17.

[28] Matt 1:18-25; Luke 1:26-38.

[29] Matt 2:1-12.

[30] Matt 3:13-17, 17:5; Mark 1:9-11; Luke 3:21-22; John 1:32-34, 12:28-30.

[31] John 2:1-11.

[32] Luke 5:1-11.

of his ministry, calming a storm at sea,[34] walking on water[35] and retrieving a coin miraculously from a fish's mouth.[36] We read that his closest disciples saw him transfigured and standing between Moses and Elijah, great prophets of divine authority from Israel's history.[37] An unexplained darkness and earthquake occurred during his crucifixion, and the Temple veil at the entrance to the Holy of Holies tore open.[38] Israelites would have seen these as strong signs from God. Matthew's Gospel records that several people came back to life when Jesus died,[39] in an incident reminiscent of the Prophet Elisha's bones bringing a man back to life.[40] Finally, the Gospel accounts of Jesus' resurrection and ascension provide unmistakable indicators of God's divine approval.[41]

Jesus fitted the historical pattern of a divinely anointed prophet and teacher because of his many healings and miracles. His cause and message resonated with the well-known prophetic tradition, and his healings and miracles provided evidence of his divine anointing. We would expect then, that people would have seen Jesus as a prophet and teacher in the course of his public ministry. According to the Gospel accounts, people thought of Jesus in exactly this way. The crowds said of him, "This is the prophet Jesus from Nazareth in Galilee."[42] We read that the crowds "regarded him as a prophet."[43] After Jesus healed a boy believed dead, the crowd responded by saying, "A great prophet has risen among us!"[44] After a different miracle they said, "This is indeed the prophet who is to come into the world," and they wanted to make him King of Israel.[45] When Jesus asked, "Who do the crowds say that I am?" some said, "John the Baptist; but others, Elijah; and still others, that one of the ancient prophets has arisen."[46] Jesus' own followers described Jesus as "a prophet mighty in deed and word before God and all the people."[47] When talking to Jesus, the Samaritan woman said "I

---

[33] John 21:1-14.
[34] Matt 8:23-27; Mark 4:35-41; Luke 8:22-25.
[35] Matt 14:22-33; Mark 6:45-52; John 6:15-21.
[36] Matt 17:23-27.
[37] Matt 17:1-13; Mark 9:2-13; Luke 9:28-36.
[38] Matt 27:45; Mark 15:33, 15:37-38; Luke 23:44-45.
[39] Matt 27:50-54.
[40] 2 Kings 13:14, 20-21.
[41] Mark 16:19; Luke 24:51.
[42] Matt 21:11.
[43] Matt 21:46.
[44] Luke 7:16.
[45] John 6:14.
[46] Luke 9:19; c.f. Luke 9:7, Mark 6:15.
[47] Luke 19:24.

see that you are a prophet."[48] After being healed by Jesus, a formerly blind man told the authorities, "He is a prophet."[49] In all four Gospels these statements appear, implying that people saw Jesus as a prophet akin to other prophets in Israel's history; such as Elijah or Moses. They reached that conclusion naturally after seeing both his miraculous works and his challenges to the authorities over social, economic and religious issues.

The Jews believed also that a *Messiah* (*Christ* in Greek) might come. The term Messiah literally means 'anointed one'. It referred to leaders of Israel whom the religious leaders had physically anointed, in a ritual that publicly recognised their God-given authority. The Old Testament refers to this term 37 times throughout.[50] These people anointed by God often brought liberation and freedom for the people. Around Jesus' time, many of the peasantry hoped that God would send a Messiah to free them from their economic and social conditions. They also expected that such a Messiah would perform many miracles.[51] Jesus fitted this pattern. His activity and message liberated people from oppressive economic and social conditions. He also amazed the crowds with many miracles. Hence, they saw him not only as a prophet, but also as the much-hoped-for Messiah. For example, after hearing some of his preaching, some in the crowd said, "This is really the prophet." Others said, "This is the Messiah."[52] After meeting Jesus, Andrew excitedly told his brother "we have found the Messiah!"[53] Simon Peter plainly told Jesus what he thought of him: "You are the Messiah, the Son of the living God."[54] A Samaritan woman suspected Jesus might be the Messiah when he told her about past events in her life that he could not possibly have known otherwise.[55] After spending two days with Jesus, the people from the village also saw him as "the Savior of the world," their Messiah.[56] People knew him by reputation as "Jesus who is called the Messiah."[57]

---

[48] John 4:19.

[49] John 9:17.

[50] Lev 4:3, 5, 16; 6:22. 1Sa 2:10, 35; 12:3, 5; 16:6; 24:6, 10; 26:9, 11, 16, 23. 2Sa 1:14, 16; 19:21; 22:51; 23:1. 1Ch 16:22. 2Ch 6:42. Psa 2:2; 18:50; 20:6; 28:8; 84:9; 89:38, 51; 105:15; 132:10, 17. Isa 45:1. Lam 4:20. Dan 9:25, 26. Hab 3:13.

[51] See for example Isa 35:5-6.

[52] John 7:40-41.

[53] John 1:41; Mark 8:29.

[54] Matt 16:16; Mark 8:29; Luke 9:20; John 6:69.

[55] John 4:28-29.

[56] John 4:42.

[57] Matt 27:17, 27:22.

The early disciples of Jesus also saw him as a Messiah, a divinely anointed leader who would bring liberation. The Gospels themselves clearly present Jesus in this light. The genealogies in Matthew and Luke[58] trace Abraham and David as his ancestors, in support of his authority as Messiah. Matthew's Gospel even introduces the record as "an account of the genealogy of Jesus the Messiah."[59] Mark begins by giving Jesus a different title which reflects the same divine mandate and authority: "The beginning of the good news of Jesus Christ, the Son of God."[60] The title 'Messiah' has strong Jewish roots, but those familiar with Greek culture would have better understood the term 'Son of God'. Both these terms carried the same significance of divine mandate and authority to their respective audiences. For example, the author of John used both terms synonymously in stating his purpose: "so that you may come to believe that Jesus is the Messiah, the Son of God."[61] Jesus is given the title 'Son of God' in several other places.[62] We can understand all these to indicate his divine authority and mandate, in the same way as the term 'Messiah'. In addition to giving Jesus these titles, the Gospels highlight ways in which his activity fulfilled various prophecies to further establish his divine commission and authority.[63] John's Gospel even depicts Jesus as the incarnation of God himself.[64] In light of all this evidence, we can conclude that Jesus' early followers saw him as a divinely appointed leader and liberator.

People also addressed Jesus by other titles that reflected his activity and mission. The style in which Jesus taught his prophetic and liberating message of economic and social reform fitted within the Rabbinic tradition common throughout Israel. 'Rabbi' was the Aramaic word for 'teacher'.[65] Israelites often gave this title to people who could teach the religion and customs of Israel. Often such Rabbis had groups of students (called disciples) whom they educated, as Jesus had. All four Gospels depict people calling Jesus 'Rabbi', using 'Rabbi' and

---

[58] Matt 1:1-17; Luke 3:23-38.
[59] Matt 1:1.
[60] Mark 1:1.
[61] John 20:31.
[62] Matt 8:29, 14:33, 16:16, 26:62-64, 27:54; Mark 3:11, 5:7, 15:39; Luke 4:41, 8:28; John 1:34, 1:49, 6:69, 9:35-38, 10:31-36, 11:27, 19:7.
[63] Matt 1:22-23, 2:1-6, 2:13-18, 2:23, 4:13-16, 8:16-17, 12:14-21, 12:39-40, 13:13-17, 13:34-35, 21:1-9, 26:54-56, 27:3-10, 27:35; Mark 14:49, 15:27-28; Luke 2:25-39, 18:31-33, 24:25-27, 24:44-46; John 2:12-17, 6:45, 11:51-52, 12:14-15, 12:37-41, 15:22-25, 18:8-9, 19:23-24, 19:31-37.
[64] John 1:1-18, 8:51-59, 10:22-38.
[65] John 1:38.

'Teacher' over fifty times in reference to him.[66] Those in the crowds also addressed Jesus respectfully as 'Master'.[67] This term recognised his honourable reputation as a wise and learned leader. Disciples of Jesus also called him 'Master', since they imitated and learned from him as students.[68] Slaves used the same term to address their owner.[69] The terms 'Teacher' and 'Master' thus reflect Jesus' publicly accepted role as a learned authority figure. Considering these titles together with those above, we arrive at a clear conclusion. The Gospels portray Jesus as a divinely appointed prophet, leader, and teacher, with a divine mandate for his message and cause.

Authority and cause

The miracles of the Old Testament prophets were seen as proof of their anointing by God, yet prophets did not perform miracles simply so that people would believe in their divine appointment. Rather, they performed miracles typically for some other cause. For example, the miracle of changing Aaron's rod into a serpent aimed to persuade Pharaoh to release the Israelites from captivity in Egypt.[70] The ten miraculous plagues brought through Moses and Aaron had the same motivation.[71] The dividing of the sea allowed the Israelites to escape slaughter by the Egyptian armies.[72] The water from the rock at Rephidim provided drink for the Israelites, and it also reinforced Moses' leadership over Israel.[73] The dividing of the Jordan under the leadership of Joshua provided a path to the other side of the river.[74] On other occasions prophets performed miracles out of compassion,[75] to provide food or water,[76] or to aid in battle.[77] Miracles such as these did

---

[66] Matt 8:19, 9:11, 12:38, 17:24, 19:16, 22:16, 22:24, 22:36, 26:25, 26:49; Mark 4:38, 5:35, 9:5, 9:17, 9:38, 10:17, 10:20, 10:35, 11:21, 12:14, 12:19, 12:32, 13:1, 14:45; Luke 3:12, 7:40, 8:49, 9:38, 10:25, 11:45, 12:13, 18:18, 19:39, 20:21, 20:28, 20:39, 21:7; John 1:38, 1:49, 3:2, 3:26, 4:17-19, 4:31, 6:25, 8:4, 9:2, 11:8, 11:28, 13:13, 13:14, 20:16.

[67] E.g. Matt 8:2, 8:6, 15:22, 17:15.

[68] E.g. Matt 8:21, 13:51, 14:28, 14:30, 18:21.

[69] E.g. Matt 18:26.

[70] Ex. 7:10-12.

[71] Ex. 7:20-12:30.

[72] Ex 14:21-31.

[73] Ex 17:5-7.

[74] Num 20:7-11.

[75] 1 Kings 17:17-24; 2 Kings 4:32-37, 5:10-27, 6:5-7.

[76] 2 Kings 3:16-20, 4:38-44.

provide evidence of God's anointing the people involved, but we should not forget that the prophets had other purposes for facilitating these miracles. The prophets typically performed miracles so that others would benefit or conduct themselves rightly in God's sight. They did not intend merely to convince people of their divine authority. In other words, their miracles provided the means to help accomplish their divine mandates.

Consider, then, the motivation Jesus had for his miracles. The stories of Jesus' healings frequently convey a motivation of compassion. He was "moved with compassion" to heal several blind beggars.[78] Compassion moved him on another occasion to heal a leper.[79] It also motivated him to heal crowds,[80] feed over 4,000 people,[81] bring to life a widow's son[82] and teach a large crowd who came to meet him.[83] On many other occasions Jesus healed people because they asked him to do so.[84] These accounts show that Jesus healed others because he wanted to see them restored to health and able to partake fully in society. However miraculous the stories of Jesus' healings, we should not forget his purpose; to help people and make them well. After all, Jesus made it clear that God had appointed him for that very purpose.[85] Jesus' miracles therefore served the dual purpose of both furthering his mission to help others and proving his divine mandate for that mission.

Jesus' miracles also furthered his cause because they persuaded people to join it. We saw earlier that people often responded to Jesus' miracles by acclaiming him as a prophet. They also thought he could be the Messiah, the Son of David, after seeing his miracles. For example, we read that when Jesus healed a blind man who could not speak, onlookers speculated "can this be the Son of David?"[86] Likewise, after Jesus had miraculously walked on water, his disciples called him the Son of God.[87] In performing these miracles, Jesus proved to them his divine authority and gave devout Jews good reason to follow him

---

[77] Josh 10:12-14.
[78] Matt 20:30-34.
[79] Mark 1:40.
[80] Matt 14:13-14.
[81] Matt 15:32-38; Mark 8:1-9.
[82] Luke 7:12-17.
[83] Mark 6:34.
[84] E.g. Matt 8:5-7, 9:27-30, 15:22-28, 20:30-34; Mark 5:22-24, 7:31-37, 8:22-25; Luke 5:12-13.
[85] Luke 4:16-22.
[86] Matt 12:22-23.
[87] Matt 14:24-33.

despite the controversy surrounding his activity. People joined his cause because his miracles persuaded them that it had divine mandate. This theme appears throughout John's Gospel, which often emphasises that God sent Jesus with divine authority so that people would follow his message.[88] John's Gospel records the crowds looking for miraculous signs from Jesus to confirm his divine authority and leadership, and[89] gives several examples of people choosing to follow Jesus as a consequence of witnessing his miracles.[90] According to John, the Pharisees plotted to kill Jesus precisely because his miracles persuaded increasing numbers of people to follow him.[91]

The miracles of Jesus gave onlookers who heard and saw them significant reason to heed his message and to follow him. His miracles had the same significance for the early Christians, who followed Jesus because his miracles proved to them his divine authority and mandate. The Gospel authors no doubt shared this view, and included so many accounts of miracles performed by Jesus because they knew that the key to persuading their readers to follow Jesus lay in showing that he had divine mandate and authority.

---

[88] E.g. John 1:1-14, 3:2, 5:36-37, 5:43, 6:29, 6:33-39, 6:44, 6:57, 7:16, 7:28-29, 7:33, 8:16, 8:18, 8:29, 8:42, 10:36, 11:42, 12:45, 12:49, 13:3, 13:20, 14:24, 15:21, 16:5, 16:27, 17:3, 17:8, 17:18-25, 16:28-30, 17:25, 20:21.

[89] John 6:30.

[90] John 1:45-51, 2:11, 2:23, 4:46-54, 10:40-42, 11:1-45, 12:1-11.

[91] John 11:46-53.

Chapter 4

Movement and martyrdom

We saw earlier that Israelites used the phrase "the Kingdom of God" to refer to their semi-Utopian dream of a better future. It represented a future in which God's will would prevail in Israel. Jesus found this phrase useful to refer to his goals of economic, cultural, social and religious reform, and this phrase occurs regularly throughout the Gospels.[1] The Gospels often summarise Jesus' ministry as preaching the good news of the coming of God's Kingdom. Jesus used the concept often, such as in his famous example prayer: "Your kingdom come: Your will be done, on earth as it is in heaven."[2]

Several movements aiming to bring the Kingdom of God had arisen before the time of Jesus. John the Baptist, for example, had led one such movement. Some Israelites of Jesus' time would have thought 'Kingdom of God' meant the military overthrow of Roman rule.[3] They hoped for a politically independent kingdom of Israel. Apparently, however, Jesus had something quite different in mind. He taught that the Kingdom of God would come not through political revolution, but through people living rightly.[4] Living in God's Kingdom meant living as individuals and communities in a way that fostered peace, love, fairness, and prosperity. The phrase represented 'how life should be'. For this reason, Jesus mentioned that pockets of God's Kingdom had already become a tangible reality of their daily lives,[5] as they lived in a community of people who helped and supported each other. This would have been truly good news to those who struggled to survive under heavy tax burdens. It would have stirred hope among the oppressed and poor by bringing to mind a better way of life. It represented the possibility of returning to a better and brighter society

---

[1] The Gospel of John translates the phrase into Greek using the words "life of the ages" (or simply "life") instead of "Kingdom of God" but essentially it has the same meaning.

[2] Matt 6:10; Luke 11:2.

[3] As mentioned in Matt 11:12.

[4] Matt 4:17; Mark 1:14-15, 2:17; John 3:1-13.

[5] Luke 17:21. See also Matt 12:28; Luke 11:20.

in which people lived rightly according to God's principles.[6] Many of Jesus' hearers had hoped and prayed for this very salvation, and he directed his activity toward this goal.

Apparently, Jesus saw that making the Kingdom of God a reality would take more than him alone, and therefore invited other people to follow his teachings and to join his movement as disciples. Jesus spoke of real opportunity, but told his disciples that it would need the work of many people.[7] For this reason he attempted to gather many followers and much of his activity focussed on leading this movement. About a third of the passages across all four Gospels relate to his movement and collecting of disciples. He did not form the movement by accident or whim, but deliberately formed and nurtured it over several years. He organised his followers, selecting twelve in particular as his closest disciples.[8] He chose a group who could relate to a wide cross-section of society, from low class fishermen to tax collectors and political Zealots. He chose twelve disciples, symbolic of the twelve tribes of Israel, to act as leaders of the new reformed Israel.[9]

Over twenty places in the Gospels record Jesus summoning followers deliberately by saying 'follow me'[10] or similar.[11] He not only trained his closest disciples, but also trained many of his followers to teach and heal as he had done, sending them out on missions exactly like his own.[12] Jesus told them that they would achieve far greater things than he himself,[13] and he used parables to describe how he expected his followers to spread, permeating society and changing it.[14] He portrayed his Kingdom movement as one that would start small but expand to benefit many people.[15] He explained that even a small number of

---

[6] See Mary Ann Beavis, *Jesus and Utopia* (Minneapolis, MN: Fortress, 2006) for a more detailed discussion of this theme.

[7] Matt 9:36-38; Luke 10:1-3; John 4:31-38

[8] Matt 4:18-22; Mark 1:16-20, 3:13-19; Luke 5:1-11, 5:27-28, 6:12-16; John 1:35-44.

[9] Matt 19:27-28; Luke 22:28-30. See R. David Kaylor, *Jesus the Prophet* (Louisville: John Knox Press, 1994), p. 187 and 176 ("fishers" of men).

[10] Matt 4:19, 8:22, 9:9, (10:38, 16:24), 19:21; Mark 1:17, 2:14, (8:34), 10:21; Luke 5:27, (9:23), 9:59, (14:27), 18:22; John 1:43, (6:28-29,10:27,12:26, 13:36, 21:19). Indirect or implied summons are bracketed.

[11] Some translations render his call to join his cause wrongly as 'believe in me': Mark 9:42, John 11:26, 12:44, 14:1, 17:20. This will be discussed further in a later chapter.

[12] Matt 10:1-15; Mark 3:13-19, 6:7-13; Luke 9:1-6, 10:1-12; John 17:18-19.

[13] Matt 28:18-20; Mark 16:15-18; Luke 24:47; John 14:12, 20:21.

[14] Matt 5:13-16; Mark 4:21.

[15] Matt 13:31-21; Mark 4:30-34; Luke 13:18-19.

people could catalyse a radical transformation of society.[16] In this way, his movement spread far and wide,[17] well beyond his immediate followers.[18]

Strength in the face of opposition

Not everyone agreed with Jesus' vision. Hence, he faced increasing opposition as his movement grew, especially from the religious leaders. His claim that God's reign would come through his teachings did more than warn of dramatic change; it also meant that the current religious leadership was not performing God's will. Jesus made this indictment clear. He spoke of God's condemnation of those who did not repent of unjust rule, and of those who opposed Jesus, his ministry, and the way of the Kingdom.[19] Jesus wanted those behaving wrongly to change their ways,[20] presenting them with the opportunity to repent and again live rightly.[21] He warned that they would bring destruction upon themselves if they did not repent,[22] as God would remove "all causes of sin and all evildoers" from his Kingdom.[23] He also told them that God would separate "the evil from the righteous."[24] In the same vein, John the Baptist had foretold earlier that Jesus' ministry would winnow out evildoers.[25] Jesus gave his sternest warnings to leaders who opposed his teachings and to the corrupt rulers oppressing the people. He announced God's displeasure against the priests and Pharisees, saying that they had failed to care for Israel properly.[26] He critiqued them for killing the many prophets that God had sent to bring Israel into the Kingdom.[27] He also criticised people who had tried to usher in the Kingdom in an incorrect way.[28] Those who disagreed with Jesus'

---

[16] Matt 13:33; Luke 13:20-21.

[17] E.g. John 12:10-11.

[18] Mark 9:38-41.

[19] Matt 11:16-24, 12:38-42, 23:14, 23:33, 12:30-37; Mark 3:28-30, 6:11, 12:38-40, 14:17-21; Luke 10:10-16, 11:27-32, 20:46-47; John 3:14-21, 3:36, 5:19-47, 8:21-24, 12:46-50.

[20] Luke 9:51-56.

[21] He illustrates this through a parable in Luke 13:6-9.

[22] Matt 7:24-27; Luke 6:46-49.

[23] Matt 13:24-30, 13:36-43.

[24] Matt 13:47-50.

[25] Matt 3:11-12; Luke 3:16-17.

[26] Matt 21:33-46; Mark 12:1-11.

[27] Matt 22:1-10, 23:37-39; Luke 13:34-35.

[28] Matt 22:11-14.

pronouncements against them had ample reason to oppose him. Even if Jesus had not criticised specific people, his challenging teachings alone would have caused conflict. He preached an unmistakable condemnation and correction for the economic, religious, cultural and moral status quo of his society. Because of all this, Jesus' movement caused huge controversy.[29]

Increasingly, his movement threatened the Jewish religious authorities who disagreed with him. They grew concerned not merely about the preaching of this one person, but about the number of people that joined his growing movement.[30] His activity had incensed them for some time,[31] and eventually the authorities sought to capture Jesus and stop him.[32] The Jewish authorities were also concerned about the possible reaction of the Roman authorities. The Romans (particularly Pilate) had a gained a reputation for suppressing political dissent brutally. If the Roman military decided that Jesus was a political threat and took action against Jesus' followers it would cost many innocent lives. This threat bolstered the resolve of the Jewish authorities to act against Jesus for the sake of their people.[33]

Jesus understood well the dangers that he and his followers faced from the religious authorities during his ministry. After all, Israel had a history of killing prophets who advocated reform.[34] In light of this, he knew he would face opposition from the religious authorities as a prophetic teacher and leader.[35] The religious leaders threatened him, but the Romans had far greater military might and would certainly have seen another Messiah as a political threat. Perhaps for both these reasons, Jesus showed concern about his reputation.[36] He took steps to keep his activity and miracles secret, and to discourage people from talking about him as a Messiah.[37] They did not always heed his warnings, however, and on several occasions Jesus obtained undesired

---

[29] E.g. John 7:11-13. People who declared openly that they followed Jesus were even expelled from the Synagogues: John 9:22, 12:42-43, 16:2.

[30] John 12:17-19.

[31] Matt 21:14-15.

[32] Matt 21:45-46, 26:3-5; Mark 11:18, 14:1; Luke 11:53-54, 19:47-48, 20:19; John 7:30-32, 7:44-45.

[33] John 11:45-53.

[34] Matt 23:29-39.

[35] E.g. Luke 6:22-23; Acts 7:52.

[36] Matt 16:13-14; Mark 8:27-28; Luke 9:18-19.

[37] Matt 16:15-20; Mark 1:25, 1:34, 1:43-45, 3:11, 8:29-30, 9:9, 9:30-32, 7:24, 8:26; Luke 9:21.

publicity.[38] Initially, he tried to avoid unwanted attention from the authorities. He tried to keep his location secret, and warned his disciples that the authorities would eventually kill him.[39] At one point Jesus had to escape a crowd who wanted to acclaim him as king,[40] since such status would have made him an obvious threat to the rulers appointed by the Romans. Jesus told his followers to be wary of King Herod and his servants,[41] as they also saw his movement as a threat.[42] Often, when Jesus discovered ominous dangers to his movement, he withdrew to different cities or less populated places.[43] We read, for example, that he withdrew when he heard news of the execution of John the Baptist.[44] Sometimes Jesus chose to keep his travel plans secret even from his close relatives,[45] and during his risky activity he sometimes only narrowly escaped capture.[46] He said that in time, though, everything would have to become public.[47] When word of his movement spread further, he told his disciples that the authorities would act to stop him.[48]

When Jesus heard that the authorities had conspired to kill him, he resolved to continue to do God's will despite knowing that it would cost him his life.[49] He knew that, since the authorities had decided to act against him, they would also eventually act against his followers.[50] Hence, Jesus warned his followers against possible persecution by the authorities.[51] He told them that they needed to prepare to show courage even in the face of death to support his cause and each other.[52] He warned them of this persecution because he wanted his followers to remain loyal to the cause and not simply run at the first sign of danger.[53]

---

[38] Mark 7:36; see also John 12:9-11.

[39] Mark 9:30-31.

[40] John 6:15.

[41] Mark 8:15.

[42] Matt 22:16; Mark 3:6, 6:14-29, 12:13; Luke 9:7-9, 13:31-32.

[43] Matt 4:12, 12:14-15, 14:1-13; Mark 3:6-7; John 7:1, 10:39-40, 11:54-57 and possibly Mark 1:34-38 and Luke 4:42.

[44] Mark 6:14-32; Matt 4:12.

[45] John 7:2-13.

[46] Luke 4:29-30; John 8:59, 10:39.

[47] Matt 10:26-27; Mark 4:21-23; Luke 8:1-18. See also Matt 5:14-16.

[48] E.g. Matt 16:21; Mark 8:31; Luke 9:22.

[49] E.g. Matt 26:39; Mark 14:36; Luke 22:41-42; John 12:27.

[50] Matt 10:16-42; Mark 13:9-13; Luke 21:7-19; John 15:18-21.

[51] In addition to those above, see also Mark 8:34-38, 10:35-40; Luke 9:23-26, 12:4-12; John 15:18-20 and possibly Mark 9:49.

[52] Luke 21:16; Mark 13:12; John 15:12-13.

[53] E.g. Matt 10:22; Mark 13:13.

His followers needed to be willing to make sacrifices for his cause. Following him would bring difficulty and derision,[54] and his followers might have to leave their families, houses and land.[55] He did not want them to leave at the first sign of difficulty, but rather to be committed followers, fully aware of the sacrifices they would have to make.[56] He warned that his cause would split families apart.[57] The families of some followers might have expelled or persecuted them.[58] He taught people to sacrifice all they owned if necessary to achieve his worthwhile cause.[59] He gave many speeches warning them of the persecutions to come and the need to remain steadfast:

> They will hand you over to councils and flog you in their synagogues; and you will be dragged before governors and kings because of me... Brother will betray brother to death, and a father his child, and children will rise against parents and have them put to death; and you will be hated by all because of my name... When they persecute you in one town, flee to the next... whoever does not take up the cross and follow me is not worthy of me.[60]

In another speech, he warned his disciples of his impending death and reiterated that they could not truly follow him unless they too were prepared to face death for his cause:

> From that time on, Jesus began to show his disciples that he must go to Jerusalem and undergo great suffering at the hands of the elders and chief priests and scribes, and be killed, and on the third day be raised... Then Jesus told his disciples, "If any want to become my followers, let them deny themselves and take up their cross and follow me."[61]

Jesus warned his followers to carefully consider the cost of following him before they decided to commit to him. He wanted them to join him only if they would willingly give up everything they had for his cause:

---

[54] Matt 7:13-14; Luke 13:23-24.
[55] Matt 8:18-22, 19:29; Mark 10:28-31; Luke 9:57-62.
[56] Luke 14:28-32.
[57] Matt 10:35-38; Luke 12:49-53, 14:25-26.
[58] Luke 12:52-53; Matt 10:36.
[59] Matt 13:44-46.
[60] Matt 10:17-38.
[61] Matt 16:21-24.

Whoever does not carry the cross and follow me cannot be my disciple. For which of you, intending to build a tower, does not first sit down and estimate the cost, to see whether he has enough to complete it? ... So therefore, none of you can become my disciple if you are not prepared to sacrifice all you have.[62]

He told his disciples not to fear being martyred: "I tell you, my friends, do not fear those who kill the body, and after that can do nothing more."[63] His speeches to his followers show that he expected many of them to suffer and even die for his cause. Unsurprisingly, Jesus encouraged them often to not surrender or despair during hardship.

Jesus promised great rewards in the afterlife for making such sacrifices and for enduring persecution to follow him.[64] He anticipated that God would reward him after death, which no doubt helped his resolve.[65] Jesus encouraged his followers to prepare to face death for the cause, reminding them that death comes to everyone but God rewards in the afterlife those who follow him.[66] Jesus stated that those who die rich leave their riches on earth, but rewards in the afterlife endure.[67] He promised his followers a resurrection[68] and rewards after death,[69] particularly if they were martyred for his cause.[70] He also promised potential rewards in this life – joy and unity with God in spirit.[71] His followers might leave their families, but the group of followers that they joined would become their new family.[72] They might lose all their old possessions and their land, but they would share in the possessions of the group.[73]

Commitment and perseverance feature as strong themes in the Gospels because following Jesus brought hardship and suffering. The Gospels emphasise consistently the need to persevere and to remain committed to Jesus through persecution and hardship in order to realise

---

[62] Luke 14:27-33.

[63] Luke 12:4.

[64] Matt 5:11-12; Luke 6:22-23; John 8:51, 10:27-29; 12:25-26.

[65] Matt 17:23; Mark 9:31; Luke 18:33; John 17:1-5.

[66] Matt 16:24-28, 10:39, 40-42.

[67] Matt 6:19-20; Mark 8:35-38; Luke 9:23-26.

[68] Matt 22:23-33; Mark 12:18-27; Luke 20:27-40.

[69] Matt 10:32, 19:21, 16:24-27, 25:31-46; Luke 12:4-10; John 3:36, 6:54.

[70] Mark 13:13; Luke 21:12-19 as well as those listed earlier.

[71] John 14:15-25, 15:1-11, 17:20-26.

[72] Luke 18:28-30.

[73] Matt 19:27-29; Mark 10:28-30.

the Kingdom of God.[74] Jesus encouraged his followers and prayed for them to persevere.[75] Seeing that his goal would take many years to realise, he encouraged his followers to endure over time. They needed to prepare for the long-haul, not simply join for a short period and then fall away at the first sign of difficulty.[76]

Jesus taught his followers to guard against those who might corrupt the group and cause others to fall away. He reproached those who betrayed him[77] or discouraged his followers from the cause,[78] warning his followers against corrupt teachers who might entice them away.[79] Yet Jesus knew his closest disciples well enough to predict how they would react in their first threatening situation.[80] His challenging teaching had already caused many to stop following him,[81] and he foresaw that persecution would also lead to disunity among his followers.[82] He advised the group to endeavour to keep itself pure and get rid of trouble-making members.[83] Jesus wanted his followers to live in the way he taught,[84] in unity and peace with one another,[85] and not to struggle for power or prestige.[86] His followers needed to unite and remain faithful during persecution to bring the Kingdom of God to fruition.

Execution of a leader

In light of Jesus' activity, his death at the hands of the authorities was predictable. The authorities had killed the leaders of dozens of similar groups. Jesus knew this and predicted in advance his own death

---

[74] Matt 24:11-13; Mark 13:9-13; John 16:1-4.

[75] John 17:6-17.

[76] Matt 13:1-23, 24:32-51, 25:1-13; Mark 4:1-20, 13:32-37; Luke 8:1-15, 12:35-48, 18:1-8.

[77] Matt 26:17-24.

[78] Matt 18:6-7, 18:10; Mark 9:42; Luke 17:1-2.

[79] Matt 7:15-20, 16:5-12, 24:4-5, 24:23-26, 25:11; Mark 13:5-6, 21-23; Luke 17:22-23.

[80] Matt 26:30-35, 26:57-58, 69-75; Mark 14:26-31, 14:50-54, 14:66-72; Luke 22:31-34, 22:54-62; John 13:36-38, 18:15-17, 18:25-27.

[81] John 6:59-68.

[82] Matt 24:9-10.

[83] Matt 5:29-30, 18:8-9; Mark 9:43-48.

[84] Matt 7:15-23; Luke 6:43-46.

[85] Mark 9:50.

[86] Matt 20:20-27, 23:8-11; Mark 10:35-44.

at the hands of the authorities,[87] which upset his disciples.[88] Jesus chose to make a very public spectacle in Jerusalem during the Passover festival, when thousands of pilgrims flocked there, entering in a procession that parodied and mocked the similar processions made by King Herod in a way that "shook the city."[89] He then denounced and disrupted the Temple publicly.[90] Jesus made it clear that he expected martyrdom for his actions and that he would give his life willingly for the sake of his cause.[91] He said that God would resurrect him,[92] and anticipated that his movement would flourish through his martyr's death and subsequent resurrection.[93]

The Jewish authorities did not have the power to carry out the death penalty, which they considered appropriate for Jesus.[94] Instead, they planned to capture him and convince the Roman authorities to kill him. Jesus' public popularity made it difficult for them to find the right time to catch him,[95] but a close follower betrayed him and made the capture possible.[96] Apparently, Jesus knew of this plot to betray him,[97] and asked his disciples to keep watch while they camped for the night at the border of the wilderness, ready to flee if necessary.[98] Those keeping watch fell asleep and, once the group of Roman soldiers arrived, Jesus chose to go with them peacefully.[99] After his capture the soldiers insulted Jesus, beat him[100] and took him to the Roman governor Pontius Pilate for sentencing.[101] The Jewish authorities presented Jesus to Pilate as a political threat to Roman rule, as the Romans stamped out the many revolutionary, bandit, and messianic movements that formed

---

[87] Matt 20:17-19, 26:1-2; 26:6-13; Mark 8:27-31, 10:32-34, 14:3-9; Luke 9:22, 17:24-25, 18:31-34; John 10:11-18, 12:1-8, 13:1, 16:5-33.

[88] Mark 8:31-33.

[89] Matt 21:1-11; Mark 11:1-10; Luke 19:28-40; John 12:12-16. See Richard A. Horsley, *The Message and the Kingdom* (Minneapolis, MN: Fortress, 2002), p. 71, 72.

[90] Matt 21:12-17.

[91] Matt 26:27-29; Mark 14:22-25; Luke 22:14-20; John 12:27.

[92] John 10:11-18; Matt 16:21, 17:22-23; Luke 9:22.

[93] John 3:14 ("lifted up"), 12:20-24, 12:31-34, and possibly John 16:19-33.

[94] Matt 26:65-66; Mark 14:61-65; Luke 22:66-71. Blasphemy meant to speak badly of someone in order to undermine their honour.

[95] Matt 26:3-5; Mark 14:1-2; Luke 22:21-23.

[96] Matt 26:14-16, 27:3-10; Mark 14:10-11; Luke 22:1-6.

[97] Matt 26:17-26; Mark 14:17-20; Luke 9:44-45; John 6:64, 6:69-71, 13:18-30.

[98] Matt 26:36-46; Mark 14:32-42; Luke 22:39-46.

[99] Matt 26:46-52; Mark 14:42-53; Luke 22:47-53, 66; John 18:1-12.

[100] Matt 26:67-68; Luke 22:63-65.

[101] Matt 27:1-2; Mark 15:1; John 18:28-32, 18:35, 19:7-8.

during their control of Israel. Pontius Pilate was the most notorious of the Roman governors in this regard,[102] and eventually the Romans replaced him because of his infamous brutal massacres of Jewish protest movements. On the other hand, although the Romans eliminated revolutionaries, they tolerated the Jewish religion and religious teachers. Jesus managed to convince Pilate[103] and King Herod[104] to view him as a religious teacher rather than as a political threat, and to view his case as an internal matter of Jewish religion.[105]

In response, the religious leaders who wanted him killed invented more political charges.[106] They claimed that he taught people not to pay the Roman tax[107] and that he had taken the political title of 'King of the Jews'.[108] Jesus is recorded as having avoided that very title once before,[109] so these claims may have been false. Regardless, the religious leaders accused him of being a political revolutionary involved in stirring up the people to rebel[110] and threatening to destroy the Jerusalem Temple.[111] They pressured Pilate to punish Jesus as a political revolutionary by crucifixion.[112] Pilate capitulated and had Jesus crucified under the title 'King of the Jews',[113] alongside two other bandit revolutionaries.[114] One of the two bandits crucified with Jesus reaffirmed his faith in Jesus' teachings, declaring that Jesus had not committed any political crimes and did not deserve death.[115]

Through his own martyrdom, Jesus taught his disciples to face suffering or even death without fear. Jesus used an analogy to describe this powerful effect of his own martyrdom: "I tell you, unless a grain of wheat falls into the earth and dies, it remains just a single grain; but if it

---

[102] Richard A. Horsley and John S. Hanson, *Bandits Prophets and Messiahs* (Harrisburg, PA: Trinity Press International, 1999), p. 66.

[103] Mark 14:55; Luke 23:4, 23:13-14.

[104] Luke 23:15.

[105] Matt 27:18; Mark 15:10.

[106] Matt 27:12-14; Mark 15:3-5.

[107] Luke 23:1-2.

[108] Mark 15:12; Luke 23:2; John 19:12.

[109] John 6:15.

[110] Matt 26:59, 27:1; Luke 23:4-5, 23:10.

[111] Matt 26:61; Mark 14:58.

[112] Matt 27:20-27; Mark 15:11-15; Luke 23:23-25; John 19:6-12.

[113] Matt 27:11, 27:27-37; Mark 15:1-2, 15:16-26; Luke 23:3, 23:11, 23:38; John 18:33-38, 19:1-5, 19:13-22.

[114] Matt 27:38; Mark 15:27-28; Luke 23:32-33. Traditionally, the Greek word translated as 'thieves' was used to describe the political revolutionaries within Israel who operated as groups of bandits.

[115] Luke 23:39-43.

dies, it bears much fruit."[116] This belief that his martyrdom would achieve something great seems to have strengthened his resolve as his death approached: "Now my soul is troubled. And what should I say— "Father, save me from this hour"? No, it is for this reason that I have come to this hour."[117] Jesus became a martyr willingly since he saw the immense effect it would have, and he went to Jerusalem knowing the authorities would kill him as they had killed the prophets before him.[118]

People rarely think of Jesus as a martyr today, but the meaning of the word very much fits the nature of his death. The American Heritage Dictionary defines a 'martyr' as: (1) "One who chooses to suffer death rather than renounce religious principles." (2) "One who makes great sacrifices or suffers much in order to further a belief, cause, or principle."[119] Jesus meets such definitions in a straight-forward manner. Thus, it is accurate to call Jesus a martyr.

The Gospels portray Jesus' death as a consequence of his ministry. They narrate his life, vision, movement and death as one continuous story. As one scholar noted concerning Jesus, "apart from the life of a martyr… the death of the martyr has no meaning."[120] In the bulk of their accounts, the Gospel writers depicted the cause for which Jesus died. They presented the meaning of Jesus' death by giving the account of his life. At the same time, we need not wonder at the considerable attention they gave to the events around Jesus' death. In the 1st century, people considered the way in which notable people died a very important part of their lives. Biographers often gave details of their deaths in accounts of their lives.[121]

A comparison with Martin Luther King Jr.

A modern-day analogy can help us to understand Jesus' ministry and movement. Jesus fits the archetype of a social reformer, martyred for his cause, so let us compare him to a similar martyred reformer; Martin Luther King Junior. Born in America in 1929, King became a Christian minister. He championed the American civil-rights movement by leading non-violent protests against racial inequality. His most

---

[116] John 12:24.
[117] John 12:27.
[118] Luke 13:33-34.
[119] *The American Heritage Dictionary of the English Language*, Fourth Edition. (Houghton Mifflin Company, 2004), Definitions 1 & 2 of 'Martyr'.
[120] Stephen J. Patterson, *Beyond the Passion: Rethinking the Death and Life of Jesus* (Minneapolis, MN: Fortress, 2004), pp. 2 – 3.
[121] Richard A. Burridge, *What Are the Gospels*, pp. 142, 160 – 11, 202.

famous speech, "I Have a Dream," described his ideal future, in which black and white people would live together in harmony as equals. He also led campaigns to help the poor, and protested against the authorities on issues of racism, poverty, militarism and materialism. His views and activity led to his assassination in 1968. Many aspects of his life compare with the life of Jesus. Looking at some of those parallels will assist us in explaining and understanding Jesus' life and ministry.

Both Jesus and King began their protests out of love. They cared about people whom their culture marginalised. Jesus focused on the ritually unclean, the sick, the poor, those with no family, and the ill-treated and excluded women in first-century Israel. King addressed the racism and poverty in a 20th-century society that excluded and neglected people because of their colour.

Jesus and King both gathered followers to support their cause. Jesus travelled around the countryside asking people to follow him, creating groups of followers in each town, structuring his followers and training them. King founded several organisations to aid in his efforts, and travelled around America organising numerous protests and rallies.

They both warned their followers of having to endure hardships, face opposition, and pay a price for the cause. King warned of arrests by authorities and of attacks by racists. Jesus warned his followers that they might face death at the hands of the authorities, and opposition even from their own families. They both stressed the need for perseverance.

Jesus and King both embarked on crusades of cultural reform, sharing a concern for the poor and marginalised. They both advocated equality and opposed the oppressive structures of social class. They attacked the social, political, and religious structures of their time. Their grass-roots movements challenged the authorities and brought social changes.

They both attempted to achieve these changes through non-violent means – they did not attempt a rebellion, revolution, or coup. Rather, they attempted to bring change by attracting followers to join their movements. Jesus wept over the violence he saw looming in Jerusalem.[122] He taught his followers, "love your enemies," which included those who might persecute them.[123] Like King, Jesus advocated non-violent resistance to oppression and organised peaceful protests.[124]

---

[122] Luke 19:41-44.
[123] Matt 5:43-48; Luke 6:27-36.
[124] See Matt 5:38-42; Luke 6:29.

Each had a vision of a better future. King said in his most famous speech, "I have a dream that my four little children will one day live in a nation where they will not be judged by the colour of their skin but by the content of their character."[125] He saw a new and better world, and he sought to make that world a reality through his efforts. Jesus spoke in the same vein of the "Kingdom of God."

In order to achieve their goals, each had to criticise and publicly confront those in power and the oppressive systems they represented. Each became recognised as a religious teacher within the culture of their time – King as a Baptist minister and Jesus as a Rabbi and Prophet. Each advocated God's will, and claimed the backing of God's authority as they challenged the authorities of their day.

Jesus and King both knew that their activity would bring persecution and death, yet both decided to follow their cause anyway, and face death for it. In a speech one day before his death, King stated that he knew of the death threats against him. He made clear his intention to continue his work, which he saw as God's will, even if it cost him his life. He was shot the next day. Jesus began his ministry secretively. He built up a movement among people in the countryside and small towns first to avoid the notice of the authorities. When he spoke in public he used cryptic stories to obscure his meaning to those threatened by his activity. Eventually, his movement grew big enough that the attempts at secrecy failed, and he confronted the authorities boldly, making the deliberate decision to continue with his cause despite knowing that it would bring about his death. The authorities arrested him in the garden of Gethsemane and killed him the next day.

The public knew King's assassination came about because of his controversial activities in the area of civil rights. Likewise, Jesus' contemporaries would have understood that the authorities had killed him because of his controversial activities.

Resurrection

The Gospels record miraculous signs accompanying Jesus' death. These indicate he had the power and authority of God in the same way that the miracles that took place at his birth and baptism did. The Gospels do not suggest that Jesus' death itself differed in kind from the deaths of the revolutionaries crucified alongside him. One thing that differed about Jesus, however, was his resurrection. According to the

---

[125] In his speech "I Have a Dream" delivered 28 August 1963.

Gospels, some of his followers took him down from the cross after he died and placed him in a tomb.[126] Yet they found his tomb empty two days later,[127] despite the two Roman guards posted at the door.[128] The initial confusion about his resurrection evaporated when the disciples met Jesus alive again,[129] which proved to them that those first visitors to the tomb had told the truth[130] – God had indeed raised Jesus from the dead. This revelation of the resurrected Jesus had a profound effect on Jesus' followers. The resurrection proved to them that God endorsed Jesus and his message.

Even more importantly for Jesus' early followers, the resurrection verified Jesus' promise of rewards from God after death. Jesus had taught his followers not to fear death in light of rewards in the afterlife. He frequently mentioned this promise of reward to encourage his followers to persevere with his cause. For example:

> Blessed are you when people revile you and persecute you and utter all kinds of evil against you falsely on my account. Rejoice and be glad, for your reward is great in heaven, for in the same way they persecuted the prophets who were before you.[131]

Another of his comments expresses this idea of reward after persever-ance: "By your endurance you will gain your souls."[132] He said this after warning his disciples that people would hate them because they followed him. The resurrection of Jesus proved to his early followers that the rewards he had promised truly existed. This encouraged them to follow him even in the face of martyrdom, since it paled in light of the expected rewards after death. His resurrection made his persever-ance even to death an even more powerful and significant example for his followers, proving to them that following Jesus would prove worthwhile despite persecution and even execution at the hands of the authorities. Taken together, Jesus' martyrdom and resurrection provided his early followers with a powerful lesson: following him was worth dying for. This lesson would see his movement grow even under fierce opposition.

---

[126] Matt 27:46-50, 27:55-63; Mark 15:34-37, 15:40-47; Luke 23:44-56; John 19:25-42.
[127] Matt 28:6; Mark 16:6; Luke 24:1-3, 24:9-12; John 20:1-10.
[128] Matt 27:62-66.
[129] Matt 28:8-10, 28:16-20; Mark 16:8-14; Luke 24:13-50; John 20:14-29, 21:1-23.
[130] Matt 28:2-7; Mark 16:5-7; Luke 24:4-8; John 20:11-13.
[131] Matt 5:11-12. See also Luke 6:22-23.
[132] Luke 21:19.

Conclusion: The challenge to follow Jesus

The four Gospels all present the same basic story of the life of Jesus and the same major points despite their different styles. 1) They all present Jesus as a divinely appointed prophet and teacher, verified by his miracles and his resurrection. 2) They all record important and memorable parts of his message, teachings and example. These reveal Jesus' cause as one of economic, social, religious and cultural reform for both individuals and the community. 3) Jesus organised a movement to further his cause and transform the economic, religious, and social realities of his day. 4) Jesus encouraged people to join his movement, despite likely persecution, because it would bring rewards both in this life and after death. 5) The Gospels tell of strong opposition to Jesus' activity, which eventually led to his execution. 6) His resurrection demonstrated to his followers that God endorsed Jesus' teachings and movement. Together, these themes in the Gospels convey a strong message – follow Jesus and commit to his movement.[133]

The Gospel authors have included in their Gospels what readers need to know in order to continue Jesus' cause faithfully. The Gospels depict the actions of Jesus, his message and his movement. They capture the way in which his teachings and activity flowed from love, leading him to challenge economic systems, social boundaries, ritual customs and religious exploitation. The Gospels portray a Jesus greatly concerned by the gap between the rich and poor. He objected to the rich landowners forcing peasants off their ancestral farmland because they could not afford to pay the high taxes. He opposed the traditional customs of purity, which labelled and marginalised many people in need and prevented love and care. He shunned the hierarchical social structure of his time and sought to form a counter-cultural group that welcomed everyone as equals. He opposed the corrupt Temple system, since it burdened the peasants financially, and he proclaimed God's impending judgment upon it. Jesus rejected the idea that God inflicted disease and illness as judgment. Instead, he freely healed people and trained his disciples to do likewise. The Gospels depict the way in which Jesus performed God's will in order to bring about the type of society that God wanted to see – the 'Kingdom of God'. Jesus became a teacher, a leader, and ultimately a martyr to make that goal a reality.

The Gospels give an account of the life of Jesus, who was martyred heroically because of his activity to help others. People in the ancient

---

[133] See John 20:31.

world commonly recounted stories of heroes who died noble deaths, retelling them not simply to entertain, nor for mere historical interest, but rather to incite people to imitate the heroes' example. The Gospels fit well within this literary tradition.[134] Early followers of Jesus would have used the stories to encourage and help people to follow him, and read them aloud at gatherings for this purpose. In all four accounts, Jesus commissions his followers to go out and preach the same Gospel of the Kingdom that he had preached during his ministry.[135] The early followers would not have missed the clear message of the Gospel accounts: that God wanted people to follow Jesus, and that following him was worth dying for. The Gospels invited people and communities to join Jesus' movement and have a place in a truly divine Kingdom.

In the last few chapters, we have endeavoured to clearly outline the way in which the Gospels portray Jesus. This overall picture of his public ministry encompasses the main content of all the Gospels. The Gospel authors probably gave the most attention to the themes most important to them. Conversely, they would have given less attention to themes they deemed less important. In the last few chapters, we have endeavoured to make the amount of space we gave to each theme comparable to the space that the Gospel writers gave them. If we have come close to achieving that aim, then this outline also indicates what the early Christians considered important about Jesus, his activity, and his movement. This picture of Jesus' public ministry seems believable and historically plausible. It fits well with what we know about the economics, culture, politics, and religious views of the time. It fits well with the Old Testament tradition of Israel's prophets. It also explains why Jesus' movement grew explosively even after his death. This picture is of Jesus as a prophet and teacher of social reform, widely believed to have performed miracles that proved his God-given authority. The movement he led and ultimately died for aimed to bring tangible change to the lives of the people of Israel.

---

[134] Richard A. Burridge, *What Are the Gospels: A Comparison with Graeco-Roman Biography* (Grand Rapids, MI: Eerdmans, 2004), p. 212, 232. See also: Lawrence Wills, *The Quest of the Historical Gospel: Mark, John and the Origins of the Gospel Genre* (New York NY: Routledge, 1997); David E. Aune, *The New Testament in its Literary Environment* (Philadelphia, PA: Westminster, 1987).

[135] Matt 24:14; Mark 16:15-16; Luke 24:47; John 20:21.

Part 2

Doctrines of the early Christians

In this section, we will look at many core early Christian doctrines fundamental to their paradigm of salvation. In particular, we will examine the early Christian beliefs that differ from modern post-Reformation views. We will draw from modern scholarship and the New Testament to explore their beliefs on a number of key topics. These early Christian ideas will build on the themes we explored in Part 1.

Chapter 5

Final judgment

Many Jews believed that God would judge the lives of everyone after death, rewarding some people but condemning others. This belief seems to have been emphasised particularly strongly during times of earthly injustices, when pious Jews were martyred and their enemies prospered. They saw this final judgment in the afterlife as explaining why God did not always reward the righteous and punish the wicked in this life. This doctrine gave many Jews hope, especially in the face of martyrdom or defeat at the hands of their enemies. Jesus and his followers continued this teaching with only minor adjustments. When we looked at the Gospel accounts, we saw how Jesus spoke of this idea in connection with his own martyrdom and the persecution his followers faced. He encouraged his followers to remain faithful and not to fear martyrdom by pointing to the rewards they would receive from God after death.

One group of Jews who believed strongly in this idea of a final judgment were the Pharisees. One scholar outlines their view:

> The Pharisees taught that sometime in the future everyone who ever lived will return to bodily life on earth. Each person will rise from the grave. Then God will judge every human being according to his or her earthly deeds. The wicked will die again, this time forever, while the righteous will receive a grant of a thousand years of life, followed by the indescribable 'World to Come.'[1]

In other words, they believed that God would base his final judgment on how humans had lived their lives. Speaking more generally about this Jewish tradition, another scholar puts it this way:

> [Ancient] Jewish texts consistently and thematically state that the criterion for survival or approbation at the Last Judgment is deeds... As indicated in their behaviour, the righteous receive

---

[1] Stephen M. Wylen, *The Jews in the Time of Jesus* (Mahwah, NJ: Paulist Press, 1996), p. 59, cf. pp. 60 – 61.

the reward of eternal life, whereas the wicked, for the same reason, receive the recompense of damnation.[2]

The Jews believed that God would judge people based on an overall assessment of their lives. He would consider the entirety of a
person's life and character. Another scholar describes this aspect of the
ancient Jewish view:

> One's works of obedience are not viewed as *merits*, each to be
> recompensed in atomistic fashion, but instead are the observ-
> able manifestations of the covenant loyalty of the unseen heart.
> One's deeds are a single whole, the *way* upon which one is
> walking, and it is this which normally forms the basis or stan-
> dard for the divine recompense.[3]

Jews believed that God would take a person's repentance and change of
character into account – he would forgive a person who repented. If a
formerly wicked person changed and became good, then God would
judge them favourably and their earlier life would "not be remembered."[4] God gave room for mercy and forgiveness, repentance and
reconciliation. He did judge not strictly, but leniently. The prophet
Ezekiel wrote of this: "Have I any pleasure in the death of the wicked,
says the Lord God, and not rather that they should turn from their ways
and live?"[5] In other words, they believed God's judgment did not
involve a legalistic count of good deeds compared to bad. Rather, it
involved a personal and intelligent judgment that took into account
repentance, forgiveness, and the entirety of a person's character and
conduct.

The Jews did not expect any surprises in the verdicts God would
give at the final judgment. The final judgment would ensure the evil
and wicked people finally got what they deserved. He would condemn
wickedness but reward righteousness. One scholar explains that "one
does not *become* righteous at this judgment, but one's righteousness is
revealed or confirmed."[6] "Rather than being necessary to *determine*
one's status as righteous or wicked before God, this judgment functions

---

[2] Chris VanLandingham, *Judgment & Justification in Early Judaism and the Apostle
Paul* (Peabody, MA: Hendrickson, 2006), p. 171.
[3] Kent L Yinger, *Paul, Judaism, and Judgment According to Deeds* (Cambridge
University Press, 1999), p. 285, cf. p. 62.
[4] Ezekiel 18:21-22.
[5] Ezekiel 18:23.
[6] Yinger, p. 286.

primarily to *reveal* this status publicly and to initiate the execution of the appropriate sentence."[7] In short, the Jews believed that God would vindicate the good and righteous at the final judgment. Their enemies who had tormented them would receive their just desserts. God would judge fairly and reasonably. As one scholar explains: "Judgment by deeds is never perceived as unfair... Quite to the contrary, judgment by deeds depicts God as fair, impartial, and righteous. The righteous gain assurance that God is a just judge. Likewise, at the same time, the wicked receive warning."[8]

Recent scholarship has revealed that no Jews thought that God required sinlessness or flawless perfection. All the Jewish sects who believed in a final judgment believed they could actually achieve a favourable judgment. Here are some quotes from two scholars explaining this aspect of Jewish belief:

> The requisite obedience (righteousness) was never viewed a *flawless perfection*, but might be better described by such terms as *consistency*, *integrity*, and *authenticity* of action... Provision was made for occasional failure, and divine patience provided for corrective chastisement upon the seriously wayward to bring them to repentance and a renewed commitment to God's way.[9]

> The "righteous" are not necessarily characterised by a *flawless* obedience, but by the proper attitude of faith and commitment, evidenced by generally consistent outward obedience.[10]

> [As far as the ancient Jewish texts are concerned:] It is misleading to say that just because one sins, one is a "sinner." The term "sinner" denotes a person who habitually sins, does not repent, and defies God. To my knowledge, no early post-biblical Jewish text describes a person as both "righteous" (or the like) and a "sinner." A person is one or the other, but not both. Sinners are often contrasted with the righteous.[11]

---

[7] Yinger, p. 93.
[8] VanLandingham, p. 171.
[9] Yinger, p. 62.
[10] Ibid., p. 96.
[11] VanLandingham, p. 32.

No evidence exists to support the position that even the right-eous are not righteous enough to be worthy of God's ultimate gifts.[12]

Unsurprisingly, Jews who believed in a final judgment seem to have been confident that they would receive a positive judgment and their enemies a negative one. Their writings tell us that, generally, faithful Jews who lived by Torah had no doubt whatsoever that they would receive a favourable judgment. They looked forward to the day when God would judge because they expected rewards for themselves and destruction for their enemies:

> In no instance have we found the note of fearful uncertainty so often associated with judgment according to deeds in carica-tures of legalistic Judaism. As noted above divine judgment ac-cording to deeds usually meant punishment of the wicked and was not even applied to the righteous. For the latter it was in-stead a day "of mercy" or "of covenant," a day awaited without fear and at which they would receive their reward.[13]

Some polemical Jewish writings dwelt on the sinfulness and wick-edness of the Gentiles and how God hated them and their evil ways. Such writings tended to teach that Jews had God's favour simply because God had chosen them as his people. The work *Wisdom of Solomon*, written about a hundred years before the time of Jesus, provides an example. It spends many pages describing the evilness of the Gentile nations and concludes that they are "deservedly pun-ished."[14] Yet Jews believed that they had God's favour simply because of their ancestry. "For even if we sin we are yours..." it reads. "But we will not sin, because we know that you acknowledge us as yours. For to know you is complete righteousness."[15] The writer claims that "the covenants given to our ancestors"[16] proved God gave his kindness exclusively to them.[17] Thus they wrote, "In everything, O Lord, you have exalted and glorified your people, and you have not neglected to help them at all times and in all places."[18] Naturally, the idea that Jews

---

[12] VanLandingham, p. 32.
[13] Yinger, p. 93.
[14] Wisdom of Solomon 16:1.
[15] Wisdom of Solomon 15:2-3.
[16] Wisdom of Solomon 18:22.
[17] Wisdom of Solomon 16:2.
[18] Wisdom of Solomon 19:22.

held greater favour in the eyes of God than other nations influenced ideas about the final judgment in some parts of Judaism.

Hence, within Judaism, two criteria existed regarding the final judgment: whether one had Jewish ancestry, and whether one performed good or evil deeds. People within Judaism held different views about just how much their descent from Abraham and participation in the covenants affected their judgment before God. Similarly, they had no unified view on what level of righteousness God required. The Gospels reflect the variety of these views within Judaism. A Jew named John the Baptist, for example, challenged other Jews about relying on their ancestry for the final judgment with the words, "Bear fruit worthy of repentance. Do not presume to say to yourselves, 'We have Abraham as our ancestor.'"[19]

Jewish literature seldom discussed the precise degree of goodness required to meet God's standards. It often took for granted that trying to follow God's will and do good would suffice to bring positive judgment. Conversely, deliberate, continual rejection of God's will combined with evil conduct would suffice to bring negative judgment. Yet God gave room for repentance. Thus, judgment depends implicitly on a person's heart and present disposition rather than a tally of their past deeds. Having a heart that desires to please God and do good places a person among the righteous, whereas intentionally rejecting God and virtue places one among the wicked. Jews viewed conduct as the outward expression of a person's true inner character. In the words of Jesus, "A tree is known by its fruit."[20] Hence, Jewish writings regularly use language about deeds and actions to indicate the inner character, and switch between references to the heart and the actions. People's righteousness or wickedness depended upon their overall life and disposition, so we cannot draw clear and definitive lines between the two. One scholar explains:

> The boundary between apostasy and fidelity is seldom legislated in unambiguous fashion, since it is a matter not of legal boundaries but of the human heart and of sovereign divine freedom. Questions as to the *quantity* of transgressions or righteous deeds are pointless.[21]

---

[19] Matt 3:8-9; Luke 3:8.
[20] Matt 12:33.
[21] Yinger, p. 285.

The New Testament writers

While Jews of the time did not all agree about whether God might resurrect the dead, the Christians believed unanimously that there would be a resurrection. Jesus' resurrection by God proved to the early Christians the doctrine of a final resurrection. Paul wrote, "Now if Christ is proclaimed as raised from the dead, how can some of you say there is no resurrection of the dead?"[22] Similarly, in Acts, the Jews who believed no resurrection would occur became "much annoyed because [the Apostles] were teaching the people and proclaiming that in Jesus there is the resurrection of the dead."[23] Paul even summarised Christian belief as the hope of resurrection from death.[24] The early Christians saw Jesus as the 'first-fruits' of the resurrection, and believed that God would also resurrect them.[25] The existence of an afterlife made the issue of attaining a positive judgment very important.

English Bibles often translate a common phrase of Paul's as "we are justified by faith not works," or similar. We will discuss brief phrases like this more carefully later, but put such statements to one side for now. Here, we will deal only with more detailed statements that more clearly relate to the concept of final judgment. About thirty passages in the New Testament provide details about the final judgment. When we examine these passages closely, we will see that they all share a common feature: the premise that God judges people based on their conduct – the outward expression of their hearts' character.

The Gospels

The Gospels make it clear that God judges according to conduct. Jesus himself spoke very clearly on the subject:

> The hour is coming when all who are in their graves will hear his voice and will come out – those who have done good, to the resurrection of life, and those who have done evil, to the resurrection of condemnation.[26]

---

[22] 1 Cor 15:12.
[23] Acts 4:2.
[24] Acts 23:6.
[25] E.g. 1 Cor 15:20; 1 Clement 24.1.
[26] John 5:28-29.

Matthew 25 records Jesus' longest and most detailed description of the last judgment. Part of it reads:

> "Come, you that are blessed by my Father, inherit the kingdom prepared for you from the foundation of the world; for I was hungry and you gave me food, I was thirsty and you gave me something to drink, I was a stranger and you welcomed me, I was naked and you gave me clothing, I was sick and you took care of me, I was in prison and you visited me. ... You that are accursed, depart from me into the eternal fire prepared for the devil and his angels; for I was hungry and you gave me no food, I was thirsty and you gave me nothing to drink, I was a stranger and you did not welcome me, naked and you did not give me clothing, sick and in prison and you did not visit me." Then they also will answer, "Lord, when was it that we saw you hungry or thirsty or a stranger or naked or sick or in prison, and did not take care of you?" Then he will answer them, "Truly I tell you, just as you did not do it to one of the least of these, you did not do it to me." And these will go away into eternal punishment, but the righteous into eternal life. [27]

According to that passage, God bases his eternal judgment on conduct. He calls those who have done good and kind deeds to the poor and suffering the 'righteous', and gives them eternal life. In contrast, he rejects those who have failed to do such things. Jesus also made it clear that God will reject those who do evil instead of God's will:

> Not everyone who says to me, "Lord, Lord," will enter the kingdom of heaven, but only the one who does the will of my Father in heaven. On that day many will say to me, "Lord, Lord, did we not prophesy in your name, and cast out demons in your name, and do many deeds of power in your name?" Then I will declare to them, "I never knew you; go away from me, you evildoers." [28]

Jesus explained that our words and deeds reflect our inner goodness or evilness, and that God will judge us based on them:

---

[27] Matt 25:31-46.
[28] Matt 7:21-23; cf. Luke 13:27.

Either make the tree good, and its fruit good; or make the tree bad, and its fruit bad; for the tree is known by its fruit. You brood of vipers! How can you speak good things, when you are evil? For out of the abundance of the heart the mouth speaks. The good person brings good things out of a good treasure, and the evil person brings evil things out of an evil treasure. I tell you, on the day of judgment you will have to give an account for every careless word you utter; for by your words you will be justified, and by your words you will be condemned.[29]

On one occasion, a rich young man asked Jesus directly to name the specific good deed or deeds he should perform to gain eternal life. Jesus had a chance to spell out his position on the subject conclusively. He affirmed the premise implicit in the man's question, that God would judge people based on conduct. Jesus' response was that the man should live in a certain way in order to receive a positive final judgment:

If you wish to enter into life, keep the commandments... You shall not murder; You shall not commit adultery; You shall not steal; You shall not bear false witness; Honor your father and mother; also, You shall love your neighbor as yourself. [30]

He clearly spelt out that moral conduct forms the criterion for eternal life. Jesus then exhorted the man to do another good deed – share his riches with the poor. In a different speech, Jesus said that when he returns people will be repaid according to how they have lived and behaved:

For the Son of Man is to come with his angels in the glory of his Father, and then he will repay everyone for what has been done.[31]

Speaking more generally, Jesus taught that people would receive the consequences of their own behaviour:

Do not judge, and you will not be judged; do not condemn, and you will not be condemned. Forgive, and you will be forgiven;

---

[29] Matt 12:33-37.
[30] Matt 19:17-19.
[31] Matt 16:27.

give, and it will be given to you. A good measure, pressed down, shaken together, running over, will be put into your lap; for the measure you give will be the measure you get back.[32]

Several of Jesus' similar comments reinforce the view that God forgives our sins on the condition that we forgive others.[33] In all these teachings, Jesus made it clear that our behaviour affects how God will judge us.

Paul

Similarly, we find some very clear statements from Paul that show he also believed God will judge according to our character and lives:

For he will repay according to each one's deeds: to those who by patiently doing good seek for glory and honor and immortality, he will give eternal life; while for those who are self-seeking and who obey not the truth but wickedness, there will be wrath and fury.[34]

He explained that people's own consciences will also bear witness to the righteousness of their deeds, and that their "conflicting thoughts will accuse or perhaps excuse them on the day when, according to my gospel, God, through Jesus Christ, will judge the secret thoughts of all."[35] He taught that God will punish the wicked and immoral:

Do you not know that wrongdoers will not inherit the kingdom of God? Do not be deceived! Fornicators, idolaters, adulterers, male prostitutes, sodomites, thieves, the greedy, drunkards, revilers, robbers – none of these will inherit the kingdom of God.[36]

Be sure of this, that no fornicator or impure person, or one who is greedy (that is, an idolater), has any inheritance in the kingdom of Christ and of God.[37]

---

[32] Luke 6:37-38; see also Matt 7:2.
[33] Matt 6:12-15, 18:21-35; Mark 11:25; Luke 6:37, 11:4.
[34] Rom 2:6-8.
[35] Rom 2:15-16.
[36] 1 Cor 6:9-10.
[37] Eph 3:5.

For the wrongdoer will be paid back for whatever wrong has been done, and there is no partiality.[38]

Even Satan disguises himself as an angel of light. So it is not strange if his ministers also disguise themselves as ministers of righteousness. Their end will match their deeds.[39]

Consequently, Paul believed that we must cease doing the things God hates so that he does not condemn us. Throughout his writings he exhorted people to cease sinning. He implored people to "put to death, therefore, whatever in you is earthly: fornication, impurity, passion, evil desire, and greed (which is idolatry). On account of these the wrath of God is coming on those who are disobedient."[40] Paul taught people to change how they lived in order to pass the final judgment, for "if you live according to the flesh, you will die; but if by the Spirit you put to death the deeds of the body, you will live."[41] Elsewhere he warned people to cease sinning, saying "the wages of sin is death."[42] Thus Paul saw it as essential that "we are disciplined so that we may not be condemned along with the world."[43]

Paul wrote that whether we receive eternal life depends on whether we continue in right conduct:

If you sow to your own flesh, you will reap corruption from the flesh; but if you sow to the Spirit, you will reap eternal life from the Spirit. So let us not grow weary in doing what is right, for we will reap at harvest time, if we do not give up.[44]

In short, Paul believed God would judge people based on their conduct:

For all of us must appear before the judgment seat of Christ, so that each may receive recompense for what has been done in the body, whether good or evil.[45]

---

[38] Col 3:25.
[39] 2 Cor 11:14-15.
[40] Col 3:5-6.
[41] Rom 8:13.
[42] Rom 6:23.
[43] 1 Cor 11:32.
[44] Gal 6:8-9.
[45] 2 Cor 5:10.

Whenever Paul expounded his views on final judgment, he always made it clear that God judges people based on their conduct. We can conclude that the concept of a final judgment according to conduct was one of Paul's firm beliefs. We will deal later with the question of how to reconcile this concept with his other beliefs and statements.

Peter

Peter took the same attitude as Jesus and Paul. He wrote to his fellow Jews:

> If you invoke as Father the one who judges all people impartially according to their deeds, live in reverent fear during the time of your exile.[46]

The book of Acts depicts Peter moving away from a belief that God only loves and rewards Jews toward a wider view. Acts reports him saying, "I truly understand that God shows no partiality, but in every nation anyone who fears him and does what is right is acceptable to him."[47]

Peter's belief in a final judgment based on conduct led him to advise others to be careful how they lived. Peter warned, "Do not repay evil for evil or abuse for abuse; but, on the contrary, repay with a blessing. It is for this that you were called – that you might inherit a blessing." He supported this advice by quoting a Psalm:

> Those who desire life and desire to see good days, let them keep their tongues from evil and their lips from speaking deceit; let them turn away from evil and do good; let them seek peace and pursue it. For the eyes of the Lord are on the righteous, and his ears are open to their prayer. But the face of the Lord is against those who do evil.[48]

Like Jesus and Paul, Peter also held that punishments and rewards given by God depend upon moral or immoral behaviour. For two chapters he exhorted his readers to do good and stay away from evil passions, and continued: "the present heavens and earth have been reserved for fire, being kept until the day of judgment and destruction of the godless." Because of this impending judgment, he told his readers

---

[46] 1 Pet 1:17.
[47] Acts 10:34-35.
[48] 1 Pet 3:9-12; Psa 34:12-16.

to consider "what sort of persons ought you to be in leading lives of holiness and godliness." They should "strive to be found by him at peace, without spot or blemish."[49] Peter thought God would punish the wicked and aid those who do good, both now and ultimately at the day of judgment:

> By turning the cities of Sodom and Gomorrah to ashes [God] condemned them to extinction and made them an example of what is coming to the ungodly; and if he rescued Lot, a righteous man greatly distressed by the licentiousness of the lawless (for that righteous man, living among them day after day, was tormented in his righteous soul by their lawless deeds that he saw and heard), then the Lord knows how to rescue the godly from trial, and to keep the unrighteous under punishment until the day of judgment – especially those who indulge their flesh in depraved lust, and who despise authority... These people, however, are like irrational animals, mere creatures of instinct, born to be caught and killed. They slander what they do not understand, and when those creatures are destroyed, they also will be destroyed, suffering the penalty for doing wrong. [50]

Revelation

The book of Revelation also depicts a final judgment according to works. In a key passage that depicts the final judgment scene, we read:

> I saw the dead, great and small, standing before the throne, and books were opened. Also another book was opened, the book of life. And the dead were judged according to their works, as recorded in the books.[51]

Similarly, Revelation includes messages from Jesus which also teach of a judgment according to people's works:

---

[49] 2 Pet 3:1-14.
[50] 2 Pet 2:6-13.
[51] Rev 20:12.

> I am coming soon; my reward is with me, to repay according to everyone's work.[52]

> I am the one who searches minds and hearts, and I will give to each of you as your works deserve.[53]

In keeping with this, Revelation teaches that those who do not meet the moral standards of the judgment will face punishment:

> But as for the cowardly, the faithless, the polluted, the murderers, the fornicators, the sorcerers, the idolaters, and all liars, their place will be in the lake that burns with fire and sulfur, which is the second death.[54]

Clearly, the New Testament authors believed that God will judge people according to their deeds at the final judgment. They believed he will reward the good and condemn the evil[55] and judge according to a person's character and behaviour.[56] He will judge favourably those who do good deeds[57] but condemn the wicked.[58] His judgment applies equally to all nations and he will judge Jews no differently from the Gentiles.[59] It was this last early Christian idea of equality between Jews and Gentiles that contrasted with the beliefs of some of their Jewish contemporaries.

Equality of Jew and Gentile

Some Jewish writings of the time disparaged the Gentiles and their chances of passing the final judgment favourably. As we saw earlier, writings such as *Wisdom of Solomon* suggested that God judges Jews positively and Gentiles negatively. The New Testament writers rejected

---

[52] Rev 22:12.

[53] Rev 2:23.

[54] Rev 21:8.

[55] Matt 12:33-37; Rom 2:14-16; 2 Cor 5:10; Gal 6:8-9; Col 3:24-25; 1 Tim 5:24-25; 1 Pet 3:10-12; 2 Pet 2:9.

[56] 1 Cor 4:5; 1 Pet 1:17; Rev 20:12.

[57] Matt 19:17; Luke 6:37-38; 1 John 4:17.

[58] Matt 7:21-23; Luke 12:47-48; 13:27; Acts 10:34-35; Rom 1:18; 1 Cor 6:9-10; 2 Cor 11:14-15; Eph 5:3-5; Col 3:5-6; 2 Pet 2:12-13; 2 Pet 3:7; Jude 1:14-15; Rev 3:15-16, 21:8.

[59] Matt 25:31-46; Rom 2:6-11, 2:14-16, 14:10-12; Acts 10:34-35; Col 3:24-25; 1 Pet 1:17.

such a view, and insisted that God judges Jews and Gentiles equally. They used the idea of a final judgment based on conduct to support this principle of equality. In two sentences in Romans, Paul repeated three times the equality of Jews and Gentiles before God in the final judgment: "There will be anguish and distress for everyone who does evil, the Jew first and also the Greek, but glory and honor and peace for everyone who does good, the Jew first and also the Greek. For God shows no partiality."[60] He explained: "It is not the hearers of the Torah [i.e. the Jewish people] who are righteous in God's sight"[61] but those who do good. He criticised anyone who thought they could behave badly because their Jewish ancestry gave them special status before God.[62] Similarly, Peter expressed his amazement after he saw the Holy Spirit descending on Gentiles. He said, "I truly understand that God shows no partiality, but in every nation anyone who fears him and does what is right is acceptable to him."[63] The New Testament differs from Jewish teachings on the subject of final judgment only in its denial that Jews have an advantage over Gentiles before God.

New Testament scholars

Biblical scholars who have studied the New Testament texts in recent years have recognised that the early Christians thought God would judge people according to their character and lives. They have begun to highlight the importance of this theme. For example, Chris VanLandingham analysed both the Jewish texts and Paul's letters comprehensively on the subject of final judgment for his thesis research, and published the results in his book, *Judgment & Justification in Early Judaism and the Apostle Paul*. He states:

> [Jews and Paul] agree that an individual's behaviour during his or her lifetime provides the criterion for this judgment: good behavior is rewarded with eternal life, bad behavior with damnation. Paul agrees with a significant number of his Jewish contemporaries on this subject.[64]

---

[60] Rom 2:9-11.
[61] Rom 2:13.
[62] Rom 2:17.
[63] Acts 10:34-35.
[64] VanLandingham, p. 15.

Paul believes that deeds not only affect one's eternal destiny, but form the ultimate criterion for determining one's eternal destiny at the last judgment. The specific deeds proscribed, permitted, or even required may differ [in Paul from Judaism], as they do, for example [within different Jewish writings]; but the idea remains the same: obedience matters to God and forms the basis for final acceptance with God, despite disagreements over what exactly God requires. Regardless of one's divine re-quital, whether eternal life or damnation, one's behaviour de-termines the outcome.[65]

In both early post-biblical Judaism and in the letters of Paul, one's eternal destiny at the Last Judgment depends on one's deeds… Other than making Christ the tribunal, Paul has not al-tered the Jewish belief in the last judgment in any significant way. Like his Jewish contemporaries Paul maintains in the clearest possible language… that an individual's eternal destiny will be adjudicated on the basis of works… Paul allowed for the possibility that God could reject Christians at the Last Judgment for moral failure.[66]

Paul, like his Jewish contemporaries, believes the Last Judg-ment is adjudicated according to deeds.[67]

Kent L. Yinger also performed a comprehensive survey recently, publishing his findings in *Paul, Judaism, and Judgment According to Deeds*. After thoroughly analysing all the relevant passages he concluded:

[Paul] thought he was saying essentially the same thing on this point as were his [Jewish] predecessors… A universal and es-chatological divine judgment awaited humanity, applicable to those within as well as without the people of God… in most in-stances this judgment results in eternal salvation or damnation. It will be according to one's deeds and not so much determine as *reveal* one's character and status as righteous or wicked.[68]

---

[65] Ibid., p. 175.
[66] Ibid., p. 240.
[67] Ibid., p. 309.
[68] Yinger, p. 16.

Paul did expect believers (along with all humanity) to face the final judgment according to works resulting in eternal life or death.[69]

Because of Paul's confidence in the Spirit's ability and readiness to bear fruit in the believers' lives, he could look forward with confidence toward the final judgment according to works.[70]

[Both Paul and Judaism teach that:] For all humanity, the righteous as well as the unrighteous, the believer as well as the unbeliever, it shall be "to each according to his deeds."[71]

In his paper *New Perspectives on Paul*, the scholar N. T. Wright provides another commentary worth quoting at length:

Final Judgment According to Works... was quite clear for Paul (as indeed for Jesus). Paul, in company with mainstream second-Temple Judaism, affirms that God's final judgment will be in accordance with the entirety of a life led – in accordance, in other words, with works. He says this clearly and unambiguously in Romans 14.10–12 and 2 Corinthians 5.10. He affirms it in that terrifying passage about church-builders in 1 Corinthians 3. But the main passage in question is of course Romans 2.1–16... here is the first statement about justification in Romans, and lo and behold it affirms justification according to works! The doers of the law, he says, will be justified (2.13).

... I am fascinated by the way in which some of those most conscious of their reformation heritage shy away from Paul's clear statements about future judgment according to works. It is not often enough remarked upon, for instance, that in the Thessalonian letters, and in Philippians, he looks ahead to the coming day of judgment and sees God's favourable verdict not on the basis of the merits and death of Christ... but on the basis of his apostolic work. 'What is our hope and joy and crown of boasting before our Lord Jesus Christ at his royal appearing? Is it not you? For you are our glory and our joy.' (1 Thess. 3.19f.; cp. Phil. 2.16f.) I suspect that if you or I were to say such a thing, we

---

[69] Ibid., p. 202.
[70] Ibid., p. 203.
[71] Ibid., p. 291; see also p. 259.

could expect a swift rebuke of 'nothing in my hand I bring, simply to thy cross I cling'. The fact that Paul does not feel obliged at every point to say this shows, I think, that he is not as concerned as we are about the danger of speaking of the things he himself has done – though sometimes, to be sure, he adds a rider, which proves my point, that it is not his own energy but that which God gives and inspires within him (1 Cor. 15.10; Col. 1.29). But he is still clear that the things he does in the present, by moral and physical effort, will count to his credit on the last day, precisely because they are the effective signs that the Spirit of the living Christ has been at work in him. [72]

Early Christian Writers

Christians the world over did not forget their core doctrines immediately after the New Testament authors penned their works. The first generation of Christians would have carefully passed their core doctrines onto the next generation. Hence, the extra-biblical texts written by the early Christians ought to contain theology that agrees largely with the New Testament on these important doctrines. Thus it is significant that the Christian writings from the early centuries attest unanimously to a world-wide Christian belief in a final judgment according to virtue, life, character and deeds. This idea features clearly and at length throughout their writings. We will confine quotations to one or two comments from each author, since space does not permit an exhaustive listing here.[73]

The Epistle of Barnabas (written in around 100 AD):

> The Lord will judge the world, playing no favourites. Each will receive according to what he has done. If he is good, his right-

---

[72] N. T. Wright, *New Perspectives on Paul*, 10th Edinburgh Dogmatics Conference: 25 – 28 August 2003. Online: http://www.ntwrightpage.com/Wright_New_Perspectives.pdf. Accessed 13/07/2010.

[73] A few additional references include: 1 Clem 31.2, 50:3; 2 Clem 5.5, 17.7; Justin *1 Apol* 12,14, 21,43,52; Tatian *Address* 7; Theo *Auto* 1.14; Clem *Strom* 6.14.108.4; Cyprian *Works and Alms* 14; Iren *A. H.* 1.10.1, 4.37.7; Hippol *Ag Greeks* 3; Tert *Apol* 48.12, *Ress of the Dead* 14.10; Origen *DP* 1, pref, 5; Lact *Div Inst* 7.21.3-8.

eousness will precede him; if evil, the reward for his wickedness will be before him.[74]

First Clement (written in around 100 AD):

> Take heed beloved [for there will be] condemnation of us all
> unless we walk worthy of Him, and with one mind do those
> things which are good and well-pleasing in His sight.[75]

> Since then all things are seen and heard [by God], let us fear
> Him, and forsake those wicked works which proceed from evil
> desires; so that... we may be protected from the judgments to
> come.[76]

Ignatius, a famous bishop and martyr (written in around 110 AD):

> All things have an end, there is set before us life upon our ob-
> servance of God's precepts, but death as the result of disobedi-
> ence, and every one, according to the choice he makes, shall go
> to his own place[77]

The Shepherd of Hermas, written around 150 AD, became used so
widely by early Christians that it almost became part of the New
Testament. It discussed the final judgment at length, exhorting
Christians to achieve extremely high standards of morality in order to
gain God's approval and achieve a positive verdict at the final judgment. Among many similar comments, it stated:

> Whoever follows [self-restraint] will be fortunate in his life, be-
> cause he will abandon all his evil deeds, believing that if he
> abandons every evil desire, he will inherit eternal life.[78]

> Do no evil in your life, but serve as the Lord's slave with a pure
> heart, keeping his commandments and proceeding in his in-
> junctions; and let no evil desire rise up in your heart... if you do

---

[74] Barnabas 4.
[75] 1 Clement 21.
[76] 1 Clement 28.
[77] Magnesians 5.
[78] *The Shepherd of Hermas* 16:4.

these things and fear [God] and are self-restrained from every evil deed, you will live to God.[79]

Second Clement (written in around 150 AD):

[God will] redeem each of us, according to our deeds.[80]

Therefore, brethren, by doing the will of the Father, and keeping the flesh holy, and observing the commandments of the Lord, will we obtain eternal life.[81]

Justin Martyr wrote two public defences of the Christian faith in around 150 AD in an attempt to stop the persecution of the Church. Explaining the Christian faith, he wrote:

[Christians] hold this view, that it is alike impossible for the wicked, the covetous, the conspirator, and for the virtuous, to escape the notice of God, and that each man goes to everlasting punishment or salvation according to the value of his actions.[82]

Let those who are not found living as He taught, be understood not to be Christians, even though they profess with the lips the teachings of Christ. For it is not those who make profession, but those who do the works, who will be saved.[83]

He defended this doctrine, saying it served the public good because it encouraged moral action.[84] He further argued that Jesus aimed to turn men from their wicked ways and lead them to godliness.[85] Justin defended freedom of choice against the views of some Romans, arguing that free will rather than fate determined righteousness or wickedness.[86]

---

[79] *The Shepherd of Hermas* 54:5; Similitude 5.1.5.

[80] 2 Clement 17.

[81] 2 Clement 13.

[82] Justin Martyr, *First Apology* XII. This is a recurring theme throughout both of Justin's *Apologies*.

[83] Ibid., XVI.

[84] Ibid., XII

[85] Ibid., XVI, amongst many other occurrences.

[86] E.g. *First Apology*, XLIII, though he discusses this several times throughout his *Apologies*.

Irenaeus, a missionary to France in around 165 AD, began his work *Proof of Apostolic Preaching* with these words:

> Knowing, my beloved Marcianus, your desire to walk in godliness, which alone leads man to life eternal, I rejoice with you...[87]

Theophius of Antioch (*Apology to Autolycus*, written in around 170 AD):

> Obeying the will of God, he who desires is able to procure for himself life everlasting. For God has given us a law and holy commandments; and every one who keeps these can be saved, and, obtaining the resurrection, can inherit incorruption.[88]

> He who acts righteously shall escape the eternal punishments, and be thought worthy of the eternal life from God.[89]

> To those who by patient continuance in well-doing seek immortality, He will give life everlasting.[90]

Melito, a renowned bishop (written in around 170 AD):

> If you follow after evil, you will be condemned for your evil deeds. But, if you follow goodness, you will receive from Him abundant good, together with immortal life forever.[91]

Athenagoras of Athens (*On the Resurrection of the Dead*, written in around 180 AD):

> [Men receive] the judgment of their Maker upon them according to the time each has lived, and according to the rules by which each has regulated his behaviour,[92]

> The examination relates to individuals, and the reward or punishment of lives ill or well spent is proportioned to the merit of each.[93]

---

[87] Irenaeus, *Proof of Apostolic Preaching* 1.
[88] Theophilusm *Autolychus* 2.27.
[89] Theophilus, *Autolychus* 2.34.
[90] Ibid., XIV.
[91] Melito of Sardis, *Apology* I.27-28.
[92] Athenagoras, *On the Resurrection of the Dead* 11.

Clement of Alexandria (written in around 200 AD):

> This is the reward of a life of goodness: Everlasting life.[94]

> Whosoever... distinguishes himself in good works shall gain the prize of everlasting life.[95]

Tertullian (*On the Resurrection of the Flesh*, written in around 220 AD):

> I affirm that God's [final] judgment must be believed to be in the first place plenary and complete, as being by that time final, and thereafter everlasting... [man is] to be judged in respect of his life as he has lived it.[96]

> [Everybody is resurrected, so] that every man may receive through his body according as he hath done, [standing before] God's judgment-seat[97]

Origen, easily the most influential writer in the early Church, taught this in his systematic theology written in around 230 AD (*On the First Principles of the Christian Faith*):

> The apostolic teaching is that the soul, having a substance and life of its own, shall, after its departure from the world, be rewarded according to its deserts, being destined to obtain either an inheritance of eternal life and blessedness, if its actions shall have procured this for it, or to be delivered up to eternal fire and punishments, if the guilt of its crimes shall have brought it down to this.[98]

Lactantius (written in around 300 AD):

---

[93] Athenagoras, *On the Resurrection of the Dead* 25. cf 18.
[94] Clement of Alexandria, *Instructor* 1.10.
[95] Clement of Alexandria, *Who is the Rich Man That Shall Be Saved* 1. See also *Rich Man* 18, 42; and *Exhortation to the Heathen* 1, 11.
[96] Tertullian, *On the Resurrection of the Flesh* 14.
[97] Ibid., 60.
[98] Origen, *On First Principles* (De Principiis), Preface 5.

By walking in [the way of righteousness] and following his Teacher, man can attain to eternal life.[99]

Athanasius (*On the Incarnation of the Word*, written in around 333 AD):

> [Jesus will] judge all, by what each has done in the body, whether good or evil; where there is laid up for the good the kingdom of heaven, but for them that have done evil everlasting fire and outer darkness.[100]

Some churches today still use the famous Athanasian Creed written in around 500 AD as a measure of orthodoxy. It presents what Christians of that time considered orthodoxy:

> At [Christ's] coming all people shall rise bodily to give an account of their own deeds. Those who have done good will enter eternal life, those who have done evil will enter eternal fire.

John of Damascus (*An Exact Exposition of the Orthodox Faith*, written in around 730 AD):

> We shall therefore rise again, our souls being once more united with our bodies, now made incorruptible and having put off corruption, and we shall stand beside the awful judgment-seat of Christ... and the impious and the sinful, will be given over to everlasting fire... But those who have done good will shine forth as the sun with the angels into life eternal.[101]

Summary

We have seen that many passages in the New Testament speak of a judgment made according to the virtuousness of a person's life and character. Christianity of both New Testament times and later periods continued to support this common Jewish doctrine. The New Testament teaches this clearly throughout: at the final judgment God will reward the good and punish the wicked. The early Christians opposed the Jewish view that descent from Abraham gave them an advantage. The

---

[99] Lactantius, *Divine Institutes* 4.26.
[100] Athanasius, *On the Incarnation of the Word* 56.4.
[101] St John Damascus, *An Exact Exposition on the Orthodox Faith,* Bk 4, Ch 27.

New Testament, recent scholarship, and the writings of early Christians all indicate that the early Christians believed that final judgment depends upon a person's life and character. Repentance, godly disposition and subsequent good conduct form the *criteria* for positive final judgment and the reward of eternal life.

Chapter 6

The imitation of Christ

The early Christians believed that God had resurrected Jesus, and saw Jesus' resurrection as divine validation of his life and message. Early Christian preaching cited the resurrection as proof of God's endorsement of Jesus. Peter used this argument in his speech to the crowd at Jerusalem, explaining: "This Jesus God raised up, and of that all of us are witnesses. [He is] therefore exalted at the right hand of God... let the entire house of Israel know with certainty that God has made him both Lord and Messiah, this Jesus whom you crucified."[1] Paul made a similar argument, saying that Jesus was "a man whom God has appointed, and of this he has given assurance to all by raising him from the dead."[2] He explained to the Romans that Jesus "was marked out to be Son of God with power... by the resurrection from the dead."[3] Elsewhere, Paul argued that God had resurrected Jesus because he had acted in obedience and submission to God's will.[4] In short, the resurrection proved to the early Christians that Jesus (and hence his controversial teachings) had God's approval.

Secondly, the early Christians also taught that, by resurrecting Jesus, God had appointed him to the position of highest authority[5] as the rightful ruler of all.[6] They believed that God had appointed Jesus as judge at the final judgement. Peter spoke of this: "They put him to death by hanging him on a tree; but God raised him on the third day... he is the one ordained by God as judge of the living and the dead."[7] Later in Acts, Paul relates the same message to the Athenians, telling them: "[God] has fixed a day on which he will have the world judged in righteousness by a man whom he has appointed, and of this he has given assurance to all by raising him from the dead."[8] Paul writes elsewhere that, according to his gospel, God would judge the secret

---

[1] Acts 2:32-36.
[2] Acts 17:31.
[3] Rom 1:4.
[4] Phil 2:8-9; see also Heb 5:7.
[5] Eph 1:20.
[6] See Acts 5:31, Rev 1:5 and other uses of the title "Lord" for Jesus.
[7] Acts 10:39-42.
[8] Acts 17:31.

thoughts of everyone through Jesus Christ.[9] He held that Jesus would judge the living and the dead,[10] and that everyone would appear before the judgment seat of Christ.[11] John shared the same view. He wrote: "The Father judges no one but has given all judgment to the Son."[12] Similarly, Revelation warns that Jesus will judge and repay people according to their works.[13]

Imitating and obeying Jesus

We saw in the previous chapter that the early Christians believed in a final judgment based on conduct. Yet this knowledge alone left a key question unanswered: what sort of conduct would lead to a positive final judgment? The resurrection of Jesus answered that question: conduct of the kind that *Jesus* taught and exemplified. The early Christians saw Jesus as their divinely appointed teacher of what correct conduct *really is*. For example, Paul wrote that God set forth Christ "as a demonstration of godly conduct at the present time."[14] This same idea persisted over a hundred years later, when Clement of Alexandria wrote about "God having made known to us the face of righteousness in the person of Jesus."[15] Paul summed up this idea of Jesus as a teacher by calling him simply, "wisdom from God."[16] This view of Jesus as a divinely appointed teacher is identical to the one we found in our earlier study of how the Gospels present Jesus.

The early Christians had confidence that following Jesus' example and teachings would bring them a positive final judgment for two reasons. Firstly, Jesus' resurrection proved that his conduct and teachings had divine approval. Secondly, if God had made Jesus the final judge, then Jesus would judge positively the sort of conduct that he had exemplified and taught. Their logic can be outlined in this manner:

---

[9] Rom 2:16.

[10] 2 Tim 4:1; c.f. 1Pe 4:5.

[11] 2 Cor 5:10.

[12] John 5:22, 27.

[13] Rev 22:12.

[14] Rom 3:25-26. We will discuss later why the phrase 'God's righteousness' in these verses means 'godly conduct'.

[15] Clement of Alexexadria, *Instructor*, Bk 1, Ch 8. Clement of Rome makes a similar comment in 1 Clem 36.

[16] 1 Cor 1:30.

1. There will be a final judgment based on conduct.
2. The kind of conduct that Jesus exemplified and taught will be judged positively, since:
    a. His conduct and teachings had divine approval.
    b. He will be the final judge.
3. Thus, Christians can obtain a positive final judgement by imitating Jesus and following his teachings.

As we noted in the previous chapter, the early Christians saw Jesus' resurrection as proof that there would indeed be a universal resurrection on the last day, followed by a judgment based on conduct. It also indicated how to obtain a positive judgment. The early Christians believed that they could obtain a resurrection and positive judgment by following and imitating Jesus.

A number of New Testament passages link imitating Jesus with obtaining positive judgement and a resurrection. Paul, for example, exhorted the Christians at Philippi to be of the same mind as Jesus. He motivated them to imitate Jesus in this way by reminding them that God glorified Jesus because of his obedience unto death. He wrote: "Let the same mind be in you that was in Christ Jesus... he humbled himself and became obedient to the point of death – even death on a cross. Therefore God also highly exalted him..."[17] Paul wanted to imitate Jesus' obedient life and death to obtain a resurrection also, as he explained in the next chapter: "I want to know Christ and the power of his resurrection and the sharing of his sufferings by becoming like him in his death, if somehow I may attain the resurrection from the dead."[18] He connected living a Christ-like life with receiving rewards after death. He said that Christians can be "joint heirs with Christ – if, in fact, we suffer with him so that we may also be glorified with him."[19] The letter to Timothy contains a shorter phrase that captures this idea: "If we have died with him, we will also live with him."[20] Paul considered imitating Jesus so important that he stated that people who failed to do this "live as enemies of the cross of Christ."[21]

John also linked imitating Jesus with the outcome of the final judgement. His letters reveal that the early Christians were confident that they could imitate Jesus well enough to gain a positive judgment. For example, he wrote: "Love has been perfected among us in this: that

---

[17] Phil 2:5-9.
[18] Phil 3:10-11.
[19] Rom 8:17.
[20] 2 Tim 2:11.
[21] Phil 3:17-18.

we may have boldness on the Day of Judgment, because as he is, so are we in this world."[22] Elsewhere he presented a similar theme, teaching that "everyone who does what is right is righteous, just as he is righteous."[23] These statements reflect the confidence the early Christians had that they could imitate Jesus adequately and thus obtain a positive final judgement.

Imitation played an important and common role in ancient cultures. Imitating someone's example was considered one of the best ways to learn how to live.[24] Students would not only learn from their teacher but also imitate him in order to become like him. Obeying teachings went hand in hand with imitating the teacher's example. One scholar has pointed out that in the Greek world, the teacher-student relationship centred mainly on imitation.[25] As Origen wrote: "A disciple resembles or imitates his master."[26] Jesus falls into a category of wise Jewish masters known as Rabbis. As we saw earlier, the Gospels record many people addressing Jesus as 'Rabbi', which means 'teacher'. Jesus affirmed the traditional Rabbinic idea that disciples should become like their teacher. He taught: "A pupil is not above his teacher; but everyone, after he has been fully trained, will be like his teacher."[27] As the disciples' teacher, Jesus deliberately used his way of life to set an example. On one occasion, he taught them to imitate his attitude of service after he humbly washed their feet. He said to them: "So if I, your Master and Teacher, have washed your feet, you also ought to wash one another's feet. For I have set you an example, that you also should do as I have done to you."[28] The Gospels show that Jesus' disciples did make an effort to follow his example and teachings.

It seems likely that the early Christians would have used the Gospels to imitate Jesus and follow his teachings. The Gospels gave them a picture of Jesus' life, virtues and teachings for them to fix their eyes on. John's Gospel, for example, presents Jesus as "the Way, the Truth, and the Life."[29] The Semitic term 'way' occurs commonly throughout the

---

[22] 1 John 4:17.

[23] 1 John 3:7.

[24] Seneca, *Epistle* 6.5-6.

[25] H. Weder, 'Disciple, Discipleship' in *Anchor Bible Dictionary* (New York: Doubleday, 1992, ed. David Noel Freedman, Volume 2), p. 209.

[26] Origen, *On First Principles* 1.2.12.

[27] Luke 6:40; see also Matt 10:24-25.

[28] John 13:14-15.

[29] John 14:6.

New Testament, and refers to a person's whole pattern of life.[30] In New Testament usage, the word for 'Truth' seems to mean 'what is right' not only in a factual sense, but also in the moral sense of right conduct. John used the final term, 'the Life', to present Jesus as the ideal role model for how people should live. So, this phrase effectively presents Jesus as "the right way in which to live." In the Gospels, the disciples also seek to imitate and obey Jesus, and in this way they provide additional role models.[31] Apparently, the Gospel authors penned their works so that people would imitate Jesus' teachings and obey his example, and they recorded so many of his actions and teachings in order to help people to do so.

Imitating Jesus is a major theme in the rest of the New Testament. Peter held up Jesus as an example of selflessness.[32] He encouraged his readers to imitate Jesus and told them, "live for the rest of your earthly life no longer by human desires but by the will of God." Like Jesus, they should not let the possibility of suffering deter them.[33] This same point is found in Hebrews, which presents Jesus' suffering as an example of perseverance through opposition to his cause.[34] Finally, consider Paul's letters. He told Christians to keep Jesus' example in mind in order to pattern their lives after his.[35] He taught that they should have the same 'mind' as Christ by developing similar thoughts and character.[36] He exhorted Christians to mature and become like Jesus in moral stature[37] and service to others.[38] He taught: "Be imitators of God, and live in love, as Christ loved us and gave himself up for us."[39] Paul also used metaphors that embodied the idea of imitating Jesus. For example, he

---

[30] H. Wolf, 'derek', in Harris, Archer, Waltke, *TWOT* (Moody, 1980), I:197. E. Merrill, 'derek', in VanGemeren, *NIDOTTE* (Zondervan, 1997), I:989-93. W. Michaelis, 'hodos', in Bromiley, *TDNT* (Eerdmans, 1985, 1-vol. ed.), 670.

[31] E.g. Richard Longenecker (ed.), *Introduction* in *Patterns of Discipleship in the New Testament* (Grand Rapids: Eerdmans, 1996), pp. 5 – 6, 75; L. Hurtado, *Following Jesus in the Gospel of Mark—and Beyond*, ibid., 13, 15, 22, 28, 37; T. L. Donaldson, *Guiding Readers—Making Disciples: Discipleship in Matthew's Narrative Strategy*, ibid., 40, 42, 44, 47-48; William Kurz, *Following Jesus: A Disciple's Guide to Luke-Acts* (Charis Books, 1984), pp. 57 – 67.

[32] 1 Pet 2:21-22.

[33] 1 Pet 3:13-4:2, 4:12-13.

[34] Heb 13:10-13.

[35] 2 Cor 4:8-10.

[36] 1 Cor 2:16; see also Phil 2:5.

[37] Eph 4:13.

[38] Eph 5:21-23.

[39] See Eph 4:20-5:2.

wrote of clothing oneself in Christ,[40] taking on his character and way of life as one would put on a garment. Elsewhere, he wrote of Christ-likeness forming within us.[41]

Students obeyed the instructions of their teacher as an important part of imitating that teacher. Unsurprisingly, the New Testament authors encouraged people to obey Jesus' teachings in order to become more like him. Paul taught his readers to make "every thought captive to obey Christ."[42] Peter provides another example, discouraging his followers from letting wrong desires govern their behaviour and encouraging them to conduct themselves correctly in the same way as Jesus had; like obedient children.[43] John made a similar connection, saying that people who truly know Jesus keep his commands.[44]

Metaphors for imitating Jesus

We have seen that many verses explicitly tell followers of Jesus to imitate and obey him. Even more verses imply this using metaphorical language. People in the first few centuries would have comprehended the idea of imitating Jesus easily through this metaphorical language. Modern readers, however, often miss or misunderstand its significance. This language includes such ideas as participating in Christ, abiding in him, and sharing in his life. Birth and family metaphors are used: being born, adopted, baptised, or named as a child of God or brother of Christ. All these different metaphors refer to imitating Jesus and being like him. We will investigate these metaphors to highlight to what extent the key idea of imitating Jesus pervaded early Christian thought, since it provided them with the way to obtain a positive judgement.

Being "in Christ"

Paul often used the metaphor of participating 'in Christ'. Variations on his 'in Christ' phrase appear 147 times in his writings.[45] Many

---

[40] Gal 3:26-27.
[41] Gal 4:19.
[42] 2 Cor 10:6.
[43] 1 Pet 1:14-15
[44] 1 John 2:3.
[45] The phrase "in Christ" appears 83 times in his writings and "in the Lord" appears a further 46 times; see Dunn, James D. G., *The Theology of Paul the Apostle* (Grand Rapids, MI: Eerdmans, 1998), pp. 396 – 7. Phrases using the pronoun "in him/whom" add at least another 18 instances. "In whom": Eph

scholars have looked to the ideas of the influential Greek philosopher Plato in order to understand this phrase. Plato believed that beyond our visible world there existed a world of perfect archetypes, called 'Forms'. These Forms were the 'blueprints of perfection'. He thought that all things in our world had their essential form because they mimicked these ideal archetypes. For example, everything circular in our world mimics the Form of a Circle. Plato used a particular Greek phrase to express this idea: he said objects participated *in* their Form. For example, he believed that circular objects were 'in' the Form of a Circle. The important aspect of this idea is that any objects that participate in a Form all *share the attributes* of that Form. Plato's ideas became very influential, and subsequent Greek writers also spoke of participating 'in' something to speak of similarity. It seems that Paul used this kind of language when he wrote of being 'in Christ'. He depicted Christ as an archetype, a Form that his followers mimic or imitate. Paul's phrase of participating 'in Christ' would have implied to his early readers a similarity between Jesus and his followers. Given that the early Christians viewed Jesus as a teacher of right conduct, the most obvious sense of this similarity is in the nature of their character and conduct. It is a *moral similarity* that comes from imitating Jesus, following his teachings, and becoming more like him. As David Brondos has argued at length regarding being 'in Christ': "This relationship is one in which the believer obeys Christ, follows his teachings, and lives under Christ as his or her Lord."[46] In other words, this relationship describes Christ-like people who imitate Jesus. They participate 'in Christ' in this ethical sense. Only by being similar to Christ in terms of character and conduct can people participate 'in him'.

Several early Christians wrote about participation in Christ in this moral sense. For example, Athanasius wrote that Christians become united with the saints in the fellowship of life by copying their deeds.[47] Similarly, Clement wrote about how Christians are "assimilated to God by a participation in moral excellence."[48] Origen too saw Jesus as "an example to all believers" and instructed Christians to let Jesus guide them to virtue so that "we may, by imitating Him, be made partakers of

---

1:7-22, 3:12; Col 1:14, 2:11-12. "In him": 2 Co 5:21, 13:4; Eph 1:4, 1:10, 4:21; Php 3:9; Col 2:6-10.

[46] David A. Brondos, *Paul on the Cross: Reconstructing the Apostle's Story of Redemption* (Minneapolis, MN: Fortress, 2006), p. 189. See also pp. 151 – 189.

[47] Athenasius, *On the Incarnation*, Chap. 9.

[48] Clement, *The Instructor* 1.12.

the divine nature."[49] A similar idea occurs in 2 Peter, which presents moral conduct as the means towards participating in Christ:

> His divine power has given us everything needed for life and godliness, through the knowledge of him who called us by his own glory and goodness. Thus he has given us, through these things, his precious and very great promises, so that through them you may escape from the corruption that is in the world because of lust, and may become participants of the divine nature.[50]

Hence, it seems likely that Paul's phrase 'in Christ' implied a similarity with Christ in moral terms of character and conduct. When Paul expanded on the idea of being 'in Christ', he did so typically in the context of moral conduct. For example, he wrote to the Romans: "Those who are in Christ Jesus walk not according to flesh, but according to Spirit." They now live morally and God will not condemn them.[51] Paul's letter to the Corinthians provides another example. He began: "If anyone is in Christ, there is a new creation: everything old has passed away; see, everything has become new!" He went on to explain that this change meant a moral transformation. It meant living for Jesus and obeying him, rather than living for oneself.[52] In his letter to the Ephesians, Paul reminded them that they had been "taught in Christ." He expanded on this by commenting on how they had learned to change their immoral conduct and thinking. Virtue and holiness characterised their new lives in the likeness of God.[53] Our final example comes from earlier in Ephesians. Here, Paul said simply that they were "created in Christ Jesus for good works."[54] In short, Paul's concept of being 'in Christ' referred to practising conduct similar to that which Christ exemplified and taught – the conduct of those who truly imitate Christ.

John's phrase of 'abiding in Christ' is very similar to Paul's 'in Christ' language. John's writings support this interpretation of Paul's

---

[49] Origen, *First Principles* 4.1.31; see also 1.3.8. Also relevant is Origen's comment: "Every one who participates in anything, is unquestionably of one essence and nature with him who is partaker of the same thing." (*First Principles* 4.1.36)

[50] 2 Pet 1:2-4.

[51] Rom 8:1-4.

[52] 2 Cor 5:17.

[53] Eph 4:17-24.

[54] Eph 2:10.

language, since clearly John viewed this participation in a moral sense. He taught: "Whoever says, 'I abide in him', ought to walk just as he walked."[55] John also stated plainly in the next chapter: "All who obey his commandments abide in him, and he abides in them."[56] Jesus' message had centred on loving conduct. Not surprisingly, John wrote that those who love others abide 'in Jesus' and 'in God',[57] and God abides 'in them'.[58] It seems that, for both John and Paul, participating 'in Christ' meant living in imitation of him and in obedience to his teachings.

Being part of the family

The second metaphor used for imitation is that of kinship. In the culture of the time, people expected sons to share similarities with their fathers and brothers to a much greater extent than in modern Western culture. Similarly, first-century people expected the members of the same household to share unified purposes, desires, and way of life. According to one Jewish writer, the great strength of this similarity meant that when fathers died they lived on through their sons, in a sense.[59] The New Testament often uses this idea of kinship to refer to similarity. For example, Jesus insulted some Pharisees by saying, "you are from your father the devil."[60] He did not refer here to a literal kinship, but a similarity of purpose and character. Paul used the phrase in a similar way, calling people children of Abraham if they demonstrated the same kind of faithfulness that he showed.[61]

The New Testament uses this metaphorical idea of kinship with Jesus and God to describe people who imitate Jesus. For example, John wrote: "If you know that Jesus is righteous you may be sure that everyone who does right has been born of him."[62] This statement demonstrates that sharing kinship with Christ implied sharing correct conduct. Elsewhere John explicitly connected these two again:

---

[55] 1 John 2:5-6.
[56] 1 John 3:24.
[57] 1 John 2:24; see also 1 John 3:11, 4:12-13.
[58] 1 John 4:12-13.
[59] Wisdom of Ben-Sirach, 30:4.
[60] John 8:44.
[61] Rom 4.
[62] 1 John 2:29.

> The children of God and the children of the devil are revealed in this way: all who do not do what is right are not from God, nor are those who do not love their brothers and sisters.[63]

Jesus also used this kind of language. He invited his disciples to live as God's children by imitating God and loving even their enemies.[64] The book of Hebrews combines both kinship and participatory metaphors. It teaches that both children of God and those who participate in his holiness require the correct conduct demonstrated by Jesus.[65]

Paul used the phrase 'heirs of God' several times. This phrase appears to combine kinship with the rewards that come through imitating Christ. Paul wrote that the children of God, who live according to his spirit, are 'joint-heirs' with Jesus. The inheritance of these 'joint-heirs' involved a resurrection to life.[66] Paul emphasised the necessity of correct conduct to receive that inheritance. On one hand he put the 'sons of disobedience'. They were characterised by immorality and would not receive inheritance. On the other hand stood the 'children of light', who exemplified virtue and pleased God.[67] This kinship language of the early Christians carried with it the importance of imitating Jesus. These Christians taught that people are God's children not because they call themselves 'Jewish' or 'Christian', but because they imitate the correct conduct of Jesus.[68]

Sharing Jesus' life and death

As the early Christians imitated Jesus and his way of life, they could say in this sense that they 'lived Christ's life'. Jesus' spirit also lived in them, since they lived by the same principles and developed a similar character. Paul used this metaphor of living Christ's life often. For example, he stated, "it is no longer I who live, but it is Christ who lives in me."[69] He combined this idea with the language of participation 'in Christ' and taught that God approves of the "life in Christ Jesus" that Christians live.[70] Christians died symbolically to their old lives and lived new lives in imitation of Jesus. Baptism 'into Christ' symbolised

---

[63] 1 John 3:10.
[64] Matt 5:44-45, 48.
[65] Heb 12:7-11. There is a similar combination in Origen, *First Principles,* 4.1.32.
[66] Rom 8:14-17; Gal 4:4-7; see also Eph 1:5.
[67] Eph 5:5-10.
[68] See Matt 7:21-23; 1 John 2:4, 6; and Paul's argument in Rom 1:18-5:2.
[69] Gal 2:20. See also 2 Cor 4:10-11 and 1 Cor 1:30 for examples.
[70] 1 Cor 1:30; Rom 8:2.

this death of their old immoral lives and the start of their new ones.[71] Like Jesus, they would face persecution for living a "godly life in Christ Jesus,"[72] and would need strength to persevere as they 'walked in Him'.[73] This concept of imitation helps to clarify Paul's more confusing writings about dying and living in or with Christ.[74] For example, it helps us to make sense of this statement from Paul: "if with Christ you died to the principles of the world, why do you live as if you still belonged to the world?"[75] In short, Paul seems to have thought of Christians 'dying with Christ' as they repented of their sinful conduct, and 'living in Christ' in the sense that their new way of life imitated that of Christ.

The early Christians changed their lives and lived like Christ in order to gain a positive final judgement and resurrection. As Paul explained: "if we have been united with him in a death like his, we will certainly be united with him in a resurrection like his."[76] Elsewhere he put it this way: "if we have died with him, we will also live with him; if we endure, we will also reign with him..."[77] The early Christians lived "the life of Jesus," and this gave them confidence that God would resurrect them as he had resurrected Jesus.[78] Paul explained it to the Colossians in this way: "When Christ who is your life is revealed, then you also will be revealed with him in glory."[79] He went on to give a long set of instructions on how they ought to live that life. The early Christians called the resurrection "the promise of life that is in Christ Jesus."[80] Their 'life in Jesus' was one lived in imitation of him, and it gave them confidence in gaining a positive final judgment.[81]

---

[71] Rom 6:1-12.

[72] 2 Tim 3:12.

[73] Col 2:6.

[74] Also, the passage in John 6:53-58 about eating and drinking Christ may be a metaphor for this idea.

[75] Col 2:20.

[76] Rom 6:5.

[77] 2 Tim 2:11-12.

[78] 2 Cor 4:7-14.

[79] Col 3:1-4.

[80] 2 Tim 1:1; see also Eph 3:6.

[81] This seems to be the idea in Phil 1:21.

The first five centuries of Christianity

We have examined the reasons why imitating Jesus was such a vital part of early Christian doctrine. We would expect Christians to have continued teaching people to imitate Jesus for several centuries, and their writings show that they did exactly that. Let us give a few brief examples. In about 90 AD, Clement of Rome wrote that we should follow the "example which has been given us" in Christ.[82] Ignatius taught that we should "live not after the manner of men, but according to Jesus Christ."[83] At about the same time, Polycarp exhorted people to "follow the example of the Lord."[84] Irenaeus too saw Christ as "an example of piety, righteousness, and submission."[85]

In about 200 AD, Tertillian described the way in which servants should obey their earthly masters. He considered it far more important, however, to imitate Jesus' character and to obey him because final judgement depended on doing so. Therefore, he exhorted Christians to obey Jesus' teachings diligently.[86] Another writer of about the same period, Clement of Alexandria, called Jesus "the Instructor." He believed that people had "a clear example of immortality in the walk and conversation of the Lord." Jesus had demonstrated and trained people in the right way of life – the "life which is best" as Clement phrased it. Clement also linked this way of life with salvation. He called it the "truly saving life of our Saviour." Elsewhere, he exhorted his readers to "perform the works of the Master" as best they could.[87] For Clement, to follow Jesus meant to imitate him:

> For it is thus that one truly follows the Saviour, by aiming at sinlessness and at His perfection, and adorning and composing the soul before it as a mirror, and arranging everything in all respects similarly.[88]

Origen shared a similar view, writing that Christ provided "a pattern of most virtuous life, in order that His disciples might devote themselves

---

[82] 1 Clem 16.17.
[83] Ignatius, *Trallians* 2.1.
[84] Polycarp, *Philippians* 10.
[85] Irenaeus, *Against Heresies* 2.22.4.
[86] Tertillian, *Of Patience*, Ch. 4.
[87] Clement of Alexandria, *Instructor*, Bk. 1, Ch. 12 and Ch. 3.
[88] Clement, *Who Is the Rich Man that is Saved* 21.

to the work of instructing men in the will of God."[89] His contemporary, Hippolytus of Rome, saw Jesus as a model for all people of all stages in life. Hippolytus added: "If you obey His solemn injunctions and become a good imitator of Him who is good, you will become like Him and will be honoured by Him."[90] He too linked imitating Christ with obtaining a positive final judgment. He said that Christians should "make Him the pattern of their conduct, and thereby win their highest glory" when God judged them.[91]

The idea that Jesus provided a blueprint for how to live was still common in the Christian tradition at the turn of the 4th century AD. Writing at that time, a teacher called Methodius explained: "For this reason [Jesus], being God, was pleased to put on human flesh, so that we, beholding as on a tablet the divine Pattern of our life, should also be able to imitate Him who painted it."[92] Several writers continued to link imitating Christ with receiving a positive final judgment. For example, Basil wrote that Jesus had lived, taught, suffered, died and rose again for us to receive salvation through imitating him.[93] Augustine also linked the idea of imitating Christ with the rewards of a positive final judgment. He wrote: "You are called a child [of God]: but if you refuse to imitate Him, why do you seek His inheritance?"[94] We can see the view of the early Christians from even this brief selection of quotes. They saw Jesus as a teacher and an example of how to live, and they continued to recognise the need to imitate his example and follow his teachings.

Other role models

It is worth recognising that the early Christians imitated not *only* Jesus, but also other people who followed his example well. In this way, Christians passed down the way of life exemplified by Jesus personally, from teacher to student. Paul, for example, considered himself as a Christ-like example to follow.[95] For this reason, he invited Christians to

---

[89] Origen, *Against Celsus* 1.68.

[90] Hippolytus, *Against All Heresies* 10.33-34.

[91] Hippolytus (c. 205, W), from surviving fragments of *On Genesis*. See *Ante-Nicene Fathers* (Buffalo: Christian Literature Publishing, 1885), 5.167.

[92] Methodius, *Concerning Chastity*, 1.4, see also 8.8.

[93] St. Basil, *De Spiritu Sancto*, 35.

[94] St. Augustine: *Sermon on the Mount; Harmony of the Gospels; Homilies on the Gospels*, Sermon LXIV, 3.

[95] 1 Tim 1:16.

not only imitate Christ, but also to imitate himself.[96] Paul held up himself and his fellow Christians as examples so that people would imitate them and "do what is right."[97] He also provided Abraham as an example. Abraham had faithfully obeyed and followed God and, as a result, God had declared him righteous and rewarded him. Hence, Paul taught that all those who "follow the example of the faithfulness that our ancestor Abraham had" could expect to receive the same rewards.[98] He described these followers as "those who share the faithfulness of Abraham."[99] In his view, scripture records Abraham's example so that people might learn from it.[100] Hebrews too exhorts readers to imitate godly role models so that they might develop in love, service, and diligence. It instructs people to imitate "those who through faithfulness and patience inherit [God's] promises."[101] Later, Hebrews spends all of Chapter 12 listing exemplary people. It concludes the list by saying: "Remember your leaders, those who spoke the word of God to you; consider the outcome of their way of life, and imitate their faithfulness."[102] Timothy and the Jewish Christians provided other Christ-like role models.[103] These brief quotations show that the New Testament writers encouraged Christians to imitate Christ-like role models to become more like him. The writings from later Christian writers show that this tradition of imitation continued for several centuries.[104]

Conclusion

The early Christians viewed imitating Jesus not as optional, but as a requirement. They considered it a vital doctrine. Jesus had revealed to them the way in which to conduct themselves correctly and live in a way that God considered righteous. They followed Jesus by learning to imitate him, by developing the same disposition he had, and by living according to his example and teachings. This imitation gave them confidence in obtaining a positive final judgment and resurrection.

---

[96] 1 Cor 4:16, 1 Cor 11:1; Phil 3:17; 1 Thes 1:6, 8.

[97] 2 Thess 3:6-13.

[98] Rom 4:12. The Greek word, *pistis*, probably means faithfulness here.

[99] Rom 4:16. *Pistis* again probably means faithfulness here.

[100] Rom 4:23-24.

[101] Heb 6:9-12.

[102] Heb 13:7-8.

[103] Timothy: 1 Tim 4:12-16. Jewish Christians: 1 Thess 2:14.

[104] In addition to the above quotes, see also 1 Clem 5-6; Athanasius, *On the Incarnation*, Ch. 9; Basil of Caeseria, *Basil to Gregory*, Letter 2, 3.

Chapter 7

Moral exhortation

Anyone familiar with the New Testament knows that it exhorts us to moral conduct. It calls us to avoid doing evil and instead to love others and do good. The question we will address in this chapter is this: *why* did the early Christians exhort people to practise moral conduct?

The post-Reformation view prevalent today considers moral conduct good, but it teaches explicitly that conduct itself does not form the basis for final judgment. It holds instead that final judgment depends only upon 'faith', which entails belief, trust, and reliance. It teaches that human conduct and effort to live rightly have no bearing on the final judgment. This post-Reformation view stands in contrast to the view of the early Christians that we have presented so far. We have argued that these Christians saw moral conduct as important not simply because it is good, but because it forms the basis for final judgment. As a result, the early Christians placed great importance on making an effort to live rightly.

These two views make opposite predictions about what we would expect to appear in the New Testament. The post-Reformation view would lead us to expect no verses that exhort moral conduct in connection with final judgment. We would not expect to find the idea of a positive final judgment used as the motivation or reward for good conduct. The thesis of this book, however, predicts that the New Testament writers *would* have linked conduct and judgment. We would expect to find frequent exhortations towards moral conduct, and expect frequent references to final judgment in this context as an incentive or reward. So, let us examine the New Testament to determine which view the evidence actually supports. We will progress through the books of the New Testament and, in each one, we will outline the passages exhorting moral conduct that use final judgment as a motivation for such behaviour.

Moral exhortation in the New Testament

Romans

Paul's letter to the Christians in Rome dealt extensively with their conduct. Early on in the letter, he explained clearly that conduct has great importance, since it forms the basis of final judgment:

> For he will repay according to each one's deeds: to those who by patiently doing good seek for glory and honour and immortality, he will give eternal life; while for those who are self-seeking and who obey not the truth but wickedness, there will be wrath and fury. There will be anguish and distress for everyone who does evil... but glory and honour and peace for everyone who does good...

He instructed them to "walk in newness of life," and do good as instruments of righteousness rather than wickedness.[1] He warned that sinful behaviour leads to death, but emphasised that righteous living brings the reward of a positive final judgment and eternal life:

> When you were slaves of sinfulness, you were free in regard to righteousness... The end of those things is death. But now that you have been freed from sinfulness and enslaved to God, the advantage you get is sanctification. The end is eternal life. For the wages of sinfulness is death, but the free gift of God is eternal life in Christ Jesus our Lord.[2]

In this passage, Paul presented his readers with two alternatives for the final judgment that depended upon their moral conduct. He continued this theme later in the letter, elaborating on the way in which following Jesus' way of life freed people from sinfulness.[3] This liberation enabled them to live rightly, so that they would receive a positive final judgment and resurrection. Paul explained it using the common Greek ethical concepts of 'flesh' and 'spirit'. We will investigate this kind of ethical language in more detail later, but here we will focus on the link he made between living according to the Spirit and obtaining a resurrection:

---

[1] Rom 6:11-14.
[2] Rom 6:22.
[3] Rom 7.

> There is therefore now no condemnation for those who are in Christ Jesus. For the law of the spirit of life in Christ Jesus has set you free from the law of sinfulness and of death... If the spirit of him who raised Jesus from the dead dwells in you, he who raised Christ from the dead will give life to your mortal bodies also through his spirit that dwells in you... if you live according to the flesh, you will die; but if by the spirit you put to death the deeds of the body, you will live.[4]

Remember that those 'in Christ' are those who imitate his example and obey his teachings. Thus, we could summarise Paul's message here like this: live according to Jesus' example and teachings, rather than doing immoral deeds desired by the body, in order to receive a positive final judgment and resurrection. Throughout chapters 12 and 13, Paul continued by giving instruction after instruction detailing the kind of correct conduct that Christians should practise.[5]

Letters to the Corinthians

In his first letter to the Corinthians, Paul instructed each Christian not to be "sexually immoral or greedy," nor an "idolater, reviler, drunkard, or robber." Paul did not consider people who did these things true followers of Jesus.[6] What incentive did Paul give?

> Do you not know that wrongdoers will not inherit the kingdom of God? Do not be deceived! Fornicators, idolaters, adulterers, male prostitutes, sodomites, thieves, the greedy, drunkards, revilers, robbers – none of these will inherit the kingdom of God.[7]

Paul's idea of 'inheriting' God's kingdom in this passage seems to refer to a positive final judgment and resurrection after death. So, here again, Paul used final judgment as an incentive for his readers to live morally.

He went on to explain his view that immoral people ought to have their lives transformed by following Jesus.[8] He gave some specific moral instructions. These concerned lawsuits among believers,

---

[4] Rom 8:1-13.
[5] Rom 12-13.
[6] 1 Cor 5.
[7] 1 Cor 6:9-10.
[8] 1 Cor 6:11.

marriage, those not married, and food offered to idols.[9] He exhorted the Corinthian Christians to strive toward self-disciplined conduct by using a metaphor from their well-known athletic competitions at Corinth:

> Do you not know that in a race the runners all compete, but only one receives the prize? Run in such a way that you may win it. Athletes exercise self-control in all things; they do it to receive a perishable garland, but we an imperishable one. [10]

Paul referred here to the imperishable prize of a positive final judgment and resurrection. He held this up as the incentive for living self-controlled, moral lives. In further support of this idea, he gave an example of God's negative judgment of Israelites, who had involved themselves in evil, idolatrous and sexually immoral behaviour.[11]

His second letter to the Corinthians covered similar themes. Paul encouraged them to focus on Jesus' example and to live a life like his.[12] He reminded them to remain faithful to Jesus, and gave the hope of resurrection as incentive: "we know that the one who raised the Lord Jesus will raise us also with Jesus."[13] They held this hope of eternal life on the grounds that the 'inner nature' of their character was being renewed every day.[14] In the next chapter, he made a clearer statement on final judgment to motivate his readers toward correct conduct:

> For all of us must appear before the judgement seat of Christ, so that each may receive recompense for what has been done in the body, whether good or evil.[15]

He taught that conversion marked a moral transformation of a person's inner character: "If anyone is in Christ, there is a new creation: everything old has passed away; see, everything has become new!"[16] He exhorted them a little later towards moral conduct and gave God's promises as a motivation: "Since we have these promises, beloved, let us cleanse ourselves from every defilement of body and of spirit,

---

[9] *Lawsuits*: 1 Cor 6:1-8. *Marriage*: 1 Cor 7:1-16. *Unmarried*: 1 Cor 7:25-40. *Food offered to idols*: 1 Cor 8.
[10] 1 Cor 9:24-25.
[11] 1 Cor 10:6-14.
[12] 2 Cor 4:1-11.
[13] 2 Cor 4:14.
[14] 2 Cor 4:16-18.
[15] 2 Cor 5:9-10.
[16] 2 Cor 5:17.

making holiness perfect in the fear of God."[17] Here, promised future rewards formed the motivation for correct conduct.

Galatians

Echoing many of the themes in Romans, Paul instructed the Christians in Galatia towards moral behaviour. He drew again on common Greek ethical ideas to exhort them to moral conduct: "Live by the spirit, I say, and do not gratify the desires of the flesh."[18] Paul connected his exhortation to avoid immoral conduct with the final judgment: "I am warning you, as I warned you before: those who do such things will not inherit the kingdom of God."[19] Once again, we see that Paul drew on the concept of final judgment as a motive for correct behaviour. Continuing this theme, he reiterated that they should live morally, by 'the spirit' rather than by 'the flesh'. Again, he highlighted the reward of positive final judgment that they would reap in reward for continuing to do what is right:

> Do not be deceived; God is not mocked, for you reap whatever you sow. If you sow to your own flesh, you will reap corruption from the flesh; but if you sow to the spirit, you will reap eternal life from the spirit. So let us not grow weary in doing what is right, for we will reap at harvest time, if we do not give up.[20]

Ephesians

Paul taught that the Ephesians' previous immoral living would have led to a negative final judgment of 'wrath': "All of us once lived among them in the passions of our flesh, following the desires of flesh and senses, and we were by nature children of wrath, like everyone else."[21] Paul pointed out that God had mercifully saved them and transformed the way in which they lived: "For we are what he has made us, created in Christ Jesus for good works, which God prepared beforehand to be our way of life."[22] Paul emphasised the importance of their new behaviour at length:

---

[17] 2 Cor 7:1.
[18] Gal 5:16; see Gal 5:16-26.
[19] Gal 5:21.
[20] Gal 6:9-10.
[21] Eph 2:3.
[22] Eph 2:10.

> Now this I affirm and insist on in the Lord: you must no longer
> live as the Gentiles live, in the futility of their minds... They
> have lost all sensitivity and have abandoned themselves to li-
> centiousness, greedy to practise every kind of impurity. That is
> not the way you learned Christ! ... You were taught to put away
> your former way of life, your old self, corrupt and deluded by
> its lusts, and to be renewed in the spirit of your minds, and to
> clothe yourselves with the new self, created according to the
> likeness of God in true righteousness and holiness.[23]

Paul provided final judgment as the incentive for this moral conduct.
He warned them that immoral people would not inherit eternal life at
the final judgment:

> Therefore be imitators of God, as beloved children, and live in
> love... But fornication and impurity of any kind, or greed, must
> not even be mentioned among you, as is proper among saints...
> Be sure of this, that no fornicator or impure person, or one who
> is greedy (that is, an idolater), has any inheritance in the king-
> dom of Christ and of God. Let no one deceive you with empty
> words, for because of these things the wrath of God comes on
> those who are disobedient.[24]

Throughout the remainder of the letter, he continued to instruct them in
moral living.[25]

Philippians

Near the start of his letter to the Philippian Christians, Paul expressed his hope that they would obtain a positive final judgment
through living rightly:

> And this is my prayer, that your love may overflow more and
> more with knowledge and full insight to help you to determine
> what is best, so that on the day of Christ you may be pure and

---

[23] Eph 4:17-24.
[24] Eph 5:1-6.
[25] Eph 5:7-18, 5:21-33, 6:1-4. 6:5-9.

blameless, having produced the harvest of righteousness that comes through Jesus Christ for the glory and praise of God.[26]

Paul continued to further emphasise the importance of living rightly,[27] holding up Jesus as an example of the way in which they should live.[28] He warned them: "Work out your own salvation with fear and trembling." This statement occurs in the context of his moral exhortations, and shows his belief that their conduct mattered greatly for salvation. Paul continued to instruct them in the nature of good conduct again, pointing to the final judgment (the 'day of Christ') as the time when this conduct would be rewarded:

> Do all things without murmuring and arguing, so that you may be blameless and innocent, children of God without blemish in the midst of a crooked and perverse generation, in which you shine like stars in the world. It is by your holding fast to the message of life that I can boast on the day of Christ that I did not run in vain or labor in vain.[29]

Paul continued with emotive pleas for his readers to live rightly, and warned them of a negative final judgment if they did not:

> Brothers and sisters, join in imitating me, and observe those who live according to the example you have in us. For many live as enemies of the cross of Christ; I have often told you of them, and now I tell you even with tears. Their end is destruction...[30]

Once again, Paul linked a negative judgment with a failure to live in the correct way. He was clearly passionate about the importance of correct conduct, saying "I tell you even with tears." He contrasted negative conduct and judgment with living in imitation of Christ-like people. Through living as 'citizens of Heaven', they would obtain a positive final judgment and resurrection on the day of Christ.[31]

---

[26] Phil 1:9-11.
[27] Phil 1:27, 2:3-5.
[28] Phil 2:5-11.
[29] Phil 2:12-16.
[30] Phil 3:17-19.
[31] Phil 3:20.

Colossians

Paul asked that the Colossians continue to "lead lives worthy of the Lord, fully pleasing to him, as you bear fruit in every good work."[32] They had transformed their lives and stopped doing evil deeds. Paul said they would stand "holy and blameless and irreproachable" before God at the final judgment, provided that they continued to live in this way.[33] Here again, Paul used final judgment as the motivation for practising correct conduct. Paul believed that, through being Christ-like, people could expect a positive final judgment. With that in mind, Paul continued instructing the Colossians in moral living.[34] He summarised this doctrine concisely as: "Christ in you, the hope of glory."[35]

Letters to the Thessalonians

In his letters to the Thessalonian Christians, Paul again linked conduct with final judgment. He urged them to "lead a life worthy of God."[36] If they lived rightly, they would stand "blameless before our God and Father at the coming of our Lord Jesus with all his saints."[37] Later, he repeated that they should "abstain from every form of evil," in order to stand "blameless at the coming of our Lord Jesus Christ."[38] In these passages, Paul exhorted them to practise moral conduct because he believed in a final judgment based on conduct.

Letters to Timothy

The letters to Timothy focus particularly on moral behaviour. The author emphasised turning away from wickedness[39] and pursuing moral virtue.[40] He spent over a chapter detailing the nature of moral conduct.[41] What motivation or incentive did the author give for living in a godly manner? This passage provides the answer:

---

[32] Col 1:9-10.
[33] Col 1:9-23.
[34] Col 3:5-12; see also Col 2:20-23.
[35] Col 1:24-29.
[36] 1 Thes 2:11-12.
[37] 1 Thes 3:12-13.
[38] 1 Thess 5:15-23.
[39] 2 Tim 2:19b-22.
[40] 1 Tim 6:3-11.
[41] 1 Tim 5.

> Train yourself in godliness, for, while physical training is of some value, godliness is valuable in every way, holding promise for both the present life and the life to come.[42]

Here, a positive final judgment and eternal life ('the life to come') is held out as an incentive for moral conduct.

Titus

The author told Titus to appoint only leaders who practised correct moral conduct[43] and to reprimand immoral people severely.[44] He instructed Titus: "teach what is consistent with sound doctrine... so that those who have become faithful to God may be careful to devote themselves to good works."[45] This passage presents good conduct as the goal of 'sound doctrine'. In Titus, we find a fascinating passage that highlights the importance of this conduct. It first outlines a time prior to salvation, in which people had lived immorally as slaves to their desires. It continues by explaining the way in which God saved them from that state through Jesus:

> For the favor of God has appeared, bringing salvation to all, training us to renounce impiety and worldly passions, and in the present age to live lives that are self-controlled, upright, and godly, while we wait for the blessed hope and the manifestation of the glory of our great God and Savior, Jesus Christ. He it is who gave himself for us that he might redeem us from all iniquity and purify for himself a people of his own who are zealous for good deeds.[46]

This passage depicts salvation entirely in terms of moral transformation. The author pointed out in this passage that they wait in hope for the afterlife because of their moral living. This passage shows that Jesus' 'own' people have a great zeal for good deeds.

---

[42] 1 Tim 4:7-10; see also 1 Tim 6:17-19.
[43] Titus 1:5-9.
[44] Titus 1:12-16.
[45] Titus 2:1-3:8.
[46] Titus 2:1-14.

Hebrews

The author of Hebrews called his readers to "provoke one another to love and good deeds" all the more as the day of final judgment approached.[47] The author encouraged readers to lay aside sinfulness[48] and emphasised the importance of disciplining themselves towards moral behaviour.[49] Twice, he reminded readers that sinful conduct would result in a negative final judgment.[50]

James

James reminded his readers that they needed to show mercy in order to receive a positive final judgment: "For judgment will be without mercy to anyone who has shown no mercy." He told them that correct beliefs alone were 'dead', and would not avail them in the final judgment if they did not live rightly.[51] After exhorting Christians to turn from wickedness and live morally,[52] he summarised true Christian religion in terms of moral conduct: "Religion that is pure and undefiled before God, the Father, is this: to care for orphans and widows in their distress, and to keep oneself unstained by the world."[53]

Peter's epistles

The bulk of Peter's epistles concern moral behaviour. His first letter opens with a strong moral exhortation:

> ... do not be conformed to the desires that you formerly had in ignorance. Instead, as he who called you is holy, be holy yourselves in all your conduct; for it is written, 'You shall be holy, for I am holy.' If you invoke as Father the one who judges all people impartially according to their deeds, live in reverent fear during the time of your exile.[54]

---

[47] Heb 10:24-25.
[48] Heb 12:1-2.
[49] Heb 12:2-13.
[50] Heb 10:26-31, 13:1-7
[51] Jas 2:13-26.
[52] Jas 1:19-22.
[53] Jas 1:27.
[54] 1 Pet 1:14-17.

Here, Peter motivated moral conduct by linking it with a final judgment based on conduct. He wrote that the threat of final judgment should lead to reverent fear and holy conduct. Yet, if they lived rightly, they could expect a resurrection and a positive final judgment.[55] Peter urged readers to rid themselves of immorality so that they "may grow into salvation."[56] He exhorted them to avoid sinful desires and instead to conduct themselves honourably. Peter called them to look to Jesus as an example.[57] He gave moral instructions for wives and husbands,[58] and gave general teaching instructing Christians to turn away from evil, do good, and seek peace. He added force to these exhortations by reminding his readers that God would hold people to account for their actions at the final judgment.[59]

In his second letter, Peter exhorted Christians to show goodness, self-control, endurance, godliness, and love in order to gain entry into the "eternal kingdom of our Lord and Saviour."[60] Again, this passage links conduct and final judgment, providing eternal life as an incentive for moral living in the present. Peter went on to warn that the coming Day of Judgment would bring the destruction of godless people. Hence, he urged Christians to live in a manner characterised by holiness and godliness.[61] Again, final judgment provided the motivation for correct conduct.

John's epistles

John, too, saw final judgment as an incentive for moral living. He wrote at length about cleansing sinfulness and transforming into more Christ-like people.[62] He exhorted them to avoid sin,[63] and warned his readers to shun sinful desires: "Do not love the world or the things in the world. ... the world and its desire are passing away, but those who do the will of God live for ever."[64] This passage states explicitly that people who practise correct conduct and perform the will of God will obtain eternal life. John used this idea to motivate his readers to follow

---

[55] 1 Pet 1:13-25.
[56] 1 Pet 2:1-2.
[57] 1 Pet 3:11-21.
[58] 1 Pet 3:1-7.
[59] 1 Pet 4:1-6.
[60] 2 Pet 1:3-11.
[61] 2 Pet 3:1-17.
[62] 1 John 1:5-10.
[63] 1 John 2:1.
[64] 1 John 2:15-17.

his teaching. Elsewhere, John explained that, if we live in a Christ-like way, we can have confidence in a positive final judgment.[65]

Jude

The letter of Jude begins with a reminder of God's judgment, citing Sodom and Gomorrah as examples of God's negative judgment of immorality.[66] The letter continues by warning that God will negatively judge people who practice immorality.[67] It warns that God will one day judge everyone and "convict everyone of all the deeds of ungodliness that they have committed in such an ungodly way."[68] With these warnings, Jude encouraged his readers to avoid indulging in immorality and to continue to live rightly. By doing this, they would remain in the love of God and could expect his merciful gift of eternal life.[69] The entire letter of Jude focusses on this theme of correct conduct, with final judgment as an incentive.

Revelation

Revelation contains short 'letters' to seven churches. These letters link moral conduct with final judgment. The writer instructed the church at Thyatira to repent of immoral behaviour, with the warning that God would judge them based on their conduct. In contrast, God would reward the people who performed good works faithfully.[70] The writer warned the church at Sardis about final judgment, adding: "I have not found your works perfect in the sight of my God." The letter urged them to remember what they first learned, to obey it and to repent.[71] The Philadelphian Christians received praise for their good works and a promise of reward from God at the final judgment as a result.[72] In these three instances, Revelation cites God's final judgment based on conduct as motivation to follow its moral exhortations. Later in Revelation, the final judgment scene itself is depicted. Those judged negatively are cast into the 'lake of fire'. Revelation presents this as the criterion of judgment: "the dead were judged according to their works,

---

[65] 1 John 4:17.
[66] Jude 5-7.
[67] Jude 8-13.
[68] Jude 14-16.
[69] Jude 1:17-21.
[70] Rev 2:18-28.
[71] Rev 3:1-6.
[72] Rev 3:7-13.

as recorded in the books." Although moral exhortation does not appear explicitly in this scene, it would certainly have motivated readers towards correct conduct!

Discussion

We have seen that many New Testament passages exhort the practise of moral conduct and mention positive final judgment as the reward or incentive for this behaviour. This evidence corresponds with the thesis we have outlined in the book thus far. In contrast, it challenges the post-Reformation view that human conduct does not affect final judgment. The early Christians viewed moral conduct as the criterion for a positive final judgment, and they saw final judgment as a motivation for right living.

The early Christians thought that doing good required effort. The New Testament authors did not shy away from instructing their readers to strive for moral change, not suggesting that this change would come easily or naturally but instead speaking of the need to make an effort. They encouraged Christians to persevere through hardship and persecution.[73] Paul wrote eloquently of how much he himself had toiled and struggled to bring about moral transformation in others so that they could develop into mature Christians.[74] He strived personally to achieve this goal of becoming Christ-like, and exhorted others to put strenuous effort into living according to Jesus' teaching and example.[75] He drew on the example of an athlete who struggles and perseveres with great effort to win a race, and instructed his readers to do likewise in order to obtain the prize of a positive final judgement.[76] This great emphasis on Christian effort to live rightly remained in the writings of the Church Fathers. They too encouraged Christians to strive their utmost.[77]

With this in mind, we can understand why the process of converting new Christians took so long in the early Church. According to a Christian document from around 215 AD, Christians carefully trained new converts in moral conduct for about *three years*. Only once the leaders had seen changes in the lives of these new converts did they

---

[73] E.g. Phil 1:27-30; 1 Pet 2:20-25.
[74] 1 Tim 4:7-10; see also Col 1:25-29.
[75] Phil 3:12-17.
[76] 1 Cor 9:24-27.
[77] As one example, see 1 Clement 1.14.

baptise them into the church.[78] Apparently, the early Christians considered it essential, not merely desirable, to live according to the teachings and example of Jesus to the best of their ability. They also believed that Christians could and should live this way successfully. Justin Martyr summed it up: "those who are not found living as He taught are not Christians – even though they profess with the lips the teachings of Christ."[79] Clement of Alexandria also taught this idea, writing that God will judge Christians negatively "unless we walk worthy of Him, and with one mind do those things which are good and well-pleasing in His sight."[80] Clearly, these early Christians did not rely on simply believing the right doctrines or 'resting in Christ's work'. In their view, only a real moral transformation and subsequent correct conduct would bring them a positive final judgment.

A note on free will and perseverance

Moral exhortation implies by its nature that the hearer has the ability to change. There is no point in encouraging people to change their character and behaviour if they cannot actually make those changes. The New Testament writers took it for granted that Christians can, by their efforts and with whatever assistance the Holy Spirit provides, live lives distinguished by moral conduct. Their whole paradigm of moral transformation takes for granted that humans have freedom and *can* repent and turn from evil to good. By implication, negative changes are also possible. People who live rightly today might cease to live rightly tomorrow. It is therefore important that they continue to live morally. If Christians stopped doing good and started performing immoral deeds, then they risked negative judgment. With this in mind, we would expect the New Testament writers to encourage perseverance strongly and to warn readers away from laziness. Persevering in right conduct to the end would have mattered greatly in light of God's final judgment of character and behaviour.

As expected, many verses in the New Testament do emphasise perseverance and warn against falling away. As we saw in our study of the Gospels, Jesus emphasised the importance of persevering to the end. The early Christians continued this teaching. Over *thirty* New Testa-

---

[78] Hippolytus, *Apostolic Tradition*, 17.

[79] Justin Martyr (c. 160, E), *Ante-Nicene Fathers* (Buffalo: Christian Literature Publishing, 1885; hereafter abbreviated *ANF*) 1.168. See also Ignatius (c. 105, E), *ANF* 1.51-55.

[80] Clement (c. 96, W), *ANF* 1.11.

ment passages outside the Gospels speak explicitly about the need for perseverance.[81] Some also warn of condemnation for those who fail to persevere in their Christian way of life. Other passages exhort Christians to stand fast until the end and not grow lax in character or conduct. For example:

> Take care, brothers and sisters, that none of you may have an evil, unfaithful heart that turns away from the living God. But exhort one another every day, as long as it is called "today," so that none of you may be hardened by the deceitfulness of sinfulness. For we have become partners of Christ, *if only we hold our first resolution firm to the end.*[82]

The importance of love

The post-Reformation tradition holds up 'faith' as the great saving virtue. It holds that a positive final judgment depends on the belief, trust and reliance of faith alone and not on conduct. This view would lead us to expect the New Testament to instruct Christians to have this kind of faith far more often than it instructs them towards practising moral conduct. It would also lead us to expect many passages expounding on the importance of such faith. When we turn to the New Testament, however, we find this is not the case. Compared to their very frequent exhortations towards moral conduct, the New Testament writers *seldom* exhorted their readers to have faith. Rather, they repeatedly held up love for others as their most important doctrine.

In the New Testament, love for others appears as the central theme from which all the ideas of correct conduct and moral transformation flow. In the Gospel accounts, love for others forms arguably the central and most distinctive theme of Jesus' actions, mission and message. Jesus opposed traditional practices out of love for those who suffered and to include and help the outcasts. Out of love for the sick, he spent at least three years roaming the countryside healing them, despite often having no home in which to sleep. Out of love for the poor, he opposed

---

[81] The clearest ones are: Gal 6:7-9; 2 Pet 2:20-21; Heb 2:1; Heb 6:4-8; 1 Heb 12:1-2; Tim 1:19-20; Matt 10:22; Mark 13:13; Gal 5:19-21; Phil 2:16; 3:12-19; 1 Thes 3:5; 1 Tim 5:8; Heb 4:1,11; 6:11-12; 2 Pet 1:8-11; 3:17; 1 John 2:24. But see also: John 15:1-2; Acts 8:12-24; Rom 6:12-18; 8:13; 11:19-23; 14:15; 1 Cor 3:16-17; 5:1-5; 6:9-11; 8:11-13; 9:27; 2 Cor 6:1; Gal 4:11; 5:4; 1 Thess 5:2-11; 2 Tim 2:16-18; Heb 3:6, 10:26-39, 12:15; Rev 3:5.

[82] Heb 3:12-14; see also Col 1:21-22; 2 Cor 13:5.

economic and temple systems that worsened their poverty. Out of love for the suffering, he demanded justice and mercy towards those unfairly treated and excluded. He was prepared both to live and, ultimately, to die for these people because of his love for them.

Jesus taught his disciples that the two greatest commandments are those which instructed them to love God and to love one's neighbour.[83] He said that these two commandments summed up all the teachings of scripture.[84] Jesus explained that your 'neighbour' means anyone one meets, including cultural enemies.[85] He emphasised that proper dealings with others mattered more than pious behaviour.[86] He said love should distinguish his followers,[87] and he taught them with that goal in mind.[88]

The New Testament also indicates that love had central importance for the early Christians. Apparently, these followers of Jesus saw love as the central principle of their spiritual lives. For example, Paul repeated three times in as many sentences that showing love fulfils God's requirements.[89] Like Jesus, Paul taught that this one command summed up all of God's commands: "You shall love your neighbour as yourself." So, Paul exhorted, "through love serve one another."[90] He called Christians to create a community characterised by "building itself up in love."[91] Paul congratulated the Thessalonian church for learning to love one another, but he urged them to love more and more.[92] In another letter, Paul concluded a long passage encouraging good conduct with these words: "Above all, clothe yourselves with love."[93] Paul even taught Christians to "become slaves to one another" out of love.[94] Love also seems to have mattered most to James. In his writings, he described the command to love your neighbour as "the royal law."[95] Likewise,

---

[83] Matt 22:37-39; Mark 12:30-33; Luke 10:27.
[84] Matt 22:40.
[85] Matt 5:43-46; Luke 6:27-35, 10:29-37.
[86] Matt 5:23-24.
[87] John 13:34-35, 15:12.
[88] John 15:17.
[89] Rom 13:8-10.
[90] Gal 5:13-14.
[91] Eph 4:1-16.
[92] 1 Thess 4:9-10.
[93] Col 3:14.
[94] Gal 5:13.
[95] Jas 2:8.

Peter pointed to love as the most important principle: "above all, maintain constant love for one another."[96]

In Paul's mind, love surpassed both knowledge and faith in importance. He explained its value:

> If I speak in the tongues of mortals and of angels, but do not have love, I am a noisy gong or a clanging cymbal. And if I have prophetic powers, and understand all mysteries and all knowledge, and if I have all faith, so as to remove mountains, but do not have love, I am nothing. If I give away all my possessions, and if I hand over my body so that I may boast, but do not have love, I gain nothing.[97]

He completed this passage by comparing love with faith and hope: "And now faith, hope, and love abide, these three; and the greatest of these is love."[98]

John the Apostle considered loving behaviour paramount also. He summed up the Christian message in one sentence: "This is the message you have heard from the beginning, that we should love one another."[99] He also taught: "Those who love God must love their brothers and sisters also."[100] For John, the teaching of love encapsulated the entire Christian message. Hence, he emphasised love and saw it as the defining characteristic of Christians.[101] In John's view, those who love people in the way Jesus loved can expect a positive final judgment:

> God is love, and those who abide in love abide in God, and God abides in them. Love has been perfected among us in this: that we may have boldness on the day of judgement, because as he is, so are we in this world.[102]

John taught that people who show love can have confidence that God will judge them favourably, and so they need not fear his judgment.[103]

The New Testament contains over 27 direct exhortations to love. These come from Jesus,[104] Paul,[105] Peter,[106] John,[107] and the writer of

---

[96] 1 Pet 4:8.
[97] 1 Cor 13:1-3.
[98] 1 Cor 13:13.
[99] 1 John 3:11.
[100] 1 John 4:21.
[101] 1 John 4:7-8, 16.
[102] 1 John 4:16-17.
[103] 1 John 4:18.

Hebrews.[108] In addition, many other passages strongly advocate love. From Jesus to Paul, from James to John, the early Christians agreed that God's greatest command is to show love toward others. This requirement fulfilled all other commands put together. They saw it as the royal law, encapsulating the message they had learned from the beginning. All the other moral teachings in the New Testament flowed from this key principle. Again and again, they made it clear that love for others lay at the core of their Christianity. While the New Testament authors often mentioned 'faith', it appears that they considered love for others more important, precisely because they were convinced that final judgment depended on conduct rather than 'faith' alone. Since the post-Reformation view denies the value of human conduct for final judgment, it clashes with this conclusion. In contrast, the moral exhortations in the New Testament provide further evidence for the paradigm of final judgment and moral conduct outlined so far in this book.

---

[104] Matt 5:44; Luke 6:27; John 13:34, 15:12.
[105] Rom 12:9-10; 1 Cor 14:1, 16:14; Eph 4:2, 5:2; Php 1:9, 2:2; Col 3:14; 1 Thess 3:12, 4:9-10; 2 Thess 3:5; 1 Tim 1:5, 4:12, 6:11; 2 Tim 2:22.
[106] 1 Pet 2:17, 3:8, 4:8.
[107] 1 John 3:18, 4:7, 4:11; 2 John 1:5.
[108] Heb 10:24, 13:1.

Chapter 8

Faithfulness

Everyone knows that 'faith' is an important concept in Christianity. English translations of the New Testament use the word 'faith' frequently, and the early Christians considered it essential. Hence, it is important to understand the concept of 'faith' accurately, in the way that the early Christians understood it.

According to the post-Reformation tradition, salvation is 'by faith alone'. The Reformers opposed the idea that positive final judgment depends upon human effort to live rightly. They insisted that final judgment does not depend upon human "strength, merits, or works."[1] Instead, they held that it depends solely on 'faith'. In post-Reformation teaching, 'faith' is generally defined as *believing in* and *trusting in* Christ alone and what he achieved for salvation. One of the most famous doctrinal confessions of the Reformation states: "the principle acts of saving faith are accepting, receiving, and resting upon Christ alone for justification, sanctification, and eternal life."[2] This 'faith' is contrasted against relying on our own efforts, character and conduct to obtain a positive final judgment. In this way, post-Reformation teaching often portrays two opposing ways of trying to obtain salvation. We can *either* trust in what Christ accomplished for us *or* trust in our ability to live in a way that will obtain a positive final judgment. It teaches that the second way will never succeed and that therefore we must accept the first. Through such teachings, the post-Reformation tradition has developed an antithesis between 'faith' and 'human effort'. Many modern Bible readers learn to interpret New Testament passages about 'faith' with this contrast in mind.

Therefore, we must spell out that this post-Reformation concept of faith *is almost the complete opposite of what the New Testament writers meant by the word*. For the writers of the New Testament, faith was not the opposite of human effort. When we read in English translations of 'faith' towards Christ (where they used the Greek noun *pistis*) they generally meant *faithfulness to* him. When we read of 'believing in' Christ (where they used the verb form, *pisteuo*) they generally meant

---

[1] Augsburg Confession of 1530 AD, Article IV.
[2] Westminster Confession of 1646 AD, Article XIV, section II.

being faithful to him. This faithfulness encompassed loyalty, obedience and perseverance. Their term for 'faith', *pistis*, implied and required human effort. The early Christians did not see a contrast between this faithfulness and human effort to live by Jesus' teachings. In their minds, being faithful to Jesus meant being committed to his movement, his teachings, his example and his cause. It meant obeying his teachings and striving to live in the way he had instructed. It meant remaining loyal to him and persevering in the way of life that he had taught. For the early Christians, living rightly and being faithful to Christ were one and the same. Hence, the post-Reformation antithesis between faith and conduct as opposing principles of salvation represents a radical departure from the early Christian teachings.

Faithfulness in the ancient world

The idea of faithfulness towards other people had great importance in the Greco-Roman culture of the first century. The performing and repaying of favours played a key role in their economic and social activities. Few people would perform favours for those who would not return them. As a result, people desired a public reputation for faithfulness in such dealings. The word *pistis* was used in this context to refer to someone's reliability, faithfulness, and commitment in returning favours.[3] This faithfulness mattered in all types of relationships, not merely those involving business. Spouses, slaves, masters, witnesses, messengers and friendships in general all needed faithfulness (pistis).[4] Because of its importance in society, people praised the virtue of faithfulness. One ancient writer labelled faithfulness "the queen of all the virtues"[5] and the "most perfect of the virtues."[6]

Greek writers used pistis widely as a political and military term for loyalty, faithfulness, allegiance and commitment. Romans translated pistis into Latin as the word *fides*, from which we derive 'fidelity' in English. The Romans valued greatly the concepts embodied by both pistis and fides. As one scholar notes: "The ancient Romans believed that to ensure their own national security they had to conquer other

---

[3] David DeSilva, *Honor, Patronage, Kinship and Purity* (Downers Grove, IL: Intervasity Press, 2000), p. 115, 145; Douglas A. Campbell, *The Quest for Paul's Gospel: A Suggested Strategy* (London: T&T Clark , 2005), p. 179.

[4] Rudolph Bultman, "pisteuo." Theological Dictionary of the New Testament, (Grand Rapids, MI: Eerdmans, 1964, Vol. 6, ed. Gerhard Kittell), p. 175, 177.

[5] Philo, *On Abraham*, 270.

[6] Philo, *Who Is The Heir Of Divine Things*, 91.

peoples with their superior military force in order to extract fides / pistis = 'loyalty' from the subjected people."[7] Many Roman coins had the word 'fides' printed on them in order to encourage loyalty to the Empire. Not everyone gave such loyalty, however. A Jew called Josephus took part in a war against the Romans and later wrote several books in Greek about his experiences. His writings provide some good examples of the way in which Greek writers used the term pistis. In his autobiography, he described a meeting with some rebels he had fought. He asked the rebels to join his army by saying, "repent and be faithful* to me."[8] Note that we have added an asterisk (*) into this quote and into similar quotes throughout this chapter to indicate usage of a Greek word from the pistis word-group. In saying, "be faithful to me," Josephus invited the rebels to change their allegiance and to give him their loyalty and commitment. Josephus' Greek words are identical to some phrases in the Gospels, which are often (misleadingly) translated as phrases like "repent and *believe** in me." Later in his autobiography, Josephus wrote of a city that had revolted against him in a military uprising rather than follow his leadership. He rebuked them for turning away, "from their faithfulness* to me"[9] – referring to their loyalty, faithfulness, and allegiance to him.

Josephus also used pistis-group words to refer to ideas of faithfulness and loyalty elsewhere in his writings. For example, we read that he obliged a multitude of people to "to take an oath of faithfulness* to him." In this oath, he "compelled them to swear that they would bear him good-will, and continue certainly so to do."[10] In another place, "he called the multitude together, and highly commended them for their faithfulness* to the Romans."[11] Elsewhere, he wrote that the Emperor knew "how loyal* the Jews were to one another."[12] He also recorded that Herod left his treasurer Joseph and Sohemus of Iturea to take care of a fortress, because "these two had been very faithful* to him from the beginning."[13] Josephus wrote of Herod, who remained firm and loyal to Antony as his "faithful* counsellor" and did not desert him after his defeat like others did. Subsequently, Herod offered his loyalty to Caesar, saying "consider how faithful* a friend, and not whose friend, I have

---

[7] Richard A. Horsley, *Jesus and Empire: The Kingdom of God and the New World Disorder* (Minneapolis, MI: Augsburg Fortress, 2003), p. 27.
[8] Josephus, *Life* 110.
[9] Josephus, *Life* 167.
[10] Ant 15:368 = 15.10.4.
[11] War 2:341 = 2.16.2.
[12] War 3:320 = 3.7.33.
[13] Ant 15:185 = 15.6.5.

been."[14] Another Greek historian wrote in the 2nd century AD of the occasion when a group betrayed Darius, the King of Persia. Some of Darius' followers refused to take part in the betrayal and remained "loyal* to Darius."[15] These examples indicate some of the ways in which Greek writers used pistis to mean faithfulness and loyalty.

Two sets of ancient writings have particular relevance for understanding what the New Testament writers meant when they used the Greek word pistis: the Old Testament in the Greek Septuagint translation, and Josephus's writings. In some recent studies, scholars have looked at each and every occurrence of pistis in these texts to better understand its meaning. These scholars tried to determine what the word meant in the context of each passage in which it occurred. While some occurrences remained ambiguous, some clear trends emerged. They found that, in the Greek Septuagint translation of the Old Testament, pistis and its variants mean 'faithfulness' in 70 to 90 percent of all occurrences. Usually, the New Testament writers quoted from the Septuagint translation of the Jewish scriptures. Hence, in *their* scriptures, pistis and its variants meant 'faithfulness' most often. The scholars found the same trend in Josephus' writings, in which pistis and its variants mean 'faithfulness' more often than any other single meaning.[16] Josephus' usage is especially relevant since he was a Jew and wrote very lengthy documents in Greek in the 1st century AD. His culture and language has much in common, therefore, with those of the New Testament writers.

Faithfulness in the New Testament

As a result of recent studies like these, a growing number of biblical scholars have concluded that pistis-group words most commonly mean faithfulness, loyalty and commitment in the New Testament itself. One scholar of Paul's writings comments that even "without claiming certain controversial instances" of pistis within the tally, the meaning of faithfulness is "the dominant one" in Paul's writings. He explains: "This is entirely predictable. It is often the most common rendering of pistis in contemporary Greek as well. It easily dominates the Septuagintal usage,

---

[14] War 1:390 = 1.20.1.
[15] Arrian, *Anabasis* III.21.4 & III.23.7.
[16] Campbell, *The Quest For Paul's Gospel*, pp. 178 – 207; David M. Hay, "Pistis as 'Ground for Faith' in Hellenized Judaism and Paul," *JBL* 18, 1989, pp. 461 – 76.

and is also the [predominant] meaning in Josephus."[17] Another scholar writes that faithfulness is "the most satisfactory translation for many texts" of the New Testament.[18] Pistis generally has this meaning of faithfulness when it is directed towards *people*. In New Testament verses that use pistis in this way, the context often makes its connotations of faithfulness and commitment clear. For example, the Pharisees failed to follow* John the Baptist,[19] and Jesus rebuked them for not following* Moses.[20] Since both John and Moses filled the roles of teachers, following them meant obeying their teachings. Presumably, Jesus had the same meaning in mind when he warned his disciples not to follow* false teachers.[21] Likewise John warned against following* ungodly spirits.[22] We also read of the faithfulness* of good servants toward their masters.[23] The concepts of faithfulness and following loyally best fit with the context of passages like these that direct pistis toward people.

In English, if someone has 'courage', we call them 'courageous'. The word 'courageous' is the adjectival form of the noun 'courage', and conveys exactly the same idea, despite being a different part of speech and having a different ending. In exactly the same way, pistis has an adjectival form, *pistos*. Almost without exception, Greek writers used pistos to describe a person or saying as 'faithful'. Even translators influenced by post-Reformation teaching rarely translate pistos as anything other than 'faithful'. The New Testament uses pistos 67 times,[24] describing both Jesus[25] and God[26] as faithful*. Paul described "faithful* Abraham,"[27] and contrasted the unfaithfulness* of people

---

[17] Campbell, *The Quest for Paul's Gospel*, p. 186.

[18] Stanley K. Stowers, *A Rereading of Romans: Justice, Jews, and Gentiles* (Ann Arbor, MI: Edwards Brothers, 1994), p. 199.

[19] Matt 21:25, 21:32; Mark 11:31; Luke 20:5.

[20] John 5:46a.

[21] Matt 24:23, 24:26; Mark 13:21.

[22] 1 John 4:1.

[23] Matt 24:45, 25:21-23; Luke 12:42-46, 16:10-12.

[24] Matt 17:17, 24:45, 25:21, 25:23; Mark 9:19; Luke 9:41, 12:42, 12:46, 16:10-12, 19:17; Acts 2:44, 5:14, 10:45, 13:34, 16:1, 26:8; 1 Cor 1:9, 4:2, 4:17, 6:6, 7:12-15, 10:13, 10:27, 14:23-24; 2 Cor 1:18, 4:4, 6:14-15; Gal 3:9; Eph 1:1, 6:21; Col 1:2, 1:7, 4:7-9; 2 Thes 3:3; 1 Tim 1:12-15, 3:1, 3:11, 4:3, 4:9-10; 2 Tim 2:2, 2:11-13; Tit 1:6-9, 3:8; Heb 2:17, 3:2-5, 10:23, 11:11; 1 Pet 4:19, 5:12; 1 John 1:9; 3 John 1:5; Rev 1:5, 2:10-13, 3:14, 17:14, 19:11, 21:5, 22:6.

[25] Acts 3:16b; Gal 2:16, 3:22; Eph 3:12, 6:23; 1 Thes 5:24; 2 Thes 3:3; 2 Tim 2:13b; Heb 2:17, 3:2, 12:2; Jas 2:1; Rev 1:5, 3:14, 14:12, 19:11.

[26] Mark 11:22; Rom 3:3; 1 Cor 1:9, 10:13; 2 Cor 1:18; Eph 6:23; 2 Thes 1:11; Heb 10:23, 11:11; 1 Pet 4:19; 1 John 1:9.

[27] Gal 3:9.

with God's faithfulness*.[28] He wrote that both he and Timothy remained faithful* to Jesus.[29] Paul instructed Timothy to teach "faithful* men, who will be competent also to teach others."[30] The New Testament also describes various teachings as faithful, using the term pistos.[31] In addition, it often uses this term to describe the loyalty of servants to their masters. In the Parable of the Talents, for example, the servants pleased the master by doing his will. He praised each, saying "well done, good and faithful* servant; you have been faithful* in a few things."[32] It contrasts the "good and faithful*" with the "wicked and lazy" a few verses later.[33] In another instance, Jesus told the story of "the faithful* and wise servant" who tended his master's house, providing a contrast to the "wicked servant" who mistreated his master's other servants.[34] Jesus grouped this wicked servant with the unfaithful*.[35] Paul taught stewards to remain faithful*,[36] and also stated: "Let slaves be subject to their own masters, well-pleasing in all things, not speaking against them, not stealing, but showing all good faithfulness*."[37] The adjective, pistos, requires a translation of 'faithful' or similar in all these cases. This evidence is once again consistent with the idea that the pistis word-group denotes faithfulness when used to speak of people.

Another way to build confidence about what the pistis word-group meant to the New Testament writers is to look at the words they used as its synonyms or antonyms. In John's Gospel, for example, Jesus contrasts those who have pistis with those who are disobedient.[38] This example suggests that disobedience is the opposite of pistis. We will investigate the major synonyms and antonyms for pistis in this way.

Obedience: Greek words that mean 'obedience' appear commonly in the New Testament as apparent synonyms for pistis. The New Testament sometimes calls good servants faithful* and sometimes obedient, indicating that these terms could take on similar meaning.[39]

---

[28] Rom 3:3; 2 Tim 2:13.
[29] Eph 1:1; 1 Cor 4:17.
[30] 2 Tim 2:2.
[31] 1 Tim 1:15, 3:1, 4:9; 2 Tim 2:11; Tit 1:9, 3:8a; Rev 21:5, 22:6.
[32] Matt 25:21, 23.
[33] Matt 25:26.
[34] Matt 24:45-51.
[35] Luke 12:46.
[36] 1 Cor 4:2.
[37] Titus 2:9-10a.
[38] John 3:36.
[39] E.g. Rom 6:16 cf. Matt 25:21.

Further confirming this, some verses speak of people as *obeying* the gospel and others speak of people as *faithfully following** it.[40] The terms obedience and pistis are used as if they are synonymous in several verses that speak of people who are blessed, saved, and subject to God's wrath.[41] Paul twice wrote of the "obedience of faithfulness*" among the nations.[42] In Luke's Gospel, the disciples ask Jesus to increase their faithfulness*, and he replies with a speech about obedience.[43] In John, Jesus contrasts disobedience and pistis by teaching, "Whoever is faithful* to the Son has eternal life; whoever disobeys the Son will not see life, but must endure God's wrath."[44] Here, pistis seems to mean exactly the opposite of disobedience. In Romans, Paul quotes a Septuagint verse containing pistis, commenting that this verse teaches about obedience.[45] In two sequential sentences, Hebrews parallels disobedience with a lack of pistis explicitly,[46] and uses these terms interchangeably thereafter.[47] In the same way, Peter and John both interchange pistis with obedience and contrast it with disobedience.[48] This evidence all indicates that, for the New Testament writers, pistis was not the opposite of human obedience but rather implied this idea.

Perseverance: The New Testament authors used pistis in ways that seem to mean 'perseverance' many times. They directly associated it with having perseverance and endurance 10 times;[49] with standing fast 11 times;[50] and with standing firm against the Devil 3 times.[51] They contrasted it with falling away 8 times;[52] with wavering once;[53] and once with growing weary and losing heart.[54] Jesus told a parable in which a woman persevered to obtain a verdict from an unjust judge,

---

[40] Acts 5:32; 2 Thes 1:8; 1 Pet 4:17 cf. Mark 1:15; Gal 3:2.

[41] Blessed: Luke 11:28 cf. Gal 3:9. Saved: Heb 5:9 cf. 1 Cor 1:21; Eph 2:8; Rom 4:5. God's wrath: Rom 2:8, 2 Thes 1:8, 1 Pet 4:17 cf. John 3:36b, Col 1:21-23.

[42] Rom 1:5, 16:26. See also Acts 6:7.

[43] Luke 17:5-10.

[44] John 3:36.

[45] Rom 10:16.

[46] Heb 3:18-19.

[47] Heb 4:1-6.

[48] 1 Pet 2:7-8. 1 John 3:11, 22-24.

[49] John 8:31; Acts 14:22; 2 Thes 1:4-5; Col 1:23; 1 Tim 1:16, 2:15, 6:11-12; Heb 6:12-15, 12:1-3; Rev 2:10.

[50] Luke 8:11-15; Rom 11:20; 1 Cor 15:1-2, 16:13; 2 Cor 1:24; 2 Tim 1:13, 4:7; Jas 1:2-4; 1 Pet 5:8-9; Heb 3:12-14, 10:36-39.

[51] Eph 6:11-17; Col 2:5; 1 Pet 5:9.

[52] Matt 13:57-58, 18:6; Mark 6:3-6, 9:42; John 6:61 cf. 6:60, 64; 1 Thes 3:2-5.

[53] Jas 1:6-8.

[54] Heb 12:1-3.

indicating that the opposite of such perseverance was a lack of pistis.[55] Elsewhere, Jesus said that servants who persevered in watching over their master's property all night demonstrated pistis.[56] When Jesus expressed hope that Peter's pistis would not fail, Peter reaffirmed his perseverance and loyalty by saying, "I am ready to go with you to prison and to death!"[57] The Gospels also record that when Jesus saw people who had persevered through difficulty to get his attention or help, he said that they had exemplified pistis.[58]

Loyalty: Many passages use pistis in a way that associates it with the idea of remaining loyal. They describe those loyal to Jesus as having pistis on 9 occasions.[59] Another 18 times they describe those who 'follow' Jesus as having pistis.[60] A further 5 times they use the word to describe those who commit to Jesus.[61] The New Testament often contrasts pistis with disloyalty – going astray, departing, turning aside or rejecting Jesus.[62] It also contrasts having pistis with betraying Jesus, wanting to kill him and following the teachings of false prophets.[63] In the Gospels, the disciples address Jesus as 'Lord', reaffirming their faithfulness and loyalty to him; yet Jesus had occasion once to ask incredulously, "Why do you call me 'Lord, Lord,' and do not do what I tell you?"[64] Jesus taught that only those who faithfully do God's will truly have him as their Lord.[65] Jesus also praised a Roman Centurion's pistis, after the man showed that he understood the connection between faithfulness and loyal obedience. The centurion explained: "I also am a man set under authority, with soldiers under me; and I say to one, 'Go,'

---

[55] Luke 18:1-8.

[56] Luke 12:35- 48.

[57] Luke 22:32-33.

[58] E.g. Matt 15:22-28; Mark 10:46-52; Luke 18:35-43.

[59] Acts 2:44, 4:4, 4:32, 5:14, 17:34; 1 Cor 6:6, 10:27, 14:23-24; Rev 17:14.

[60] Compare *akoloutheo*: Matt 8:22, 9:9, 10:38, 16:24, 19:21; Mark 2:14, 8:34, 10:21; Luke 5:27, 9:23, 9:59, 18:22; John 1:43, 12:26, 21:19-22; *deute opiso*: Matt 4:19; Mark 1:17; *erchetai opiso*: Luke 14:27 with *pistis*: John 12:44, 14:1, 16:9, 17:20. See also John 10:26-27.

[61] John 6:35, 7:37-38, 5:40-47, 1:12; Acts 11:21.

[62] Going astray: Matt 24:23-24; Mark 13:21-22; John 7:48; 1 Tim 6:10; Heb 3:10-12. Departing, as: *Aphistemi*: Heb 3:12; Luke 8:13; 1 Tim 4:1. *Hupostello*: Heb 10:38-39. *Diakrino*: Matt 21:21; Mark 11:23; Rom 4:20, 14:23; Jas 1:6. Turning aside: Matt 17:17; Luke 9:41, Acts 13:8. Rejecting Jesus: Luke 22:32-34; John 6:60-66, 12:47-48, 14:1.

[63] Betrayal: John 6:64, 6:71. Wanting to kill Jesus: John 8:37-47. Following false prophets: Matt 24:26; 1 John 4:1.

[64] Luke 6:46.

[65] Matt 7:21-23.

and he goes, and to another, 'Come,' and he comes, and to my slave, 'Do this,' and the slave does it."[66] These passages show that the New Testament authors used pistis to describe the concepts of loyalty and fidelity towards Jesus.

Correct conduct: The New Testament also parallels having pistis toward Jesus with correct conduct. These parallels suggest that they used pistis synonymously with morally virtuous conduct, which makes sense if pistis refers to faithfulness to Jesus and his moral teachings. Jesus described those who those who love darkness more than light as lacking pistis. He taught that those who love darkness work evil and practice wickedness, and he contrasted them with those who live rightly.[67] Elsewhere, he said that those who performed good deeds had pistis. He contrasted these people with others who had practised evil,[68] and contrasted pistis with unrighteousness.[69] Those who have pistis no longer practise sin,[70] but he called those who lacked pistis "children of the Devil."[71] Paul also paralleled pistis with moral behaviour. He wrote of those who do not have pistis toward what is right, but instead delight in immoral conduct.[72] He called people who lack pistis "evil and wicked men."[73] He described children of God by using the word pistis, saying that right conduct and 'light' characterised them. Conversely, iniquity and 'darkness' characterised people without pistis.[74] Paul linked having pistis with having good moral sense,[75] and contrasted it with having a corrupted mind, having counterfeit pistis, and opposing what is right.[76] He taught that people without pistis have a corrupt sense of morality and deny God by their disobedient actions.[77] Paul encouraged Timothy to exercise himself in godliness, which he implied should characterise those with pistis. He also included pistis regularly in his lists of virtues that characterise godly and right living.[78]

---

[66] Luke 7:8-9; see also Matt 8:10.
[67] John 3:12-21.
[68] John 5:24-29.
[69] Luke 16:10.
[70] John 8:31-34.
[71] John 8:44-45.
[72] 2 Thes 2:12.
[73] 2 Thes 3:2.
[74] 2 Cor 6:14-18.
[75] 1Tim 1:19.
[76] 2 Tim 3:8.
[77] Titus 1:10-16.
[78] Gal 5:22; 1 Tim 4:7-12, 3:8-11; 2 Tim 2:22.

Peter also described those with pistis as obedient to what is right.[79] In contrast, Revelation counts those without pistis to Jesus among "the cowardly... the polluted, the murderers, the fornicators, the sorcerers, the idolaters, and all liars."[80] These verses illustrate how closely the New Testament authors associated having pistis toward Jesus with living rightly according to his teachings.

Conclusion

Scholars who have looked at how the ancient Greek word for 'faith' (pistis) was used have concluded that it most often meant faithfulness, obedience, loyalty and perseverance. In the Greek translation of the Old Testament used by the New Testament authors, 'faithfulness' is the standard meaning of the word. Similarly, the notion of 'faithfulness' is the dominant meaning in other Greek texts from around the time. As a result, many recent scholars have agreed that 'faithfulness' is probably the single best translation for pistis throughout most of the New Testament. We have looked at the words the New Testament writers used as synonyms and antonyms for pistis in order to better understand the way in which they used the word. We have seen that the synonyms and antonyms they used point frequently and strongly to four primary concepts: obedience, perseverance, loyalty and moral conduct. These four ideas seem to summarise what the early Christians thought it meant to have faithfulness (pistis) towards Jesus. In Greek literature, pistis toward a person meant faithfulness, loyalty, commitment and obedience to the person, to their commands and to their teachings. The New Testament writers also used the word in exactly this way to speak of faithfulness to John the Baptist, Moses, false teachers and slave masters. The word pistis had exactly same connotations when they directed pistis toward the person of Jesus. It did not take a special meaning when directed toward Jesus. It meant faithfulness, obedience, loyalty and commitment to Jesus and his teachings.

The New Testament writers did not see any contrast between faithfulness and effort. On the contrary, they saw 'faith' as involving the effort to live faithfully according to Jesus' teachings.

Two definitions of pistis that survive in the writings of Christians from the second century support this understanding of the term. Irenaeus explained to his readers that to have pistis towards Jesus "is to

---

[79] 1 Pet 1:21-22.
[80] Rev 21:8.

do His will."[81] Similarly, Clement of Alexandria stated that Christians used the word pistis to speak of obedience to Jesus.[82] It seems that these early Christians also shared the understanding of pistis toward Jesus as faithful obedience to him and his message.

The post-Reformation concept of 'faith' differs markedly from what the early Christians and other Greek-speaking people of their time meant by the word pistis. The post-Reformation tradition takes pistis toward Jesus to mean not 'faithfulness' to Jesus *the person*, but 'belief, trust, and reliance' in *ideas* concerning Jesus and his accomplishments. Such an interpretation redirects 'faith' away from the stated target (Jesus) and onto *unstated ideas* about the things that Jesus did. Rather than interpret the Greek words straightforwardly as "faithfulness toward Jesus," the post-Reformation tradition tries to read them as if they meant "believing the idea that Jesus' atoning death on the cross saved us and trusting in that alone to save us." The way that Greek speakers typically used pistis gives no support for such a creative interpretation. When Greek writers directed pistis towards a person, they seem to have referred to faithfulness towards that person, their instructions, and their cause. There is no hint that they usually used such phrases to refer to belief and trust in *ideas* concerning the person. Likewise, there is no hint that the New Testament writers had the post-Reformation idea of 'faith' in mind when they wrote of pistis toward Jesus. When they elaborated on pistis, or paralleled it with other ideas, they seem to have had the concept of 'faithfulness' in mind, rather than beliefs in a series of doctrines regarding Jesus and his accomplishments. If the New Testament writers had supported post-Reformation ideas about pistis, we would expect them to have paralleled it with Greek synonyms or antonyms for belief, trust, or reliance. However, very few, if any, such parallels exist. The early Christians considered pistis towards Jesus essential; yet, for them, the term meant faithfulness to Jesus, not belief and trust in doctrines about him and how he saved people.

---

[81] Irenaeus, *Adversus Haereses*, 4.6.5.

[82] Clement of Alexandria, *Instructor* 1.13, *Stromata* 2.4. In the pre-Nicene Fathers, the word *pistis* is used as a theological term in two general ways. (1) To speak of the faithfulness and obedience of the Christian towards the commandments of God revealed through Christ. (2) To speak of monotheism – belief in and worship of only one God – which is usually ranked as a virtue in lists alongside almsgiving and love for one's neighbour.

A more nuanced understanding of pistis

Faithfulness is the most common meaning of the pistis word-group in both the New Testament and ancient Greek in general. These words, however, can acquire a number of other meanings when used in different contexts. The remainder of this chapter describes the way in which we can have confidence that pistis means one thing and not another in a given instance. This discussion will provide more insight into why pistis means 'faithfulness' rather than 'belief, trust and reliance' when it is directed towards Jesus. Readers not interested in these details should feel free to skip to the next chapter.

The English word 'suit' provides an example of a word that can mean several different things when used in different ways. It can refer to a legal trial, a matched set of business clothes, playing cards, something looking attractive or something seeming convenient. Native English speakers can discern easily the intended meaning of the word 'suit' in an English sentence, despite its many different uses and meanings. Similarly, "pistis had a range of meanings in ancient usage: loyalty, honesty, good faith, faithfulness, trust, trustworthiness, belief, proof, and confidence."[83] Early readers of the New Testament texts would have discerned the right meaning of pistis from the context. Since most people today do not speak the original language of the New Testament fluently, however, it is harder for them to determine its intended meaning.

Here we will outline a framework to help discern the intended meaning of pistis in a given context. All the usages of pistis share the underlying meaning of a firm and steadfast connection between two entities. Pistis describes connections of *firmness* that can form between a wide variety of entities: people, traditions, practices, groups, purposes, facts or propositions. In English, we use several different words to describe such connections depending on the types of entities we are talking about. The appropriate English translation of pistis is thus almost entirely dependent on what types of entities the Greek speaker is connecting with the word. The subject and the object of the sentence provide, therefore, the most useful indicators of the precise meaning of pistis in any instance. *Who* or *what* has 'pistis', and *whom* or *what* do they have it *toward*? The different English words appropriate for translating pistis depend on the entities that it connects, as follows:

---

[83] Stowers, *A Rereading of Romans*, p. 199.

From (the subject)	To (the object)	English words typically relating to the connection
Person	Person	Faithfulness, obedience, loyalty, commitment, fidelity, allegiance, following a person, a pledge to a person
Person	Idea, proposition	Belief, assent, trust
Person	Thing, message, teaching, purpose, tradition	Commitment, faithfulness, perseverance, endurance, trustworthiness, being entrusted
Person / Idea	N/A (intransitive)	Faithful, persevering, reliable, trustworthy
Proposition / Fact	Conclusion	Evidence, proof

Pistis takes on meanings of faithfulness, loyalty, and fidelity when directed towards someone by another person. In this usage, pistis denotes a commitment to a person – faithfulness, loyalty, and willingness to follow that person obediently. One scholar puts it this way: "Relative to persons, faith is reliability in interpersonal relations; it thus takes on the value of enduring personal loyalty, of personal faithfulness... 'faith' primarily means personal loyalty, personal commitment to another person, fidelity and the solidarity that comes from such faithfulness."[84] People used pistis in situations that involved the need for loyalty. These might include a master to servant relationship; a teacher to disciple relationship; ruler to subject loyalty; commander to soldier fidelity; a marriage; or a friendship.

Sometimes, the target of the pistis is an idea rather than a person. In this context it still denotes commitment, but that commitment now focusses upon the idea rather than on a person. In English, we describe

---

[84] John J. Pilch (ed.) and Bruce J. Malina (ed.), *Handbook of Biblical Social Values* (Peabody, MA: Hendrickson, 1998), pp. 72 – 75. See also G. Howard, "The 'Faith of Christ'," *ExpTim* 85, 1974, 214.

commitment toward ideas with words like 'belief', 'assent' and 'trust'.[85] We can usually discern this usage of pistis easily because the writer supplies an idea, statement, or proposition as the target of the belief.

The target of the pistis can also be a purpose, tradition, or teaching.[86] This usage conveys the idea of commitment, faithfulness, and perseverance to the objective concerned – pursuing a goal, keeping a tradition, or obeying a teaching. Occasionally, writers used the verb in the 'passive' Greek form to reverse the relationship. Thus, instead of denoting a person committing to a cause, the cause is 'entrusted' to the person. Paul used the verb several times in this way to talk about how God had entrusted him with the gospel.[87]

Sometimes, pistis-group words do not connect two entities but instead denote a characteristic of a single entity. For example, a writer can describe a person as 'faithful', or as characterised by 'faithfulness'. Here, the pistis has no target. The writer does not mention what the person is faithful toward, and instead focusses on the person's characteristic of faithfulness. Likewise, writers can describe sayings or teachings as reliable and trustworthy using pistis-group words.

Greek philosophers sometimes used the word pistis to refer to the evidence or proof for certain conclusions in logical arguments. In this sense, a premise 'faithfully' leads to its conclusion and provides it with 'firm support'. This usage does not involve people. While such usage appears commonly in certain extra-biblical philosophical writings,[88] it occurs only once in the New Testament.[89]

Unlike in Greek, the English word 'faithfulness' does not possess a directly matching verb form. Depending on the particular relationship, we use different words to describe faithfulness in action. For example, in a master-servant scenario, we say that the faithful servant *obeys* the master. In a marriage, a wife wants her husband to *be faithful* to her. In a disciple-teacher relationship, the disciples *follow* the teacher. So, in English, we use several different words for the verb form of 'faithfulness' where the ancient Greeks would always use *pisteuo*. This means

---

[85] Pilch and Malina, *Handbook of Biblical Social Values*, p. 74; Campbell, *The Quest for Paul's Gospel*, p. 179.

[86] John Dominic Crossan and Jonathan L. Reed, *In Search of Paul: How Jesus' Apostle Opposed Rome's Empire with God's Kingdom* (New York, HarperCollins, 2004), pp. 385 – 86.

[87] Generally: Titus 1:3. With the Words of God: Rom 3:2. With the gospel: Gal 2:7; 1 Thes 2:3-4, 1 Tim 1:11-13. With a stewardship: 1 Cor 9:17.

[88] E.g. in the writings of Philo. See Campbell, *The Quest For Paul's Gospel*, pp. 178 – 207 and Hay, 'Pistis as "Ground for Faith"', pp. 461 – 76.

[89] Acts 17:31.

that, where New Testament authors used pisteuo, the relationship dictates the most appropriate English translation. Many English Bibles translate pisteuo inaccurately as 'believe' (a connection to an idea) in verses where it describes a firm connection between *people*. Words or phrases like 'follow', 'obey' or 'be faithful' would provide more accurate translations in these verses.

Of all the ways in which the New Testament writers used pistis, they directed it most commonly toward people. These people include John the Baptist,[90] Moses,[91] false teachers[92] and slave masters.[93] More importantly and much more often, they wrote of faithfulness* toward God (20 times)[94] and toward Jesus (94 times).[95] Having pistis toward Jesus is the most important idea concerning pistis in the New Testament, so it is vital that we understand this particular usage correctly. As we have argued throughout this chapter, having pistis towards Jesus meant being faithful, loyal, obedient and steadfast in following him. Many English Bible translations can be very misleading in this context, since phrases like 'believe in Jesus' would be better translated as 'be faithful to Jesus' or 'follow Jesus'.

Sometimes, the New Testament authors wrote of pistis toward certain teachings when trying to encourage faithfulness to those teachings. Such teachings include the commands of God and the teachings of Jesus, Moses, Isaiah, and the gospel.[96] Paul used the word pistis when encouraging people to faithfully follow his message, word

---

[90] Matt 21:25, 21:32; Mark 11:31; Luke 20:5.

[91] John 5:46a.

[92] Matt 24:23, 24:26; Mark 13:21. See also 1 John 4:1.

[93] Matt 24:45, 25:21-23; Luke 12:42-46, 16:10-12.

[94] John 5:24, 12:44b, 14:1a; Acts 16:34, 27:25; Rom 4:3, 4:5a, 4:17, 4:18, 4:19, 4:20, 4:24; Gal 3:6; 1 Thes 1:8; Tit 3:8b; Heb 6:1; 1 Pet 1:21; 1 John 5:10.

[95] By name: Matt 18:6, 27:42; Mark 9:42; Luke 20:5; John 2:11, 3:15, 3:16, 3:18a, 3:36, 4:21, 4:39, 5:38, 5:46b, 6:29, 6:30, 6:35, 6:40, 6:47, 7:5, 7:31, 7:38, 7:39, 7:48, 8:30, 8:31, 8:45, 8:46, 9:35, 9:36, 10:37, 10:38a, 10:42, 11:25, 11:26, 11:45, 11:48, 12:11, 12:37, 12:42, 12:44a, 12:46, 14:1b, 14:11, 14:12, 16:9, 17:20; Acts 9:42, 10:43, 11:17, 11:21, 3:39, 14:23, 16:15, 16:31, 18:8, 19:4, 20:21, 22:19, 24:24, 26:18; Rom 9:33, 10:11, 10:14; 1 Cor 4:17; Gal 2:16, 2:20, 3:26; Eph 1:1, 1:13, 1:15; Php 1:29; Col 2:5; 1 Tim 1:14, 3:16; 2 Tim 3:15; Phm 1:5; 1 Pet 2:6; 1 John 5:10a. As the Light: John 12:36. As God's witness: 1 John 5:10c; Rev 1:5, 2:13, 3:14. As the name of Jesus: John 1:12, 2:23, 3:18; Act 3:16, 8:12; 1 John 3:23, 5:13.

[96] God: Acts 4:32; Rom 3:2. Jesus: John 2:22 (also towards the scripture referred to), 3:12, 4:50, 5:47; Acts 13:48. Moses: John 5:47. Isaiah: John 12:38; Rom 10:16. The gospel: Mark 1:15, 16:16, 16:17; Luke 8:12-13; Acts 15:7; Heb 4:2; Rom 1:16 (of Christ).

and testimony rather than the wisdom of men.[97] In these passages, the authors used pistis when encouraging their readers to follow those teachings faithfully, not simply to believe or trust that they were true. Hence in these cases, the idea of faithfulness again provides the best translation of pistis.

In the New Testament, the target of pistis is rarely an idea or proposition. Hence, a translation of pistis as belief or trust is not often appropriate. The New Testament mentions people believing* or disbelieving* that events had truly occurred[98] or that others' statements were true only occasionally.[99] In other cases, the beliefs concerned whether events like resurrection could actually occur,[100] or whether people truly held some claimed position.[101] The New Testament authors also encouraged their readers to believe* that Jesus had divine authority, died, and rose again.[102] They encouraged their Christian readers to believe* that God would resurrect them also.[103] These straightforward references are, arguably, the only occasions in the New Testament where pistis is directed toward ideas or statements of fact.

There is no doubt that the early Christians considered beliefs concerning Jesus important, but they did not refer to these beliefs when they spoke of 'faith' toward him. Their message was that people can obtain eternal life through being faithful to Jesus, his example, and his teachings. Indeed, we have seen that many passages mention such conduct as the basis for final judgment. In contrast, no New Testament passages advocate belief, trust or reliance in ideas about what Christ achieved as the grounds for final judgment. The early Christians did not speak of "resting in Christ alone for justification, sanctification, and eternal life," and they did not understand 'faith' in that way. For them, 'faith' meant faithfulness, and faithfulness required human effort.

---

[97] Message: Acts 17:34, 28:24; 1 Cor 15:11. Word: 1 Cor 15:2. Testimony: 2 Thes 1:10, c.f. 1 Cor 2:5.

[98] John 9:18, 20:8; 1 Cor 11:18.

[99] Luke 1:20, 24:25.

[100] Matt 9:28, although an alternative interpretation is that they had pistis towards Jesus because the report about his miraculous healing ability had reached them, as verse 26 may indicate.

[101] Mark 15:32; Acts 9:26,

[102] Divine authority: Luke 22:67; John 8:24, 10:38, 11:27, 11:42, 13:19, 14:10, 16:27, 16:30, 17:8, 17:21, 20:31; Acts 17:31; 1 John 5:1, 5:5. Died: John 19:35. Rose again: Mark 16:11, 16:13, 16:14; Luke 24:11, 24:41; John 20:25, 20:27, 20:29; Rom 10:9; 1 Thes 4:14.

[103] Acts 26:8; Rom 6:8; 1 Thes 4:14.

Chapter 9

Righteousness and the Torah

The previous chapter showed the importance of understanding the way in which the early Christians understood New Testament words. Now we turn to another important yet often misunderstood term – 'righteousness'. People of the 1st century spoke often of righteousness, using the Greek word *dikaiosyne*. Their culture cared about correct behaviour far more than the modern West does. Scholars who have studied the word dikaiosyne in Greek culture agree that it meant "correct behaviour according to some set of social norms, customs, or laws."[1] It occurs many times in the Greek Septuagint (LXX) translation of the Old Testament that the New Testament authors used for their scriptures. One scholar observes, "Dikaiosyne occurs over 300 times in the LXX... indicating conduct that is pleasing to God, in accord with the Law, and morally correct... It is often used of a godly and moral person."[2] Plato wrote one of the most famous works of ancient Greek philosophy, his 300-page *Republic*, on moral virtue, using dikaiosyne as the term for moral virtue. A particularly experienced translator of Greek works decided to use the English word 'morality' as the best translation for dikaiosyne throughout his recent translation of the *Republic*.[3] Scholars have reached similar conclusions about what the term means in the New Testament. Apart from Paul, Matthew used the word dikaiosyne more than any New Testament writer. One scholar states that, in Matthew's Gospel, righteousness means "the conduct which God expects of his people."[4] Another scholar explains: "righteousness is seen as God's demand upon man. Righteousness refers to proper conduct before God."[5]

---

[1] See e.g. L. Morris, *The Apostolic Preaching of the Cross* (Grand Rapids, MI: Eerdmans, 2000), p. 252; Malina, Bruce J. and John J. Pilch, *Social-Science Commentary on the Letters of Paul* (Minneapolis: Fortress, 2006), pp. 227 & 237.

[2] Ben Witherington III, *Paul's Letter to the Romans: A Socio-Rhetorical Commentary* (Grand Rapids, MI: Eerdmans, 2004), p. 52.

[3] Plato, *Republic*, trans. Robin Waterfield (New York: Oxford, 1998), p. xii.

[4] R. T. France, *The Gospel of Matthew* (Grand Rapids: Eerdmans, 2007), p. 119.

[5] B. Przybylski, *Righteousness in Matthew and His World of Thought* (Cambridge: University Press, 1980), p. 99.

The New Testament authors used righteousness as a moral term. It concerned thinking and behaving in the right way, and they used it to write about correct behaviour. We must clarify here why the post-Reformation tradition tends to misunderstand righteousness as a legal term; the ancient Greek writers sometimes used dikaiosyne in the context of law court decisions pertaining to whether someone had acted rightly or wrongly. When translators created a Latin version of the Bible, they translated the Greek word *dikaiosyne* into the Latin word *iustitia*, which means 'justice'. Around 1600 AD, Law was the most advanced degree at universities, and students studied it in Latin. Biblical scholars who trained in law saw this word 'justice' in their Latin Bibles and interpreted many verses through a legal paradigm rather than an ethical one. They believed this 'justice' concerned a person's *legal standing* of guilt or innocence, rather than a person's actual conduct. Recent studies have begun to correct this misunderstanding. By focusing on the Greek word dikaiosyne rather than its Latin translation, scholars have found that the word generally has little to do with courts of law. Generally, in the Old Testament, dikaiosyne concerns correct behaviour – moral virtue and good conduct – with virtually no mention of a legal meaning. As one scholar comments about the meaning of *dikaiosyne* in the LXX: "There can be little doubt that as applied to human beings the term usually has an ethical rather than forensic [law-court related] flavour."[6] Studies in the New Testament have reached similar conclusions. For example, a scholar of Matthew's Gospel notes that it is a "strictly ethical concept."[7] Both the Bible and other Greek texts use the term most often while discussing moral virtue and correct conduct. *Dikaiosyne* concerns a person's actual conduct and not merely their legal standing of guilt or innocence.

Unfortunately, the legal concepts of the 17th century linger in our modern English Bibles. Some translators have tried to solve this by translating dikaiosyne as 'righteousness' rather than 'justice',[8] but the legal tradition has also influenced how people understand the term 'righteousness'. Furthermore, English Bibles use the terms 'justify' and 'justification' typically as translations for two of the forms of dikaio-

---

[6] Ben Witherington III, *Paul's Letter to the Romans*, p. 52.
[7] R. Mohrlang, *Matthew and Paul: A Comparison of Ethical Perspectives* (Cambridge: University Press, 1984), pp. 113 – 114.
[8] ... which is better. Yet modern English lacks a verb form of righteousness (in older English it was "to rightwise") so the verb form of 'righteousness' ends up as 'justify'.

syne.[9] Hence, modern English readers assume all too often that righteousness concerns primarily one's *legal standing before God*, regardless of conduct. The New Testament authors, however, would have used these exact words to describe living in accordance with God's moral requirements. Early Christians would have thought of dikaiosyne as morality, not as legal standing before God, and we must interpret the words as they did in order to correctly understand their message.

Just as the word dikaiosyne referred to correct conduct, *hamartia* referred to incorrect conduct. The Greeks used this word as the standard term for an error, flaw, mistake, or wrongdoing. Usually, modern English translations interpret it as 'sin', which has become a technical Christian term. Many people, however, do not realise that *hamartia* had a normal meaning in everyday speech, just as dikaiosyne did. Greek speakers used these terms daily without meaning anything particularly theological or technical. When wrongdoing characterised someone, people termed that person a 'sinner' (*hamartolos*). When correct conduct characterised someone, they called that person 'righteous' (*dikaios*). Jesus contrasted people characterised by hamartia with those characterised by dikaiosyne, explaining: "I have come to call not the righteous but sinners."[10] Elsewhere he taught: "there will be more joy in heaven over one sinner who repents than over ninety-nine righteous people who need no repentance."[11] Early Christian readers would have understood these statements made by Jesus in a moral sense. Paul contrasted righteousness with sinfulness frequently in a similar sense,[12] using sinfulness as a moral term. He wrote of the power of sinfulness, referring to ensnaring desires that cause immoral conduct and describing people held "captive to the rule of sinfulness."[13] Paul argued that no nation is free from "the power of sinfulness,"[14] and wrote of sinfulness reigning over human lives,[15] enslaving them.[16] We must keep in mind that the early Christians thought of sinfulness in terms of a person's *current* moral character and conduct. It was not a list of past wrongs, nor guilt from those past wrongs.

---

[9] For more information on the history and influence of the Latin "Iustitia" see the recent history given in Alister McGrath, *Iustitia Dei: A History of the Christian Doctrine of Justification* (Cambridge, University Press, 2005, 3rd ed.).

[10] Matt 9:13; Mark 2:17; Luke 5:32.

[11] Luke 15:7.

[12] E.g. Rom 5:19, 21; 6:13, 16, 18, 20.

[13] Rom 7:23.

[14] Rom 3:9.

[15] Rom 5:21.

[16] See especially Rom 6-7.

Righteousness through faithfulness, not Torah

Jesus' activity had led people into a way of life characterised by correct thought and behaviour. His message aimed to turn people away from wrong ways of living (sinfulness), and to set them on a new path of loving and helping others (righteousness). Hence, the early Christians naturally used the Greek terms for sinfulness and righteousness to discuss the importance of following Jesus. They believed that righteousness came through following his teachings and example faithfully. This claim caused controversy, since many Jews believed that one had to follow the Jewish Torah in order to be righteous. Acts and Galatians record much controversy surrounding this issue within the early church.

The controversy had two main aspects. The first concerned the question of whether Christians needed to follow the Jewish way of life dictated by the Torah. Widespread Hellenisation had threatened the Jews' way of life and made this a sensitive issue. On one end of the spectrum lay Paul's view. Jesus' ministry and resurrection proved to Paul that people did not need to follow the ritual requirements of the Torah. He argued that Gentile Christians need not follow Torah, and that Jews could ignore the purity requirements of the Torah in order to have fellowship with Gentiles. At the other end of the spectrum, some Jewish Christians believed firmly that everyone should follow all of Torah. This difference of opinion created problems, since the Torah impinged on church unity during events like shared meals.[17] The leaders reached a pragmatic compromise to preserve unity. Gentile converts would adopt some very basic Torah food practices, but would otherwise not need to follow Torah.[18]

The second aspect of this controversy proved more difficult to resolve and was a matter of contention for many Jews outside the church. The idea that God would include in his people those who did not follow Torah upset some Jews. Some Christians did not even have Israelite ancestry. Jews felt that God had chosen their nation,[19] and to include Gentiles threatened their sense that God considered them special. Their God was the God of *Israel* and not of other nations. Perhaps more importantly, though, they felt the Christian movement threatened their covenant with God. This covenant given through Moses required them

---

[17] An issue Paul raises in Gal 2:12-13.
[18] Act 15:19-31.
[19] This was their "boast," as Paul puts it. See Rom 2:17, 2:23, 3:27, 4:2; Eph 2:9.

to maintain purity and keep the Torah as a nation. Paul and other Christians, however, told Jews that they should not follow its purity regulations, since those rules marginalised some people. To devout Jews, Paul's preaching seemed to oppose the Torah of the Covenant. The same issue had angered the authorities about Jesus' teaching and led them to kill him. Decades after Jesus, this issue had become even more widespread as the Jesus-movement had grown. To non-Christian Jews, the Christian message threatened the legitimacy of their tradition and identity by saying that people need not and sometimes should not keep the Jewish tradition.

Paul's view of Torah

Paul had dealt with this issue of Torah extensively. In his earlier life as a Pharisee, he had encouraged Israelites strongly to follow Torah, the purity regulations in particular. Jesus, however, had rejected parts of Torah concerning ritual purity radically during his ministry. He valued the wellbeing of others over the customs that stood in the way of showing them compassionate love. The Pharisees had plotted to kill him because they saw his teachings as incompatible with the Torah. As a Pharisee, Paul had opposed followers of Jesus for the same reasons. He recounted to the Galatians:

> You have heard, no doubt, of my earlier life in Judaism. I was violently persecuting the church of God and was trying to destroy it. I advanced in Judaism beyond many among my people of the same age, for I was far more zealous for the traditions of my ancestors.[20]

The word 'Judaism' referred to following the Torah. We learn from the book of Acts and his own letters that Paul persecuted Jesus' followers out of zeal for the Torah. He arrested them and approved of their execution.[21] Speaking of his previous enthusiasm for Torah, he wrote:

> [I was] circumcised on the eighth day, a member of the people of Israel, of the tribe of Benjamin, a Hebrew born of Hebrews; as

---

[20] Gal 1:14.
[21] Act 22:3-5.

to Torah, a Pharisee; as to zeal, a persecutor of the church; as to righteousness under Torah, blameless.[22]

No one could be more Jewish than Paul. He had the right ancestors; he had followed Torah from birth; and had firmly opposed those who had taught against it.

When Paul had a vision of the risen Jesus, he abandoned his strict Judaism. That vision proved to Paul that God wanted people to live according to the teachings of Jesus – Jesus had taught that the customs and rituals of Torah did not matter in God's eyes. This revelation became central to Paul's theology and caused great controversy among Jews. Paul argued that their enthusiasm for Torah was not "according to knowledge." They were "ignorant of the way of living God considers right."[23] Furthermore, he argued that Gentile Christians did not need to follow the customs of the Torah.[24] He taught that Jesus had put an end to those customs.[25] Like Jesus, Paul argued instead that, "the one who loves another has fulfilled Torah."[26] Again echoing Jesus, he taught that "the whole Torah is summed up in a single commandment, 'You shall love your neighbor as yourself'."[27] Paul believed that God wanted people to follow Jesus' teachings of love for others, not the customs of the Torah.

Paul announced dramatically in his letter to the Philippians that he now considered worthless all the previous Torah-following he had done. "Whatever gains I had," he wrote of his past Judaism, "these I have come to regard as loss because of Christ."[28] When some of his converts started observing some customs of the Torah, he feared he had wasted his efforts.[29] He also taught the Colossians that they did not need to keep the rituals of the Torah: "do not let anyone condemn you in matters of food and drink or of observing festivals, new moons, or sabbaths."[30] Indeed, many of his writings bear witness to his fight against 'the Judaisers' – Jews who insisted that people follow the customs of the Torah.

---

[22] Phil 3:5-6.
[23] Rom 10:2-4.
[24] For example, see Gal 2:14.
[25] Col 2:13-14.
[26] Rom 13:8-10.
[27] Gal 5:14.
[28] Phil 3:7.
[29] Gal 4:10-11.
[30] Col 2:16.

This message did not make Paul a popular figure among Jews, to say the least. Some Jerusalem Christians did not like his message either, since they were still "zealous for the Torah."[31] A rumour circulated that Paul encouraged *Jews* and not merely Gentiles to abandon Torah.[32] In order to avoid trouble, Paul observed the Torah carefully and publicly while visiting Jerusalem. Even this, however, failed to prevent Jews angered by his views on Torah from mobbing him. He told them he was "brought up in this city at the feet of Gamaliel [a famous Pharisee], educated strictly according to our ancestral law, being zealous for God, just as all of you are today."[33] But when he announced that God had told him to leave Judea and preach to Gentiles, they screamed for his blood again. They felt Paul's liberal views on Torah threatened their Torah-based covenant with God. One group of Jews even vowed to assassinate Paul because of this very issue.[34]

Paul's argument against righteousness through Torah

The issue of what made people righteous in God's sight filled much of Paul's writings, since it caused such controversy. Did people need to follow the Torah to be righteous? The followers of Jesus needed to clarify this in order to resolve their internal disagreements over customs. The answer to this question also affected the rate at which Greeks converted to Christianity, since many objected to adopting the Jewish customs. Gentile converts filled Paul's churches and wanted a clear answer on the subject. Hence, Paul discussed the topic at length in several of his letters. He argued that the rituals of the Torah did not make people righteous in God's sight. Some Christians had told the Galatian converts they ought to follow Torah. Paul condemned this as "another gospel," since Jesus had not required people to keep the rituals of the Torah.[35] He felt that this compromised some of Jesus' core teachings. Paul devoted a substantial amount of his two most deeply theological letters to clarify the matter – Romans and Galatians. We will focus here on his argument in Romans, chapters one to four.

The Jews saw themselves as God's chosen nation and were deeply divided in how they viewed themselves in comparison to Gentiles. Some Jews considered themselves much better off before God than the Gentiles were. This group believed that, as they were descendents of

---

[31] Acts 21:20; see also Act 15:1-11.
[32] Acts 21:21.
[33] Acts 22:2-3.
[34] Acts 23:12-30.
[35] Gal 1:6-8.

Abraham, God would guard them and care for them, punishing their Gentile enemies. A Jewish work called *Wisdom of Solomon*, written about a hundred years before the time of Jesus, expressed this view. It said that the Jews possessed God's favour inherently and that God gave them special protection from sin and punishment. One passage explains, "even if we sin we are yours, knowing your power; but we will not sin, because we know that you acknowledge us as yours. For to know you is complete righteousness, and to know your power is the root of immortality."[36] They believed, therefore, that if they sinned, God would not punish them because of his covenant with their people. Another passage mentions this exact idea: "instead of this punishment [which the Gentiles received] you showed kindness to your people."[37]

Just as John the Baptist[38] and Jesus[39] had done, Paul strongly opposed this view. Paul wrote much of the book of Romans in dialogue format in order to debate opponents, probably choosing this format because he had no direct authority over the church in Rome and therefore had to convince them rather than command them. He began his argument with a lengthy paraphrase of his opponent's position. Scholars have long observed that in Romans 1:18-32, Paul paraphrased from *Wisdom of Solomon*.[40] Sudden changes of voice occur both before and after this quote. Immediately following the quote, Paul condemned the previous speaker.[41] He criticised him for judging others when he did the same things.[42] Paul continued by presenting his thesis that Jews did not have an inherent advantage before God in comparison to Gentiles:

> There will be anguish and distress for everyone who does evil, the Jew first and also the Greek, but glory and honor and peace for everyone who does good, the Jew first and also the Greek. For God shows no partiality.[43]

He reiterated three times in these two sentences that God treats Jews and Greeks equally, and once more in the sentence that follows. Paul

---

[36] Wisdom of Solomon 15:1-3.
[37] Wisdom of Solomon 16:2.
[38] Matt 3:8-9, Luke 3:7-8.
[39] John 8:39-44.
[40] Wisdom of Solomon 13-14.
[41] Rom 2:1
[42] There were plenty of times in Israel's history where it had strayed from God and engaged in the various evils that the account (in Rom 1:18-32 / Wisdom of Solomon 13-14) accuses Gentiles of committing.
[43] Rom 2:9-11.

argued that God judges a person on his or her individual moral conduct and not on customs or ancestry. Paul preached this message as part of his gospel.[44] He restated this principle throughout his letter to the Romans, as he built more and more support for it.

Paul argued against his opponents' belief that Jews had special protection from sinfulness, beginning the next section of his argument by alluding to incidents that had occurred in Rome several years earlier. In one high-profile case, a Jew had been caught practising adultery. Not long after, some Jewish teachers were caught stealing money from donations to the Jewish Temple. These caused such a public scandal that the Emperor expelled all Jews from Rome in 19 AD.[45] Further controversies led to a subsequent Emperor expelling the Jews from Rome again in 49 AD. The Jews began returning about five years later,[46] which some think prompted Paul to write Romans.[47] Paul reminded his opponent of the Jews' imperfect history in his dialogue: "You that forbid adultery, do you commit adultery? You that abhor idols, do you rob temples? ...The name of God is blasphemed among the Gentiles because of you."[48] Paul used these events of their recent past to remind his Jewish readers that the Torah did not make them any more immune from immorality than the Gentiles were. After a brief dialogue with his opponent, Paul returned to this line of argument.[49] He cited historical examples in which the Old Testament condemned groups of Israelites or Gentiles for immoral action.[50] He explained that Scripture itself uses similar terms to describe Israelite and Gentile immorality. This demonstrated that Jews did not have immunity from sin and that their Israelite ancestry did not make them more righteous than the Gentiles. Paul explained that God condemns both Jews and Gentiles when they do evil, "for there is no distinction."[51] Similarly, he argued that God accepts both Jews and Gentiles when they show moral virtue.

In the next section of Romans, Paul targeted the central issue: what makes a person righteous? He pointed to Jesus and Abraham as

---

[44] Rom 2:16.
[45] Josephus, *Antiquities* 18:65-84.
[46] There is no documented evidence regarding the return date; however, generally scholars believe that the decree would have expired upon the death of the Emperor Claudius in 54 AD.
[47] Generally, Romans is dated 55 – 57 AD.
[48] Rom 2:22-24.
[49] Rom 3:9-20.
[50] Rom 3:10-18.
[51] Rom 3:22.

examples of righteousness,[52] and argued that God will also deem as righteous anyone who follows their examples. He argued that true, godly righteousness comes through following Jesus rather than following the Torah. He put it this way: "no human being will live rightly in [God's] sight by deeds prescribed by the Torah."[53] He restated this position only a few verses later: "a person lives rightly by faithfulness apart from the works prescribed by the Torah."[54] He used a similar phrase to the Galatians: "we know that a person lives rightly not by following Torah but through faithfulness like Jesus Christ's."[55] Paul reminded the Romans of Abraham's story. God deemed Abraham righteous because he was faithful to God even though he was not circumcised and thus not following Torah, since the Torah had not yet been given through Moses.[56] Paul explained that God can deem as righteous the Gentiles deemed 'ungodly' by the Torah.[57] (*Wisdom of Solomon* often used the derogatory label 'ungodly' to describe Gentiles.[58] Paul played on this term to explain that God considered righteous some of the supposedly 'ungodly' – the Gentiles.) Paul also referenced a Psalm by David. David had committed murder and adultery, for which the Torah gave no forgiveness, yet that did not stop God from forgiving David out of love. This story illustrated Paul's point: those faithful to God need not follow the rituals of the Torah in order for God to forgive them.[59] The Torah might distinguish between Jew and Gentile, but God does not. Paul argued that *both* Jews and Greeks could become righteous by following Jesus faithfully, since righteousness does not come from following Torah.

We saw earlier that righteousness means "correct behaviour according to an agreed norm or standard." The prescribed behaviours can differ markedly depending on the standard or norm one applies. In modern ethical debates, people disagree often on what is right and what is wrong, since they judge the actions by different standards. Similarly, the standards of different religious teachings and secular laws can often judge the same acts quite differently. For example, people label acts of terrorism, abortion, and prostitution as acceptable or unacceptable depending on which standard they use. In the same way, people in the

---

[52] Rom 3:26, 4:1-22.
[53] Rom 3:20.
[54] Rom 3:28.
[55] Gal 2:16.
[56] Rom 4:10.
[57] Rom 4:5.
[58] E.g. Wisdom of Solomon 14:9, 16; 16:16, 18; 19:1.
[59] Rom 4:7-8; Psalm 32.

ancient world could apply different standards for righteous conduct. Jewish literature from around the time of Paul contrasted regularly different standards and levels of righteousness.[60] One document contrasts the righteousness of God with the righteousness of the Devil. According to the Devil, correct behaviours for humans include gaining wealth, lusting, and defiling the sacred.[61] Jews evidently referred to the standard of conduct advocated by person 'X' by speaking of 'the righteousness of X'. Hence, the righteousness of the Devil and the righteousness of God referred to contrasting standards of conduct for humans. In Jewish literature of the time, the 'righteousness of God' denoted the standard of conduct for humans that God considers correct.[62] Matthew's Gospel uses the phrase in a way consistent with that meaning, as does the letter of James.[63] This helps us make sense of Paul's use of the phrase, 'righteousness of God', which has long caused confusion and debate. Paul used this phrase to contrast the two standards of behaviour he discussed – one advocated by Torah and another that God wants people to follow. Throughout Romans, Paul argued that real righteousness, the righteousness of God, does not require a person to follow Torah. Instead, he argued that such right-eousness comes through following Jesus faithfully. He contrasted the 'righteousness from Torah' with the 'righteousness from God' again in his letter to the Philippians. He argued that the first has no worth, while he strived with all possible effort to achieve the second.[64]

Some theologians have claimed that Paul saw God's righteousness in a legal paradigm as a free gift *from* him. They imagine that God imputes this state of righteousness to us through Christ, independently of the way in which we live. This idea, however, does not correspond with what Paul wrote. Throughout Philippians 3, Paul contrasted two codes of conduct that God could use to judge whether we live right-eously. The first was revealed "from God" through Jesus, and the second was revealed "from Torah." When Paul wrote of righteousness from Torah, he did not mean that the Torah 'imputes righteousness' to those who do not live rightly. Rather, he meant that people who follow the Torah are righteous according to its code of conduct. Paul explained that, in his past as a Pharisee, he was faultless in terms of the way in which the Torah defined righteousness. The resurrection of Jesus, however, revealed 'God's righteousness' to him. Paul saw that God had

---

[60] B. Przybylski, *Righteousness*, pp. 22, 38, 44 – 46.
[61] Damascus Document 4:17.
[62] B. Przybylski, *Righteousness*, pp. 32, 35, 90.
[63] Matt 6:33, Jas 1:20, cf Przybylski, *Righteousness*, p. 90.
[64] In Phil 3.

raised Jesus from the dead, and it convinced him that God approved of the code of conduct taught by Christ. Therefore, Paul abandoned his old 'righteousness of Torah' and strived to live according to the 'righteousness of God' made known through Jesus. Such a reading of Paul explains both what he emphasises and what he contrasts. He and the early Christians preached that, in God's sight, correct conduct did not involve living merely by the rituals and customs of the Torah. Rather, it involved faithfully following the teachings of Jesus.

Some common mistakes

Biblical scholars have only started to understand Paul's above argument about Torah well in the last thirty years. Their insights have followed considerable recent research into ancient Judaism and Paul's terminology. Unfortunately, this means that several older guesses about what Paul meant were mistaken. Here, we will look more closely at two mistaken ideas: that the New Testament teaches against making *effort* to live rightly ourselves, and that God considers no one righteous on the grounds of their conduct. If the detailed discussion that follows does not interest you, though, feel free to skip to the conclusion of this chapter.

Human effort

The first mistake concerns a phrase of Paul's that appears often in English Bibles as 'works of the law'. The phrase is translated more accurately as 'works of the Torah,' since Paul used the term 'law' to refer to the Torah. Unfortunately, the older translation of 'works of law' has led many people to interpret it generally as 'good works' or even 'human effort'. This reading would have Paul denying the need to do good, or even the need to make an effort to be righteous before God. In other words, it suggests that moral behaviour and human effort to live rightly have no influence upon final judgment.

In Romans 2:6 – 10, however, we see clearly that Paul placed great importance upon correct moral behaviour. He stated plainly that God "will repay according to each one's deeds," and implored his readers to strive to live rightly and avoid sin. Likewise, in Galatians, Paul attacked the value of 'works of the Torah'. In the last one and a half chapters, however, he spelled out the importance of correct conduct, clarifying that an immoral life brings negative judgment[65] while godly behaviour brings eternal life. He explained: "if you sow to the Spirit, you will reap eternal life from the Spirit. So let us not grow weary in doing good, for we will reap at harvest time, if we do not give up."[66] It seems unlikely that Paul would have written four and a half chapters against the importance of living rightly, and then endorsed its importance over the next one and a half chapters. Rather, Paul seems to have had cultural customs and practices in mind when he wrote of 'works of the Torah'. This phrase referred to the issue of following Torah, and not did not refer to 'good works' or 'human effort'. On understanding Paul's argument against the Torah, we see that Paul never denied the value of effort nor the value of human conduct. He held the view that by living rightly we *are* righteous, and thus God recognises us as such. The customs of the Torah did not define that right way to live – Jesus did. Thus, Paul exhorted us to strive to follow *Jesus'* example and teachings in order to become righteous.

Paul made a similar argument in Philippians 3. He emphasised his Jewish past, and the fact that he had met all the requirements of the Torah. Yet as a result of encountering the risen Jesus, Paul rejected those requirements as meaningless.[67] Instead, Paul put his efforts into imitating Christ so that he might achieve a resurrection like Christ's.[68] A careful reading of this passage shows that Paul did not oppose the value of human effort here. Half of Paul's righteousness according to Torah had come from his ancestry. The other half had come from his diligence in obeying it. In contrast, Paul depicted his Christianity in terms of far greater effort to obey Jesus' teachings, comparing it to the effort needed to win a race.[69] Paul and the early Christians taught that following Jesus involved considerable effort. No verses in the New Testament teach otherwise.

"No one is righteous"

Another more serious mistake about New Testament doctrine is to think that people cannot actually achieve righteousness before God through godly living. The major implications of this common view demand that we give it a detailed treatment here. We have already seen that the Jews believed righteousness and wickedness depended upon

---

[65] Gal 5:21.
[66] Gal 6:8-9.
[67] Phil 3:4-7.
[68] Phil 3:10-21.
[69] Phil 3:12-16.

people's conduct, the outward expression of the character of their hearts. God deemed as righteous those who sought truly to live according to his will. Occasional mistakes did not make them 'sinners'. Rather, they became sinners only if they rejected God and his will deliberately and consistently. The Jews used the terms 'sinner' and 'righteous' in a way similar to the way in which we contrast good and bad people today. The New Testament authors used the terms this way consistently, and so did Jesus himself. As we noted earlier, he said he came to call not the righteous but sinners,[70] and that more rejoice over one sinner who repents than 99 righteous people who need no repentance.[71] Jesus implied that righteous people can indeed exist. Throughout the Old and New Testaments, over 80 passages in the Bible contrast the wicked or sinners with the righteous explicitly.[72] Evidently, the writers of the Bible believed that there *were* people who lived rightly, whom God considered righteous. Passages concerning righteous people speak of them very positively and depict God as being pleased with them. Misunderstandings of Judaism and Paul's writings over the centuries, however, have led some people to argue against the teaching of these clear biblical statements. They give misunderstood passages and mistaken ideas priority over other, clearer passages. Here we will endeavour to shed light on some of these misunderstandings.

The view that no one can live righteously often goes hand-in-hand with a misunderstanding of Judaism, with many modern Christians imagining ancient Jews striving and failing to follow an impossible law. They imagine the Torah as God's perfect standard of morality that no one *could* follow because of sin. This view misunderstands the nature of the Torah greatly. While the Torah did include moral commands, it encompassed not merely a system of morality but an entire *culture*. The Torah was the Jewish way of life. Jews could choose to adopt it or not,

---

[70] Mark 2:17; Luke 5:31-32; Matt 9:13.

[71] Luke 15:7.

[72] Genesis 6:9; 7:1. 2 Samuel 4:11. Job 1:1, 8. Psalms 1; 5:12; 7:9; 11:3, 5, 7; 14:5; 31:18; 32:11; 33:1; 34:15,17,19,21; 37:12-17,21,25,28-30,32,39; 52:6,22; 58:10-11; 64:10; 68:3; 75:10; 92:12; 94:15,21; 97:11-12; 112:4,6; 118:15,20; 125:3; 140:13; 141:5; 142:7; 146:8. Proverbs 3:33; 4:18; 9:9; 10:3,6,7,11,16,20-21,24-25,28,30-32; 11:8-10,21,23,28,30-31; 12:3,5,7,10,12-13,21,26; 13:5,9,21-22,25; 14:19,32; 15:6,28-29; 18:10; 20:7; 21:15,18,26; 23:24; 24:15; 28:1,12,28; 29:2,6-7,16,27. Ecclesiastes 3:17; 7:15; 8:14; 9:1-2. Isaiah 26:7; 57:1; 58:2. Lamentations 4:13. Ezekiel 3:20-21; 13:22; 18:9,20,24,26; 33:12-13,18. Amos 2:6; 5:12. Habakkuk 1:4; 2:4. Zephaniah 3:5. Malachi 3:18. Matt 1:19; 5:45; 9:13; 10:41; 13:17; 13:49; 23:29; 23:35; 25:37,46. Mark 2:17; 6:20. Luke 1:6; 2:25; 5:32; 15:7; 23:50. Acts 24:15. Hebrews 11:4. James 5:16. 1 Peter 3:12; 4:18. 2 Peter 2:7-8. 1 John 3:7,12. Revelation 19:8; 22:11

just as people today can choose to live by Western customs. It is senseless to speak of *trying* to observe it but failing to do so 'because of sin'. If a person chose to follow it, then they did. If a person did morally err in some minor way, the Torah outlined procedures to follow. A Jew who sinned but repented and offered the prescribed sacrifice still followed Torah entirely. Jews saw keeping the Torah as entirely possible. Paul wrote about his life as a Jew, saying that "as to righteousness under the Torah, [he had been] blameless."[73] He did not conclude from his life following Torah that humans could never keep God's commands – far from it. Paul viewed keeping the Torah as very possible, and he never suggested that people could not live in the right way. Rather, he argued about what the right way to live *was*. He taught that Jesus defined it, rather than the Torah.

The idea that people cannot live righteously grows also from another misunderstanding about Paul's contrast between the 'spirit' and the 'flesh'. Some people think that the verses in which Paul made this contrast indicate that humans have a 'sinful human nature,' which prevents them from living in a way that God would deem righteous. In reality, Paul made the opposite point in these verses. When discussing ethics, Greeks represented the mind commonly as comprising two or more conflicting parts. Centuries earlier, the Greek philosopher Plato had noted the competing desires that people sometimes experience and concluded that these came from two different parts of the mind.[74] He likened the mind to a chariot pulled by two horses. One of the horses represented bodily desires for food, drink and sex. The other horse represented spiritual desires for abstract goods like love, honour and justice. These two battled for control of the mind. Plato considered it acceptable to satisfy the bodily desires in moderation. Giving these desires free reign, however, would lead to greed, sexual immorality, selfishness, and so on. Hence, in order to have 'self-control', the part of the mind that sought spiritual things must control the part that desired fleshly things. By Paul's time, the Stoic philosophies that drew on Plato's ideas had become popular among the educated higher classes. Stoicism concerned ethics, freedom from desire, and self-control. The Stoics believed that, "No man is free who is not master of himself."[75] The Greek philosophers believed that people could learn to follow the good desires for virtue, rather than their bodily desires.

---

[73] Phil 3:6.

[74] Plato, *Republic*, 434d-441c, *Phaedrus* 246b ff.

[75] Epictetus, Fragments, 15.

In both Acts and Corinthians, we read that Paul liked to explain his message using concepts familiar to his hearers.[76] Unsurprisingly, therefore, he drew on these Platonic and Stoic ideas. He used Greek ethical terminology when he wrote to his readers in Rome about freedom from 'slavery' to the 'fleshly desires'.[77] They understood that following fleshly desires led to wrongdoing. Paul contrasted this with the righteousness and freedom from sinfulness that resulted from following the spirit of Jesus. In Romans 7:14-8:16, Paul portrayed the struggle between the fleshly and spiritual desires within people. Even though people want to do good with part of their mind, their bodily desires control them instead.[78] Paul explained that through Jesus, people could achieve freedom from bodily desires to live righteously.[79]

Paul, like the Greek ethicists, thought that his readers could choose to follow their desires to do good rather than their selfish desires. Otherwise, his moral exhortations would have made little sense. He instructed them, "live by the spirit, I say, and do not gratify the desires of the flesh."[80] According to Paul, the message of the gospel should lead those who follow their fleshly desires to follow spiritual desires instead.[81] By 'sinful flesh,' Paul did not refer to some kind of 'unregenerate human nature'. Rather, he spoke of desires that can lead to sin if fulfilled without moderation. He did not think people were entirely and irrevocably sinful. He framed his discussion in the common terminology of Greek ethical philosophy and exhorted them to choose the set of desires taught and exemplified by Jesus. Through Jesus' spirit, people could be freed from their sinful desires and instead live rightly.

It is sometimes assumed that several other Biblical passages indicate that no one *actually* lives according to God's standard of correct conduct. Thus, it follows that no one *is* righteous in this sense. These passages, however, provide no support for such a view when understood correctly. Firstly, consider Psalm 51:5: "Behold, I was brought forth in iniquity, and in sin my mother conceived me."[82] Some claim

---

[76] Acts 17:22-31; 1 Cor 9:22 etc.

[77] Rom 7:24; 8:2.

[78] Rom 7:14-23. For a comparison of Romans 7 with ideas from Greek moral philosophy see Emma Wasserman, *The Death of the Soul in Romans 7: Sin, Death, and the Law in Light of Hellenistic Moral Psychology* (Tübingen: Mohr Siebeck, 2008), and also Stanley K. Stowers, *A Rereading of Romans: Justice, Jews, & Gentiles* (Ann Arbor, MI: Yale University Press, 1997).

[79] Rom 8:1-3.

[80] Gal 5:16.

[81] Gal 5:19-24.

[82] Other verses include Psalm 58:3 and Eph. 2:3.

that this verse supports the doctrine of original sin, holding it up as proof that humans are sinners from birth. Yet, the verse taken literally attributes sin to the mother, not the child. One scholar likens it to the phrase, 'in anger my father whipped me,' in which no one would attribute the anger to the child.[83] Hence, it is possible that the writer may have lamented in this verse his illegitimate conception outside of marriage. Alternatively, he may have meant that his birth brought him into a sinful environment. As yet another alternative, he may have felt racked with guilt and exaggerated his sinful deeds poetically. He may have expressed something like, "it seems like I have been doing serious wrongs since I was born." Given these alternatives, this verse hardly provides convincing support for original sin, or definitive proof that God sees everyone as sinful. Indeed, even some who have supported the doctrine of original sin have agreed that this passage does not support the idea.[84]

Another passage that people quote as 'proof' that no one can ever be righteous comes from Isaiah 64: "We have all become like one who is unclean, and all our righteous deeds are like a filthy cloth."[85] Yet in this passage, Isaiah lamented that Israel once served God but had since rebelled. The Israelites' degree of righteousness had become very low indeed. Note the 'become' – Israel had changed from righteous to unrighteous. The passage did not imply that God sees all of humanity's attempts at righteousness as like a filthy cloth. Rather, it referred to the unusually low level of righteousness held by a particular nation in a particular point in history. Only one verse earlier, the prophet had written that God meets "those who gladly do right." That phrase implies that people can indeed conduct themselves correctly in God's sight.

We must address the most influential passage and most commonly misunderstood passage – Romans 3:9-18. Some people believe it teaches that God sees all people as sinners. Let us read what Paul wrote:

> Are we [Jews] any better off? No, not at all; for we have already charged that all peoples, both Jews and Greeks, are under the power of sinfulness, as it is written:

---

[83] T. W. Brents, *The Gospel Plan of Salvation* (Gospel Advocate Company, 2001), pp. 133-134.
[84] E.g. Albert Barnes, *Notes on the Psalms*, ed. Robert Frew (Grand Rapids, Baker Book House, 1979), Vol. 2, p. 138.
[85] Isa 64:6.

"There is no one who is righteous, not even one; there is no one who has understanding, there is no one who seeks God. All have turned aside, together they have become worthless; there is no one who shows kindness, there is not even one."
"Their throats are opened graves; they use their tongues to deceive."
"The venom of vipers is under their lips."
"Their mouths are full of cursing and bitterness."
"Their feet are swift to shed blood; ruin and misery are in their paths, and the way of peace they have not known."
"There is no fear of God before their eyes."

Up to this point, Paul had tried to persuade his audience that having Jewish ancestry and following the Torah does not make a person righteous. Instead he insisted that God judges both Jews and Gentiles equally on the basis of their conduct. He continued his argument in this passage by highlighting that, throughout history, both groups of Jews and groups of Gentiles had sinned to the same extent. Paul took the six scriptural citations here from specific places and times in history when particular groups of Gentiles or Israelites had acted unrighteously. In Paul's time, people had not yet added chapter and verse numbers to identify scripture passages, so he referenced these passages in the common way by quoting memorable phrases. Jews memorised the scriptures at an early age, so Paul's quotes would have brought each passage to mind readily. To make his point, Paul drew attention to the specific groups of unrighteous people at the centre of these stories. Each of the six passages from which Paul quotes contrasts a particular group of sinners with a particular group of righteous people. Hence, the passages all imply that righteous people exist.

The first passage (3:10-12) quotes from Psalm 14, which concerns Gentile nations attacking Israel. It reads:

Fools say in their hearts, "There is no God." They are corrupt, they do abominable deeds; there is no one [of them] who does good. The Lord looks down from heaven on humankind to see if there are any who are wise, who seek after God. They have all gone astray, they are all alike perverse; there is no one [of them] who does good, no, not one. Have they no knowledge, all the evildoers who eat up my people as they eat bread, and do not call upon the Lord? There they shall be in great terror, for God is with the company of the righteous [Israel]... When the Lord restores the fortunes of his people, Jacob will rejoice; Israel will be glad.

The Psalmist criticised the unbelieving Gentile nations attacking Israel at that time. *They* were the corrupt people. Yet the Psalmist said that, as a nation, Israel was righteous at that time. Hence, Israel could have confidence that God would protect them. The second quote (3:13a) comes from Psalm 5. The relevant parts read:

> For there is no truth in [my enemies'] mouths; *their* hearts are destruction; *their* throats are open graves; *they* flatter with their tongues... For *you bless the righteous,* O Lord; you cover them with favor as with a shield.

This Psalm contrasted the lying enemies with the righteous people that God would bless. Clearly, the Psalmist did not believe that God deemed everyone unrighteous. The third quote (3:13b) comes from Psalm 140, which reads:

> Deliver me, O Lord, from *evildoers*... *They* make their tongue sharp as a snake's, and under *their* lips is the venom of vipers... I know that the Lord maintains the cause of the needy, and executes justice for the poor. Surely *the righteous* shall give thanks to your name; *the upright* shall live in your presence.

Here, the psalmist complained about certain evil people, and again implied that God saw other people as righteous. Romans 3:18 quotes from Psalm 36:

> Transgression speaks to *the wicked* deep in their hearts; there is no fear of God before *their* eyes... O continue your steadfast love to those who know you, and your salvation to *the upright of heart*!

Here the Psalmist clearly believed that God aids the people with upright hearts – who do actually exist.

The following table categorises the important references in these six passages quoted by Paul. The first column indicates the verse number in Romans 3 where Paul cited the scripture. The second gives the Old Testament verse he cited. The third column lists the verses in the Old Testament passages that show most clearly that the wickedness had a limited extent contained within a specific group. The fourth column gives the corresponding verse in the Old Testament passage that indicates that righteous people also existed.

Verse in Romans 3	Quoted passage	Verses indicating the sinfulness was limited	Verses indicating that righteous people also existed
10-12	Psa 14:1-3/53:1-3	14:4/53:4	14:5
13a	Psa 5:9	5:8	5:12
13b	Psa 140:3	140:4	140:13
14	Psa 10:7	10:2,8	10:12,14,17-18
15-17	Isa 59:7-8	59:2,9,15,20	59:20
18	Psa 36:1b	36:1a	36:10

From this evidence, we can see that all six quotes come from passages contrasting a particular group of evildoers with a particular group of righteous people. All of the passages quoted by Paul affirm both the wickedness of some people and the righteousness of others. If we interpret these quotes to mean that *all* people are sinners, then Paul would have contradicted all six passages he quoted in support of his point. Hence, the evidence from these passages suggests that Paul believed God does not see *all* people as unrighteous sinners.

Interpreting Paul's quotes as a broad generalisation that God sees every single person as a sinner also places Paul in serious conflict with what the Bible says elsewhere. For example, scripture refers to righteous people,[86] contrary to a generalisation that God sees no one's life as righteous. We read of people who "seek God,"[87] contrary to the generalisation that "there is no one who seeks God." It tells of people who "feared God," contrary to the generalisation that "there is no fear of God before their eyes."[88] Hence, if Paul meant that God sees every single human as sinful, he would have contradicted both the passages he quoted, the rest of the Bible and what he himself wrote elsewhere. A number of passages show that, after his conversion, Paul thought of

---

[86] Gen 6:9; Luke 1:6.
[87] 2 Chr 19:3, 26:5.
[88] Ex 1:17; Acts 10:2.

himself as a good person, righteous before God.[89] Paul strived for righteousness, so that he would not be disqualified at the final judgment.[90] This shows that, after his conversion, Paul did not think the generalisation that "no one is righteous" applied to him.

The last commonly misunderstood passage that we will discuss comes from the letter of James. James wrote, "whoever keeps the whole law but fails in one point has become accountable for all of it."[91] People sometimes take this to mean that, since no one lives perfectly throughout their lifetime, God deems everyone as sinful as if they had broken all of his commandments. It was common in Jewish literature to find sayings about rewards and punishments for keeping or breaking 'even one' commandment. As one scholar explains, they provided "an effective way of urging people to obey the commandments as best they can and insisting on the importance of doing so."[92] The book of James fits well with this common feature of Jewish wisdom literature. He made the point here that even our smallest deed reflects our attitude of contempt or love toward God.[93] James spurred his readers to choose correct conduct deliberately and not to neglect God's will in minor matters. He could not have meant, "one mistake and you've fallen short forever." Such an idea would have defeated the whole purpose of his argument. He wrote this passage to *encourage* his readers toward correct moral conduct, not to tell them it was pointless even to try. He exhorted his readers to righteous conduct, using a standard idiom of Jewish rhetoric to do so.

Having examined the above passages, therefore, we can see that the early Christians believed it was possible to live according to God's code of conduct. Jesus had exemplified and taught them this; the way of righteousness. Once we understand the above passages in their proper context, no verses indicate anything to the contrary. Indeed, the idea that people cannot live righteously would completely contradict the other important doctrines of the early Christians. They taught that people could really live in the way that Jesus taught and thus receive positive final judgment and a resurrection like his. Their clear and unanimous message: God would see people as righteous if they followed the example and teachings of Jesus.

---

[89] Acts 23:1, 24:15-16; 1 Cor 4:4; 2 Cor 1:12, 5:8-11.

[90] 1 Cor 9:27.

[91] James 2:10.

[92] E. P. Sanders, *Paul and Palestinian Judaism* (Philadelphia: Fortress, 1977), p. 141.

[93] E. P. Sanders, *Paul and Palestinian Judaism*, pp. 133 – 141.

Conclusion

The early Christians believed that God saw people who lived rightly – who practised correct conduct – as righteous. Jesus had shown them what correct conduct involved, and thus by following his example and teachings they could become righteous. However, many Jews thought that God would only deem people righteous if they followed the Torah. Paul dealt with this issue often, and stressed that people become righteous by exhibiting the kind of faithfulness Jesus had, not by following all the customs of the Torah. Paul argued that the Torah did not stop people from sinning, nor did following it guarantee that people lived rightly – since both Jews and Greeks had sinned in the past. Therefore, following neither Jewish nor Greek customs made people righteous automatically.

Paul and the early Christians taught that God considers people righteous if they faithfully follow Jesus and live according to his example and teachings. We have shown that the early Christians believed they could achieve this. With the previous chapter on faithfulness in mind, we can understand Paul's teaching of 'justification by faith' in this context. This phrase conveyed Paul's central idea that God considered righteous the people who faithfully followed the example and teachings of Jesus. Thus, no conflict exists between this doctrine and the early Christian doctrine of final judgment based on one's conduct. Both righteousness and positive judgment depend upon the same criterion.

Chapter 10

Forgiveness and favour

First-century Jews held a common view of repentance and forgiveness. They believed that, if people repented of their sinfulness and turned to live righteously, God would graciously forgive their past wrongs.[1] They used the common phrase, 'repentance and forgiveness', to express this idea. The book of Ezekiel spelled this principle out carefully.[2] By the time of Jesus, the concept of repentance and forgiveness had become ingrained. No Jew worried about how they could escape the guilt of their sins before God. They knew how – through repentance and forgiveness. No sacrifices existed within the Jewish sacrificial system for deliberate moral sins.[3] The only way to deal with a deliberate sin was repentance. When sinners truly repented, they began by confessing their sins to God. They asked him for mercy and forgiveness, and pledged to live faithfully again according to his will. Out of his great love, God would accept their prayers and forgive them freely because of their sincere repentance.

The Gospels

The Gospels illustrate the widespread influence of this doctrine of repentance and forgiveness. John the Baptist preached "a baptism of repentance for the forgiveness of sins."[4] He told people to "repent"[5] and to "bear fruits worthy of repentance."[6] His hearers would have understood his message clearly, as their tradition already contained the

---

[1] For example see E. P. Sanders, *Paul and Palestinian Judaism* (Philadelphia, PA: Augsburg Fortress, 1977), pp. 5-7, 499-550. Sanders and others seem confused as to why Paul does not use much repentance terminology. The idea of turning from wickedness to righteousness is key in Paul's theology even though he does not use the actual word 'repentance' often. The best explanation for this is probably that Paul is writing to Gentiles rather than Jews, and so expresses the Jewish concept of repentance using different terminology.

[2] Ezek 18:21-23, 33:14-16.

[3] The sacrifices were for cleansing ritual impurity or unintentional moral sins.

[4] Matt 3:11; Mark 1:4; Luke 3:3; Acts 13:24, 19:4.

[5] Matt 3:2, 3:11; Luke 3:11.

[6] Matt 3:8; Luke 3:8.

idea of repentance and forgiveness. To signify repentance and forgiveness, John gave his followers a ritual washing (baptism) to symbolise the washing away of their sins.[7]

Jesus too spoke of repentance and forgiveness. Many times he urged people to repent,[8] and he warned of divine judgment against those who failed to do so.[9] Jesus also applied the doctrine of repentance and forgiveness to relationships between people. He taught his disciples that if someone repented, even after sinning against them many times, "you must forgive."[10] He instructed his disciples to proclaim "repentance and forgiveness of sins" throughout the world.[11] In a parable of a tax collector and a Pharisee praying at the temple, Jesus illustrated this concept of repentance and forgiveness.[12] In great remorse over the wrongs he had done, the tax collector "beat his breast" to show his repentance and cried out to God for mercy. Jesus said that the tax collector went home forgiven and right with God.

Jesus endorsed the 'repentance and forgiveness' concept described above often. Sometimes, however, he taught that people had to forgive others before God would forgive them. At first, this idea seems to present a different argument, so let us explore it further. It appears most prominently in Matthew's Gospel. Jesus said in the Lord's Prayer, "Forgive us our debts, as we also have forgiven our debtors."[13] Immediately after the prayer he explained, "For if you forgive others their trespasses, your heavenly Father will also forgive you; but if you do not forgive others, neither will your Father forgive your trespasses."[14] Later, Jesus told a parable in which a servant owed a huge monetary debt to his master and could not repay it.[15] The master responded by releasing the servant from the debt – by forgiving the debt. (The same Greek word means both 'release' and 'forgive' in English.) The servant then went out and refused to forgive another servant who owed him a much smaller debt. News of this angered the master, and he revoked the forgiveness he had granted.

Both of Jesus' examples about forgiveness of others focus on remitting monetary debts. Jesus lived in a time of serious economic trouble

---

[7] Mark 1:5; Matt 1:6.

[8] Matt 4:17; Mark 1:15, 6:12; Luke, 5:32, 15:7, 16:30.

[9] Matt 11:20; Luke 13:3, 13:5.

[10] Luke 17:3-4.

[11] Luke 24:47.

[12] Luke 18:9-14.

[13] Matt 6:12; Luke 11:4.

[14] Matt 6:14-15; Mark 12:25-26; Luke 6:37-39.

[15] Matt 18:23-35.

and part of his mission was to combat the life-threatening poverty that those around him suffered. Debts both forced people into poverty and kept them there. Jesus taught that God would not look kindly upon the creditors who foreclosed on loans and took everything from the poor. Those who oppressed the poor opposed God's wishes, and they needed to repent of their exploitation for him to judge them favourably. For the rich, repentance meant ceasing to exploit the poor and waiving their debts. Jesus' teaching that God would only forgive those who forgave others makes a lot of sense in this context. For God to forgive these 'moral debts' of the rich, they had to forgive the monetary debts that burdened the poor. Jesus gave a similar message a rich young ruler who asked what God required of him. He told him, "sell your possessions, and give the money to the poor, and you will have treasure in heaven."[16] Jesus looked for this kind of repentance from those who had become rich through exploiting the poor. If they repented, God would forgive their past exploitation. Outside the Gospels, James expressed a similar message. He wrote: "Judgment will be without mercy to anyone who has shown no mercy [to the poor],"[17] again in the context of concern for the poor. The economic situation at the time thus makes sense of Jesus' message to 'forgive others their debts and God will forgive you'. He did not depart from the Jewish concept of repentance and forgiveness. He did not adopt a 'forgive and be forgiven' slogan in opposition to the previous thinking of 'repent and be forgiven'. Rather, he used the phrase to apply the principle of repentance and forgiveness to the specific problem of poverty.

The New Testament letters

Other New Testament authors also shared the doctrine of repentance and forgiveness. Acts records Peter preaching: "Repent, and be baptized every one of you in the name of Jesus Christ so that your sins may be forgiven."[18] Like Jesus, Peter taught that people needed to repent in order to receive forgiveness. He urged: "Repent, therefore, and turn to God so that your sins may be wiped out."[19] He preached that God exalted Jesus "so that he might give repentance to Israel and forgiveness of sins."[20] Peter also instructed Simon to repent from his

---

[16] Matt 19:21; Mark 10:21; Luke 18:22.
[17] James 2:13.
[18] Acts 2:38.
[19] Acts 3:19.
[20] Acts 5:31.

wickedness before petitioning God to forgive the thoughts of his heart.[21] In his second epistle, Peter wrote that God is slow to punish sinners because he wants them to "come to repentance."[22] Peter convinced the Jerusalem Christians that they could also include Gentiles in their group. They concluded: "God has given even to the Gentiles the repentance that leads to life."[23] In this case, repentance appears synonymous with becoming a Christian.

Paul summarised his teachings using two concepts: repentance and faithfulness. He explained, "I testified to both Jews and Greeks about repentance toward God and faithfulness toward our Lord Jesus."[24] Later in another summary, he taught "that they should repent and turn to God and do deeds consistent with repentance."[25] The connection between repentance and deeds shows that repentance consisted of not merely an internal attitude but of a real change in lifestyle. Paul taught that God forgives people who change their hearts and turn away from wickedness. In his letter to the Romans, he listed many ungodly and wicked behaviours that anger God,[26] pointing to repentance as the way in which to escape God's negative judgment.[27] God would not condemn someone who had repented and begun living rightly. Paul's emphasis on the need for repentance made him concerned about the Corinthian Christians. He feared that some may have not "repented of the impurity, sexual immorality, and licentiousness that they have practised."[28] He contrasted the repentant Corinthians' old way of life with their new Christian way of life, and likened this great change to going from death to life. Because of this change, he explained, God forgave them their trespasses.

The repentance and forgiveness theme also appears in New Testament books by other authors. Hebrews lists "repentance from dead works and faithfulness towards God" as key ideas that new Christians needed to learn.[29] The letter of 1 John discusses repentance and forgiveness, saying that those who confess their former sins and cease to live wrongly will receive God's forgiveness.[30] The book of Revelation

---

[21] Acts 8:22.
[22] 2 Pet 3:9.
[23] Acts 11:18.
[24] Acts 20:21.
[25] Acts 26:20 cf. 26:18.
[26] Rom 1:18-32.
[27] Rom 2:3-10.
[28] 2 Cor 12:21.
[29] Heb 6:1-2.
[30] 1 John 1:9.

also presents this concept: Jesus told the church in Ephesus to "repent, and do the works you did at first."[31] He gave the same message to the churches in Sardis[32] and Laodocia.[33] Revelation threatens destruction and judgment against people who do evil and fail to repent.[34]

The above examples indicate that Jesus and the early Christians endorsed the Jewish teachings of repentance and forgiveness that portrays a loving God who forgives his children freely when they repent sincerely. He forgives their past mistakes when they commit to doing his will. From another perspective, such forgiveness came at a price, in the sense that it depended upon a real change in the sinner's way of life. Neither Jews nor the early Christians thought that they could make no effort to live rightly and simply invoke God's forgiveness repeatedly. They did not see God as an indulgent father, blinded by insincere requests for forgiveness from people who did not intend to live rightly. Rather, they believed that God could discern the true intent of the human heart. They saw authentic repentance and a sincere intention to live rightly as the conditions for God's forgiveness.

Baptism

Let us look briefly at where baptism fitted in to the early Christians' idea of forgiveness. They associated baptism closely with repentance, from the time of John the Baptist through to the 3rd century. One Christian writer from early in the 3rd century wrote about the Christian conversion processes; apparently those who wanted to convert underwent three years of training in the Christian way of life. Church leaders watched their life closely during this period. Once their lives demonstrated a strong commitment to Jesus and his teachings, the leaders baptised them and accepted them formally into the church.[35] The baptism thus sealed the repentance and moral transformation that had occurred in their lives, signifying their repentance and God's forgiveness. Early Christian writers expected repentance to accompany baptism.[36] Writing in around 230 AD, "Origen emphasized that moral conversion had to take place before baptism for any benefit to be

---

[31] Rev 2:5.

[32] Rev 3:3.

[33] Rev 3:19.

[34] Rev 2:5, 16, 21-22, 9:20, 21, 16:9, 11.

[35] Hippolytus (~215AD), *The Apostolic Tradition* 16-20.

[36] See Justin Martyr, *First Apology* 111, *Dialogue with Trypho* 14, Theophilus *To Autolycus* 2.16; Clement of Alexandria *Instructor* 1.4, 1.6.

derived from the rite."[37] At around the same time, Tertullian argued that baptism itself did not remove sin; the repentance accompanying it removed sin. He explained: "We are not washed in order that we may cease sinning, but because we have ceased, since in heart we have been bathed already [through repentance]."[38]

Repentance and judgment

The early Christians' doctrine of forgiveness through repentance fitted with their idea of judgment based on character and conduct. They believed that God would reward good and punish evil. At the same time, a person's character could change from evil to good, or vice versa. The two ideas fitted together, in their view, without contradiction. They saw God as interested in a person's *current* moral character, and they believed that he cared about the present state of a heart rather than its past. Hence, whenever a person truly changes his or her character, God dismisses past mistakes. According to this view, God has no interest in exacting retributive justice for past actions if moral character has since changed for the better. God is seen as interested in a person's deeds insofar as those deeds testify to the current character of their heart. Any deeds that occurred prior to the most recent character change are deemed irrelevant. So, people who authentically repented, changed their hearts and began a new way of life could expect God to forgive their previous deeds. In this way, the doctrine of judgment based on character and conduct fitted with the idea of repentance and forgiveness. Together, these two concepts motivated repentance and subsequent moral transformation.

The early Christians did not change the long-established Jewish view of the relationship between repentance and judgment. Jewish literature time and again links the concepts of repentance, forgiveness and judgment, presenting the view that God will condemn people who fail to live rightly but forgive those who turn from their evil ways. Take this passage from Ezekiel, for example, in which God says:

> But if the wicked turn away from all their sins that they have committed and keep all my statutes and do what is lawful and right, they shall surely live; they shall not die. None of the

---

[37] Thomas P. Scheck, *Origen, Commentary on the Epistle to the Romans Books 1-5,* The Fathers of the Church, Vol. 103 (Washington, DC: Catholic University of America Press, 2001), p. 354 fn. 411. See Origen's *Comm Rom* 5.8.2-3, 5.7.3; *Hom in Lv* 6.2; *Hom in Lk* 21; *Hom in Ezek* 6-10; *Comm in Jn* 6.17.

[38] Tertullian, *On Repentance* 6.

transgressions that they have committed shall be remembered against them; for the righteousness that they have done they shall live. Have I any pleasure in the death of the wicked, says the Lord God, and not rather that they should turn from their ways and live? But when the righteous turn away from their righteousness and commit iniquity and do the same abominable things that the wicked do, shall they live? None of the righteous deeds that they have done shall be remembered; for the treachery of which they are guilty and the sin they have committed, they shall die.[39]

A scholar writing on the subject of the Jewish doctrine of judgment by conduct has commented:

A radical understanding of retribution, where *all* one's deeds without exception are brought together and judged by weighing good against evil deeds, does not characterize the [Old Testament]. Mercy could be applied as God determined, and repentance could bring a new beginning, a clean state as it were.[40]

The Jewish literature in the intertestamental period echoed such thinking regularly throughout. The same scholar noted that, in Jewish works of this period:

When it is said that individuals will be recompensed or judged "according to their deeds," this presumes a holistic or unitary view of human works. It is not a deed for deed inspection, but rather one's entire pattern of life is in view, one's "way." Not even all one's deeds in a lifetime need to be considered, since repentance and forgiveness could eliminate the relevance of past misdeeds and mark the beginning of a new way.[41]

Another scholar examining Jewish literature on the subject emphasised that there is no contradiction between "a Last Judgment according to deeds... [and] God's mercy, forgiveness, and love."[42] No conflict or

---

[39] Ezek 18:21-24.

[40] Kent L. Yinger, *Paul, Judaism, and Judgment According to Deeds* (Cambridge: Cambridge University Press, 1999), p. 62.

[41] Yinger, p. 284.

[42] Chris VanLandingham, *Judgment & Justification in Early Judaism and the Apostle Paul* (Peabody, MA: Hendrickson, 2006), p. 171.

contradiction existed between the teachings of 'judgment by conduct' and 'repentance and forgiveness' in Judaism. The same held true in early Christianity. The teachings of repentance, forgiveness and final judgment by conduct went hand-in-hand.

Favour

God's willingness to forgive people illustrates his graciousness. The New Testament portrays consistently a gracious God, ready to forgive the sins of those who try to do his will. The word 'grace', however, has become a theological term meaning far more than God's graciousness. In post-Reformation teaching, the paradigm of grace is contrasted with the paradigm of human effort. The idea of 'salvation by grace' is understood to mean that righteousness and final judgment do *not* depend on our lives and character. We will argue here that this idea of grace is not at all what the biblical authors had in mind. We will show how the early Christians saw grace in a way entirely consistent with judgment based on conduct and character. To begin, we must clarify what the Greek word often translated as 'grace' actually meant. That word was *charis*. This commonplace word meant 'favour'. We will look at the culture of the 1st century again to decipher the way in which they used and understood this word.

Charis and the Reciprocity System

An informal system of trade governed people's dealings in the ancient world. Scholars call it the Reciprocity System,[43] as reciprocal exchanges formed the basis of this system. One party would do a 'favour' for a second party, who would repay it later with a favour of similar value. A carpenter, for example, might make implements for farmers to use. In return, the farmers would repay him at harvest time

---

[43] For more information on the Reciprocity System in the context of first-century Palestine, see for example: K. C. Hanson and Douglas E. Oakman, *Palestine in the Time of Jesus*, (Minneapolis, MN: Augsburg Fortress, 1998); James S. Jeffers, *The Greco-Roman World of the New Testament Era*, (Downers Grove, IL: Intervasity, 1999); David A. Desilva, *Honor, Patronage, Kinship & Purity* (Downers Grove, IL: Intervasity Press, 2000); Bruce Malina, *The New Testament World* (Louisville, KY: Westminster John Knox, 3rd ed., 2001); Stegemann, Malina & Theissen, *The social setting of Jesus and the Gospels* (Minneapolis, MN: Augsburg Fortress, 2002); James R. Harrison, *Paul's Language of Grace in its Graeco-Roman Context* (Tübingen: Mohr Siebeck, 2003).

with a share of the crop. A nobleman might request his influential friend to appoint him as a governor. Later, he would use his power to benefit his friend in order to repay the favour. A rich man might donate money to a city for the building of an aqueduct. In repayment, people would place a statue of him in a public square to extol his virtues and give him 'everlasting fame'. In this Reciprocity System, people expected repayment. They considered failure to repay a favour a serious moral failing, and sometimes even a public scandal.

The Reciprocity System extended to interactions between humans and the gods also. The Greeks thought this system of repaid favours governed their interactions with the gods. Favours from the gods obliged people to repay them, with potential for disaster if they failed to do so. Likewise, they believed that the favours they did for the gods through acts of piety, sacrifices, or temple donations obliged the gods to respond. A favour done deserved a favour in return. They thought that the gods acted according to these same social conventions of reciprocity that bound human behaviour.[44]

During Jesus' lifetime, very few coins existed in circulation within Israel, and few people could use currency to trade. The Reciprocity System, therefore, provided a primary means of trade. Yet it had more flexibility than money, since it related not only to material goods, but also to more abstract goods – such as honour. Hence, it governed a very broad range of interactions. Hundreds of surviving documents from the ancient world discuss the proper exchange of favours. As one scholar has noted, people placed such great importance on this Reciprocity System that it "dominated first-century Jewish and Graeco-Roman civic life."[45]

This Reciprocity System provided the context in which the Greek word for favour, *charis*, had its everyday meaning. While many English Bibles translate this word as 'grace', a major theological term in post-Reformation theology, it had no special theological significance in the 1st century. Variations of this word could refer to acts of both giving and receiving favours. The word could refer to the favour given, or to the thankfulness of the receiver, or to the favour performed in return. For example, Acts records that Felix left Paul imprisoned because he wished to "do the Jews a favor [charis]."[46] One of Jesus' teachings discusses the repayment of favours:

---

[44] Harrison, *Paul's Language of Grace*, pp. 53 – 56, 85 – 87, 196, 210, 284.

[45] Harrison, *Paul's Language of Grace*, p. 110.

[46] Acts 24:27. See also Acts 25:3, 25:9.

> When you give a luncheon or a dinner, do not invite your friends or your brothers or your relatives or rich neighbors, in case they may invite you in return, and you would be repaid. But when you give a banquet, invite the poor, the crippled, the lame, and the blind. And you will be blessed, because they cannot repay you, for you will be repaid at the resurrection of the righteous.[47]

In this passage, Jesus taught that God would repay people for the favours they did for the poor. Likewise, Jesus promised elsewhere to repay the favours that people did for the poor as if they had done these favours for him.[48]

In the 1st century, charis did not come 'free' any more than a bank loan or credit card payment today comes 'free'. A favour came with an obligation to repay it. Thus, people wanted generally to perform favours for only those whom they deemed likely to repay them (who had a reputation for faithfulness). This disadvantaged those unable to repay favours. Therefore, Jesus challenged this attitude as part of his ministry in support of the poor. Those people most stricken by poverty needed support from others, yet they seldom received favours since they could not repay their benefactors.[49] The System of Reciprocity underpinned their economy and culture, creating a deeply embedded problem, as people had to repay those who had done them favours in order to preserve their good reputation. One example comes from the Gospels, when a group of Jews came to Jesus on behalf of a Roman Centurion. They tried to persuade Jesus to do a favour for the Centurion – to heal his slave. They explained to him: "He is worthy of having you do this for him, for he loves our people, and it is he who built our synagogue for us."[50] In their view, the Centurion deserved a favour from Jesus because he had done a favour to the Jews. This example shows how people often saw others as deserving of the favours they received.

Like the English word 'favour', the term charis could also refer to having another's favour; that is, to being regarded favourably.[51] For example, Luke recorded that the angel told Mary, "Do not be afraid, Mary, for you have found favour with God."[52] Similarly, many passages

---

[47] Luke 14:12-14.
[48] Matt 25:31-46.
[49] Luke 6:31-35. See also *charis* in Luke 17:9.
[50] Luke 7:4-5.
[51] Harrison, *Paul's Language of Grace*, pp. 47 – 48.
[52] Luke 1:30.

throughout the Bible present people who had favour in the eyes of others or with God.[53] People thought generally that whoever had found favour with God deserved it. The first-century Jewish writer Philo discussed this issue. He concluded that God gives favours to those worthy of them.[54] Josephus too wrote that the Patriarchs were worthy of the divine favour they found.[55] As an example, he wrote that God repaid Jacob's piety with the enduring honour he deserved.[56] But Philo also added that God shows generous and benevolent love to all, and can bestow favours upon people simply out of kindness. So, nothing in the word *charis* itself tells us whether a favour is deserved or undeserved. Rather, the word means simply *favour*, and we must understand its significance from the context.

Having God's favour

We have already seen that the early Christians thought that, if they followed faithfully Jesus' example and teachings, God would regard them favourably and judge them positively. In this sense, they believed they deserved God's favour, since by following Jesus they lived according to his will. The notion that they felt *undeserving* of God's favour does not fit with their other doctrines. At the heart of their message lay the idea that people would find favour in God's eyes by following Jesus. Paul called this the "favour in which we stand."[57] Clement explained this principle in the late 2nd century: "Rightly, then, to those who have become faithful and obey, [God's] favour will abound beyond measure."[58] Obtaining God's favour by living rightly also meant that they could fall out of favour if they turned away from living rightly. The author of Hebrews warned his readers of this possibility: "Pursue peace with everyone, and the holiness without which no one will see the Lord. See to it that no one fails to obtain God's favour."[59]

---

[53] E.g. Luke 2:52; Act 2:46-47, 4:33, 7:9-10, 7:46.
[54] Harrison, *Paul's Language of Grace*, pp. 114 – 131.
[55] Josephus, *Antiquities of the Jews* 2.27-28.
[56] Josephus, *Antiquities of the Jews* 2.196.
[57] Rom 5:2.
[58] Clement (~195, E), *ANF* 2.196.
[59] Heb 12:14-15.

The favour of God sending Jesus

The early Christians also used the word 'favour' to speak of the one great favour God had done for them: sending Jesus to save them. In the New Testament, this favour of God sending Jesus dominates the major theological usages of charis. They viewed this favour simply. People had been living wrongly, yet, out of love, God did them the favour of sending Jesus to teach them how to live rightly instead. This favour was *undeserved*, since until then they had lived in ways that God did not view favourably. God sent Jesus to transform people's lives not because of the good that they did, but rather because of the *bad* they had done. The letter to Titus summarises this idea:

> For the favour of God has appeared, bringing salvation to all, training us to renounce impiety and worldly passions, and in the present age to live lives that are self-controlled, upright, and godly... Jesus Christ gave himself for us that he might redeem us from all iniquity and purify for himself a people of his own who are zealous for good deeds... For we ourselves were once foolish, disobedient, led astray, slaves to various passions and pleasures, passing our days in malice and envy, despicable, hating one another. But when the goodness and loving kindness of God our Savior appeared, he saved us, not because of any works of righteousness that we had done, but according to his mercy, through the water of rebirth and renewal by the Holy Spirit... so that, having become righteous through his favour, we might become heirs according to the hope of eternal life.[60]

The same theme appears in a similar passage exhorting Timothy to endure for Jesus' cause:

> Join with me in suffering for the gospel, relying on the power of God, who saved us and called us with a holy calling, not according to our works but according to his own purpose and favour. This favour was given to us in Christ Jesus... who abolished death and brought life and immortality to light through the gospel.[61]

---

[60] Titus 2:11-3:7.
[61] 2 Tim 1:8-10.

Peter stated this message of God's favour simply. He preached that God had saved Christians through "the favour of the Lord Jesus Christ."[62] God had not simply left sinners to wallow in their unrighteousness, but had done them a favour by sending Jesus to save them. Paul illustrated this favour using his own story:

> I am grateful to Christ Jesus our Lord, who has strengthened me, because he judged me faithful and appointed me to his service, even though I was formerly a blasphemer, a persecutor, and a man of violence. But I received mercy because I had acted ignorantly in unfaithfulness, and the favour of our Lord overflowed for me with the faithfulness and love that are in Christ Jesus. The saying is sure and worthy of full acceptance, that Christ Jesus came into the world to save sinners – of whom I am the foremost.[63]

Variations of this Greek word charis can also mean 'gratefulness' or 'thanks'. In first-century culture, people could reciprocate a favour by giving public thanks and praise. This thankfulness went beyond a feeling of gratitude; it involved praising the benefactor publicly. The New Testament authors thanked God for sending Jesus to save them from sinfulness. As a favour, God had freed sinners from sinfulness[64] and given them victory over sinfulness and death.[65] Hence, they saw it as appropriate to give thanks and praise to God frequently. For example, Paul encouraged his Gentile converts in Colossae to give "thanks to the Father, who has enabled you to share in the inheritance of the saints in the light." Paul continued, explaining the favour for which they should give thanks: "He has rescued us from the power of darkness and transferred us into the kingdom of his beloved Son, in whom we have redemption, the forgiveness of sins."[66] We find another example in Paul's letter to the Corinthians. He thanked God for the favour of sending Jesus to save them: "thanks be to God, who gives us the victory through our Lord Jesus Christ" over sinfulness and death.[67] Likewise, in his letter to Rome, Paul thanked God for the favour of saving them from sinfulness:

---

[62] Acts 15:11.
[63] 1 Tim 1:12-15.
[64] Rom 6:17-18.
[65] 1 Cor 15:56-57.
[66] Col 1:12-14.
[67] 1 Cor 15:57.

> Thanks be to God that you, having once been slaves of sinfulness, have become obedient from the heart to the form of teaching to which you were entrusted, and that you, having been set free from sinfulness, have become slaves of righteousness.[68]

Paul emphasised sometimes that God had sent Jesus as an initiating favour, rather than the repayment of any previous favour. He indicated this by calling it a "freely given gift [*dorea*]." To the Romans, he spoke of "the favour of God and the freely given gift in the favour of the one man, Jesus Christ." He explained that, because of Jesus, "those who receive the abundance of favour and the freely given gift of righteousness" will "exercise dominion in life."[69] Paul explained that God had given them this gracious gift of sending Jesus in order to save undeserving sinners:

> For while we were still weak, at the right time Christ died for the ungodly. Indeed, rarely will anyone die for a righteous person – though perhaps for a good person someone might actually dare to die. But God proves his love for us in that while we still were sinners Christ died for us. Much more surely then, now that we have been justified by his blood, will we be saved through him from the wrath of God. For if while we were enemies, we were reconciled to God through the death of his Son, much more surely, having been reconciled, will we be saved by his life. But more than that, we even boast in God through our Lord Jesus Christ, through whom we have now received reconciliation.[70]

The above passage explains how sinners had become righteous through God's favour of sending Jesus to lead them in a new way of life. It clarifies Paul's statement earlier in Romans that God justified people "by his freely given favor, through the redemption that is in Christ Jesus."[71] Paul expressed a similar sentiment in his letter to the Corinthians. He told them: "For you know the favor of our Lord Jesus Christ, that though he was rich, yet for your sakes he became poor, so that by his poverty you might become rich."[72] The same theme lies behind many more of Paul's statements. He reminded the Gentile Christians at

---

[68] Rom 6:17-18.
[69] Rom 5:15-17.
[70] Rom 5:6-11.
[71] Rom 3:24.
[72] 2 Cor 8:9.

Corinth of the favour God had given them in Christ Jesus. This favour involved God inviting them "into the fellowship of his Son," which meant they could become "enriched in him, in speech and knowledge of every kind."[73] Later, Paul encouraged them to follow Jesus in order to become righteous and reconciled to God. "Now is the day of salvation," he wrote, urging them "not to accept the favour of God in vain" by failing to reciprocate and follow Jesus.[74]

The Torah versus favour to the Gentiles

In the previous chapter we saw how the New Testament depicts Jesus as revealing a new standard of righteousness. The early Christians believed that God had demonstrated that righteousness came through following Jesus' teachings, not through following the popular interpretation of the Torah. God's favour of sending Jesus to teach a righteous way of life stands in contrast to trying to live righteously through Torah. Paul expressed the idea to the Galatians in this way: "I do not nullify the favour of God; for if justification comes through the Torah, then Christ died for nothing."[75] Later in the letter he restated the same basic message: "You who want to be justified by the Torah have cut yourselves off from Christ; you have fallen away from favour."[76] The Apostle John also contrasted the Torah with the favour and message of Jesus. He wrote: "The Torah indeed was given through Moses; favour and what is right came through Jesus Christ."[77]

Many Jews had thought that God's chosen people included only Torah-following Jews and excluded non-Jews who followed Greek customs. Jesus' message challenged that view. It stated that being Jewish and following Torah did not make people righteous automatically. Rather, following Jesus made people part of God's people, regardless of whether they were Jew or Greek. Greeks could follow Jesus' teachings as easily as Jews could. Thus, Paul realised that God's favour also extended to the Greeks, who could become righteous in God's sight irrespective of Torah.

He wrote of this idea to the Christians at Rome, and explained that God saw "no distinction" between Jews and Greeks. God had led both groups into righteousness "by his favour as a freely given gift, through the redemption that is in Christ Jesus." Paul argued that this action

---

[73] 1 Cor 1:4-8.
[74] 2 Cor 5:20-6:5.
[75] Gal 2:21.
[76] Gal 5:4.
[77] John 1:17.

removed any grounds on which Jews could boast of a superior standing before God. Paul saw God as "God of the Gentiles also." He taught that God deems righteous the "[Jews] on the ground of faithfulness and [Gentiles] through that same faithfulness."[78] Paul challenged strict adherence to the Torah's rituals because it excluded Gentiles from God's people. He argued that God does not limit his rewards only to those people who live by the customs of the Torah, since his favour also extends to the Gentiles.[79] He elaborated further:

> If it is [only] the adherents of the Torah who are to be the heirs [of Abraham], faithfulness is null and the promise is void... For this reason it depends on faithfulness, in order that the promise may rest on favour and be guaranteed to all his descendants, not only to the adherents of the Torah but also to those who share the faithfulness of Abraham...[80]

In light of the message Jesus brought, Paul realised that God's favour extended to people outside the boundaries of the Torah. For this reason, Paul wrote that God's favour "abounded for many."[81] The Gentile Christians did not follow Torah, but God's favour extended to them.[82]

Paul expressed a similar idea of favour to the Christians at Ephesus.[83] Paul explained that God had saved them mercifully from their previous unrighteous way of life: "by a favor you have been saved through faithfulness." The flexibility of the Greek word charis makes the giver and receiver of a favour ambiguous in this case. Hence, Paul clarified that the favour came as a gift from God, not us: "this favor is not your doing, the gift is from God." Paul emphasised that Jewish heritage had not saved them – God had not done this because they followed Torah. One of Paul's key insights was that Jesus' message did away with the distinction between 'Jew' and 'Gentile'. In this sense, he explained that God had united Jews and Gentiles together under Christ:

> You Gentiles by birth... were at that time without Christ, being aliens from the commonwealth of Israel, and strangers to the covenants of promise, having no hope and without God in the world. But now in Christ Jesus you who once were far off have

---

[78] Rom 3:21-30.
[79] Rom 4:4. See also Rom 11:5-6.
[80] Rom 4:13-16.
[81] Rom 5:12-21.
[82] Rom 6:14-15.
[83] Eph 2:1-16.

been brought near by the blood of Christ. For he is our peace; in his flesh he has made both groups [Jews and Gentiles] into one and has broken down the dividing wall, that is, the hostility between us. He has abolished the Torah with its commandments and ordinances, so that he might create in himself one new humanity in place of the two [Jews and Gentiles], thus making peace, and might reconcile both groups to God in one body through the cross, thus putting to death that hostility through it.[84]

This revelation that God's favour extended equally to both Jews and Gentiles had great importance for more than only Paul. Acts records it as a turning point in the history of the church that led to the inclusion of Gentiles in the Jesus-movement.[85] This account begins with Peter's vision. He told a group of Gentiles what it meant: "You yourselves know that it is forbidden by our customs for a Jew to associate with or to visit a Gentile; but God has shown me that I should not call anyone profane or unclean."[86] He continued to spell out the implication that God shows no partiality to Jews nor Gentiles, "but in every nation anyone who fears him and does what is right is acceptable to him."[87] This idea caused great controversy when it reached the Jewish disciples in Jerusalem. Peter had to persuade them that God's favour really did extend to the Gentiles.[88] When he explained that the Gentiles had received the Holy Spirit, Jewish followers of Jesus believed that God had indeed accepted Gentiles into the Jesus-movement.[89] As a result, Jesus' message spread to other Gentile cities like Antioch.[90] Later, when Barnabas visited the city and saw that the Jesus-movement included the Gentiles, he rejoiced because he "saw the favour of God."[91] Consequently, the followers of Jesus adopted the label *Christian*, a term that could include both Jews and Gentiles.[92] Despite Paul and Barnabas's teaching, some Jews rejected the idea that God's favour extended to the Gentiles. These Jews "stirred up persecution against

---

[84] Eph 2:11-16.
[85] Acts 10:1-11:26.
[86] Acts 10:28.
[87] Acts 10:34-35.
[88] Acts 11:1-2.
[89] Acts 11:18.
[90] Acts 11:19-21.
[91] Acts 11:22-23.
[92] Acts 11:25-26.

Paul and Barnabas, and drove them out of their district."[93] Zealous Jews persecuted Paul many other times for claiming that God's favour extended to those who followed Greek customs. Peter and Paul kept this controversy in mind when they wrote to their mainly Gentile readers, and perhaps this is why they began their letters by reaffirming that God's favour did indeed extend to their readers.[94]

Conclusion

The early Christians believed that God had sent Jesus graciously to save them from sinfulness. Through following Jesus' teachings they could live rightly and receive a positive judgment from God. They understood that they could not have saved themselves from sinful ways of life. They knew that they had needed God's help, a favour from him. Jesus graciously gave them this help that they needed, and led them into a new, righteous way of life. For this reason, the early Christians thanked God greatly for sending Jesus graciously to save them. Sinners had done nothing to deserve the intervention Jesus provided; God had done them an undeserved favour. Through Jesus, God's favour extended also to Gentiles and placed them on equal standing with Jews before God.

This idea of God's favour did not conflict with the early Christians' doctrines of righteousness and final judgment. In their view, God sent Jesus to help people live rightly precisely because of his concern for the way in which they lived. If they followed Jesus' teachings and example, they would become righteous and God would judge them favourably. The idea of God's graciousness, therefore, meant more to the early Christians than his willingness to forgive the repentant. Rather, it meant the active involvement by God (and his agents) in order to free people from the power of sinfulness and to lead them into a righteous way of life. Clement of Alexandria wrote on this topic in about 200 AD:

> "For by favour we are saved" – but not, indeed, without good works. Rather, we must be saved by being molded for what is good, acquiring an inclination for it. And we must possess the healthy mind that is fixed on the pursuit of the good. For this, we have the greatest need of divine favour, of right teaching, of

---

[93] Acts 13:42-51.
[94] Rom 1:7; 1 Cor 1:3; 2 Cor 1:2; Gal 1:3; Eph 1:2; Php 1:2; 1 Thes 1:1; 1 Tim 1:2; Tit 1:4; Phm 1:3; 1 Pet 1:2; 2 Pet 1:2.

holy susceptibility, and of the drawing of the Father to Him-self.[95]

Jesus, too, taught his disciples that people needed salvation from sinfulness to live rightly. After training his disciples, therefore, he commissioned them to continue his mission. Just as Jesus had gra-ciously and selflessly helped and loved people, he instructed his disciples to graciously and selflessly do the same. It would require them to cross social boundaries as Jesus had done, and to endure persecution and even death for the sake of helping others. As history shows, Jesus' disciples took up this cause that Jesus entrusted to them. Jesus had been the agent of God's favour to his early followers and, in the same way, his followers continued to act as agents of God's favour to countless more people across the world.

---

[95] Clement (c. 195, E), *ANF* 2.445.

Part 3

The importance of Jesus

The post-Reformation ideas about what Jesus achieved often centre upon his death as a substitutionary punishment. In this section of the book, we will explore what the early Christians wrote about Jesus' accomplishments. We will find that their ideas contrast sharply with the teachings of the post-Reformation tradition. We will also address some common misunderstandings about sacrifice and look more closely at Jesus' death as a martyr.

Chapter 11

What Jesus achieved

What did the early Christians think that Jesus had done for them? We will investigate this question here, and see that they believed he had changed their lives and characters by freeing them from sinfulness and showing them how to live rightly. As a result, they expected God to judge them positively and resurrect them. The New Testament writers used several ideas and metaphors to explain this one theme. We will explore each in turn, since they shed light on what Jesus accomplished.

Salvation

The New Testament authors used the term 'salvation' to write about the way in which Jesus had led his followers into a new way of life. Among the followers of Jesus, the rich shared their wealth with the poor.[1] Those excluded previously from society gained a new family that treated them with equal dignity and privilege. In the new Kingdom communities founded by Jesus, people saw the benefits of this new way of life. They saw that Jesus had saved them from the wrong and harmful ways in which they had lived formerly.

The New Testament authors wrote often about this salvation from sinfulness, sometimes referring to it simply as 'salvation'. Let us look at a few examples:

Paul. Paul wrote that Jesus appeared, "bringing salvation to all, training us to renounce impiety and worldly passions, and in the present age to live lives that are self-controlled, upright, and godly."[2] Paul used the word 'salvation' here to refer to moral transformation. He did this again later in the same letter: "We ourselves were once foolish, disobedient, led astray, slaves to various passions and pleasures, passing our days in malice and envy, despicable, hating one another. But when the goodness and loving kindness of God our

---

[1] Acts 2:44-45.
[2] Titus 2:11-13.

Savior appeared, he saved us."[3] Paul wrote a long passage to the Ephesians about God saving them. He commented that, previously, they had lived sinfully – yet, out of God's kindness, God had transformed them through Jesus and taught them to live well. Paul referred to this whole process as salvation.[4]

Peter. Peter also referred to moral transformation as salvation. He wrote that God had sent Jesus for this reason: "to bless you by turning each of you from your wicked ways."[5] In his letters, he instructed: "rid yourselves, therefore, of all malice, and all guile, insincerity, envy, and all slander. Like newborn infants, long for the pure, spiritual milk, so that by it you may grow into salvation."[6] In his view, Christians ought to have "escaped the defilements of the world through the knowledge of our Lord and Savior Jesus Christ."[7] He instructed them not to let sinfulness corrupt them again after their salvation. If they did, "it would have been better for them to have never known the way of righteousness."[8] After Pentecost, Peter exhorted people to be saved from corruption by repenting and following Jesus.[9] Peter likened Jesus to a shepherd who leads people away from sinfulness and back to righteousness.[10] (Jesus himself had used this same metaphor to describe his mission.[11]) Peter explained that Jesus had done this through his example and teachings, so that people would "follow in his steps."[12]

The Gospels. The Gospels sum up the ministry of Jesus often with the concept of salvation from sinfulness. For example, the angel told Mary that her son "will save his people from their sinfulness."[13] We have seen in our study of the Gospels that this salvation came though Jesus' activity for social and personal reform. He challenged oppressive people and institutions, healed those who suffered and gave moral teachings about love and justice. Jesus himself used the

---

[3] Titus 3:3-5.
[4] Eph 2:1-10
[5] Acts 3:26
[6] 1 Pet 2:1-2
[7] 2 Pet 2:20
[8] 2 Pet 2:21
[9] Acts 2:40
[10] 1 Peter 2:25
[11] Matt 18:12-14
[12] 1 Peter 2:20-23
[13] Matt 1:21

term 'salvation' to describe Zacchaeus' moral change in behaviour. Zacchaeus repented of his greedy, fraudulent behaviour because of his meeting with Jesus. Jesus declared consequently: "Today salvation has come to this house... for the Son of Man came to seek out and to save the lost."[14] Conversely, when a rich person found it hard to follow Jesus' teaching of generosity, Jesus said that salvation is difficult for such people.[15]

The idea that Jesus saved people from sinfulness also appears in verses that do not even mention the term 'salvation.' For example, John wrote that God revealed Jesus "to take away sinfulness," and that we should therefore purify our conduct.[16] John the Baptist echoed this idea when speaking about Jesus.[17] We find another example in Revelation, which praises Jesus for loving people and freeing them from sinfulness.[18] The writer of Hebrews also wrote that Jesus came to remove sinfulness and to eradicate people's sinful ways.[19] These examples show the variety of ways in which the early Christians wrote of how Jesus had saved them from sinfulness.

That salvation from sinfulness also had consequences for the final judgment and resurrection after death. The early Christians hoped for a resurrection through obeying and imitating Jesus.[20] Paul wrote of this, explaining that Jesus "abolished death and brought life and immortality to light through the gospel."[21] James wrote too that whomever brings a sinner back from error "will save the sinner's soul from death."[22] The early Christians saw Jesus as "the source of eternal salvation for all who obey him."[23] These verses correspond with the other 'salvation' verses in the New Testament that refer more clearly to the moral transformation Jesus brought. Jesus saved people from sinfulness and led them towards righteousness, which in turn leads to positive final judgment and resurrection.

---

[14] Luke 19:8-10.
[15] Matt 19:23-26.
[16] 1 John 3:2-6.
[17] John 1:29.
[18] Rev 1:5.
[19] Heb 9:26.
[20] John 3:16-17.
[21] 2 Tim 1:8-10.
[22] Jas 5:19-20.
[23] Heb 5:9.

Present sinfulness versus the guilt of past wrongdoings

The post-Reformation tradition focusses strongly on the concept of guilt. It teaches that, through wrongdoing, humans become guilty before God and deserving of punishment. It is from this guilt and punishment that Christ needs to save them. This view appears to have inclined many modern Christians to interpret the word 'sin' in the Bible as 'guilt'. They take phrases like "Jesus saves us from our sins" to mean that Jesus saves people from the guilt and future punishment that they have incurred as a result of past wrongdoings.

A very different way of thinking about sin emerges from a focus on future behaviour. A person with an immoral character will behave badly in the future. A moral person will behave well in the future. A person's character and pattern of behaviour can be thought of as 'sinful' or 'righteous'. Viewing sin in this sense, salvation from sin means a transformation of character, thoughts and behaviour. Many Jewish and early Christian writings appear to focus more on this aspect of sin than on guilt. It was not the guilt of past wrongs that made people sinners but rather the wrongdoings they continued to perform in the present and future. This idea of sin corresponds with the way in which Paul portrayed sin. He did not write of sin as something accrued from the past, but rather as being a power that rules over people in the present and shapes their future actions.

The Jews and early Christians believed that God is interested in people's current character and behaviour, and that he forgives past sinful acts freely once that person repents and begins to live rightly. The New Testament writers did not mention the concept of guilt particularly often, and distinguished it from 'sin'.[24] They did not focus on the guilt of past wrongs, instead focussing on people's present character and conduct, since that determined whether would God judge them as sinners or as righteous.

When the New Testament speaks of 'forgiveness of sins' it is not always obvious whether the writers have in mind the 'past guilt' or 'future behaviour' aspect of sin. The Greek word translated as 'forgiveness' (*aphesis*) in these phrases is the standard Greek word for 'release'. Release from sin could mean having the guilt of your past sins remitted – hence 'forgiveness'; or it could refer to release from the power of sinfulness and sinful patterns of behaviour. We must consider the

---

[24] Distinguished from sin: Jas 2:9-12, Rom 5:13. Other verses that mention the concept of guilt: Matt 5:21, 22; 26:66; Mark 3:29; 14:64; 1 Cor 11:27; Heb. 2:15; Phm 1:18; James 2:10.

context of any particular passage to determine the intended meaning. Both concepts of forgiveness and salvation from sinfulness fit with the early Christian paradigm we have outlined.

Salvation from God's negative judgment

Earlier we examined how God opposes sinfulness and judges evildoers negatively. By transforming people's lives and turning them away from sinfulness, Jesus made his followers righteous in God's sight. As a result, Jesus also saved them from God's wrath – God's anger against evildoers. Paul mentioned this idea in his letters to the Thessalonians, writing that Jesus rescued people "from the wrath that is coming."[25] He explained: "God has destined us not for wrath but for obtaining salvation through our Lord Jesus Christ."[26] He spoke of God's vengeance on those who do not obey Jesus' message, but of God's favourable judgment on those obedient to it.[27] To the Romans, Paul explained that God is wrathful towards the unrighteous. He warned that God had delayed his judgment to give evildoers a chance to repent from their wicked ways.[28] Those who had followed Christ into righteousness, however, were saved from God's wrath.[29] Paul gave a similar message to the Ephesians. He explained that God would forgive those who repented and followed Jesus, and that these people would escape a negative final judgment.[30] Likewise, Jesus said God would judge those who repented and followed his teachings more favourably than those who continued in sinful ways.[31] The salvation from God's wrath offered by Jesus required a change in behaviour. Indeed, the authors of Hebrews warned that if the followers of Jesus did not forsake sinful ways then they would receive a negative judgment.[32]

The verses referred to above cover arguably all of the explicit New Testament references to salvation from God's wrath. Note that they all link salvation from God's wrath with moral transformation. There are also very few of them compared to other verses concerning Jesus' accomplishments. Both of these observations do not support post-Reformation teaching. That teaching sees Christ's primary work as

---

[25] 1 Thes 1:9-10.
[26] 1 Thes 5:8-10.
[27] 2 Thes 1:7-8.
[28] Rom 2:1-11.
[29] Rom 5:9-10.
[30] Eph 5:1-6.
[31] Matt 11:20-24, 12:41; Luke 10:13-14, 11:32.
[32] Heb 10:26-27.

saving us from God's wrath, with human effort playing no part in the process. It rejects explicitly the notion that salvation from God's wrath results from *changing our behaviour*. In such a view, we would expect the idea that Jesus saved us from God's wrath to appear very frequently in the New Testament. Only a handful of verses, however, mention this idea – and, when they do, they explain it in terms of moral transformation. By contrast, in the moral transformation view, salvation is primarily from *sinfulness*, and it results from following Jesus and living rightly. Salvation from God's wrath then follows as a secondary effect – we are saved from God's wrath by a positive change in our behaviour. This paradigm corresponds much better with the biblical passages concerning God's wrath and judgment. It also explains why the New Testament does not seem to emphasise salvation from God's wrath as the primary effect of Christ's saving work.

Freedom from slavery and captivity

The New Testament authors wrote often of freedom from the 'slavery' of sinfulness. Greek ethical philosophers spoke commonly of how desires enslaved people, and of how people could break free from this slavery.[33] One such philosopher, Justin Martyr, converted to Christianity in the 2nd century AD. He wrote: "to yield and give way to our passions is the lowest slavery, even as to rule over them is the only liberty. The greatest of all good is to be free from sinfulness."[34] The New Testament authors used this theme to write of Jesus freeing people from sinfulness. Let us look at some examples:

Romans. In Romans chapters 6 through 8, Paul wrote extensively of Jesus freeing people from slavery to sinful desires. He described his Christian readers as former "slaves of sin," who had become "free from sin" and instead were "slaves of righteousness." They were "freed from sin and enslaved to God," which led to sanctification and eternal life.[35] Jesus had freed them "from the rule of sin and of death."[36] Paul even described creation itself as waiting in the hope that God would set it "free from its bondage to decay."[37] Paul wrote

---

[33] Stanley K. Stowers, *A Rereading of Romans: Justice, Jews, & Gentiles* (Ann Arbor, MI: Yale University Press, 1997), pp. 42 – 82, 260ff.
[34] Justin Martyr, *Other fragments from the lost writings of Justin*, 13.
[35] Rom 6:16-23.
[36] Rom 7:21-8:4.
[37] Rom 8:19-21.

also of baptism as being a symbol that "our old self was crucified with him so that the body of sin might be destroyed, and we might no longer be enslaved to sin."[38] He implored his readers to strive for moral virtue and maintain their freedom from sinfulness:

> Do not let sin exercise dominion in your mortal bodies, to make you obey their passions. No longer present your members to sin as instruments of wickedness, but present yourselves to God as those who have been brought from death to life, and present your members to God as instruments of righteousness. For sin will have no dominion over you.[39]

Ephesians. This letter teaches that Jesus freed his followers from "captivity to sinfulness."[40]

Galatians. Paul explained that Jesus "gave himself for our sinfulness to set us free from the present evil age."[41] He wrote that Jesus freed us from slavery to the fundamental principles of the world[42] and also freed us from idols.[43]

Timothy. This letter links freedom from sinfulness with repentance. We read that Timothy's opponents should "repent and come to know what is right, and that they may escape from the snare of the devil, having been held captive by him to do his will."[44]

Peter. Jesus gave us "everything needed for life and godliness." Thus, we may "escape from the corruption that is in the world because of lust, and may become participants of the divine nature."[45] Peter contrasted people who have "escaped the defilements of the world" by following Jesus with the "slaves of corruption."[46]

---

[38] Rom 6:6.
[39] Rom 6:12-14.
[40] Eph 4:8, quoting Psalm 68.
[41] Gal 1:3-4.
[42] Gal 4:3-6.
[43] Gal 4:8-9.
[44] 2 Tim 2:24-26.
[45] 2 Pet 1:3-4.
[46] 2 Pet 2:18.

Hebrews. Jesus freed people "held in slavery by the fear of death."[47]

The Gospels. Jesus himself used slavery metaphors to describe his mission. He said he God had appointed him to "proclaim release to the captives" and "let the oppressed go free."[48] Elsewhere, he said that he would free people by teaching them what is right. He explained: "everyone who commits sin is a slave to sin." Yet, he offered them freedom, saying, "if the Son makes you free, you will be free indeed."[49] Note the similarity of this statement to one by Paul: "where the Spirit of the Lord is, there is freedom." Paul explained that this freedom came through Jesus, as his followers "changed into his image with ever-increasing glory."[50]

From the above passages, we see that the New Testament authors believed that Jesus had freed them from slavery to sinfulness. The process of freeing slaves was called 'redemption' or 'ransoming'. The early Christians used these terms to describe what Jesus achieved for them, and we will investigate passages that use these specific terms. Keep in mind that, as the previous passages show, the early Christians believed that Jesus had freed them *from sinfulness*. Thus, when they wrote of Christ redeeming or ransoming them, they had in mind this same liberation from sinfulness – this same moral transformation. For example, Paul said Jesus "gave himself for us that he might *redeem* us from all iniquity and purify for himself a people of his own who are zealous for good deeds."[51] Elsewhere, he said that Jesus had rescued and redeemed us "from the power of darkness and transferred us into the kingdom of his beloved Son."[52] John the Baptist's movement preceded that of Jesus, and Luke described John's ministry in similar terms.[53]

It was possible to redeem or 'ransom' slaves by first purchasing them and then setting them free. The price paid to free a slave was called the 'ransom'. In Jesus' case, his mission to free people from sinfulness cost him his life. He paid the price of martyrdom. Naturally, therefore, the New Testament portrays his martyrdom as the price Jesus paid to 'ransom' people from sinfulness. Jesus himself spoke of this.

---

[47] Heb 2:14-15.
[48] Luke 4:18-21.
[49] John 8:31-36.
[50] 2 Cor 3:9-18.
[51] Titus 2:11-14.
[52] Col 1:13-14.
[53] Luke 1:68-75.

Foreseeing his death at the hands of his opponents, he spoke of how he "did not come to be served, but to serve, and to give His life [as] a ransom for many."[54] He also taught his disciples, "I lay down my life for the sheep."[55] In keeping with these statements, the rest of the New Testament portrays his martyrdom as the price paid to free humanity. For example, a hymn in the book of Revelation praises Jesus' self-sacrificing death for ransoming people from all nations and enabling them to join the Church.[56] Similarly, Paul wrote that Jesus "gave himself as a ransom for all."[57] He wrote that Jesus became 'poor' for our sakes so that we might become rich.[58] His followers should therefore live in a righteous way since they had been "bought with a price."[59] Thus, the 'ransom' terminology in the New Testament fits comfortably within the paradigm of Jesus bringing moral transformation. The New Testament authors used 'ransom' terminology to link Jesus' martyrdom with his efforts to free people from sinfulness.

Paul also used the language of freedom in relation to the Torah. Paul explained that the Torah had taught the difference between right and wrong, but that it had little power to transform lives.[60] Instead, it had acted as a temporary half-measure.[61] Followers of Jesus gained the freedom from sinfulness that the Torah could not bring.[62] New Testament writers also saw great significance in the fact that Jesus had set people free from having to follow the ritual requirements of the Torah.[63] They contrasted Torah unfavourably with the new covenant Jesus had ushered in,[64] as the Torah brought death, but the new covenant of Jesus brought life.[65] Jesus provided the "guarantee of a better covenant."[66] He had rescued Jews "from the futile ways inherited from [their] ancestors."[67] Paul explained: "we are discharged from the Torah, dead to that which held us captive." This change meant that the

---

[54] Matt 20:28; Mark 10:45.
[55] John 10:15.
[56] Rev 5:9-10.
[57] 1 Tim 2:5-6.
[58] 2 Cor 8:9.
[59] 1 Cor 6:9-20.
[60] Gal 3:21-23; Rom 7.
[61] Gal 3:24.
[62] Acts 13:39.
[63] Eph 2:15.
[64] John 1:17.
[65] 2 Cor 3:6.
[66] Heb 7:22.
[67] 1 Pet 1:18.

early Christians no longer had to follow the rituals of the Torah, but instead could follow the new way of life that Jesus taught.[68] Jesus had set his followers free "from the law of sin and of death" and from walking "according to the flesh." Thus, they could fulfil the important spiritual aspects of the Torah.[69] They had metaphorically 'died' to their obligations under the Torah so that they might "live to God."[70] Jesus had rescued them "from the curse of the Torah."[71] Paul argued that if Gentile Christians started following the Torah they would betray Jesus' message.[72] Jesus had freed them, so they ought not to return to being slaves of the Torah.[73] The Torah had also created a division between Jew and Gentile, and Jesus' teachings freed them from this division. His movement unified Jews and Gentiles in the Church, removing the barrier created by the Torah.[74] Hence, Paul taught them to distinguish no longer between "Greek and Jew, circumcised and uncircumcised."[75] In this way, Paul used the language of redemption, ransom and rescue from slavery to speak of how his Gentile churches were not obliged to follow Torah.

New life

The early Christians also used the idea of a 'new life' in Christ to refer to moral transformation. Jesus had changed their way of life, and they spoke of this change as a new birth, a renewal, and a restoration. Let us look at some examples:

Ephesians. Paul wrote of the stark contrast between the Ephesians' old way of life and their 'new life' as followers of Jesus. They had lived wrongly in the past, following their sinful desires and living in disobedience to God. Upon becoming followers of Jesus, however,

---

[68] Rom 7:6.
[69] Rom 8:1-4.
[70] Gal 2:17-21.
[71] Gal 3:13, 4:5.
[72] Gal 4:10-11.
[73] Gal 5:1.
[74] Eph 2:12-17.
[75] Col 3:11. See also Gal 3:28 and Rom 10:12.

they gained a new, righteous way of life.[76] They each took on a 'new self' characterised by correct conduct and a godly way of thinking.[77]

Colossians. For the Colossians, following Jesus meant ending their old lives governed by the "principles of the world."[78] They needed to rid themselves of the wicked practices of the 'old self', and clothe themselves with the 'new self'. In literal terms, this meant ceasing to live immorally and instead following the example and teachings of Jesus.[79] Paul considered these two ways to be as different as death and life.[80] He wanted to "present everyone mature in Christ,"[81] which involved a tangible moral transformation.

Romans. Paul instructed the Roman Christians to live a new life in various ways: by becoming "alive to God" and considering themselves "dead to sin," rather than its slave;[82] by serving sin no longer;[83] by living in virtue according to Jesus' teachings and example; and by practising sinful deeds of the flesh no longer.[84] They needed to live a new kind of life: "Do not be conformed to this world, but be transformed by the renewing of your minds, so that you may discern what is the will of God – what is good and acceptable and perfect."[85]

Corinthians. Paul wrote that anyone who follows Jesus should live as "a new creation." A new way of life should replace the old way of life.[86] This life should be lived according to the "Spirit that is from God" not the "spirit of the world."[87]

Galatians. Paul wrote that "those who belong to Christ Jesus have crucified the flesh with its passions and desires."[88] He described this

---

[76] Eph 2:1-5.
[77] Eph 4:17-24.
[78] Col 2:20 c.f. Gal 4:9, Eph 2:2.
[79] Col 3:5-11.
[80] Col 2:13-14.
[81] Col 1:28.
[82] Rom 6:11.
[83] Rom 6:1-6.
[84] Rom 8:1-13.
[85] Rom 12:2.
[86] 2 Cor 5:17.
[87] 1 Cor 2:12.
[88] Gal 5:24 .

old fleshly life as one of "fornication, impurity, licentiousness, idolatry, sorcery, enmities, strife, jealousy, anger, quarrels, dissensions, factions, envy, drunkenness, carousing, and things like these." In contrast, he characterised the new life of Christians as possessing traits of "love, joy, peace, patience, kindness, generosity, faithfulness, gentleness, and self-control."[89] He reiterated that he had died to his old life through the cross of Christ and become a "new creation."[90]

Titus. This letter speaks of a "rebirth and renewal." Through this rebirth, Christians turned away from an old life of sinfulness. In their new life they should "devote themselves to good works."[91]

John. John also used the metaphor of rebirth in both his Gospel and letters. In his Gospel, he depicted Jesus teaching that "no one can see the kingdom of God without being born from above." People needed to be reborn – "born of water and Spirit."[92] John touched on this idea in a letter also: "those who have been born of God do not sin."[93] Here, he tied this idea of rebirth to the concept of moral change – Christians no longer commit sin.

Peter. Peter also used the concept of a "new birth."[94] He wrote that followers of Christ had "finished with sin." They would now live the rest of their earthly lives "no longer by human desires but by the will of God."[95]

The early Christians used the metaphors of dying to the old life, rebirth, and experiencing a new life to speak of how Jesus had affected their lives and the great moral transformation which had occurred.

Light and darkness

The early Christians also used the metaphor of going from darkness into light to describe the moral transformation that Jesus had accomplished in their lives. This language emphasised the concept of

---

[89] Gal 5:19-23.
[90] Gal 6:14-15.
[91] Titus 3:3-7.
[92] John 3:3-8.
[93] 1 John 3:7-9, 5:1-4; c.f. John 1:12-13.
[94] 1 Pet 1:3-4.
[95] 1 Pet 4:1-2.

Jesus as a teacher who 'enlightens'.[96] John used this language often, calling Jesus "the Light,"[97] and describing his life as "the light of all people."[98] In John's Gospel, Jesus called himself the "light of the world" three times.[99] According to John, Jesus overcame darkness, enlightened humanity[100] and brought attention to the evil in the world.[101] John linked darkness and wrongdoing. He explained: "people loved darkness rather than light because their deeds were evil."[102] In contrast: "those who do what is right come to the light."[103] Walking in the light meant living according to Jesus' teachings. John explained that people who follow his teachings "will never walk in darkness but will have the light of life."[104] In contrast, the people who fail to keep his teachings "remain in darkness."[105] In a letter, John made use of this metaphor of light and darkness again, saying that the light of Jesus' teaching cleanses those who walk in it from all sin.[106] Jesus' teachings were characterised by love. Hence the people "still in the darkness" lacked love, while those living "in the light" loved others.[107]

Paul also used the metaphor of light and darkness to explain his message. He wrote that Jesus' mission had been to "proclaim light" to both the Jews and Gentiles.[108] He explained that Jesus had rescued his followers "from the power of darkness" and transferred them "into the kingdom of his beloved Son."[109] Paul saw himself as championing that mission to bring people into God's kingdom. He aimed to "open their eyes so that they may turn from darkness to light and from the power of Satan to God, so that they may receive forgiveness of sins."[110] He preached to them "the light of the gospel," which God had shone into their hearts through Jesus.[111] Like John, Paul thought that people could

---

[96] The use of 'light' as a metaphor for moral teachings seems to have been a common one. See, for example, Rom 2:19-20 and Matt 5:15.

[97] John 1:5, 8-9, 3:19-21, 8:12, 9:5, 12:35-46.

[98] John 1:4.

[99] John 8:12; 9:5; 12:35-46.

[100] John 1:3-9.

[101] John 7:7.

[102] John 3:19-20.

[103] John 3:21.

[104] John 8:12; see also John 12:35.

[105] John 12:46-50.

[106] 1 John 1:5-7.

[107] 1 John 2:9-11.

[108] Acts 26:23.

[109] Col 1:13-14.

[110] Acts 26:17-18.

[111] 2 Cor 4:3-6; Eph 5:14.

go from darkness into light by following Jesus' teachings and example. The following quote from Paul illustrates this attitude well:

> Lay aside the works of darkness and put on the armor of light; let us live honorably as in the day, not in reveling and drunkenness, not in debauchery and licentiousness, not in quarreling and jealousy. Instead, put on the Lord Jesus Christ, and make no provision for the flesh, to gratify its desires.[112]

Paul gave the Ephesians a similar message. He explained that anyone who practiced fornication, impurity of any kind, greed, and inappropriate talk lived "in darkness" and would not inherit the Kingdom of God. He exhorted his readers, therefore, to "take no part in the unfruitful works of darkness," but instead to "live as children of light." He explained: "the fruit of the light is found in all that is good and right and true." He implored his followers to "try to find out what is pleasing to the Lord." He encouraged them to change their ways by imitating Christ: "Be imitators of God, as beloved children, and live in love, as Christ loved us." He concluded, "Be careful then how you live, not as unwise people but as wise."[113] In Paul's view, Jesus had "illuminated" the way in which to live rightly. This enlightenment brought freedom from the "darkness" of sinful behaviour.

This theme of light and darkness occurs elsewhere in the New Testament. Luke used it to explain John the Baptist's ministry, saying that he gave "light to those who sit in darkness and in the shadow of death, to guide our feet into the way of peace."[114] He used similar language to speak of Jesus.[115] Later in Luke, it is recorded that Jesus rebuked his generation as evil for not repenting. He exhorted them to become full of light rather than darkness.[116] Matthew described Jesus' preaching of repentance in this way: "the people who sat in darkness have seen a great light, and for those who sat in the region and shadow of death light has dawned."[117] Peter shared this view, and wrote that Jesus called his followers "out of darkness into his marvellous light."[118]

---

[112] Rom 13:12-14.
[113] Eph 5:1-15.
[114] Luke 1:79.
[115] Luke 2:30-32.
[116] Luke 11:29-36.
[117] Matt 4:16-17; Isaiah 9:1-2.
[118] 1 Pet 2:9.

Many New Testament authors used the theme of light and darkness to speak of Jesus' work; he had taught people a new, right way of living that transformed their lives away from sinfulness.

Purification

New Testament writers sometimes drew on the vocabulary of 'purity' and 'impurity' that existed within their culture. Their culture deemed something things 'ritually pure' and others 'ritually impure'. Many sources of ritual impurity existed, such as contact with corpses or with certain skin diseases. Objects and people could be purified ritually through following the correct procedures. Pure things were 'holy' and 'sanctified'. The New Testament writers adopted this purity language to speak not of ritual purity but of morality, using these words to describe the moral transformation which had come through Jesus. He had 'purified' their hearts – transforming them morally.

Peter used the term 'holy' to speak of this moral goodness. He wrote: "be holy yourselves in all your conduct." This 'holiness' in conduct involved practising self-discipline and turning from sinful desires.[119] He urged his readers to be "leading lives of holiness and godliness." They needed to do this because of the coming judgment of God upon the godless and lawless.[120]

The letter of Titus also uses the language of purity to speak of the moral transformation brought by Jesus, saying that Jesus taught people to live rightly in order to "*purify* for himself a people of his own who are zealous for good deeds."[121] Paul expressed this same idea to the Corinthians, who became 'washed' and 'sanctified' from sinful behaviour through following Jesus.[122] The Colossians experienced a similar transformation in becoming reconciled to God. They had become "holy and blameless and irreproachable" before God, provided they remained committed to following Jesus.[123] Paul saw each follower of Jesus as being like God's temple. Each should remain holy in a moral sense just as the temple should remain holy in a ritual sense. Paul used this analogy to exhort his followers to flee from sinfulness.[124]

---

[119] 1 Pet 1:13-16.
[120] 2 Pet 3:1-18.
[121] Titus 2:11-14.
[122] 1 Cor 6:9-11.
[123] Col 1:20-23.
[124] 1 Cor 6:17-19.

Paul taught the Ephesians that Jesus loved the church and died to make it holy. It became holy and cleansed as people were 'washed' by obeying the message of his teachings. Those who followed Jesus became "without a spot or wrinkle or anything of the kind," "holy and without blemish."[125] Paul used similar language when he wrote to the Thessalonians about final judgment. Those who did what was right faithfully had received "salvation through sanctification." In contrast, Paul warned that God would condemn those who did not do what was right. Paul adopted the word 'sanctification' here from the background of purification rituals and used it instead to speak of moral transformation.[126]

The book of Hebrews deals with the Torah at length. The Torah contained many teachings on ritual purity, and so Hebrews adopts this language as a metaphor for morality, describing Jesus as the pioneer of salvation who "sanctifies" those who obey his teachings.[127] Christians can remain "holy partners of Christ" if they do not develop an evil, unfaithful heart that turns away from God.[128] Later, Hebrews explains that the gifts and sacrifices of the Jewish sacrificial system "cannot perfect the ethics of the worshipper,"[129] since they would have otherwise ceased sinning and not have needed to offer continual sacrifices.[130] In contrast, Jesus taught true purity, which came through performing God's will rather than performing sacrifices.[131] In this way, he removed the sinful character of those who follow him and "perfected for all time those who are sanctified,"[132] ushering in a new covenant in which God had "put his laws in their hearts," and "written them on their minds."[133] Followers of Jesus had their minds "sprinkled clean from an evil ethic" and their bodies "washed with pure water" so that they could love others and perform good deeds.[134] The author of Hebrews explained that Jesus suffered in order to 'sanctify' Christians

---

[125] Eph 5:25-27.

[126] 2 Thes 2:7-17.

[127] Heb 2:10-11 and Heb 5:9.

[128] Heb 3:1-14.

[129] Heb 9:9-14. The Greek word *suneidesis* has been translated as 'ethics' rather than 'conscience' here since it refers not to the idea of guilt but to a person's moral sense of right and wrong that motivates future behaviour.

[130] Heb 10:1-4.

[131] Heb 10:5-10.

[132] Heb 10:11-14.

[133] Heb 10:15-16.

[134] Heb 10:19-25.

in this way.[135] As a result of this sanctification brought about by Jesus, they would avoid God's condemnation unless they persisted wilfully in sinful ways.[136]

The verses we have examined above used the language of purification to speak about moral transformation. The New Testament authors used this language to discuss the moral purity that Jesus had brought them.

Conquest of evil powers

The early Christians believed that the Devil ensnared people into living in sinful ways. Hence, the New Testament authors also used the language of 'defeating the Devil' to describe the freedom from sinfulness that Jesus brought. Jesus had overcome the Devil's temptations during his time in the wilderness.[137] New Testament writers, however, took the idea of defeating the Devil much further. According to the Genesis account, sinfulness entered the world as a result of the Devil's temptation. It was believed that from then on, the Devil continued to tempt people actively into wrongdoing. Jesus' mission of turning people away from sinfulness, therefore, stood in clear contrast to the Devil's mission of leading people into sinfulness. This idea appears often in the New Testament. For example, John explained that Jesus came "to take away sinfulness" and thus "to destroy the works of the devil."[138]

Christians did not have victory over sinfulness and the Devil automatically, however. Their faithfulness in following and imitating Jesus aided them in conquering sinfulness.[139] John wrote that mature Christians who were strong in their faithfulness had "conquered the evil one."[140] James too wrote of the problem of the Devil, warning readers to resist the Devil and avoid sinful behaviour and thoughts.[141] Paul also warned Christians against the traps laid by the Devil. He warned them to avoid evil,[142] the snares of the Devil,[143] deceitful spirits

---

[135] Heb 13:12-13.
[136] Heb 10:26-39.
[137] Matt 4:1-11; Mark 1:13; Luke 4:1-13.
[138] 1 John 3:5-10. Likewise see Heb 2:14.
[139] 1 John 4:4, 5:4-5.
[140] 1 John 2:12-14.
[141] Jas 4:7-8.
[142] Rom 12:21.
[143] 1 Tim 3:6-7.

and the teachings of demons.[144] He warned them against following Satan[145] and against harmful desires that might tempt them.[146] Paul wrote of the struggle Christians experienced continuously against evil influences. He encouraged his readers: "be strong in the Lord" and "put on the whole armor of God, so that you may be able to stand against the trickery of the devil."[147] He wrote of striving against unrighteousness through self-discipline in order to bring one's thoughts into line with Jesus' teachings.[148] In these ways, the New Testament writers wrote of Christ having helped Christians to defeat the Devil in their lives, using this language to speak of the moral transformation that Jesus had brought about.

Conclusion

The New Testament authors used a variety of imagery in their language to express Jesus' accomplishments. They drew on a number of metaphors from their culture to express the same basic conviction: Christ had transformed their lives, by leading them away from sinfulness and teaching them to live rightly. Again and again, the New Testament authors wrote of this moral transformation that Christ had wrought in their lives. This transformation lay at the heart of what they believed Jesus had achieved for them.

---

[144] 1 Tim 4:1.
[145] 1 Tim 5:14-15.
[146] 1 Tim 6:9-10.
[147] Eph 6:10-17.
[148] 2 Cor 10:3-5.

Chapter 12

Sacrifice

To understand how the New Testament authors used sacrificial language to describe what Jesus had accomplished, we must first find out the way in which their culture understood sacrifices. Let us start with some background. Sacrificial practices predated the formation of ancient Israel. Both biblical narratives and studies of ancient cultures reveal that people made sacrifices long before the Jews received the sacrificial laws of the Torah. The covenant between God and Israel at Sinai did not introduce sacrificial practices, but rather provided formal guidelines and strict limits in order to control an already existing system. Generally, early Christian writers believed that God had never approved of ritual sacrifices and desired to phase them out. In their view, he regulated their practice first at Sinai and then critiqued them over time through the Prophets. Finally, he abolished them entirely following the life of Jesus and the destruction of the Jerusalem Temple.[1] As one scholar explains: "Early Christian writers collected together the anti-sacrificial passages in the prophets in order to show that God did not need or want the sacrifices of the Jews, but rather demanded obedience, learning to do good, desisting from evil, seeking justice, correcting oppression, and supporting the widow and orphan."[2]

In the last few centuries, many Christians have believed that Jesus died a substitutionary death on behalf of others to atone for their sin. This idea has become connected with the New Testament sacrificial language used to speak of Jesus' death. Without understanding how ancient Israelite sacrifices actually worked, Christians often assume they worked through substitutionary atonement. One scholar explains it like this: "ideas that form the basis for certain interpretations of Jesus' death are read back into the biblical texts regarding sacrifice so as to argue that the same ideas are behind ancient Jewish beliefs concerning sacrifice... it is argued that in ancient Israel, sacrifices were understood as involving the death of an animal as a substitute for the person who had sinned and thus deserved death: sinners themselves were spared

---

[1] E.g. *Barnabas* 2.7-8; Irenaeus *Against Heresy* 4.17.1-4; Origen *Homilies on Leviticus* 2.5, 4.5.
[2] Frances M. Young, *Sacrifice and the Death of Christ* (London: SPCK, 1975), p. 55.

this penalty when the animal victim endured it in their place."[3] We could imagine that people offered sacrifices because they felt guilty of sin and worthy of death. The animals died in their place as substitutes, and took the punishment they deserved. Such an account has appeared widely in recent Christian literature, and it probably sounds familiar to many Christians today.

As plausible as such a view might sound, recent scholarship shows that the Israelites understood their sacrifices very differently. "A deepening scholarly appreciation of ancient animal sacrifice has revealed that later Christian conceptions of sacrificial atoning death have been systematically projected back onto Judaism."[4] We know this because scholars have studied the ancient texts carefully. They have examined how the people practising those sacrifices described what they did and why they did it. Largely, these scholars have reached agreement. Even anthropologists who study modern cultures that perform sacrifices report the same findings. It does not seem to matter what culture we study – Israelite or Greek, Indian or Hawaiian, ancient or modern – the same basic sacrificial principles and motivations appear around the world and throughout history. Modern scholars have studied ancient Jewish texts carefully (including the scriptures and other texts). They have found that the principles and motivations held by the Israelites have striking parallels in many other cultures – yet modern Westerners would find their ideas completely foreign!

One scholar investigated the way in which the early Christians understood sacrifices as part of her doctoral research. She has also published several books on early Christianity. She noted this problem of misunderstanding the meaning of sacrifice, and explained it in this way:

> [Christians today] live in a culture in which the practice of sacri-fice is totally foreign – no doubt largely because of the influence of Christianity down the centuries. But the result is that we no longer seem to be in a position to know instinctively what the sacrifice language of our traditions really means. In fact, we get certain preconceptions about the meaning of sacrifice and so misinterpret the real point of the language we are using. Many books on the subject expound theories of sacrifice which are in fact modern reconstructions with little evidential basis in the

---

[3] David A. Brondos, *Paul on the Cross: Reconstructing the Apostles's Story of Redemption* (Minneapolis, MN: Augsburg Fortress, 2006), p. 19.

[4] Stanley K. Stowers, *A Rereading of Romans: Justice, Jews and Gentiles* (Ann Arbor, MI: Edwards Brothers, 1994), p. 206.

ancient texts. The most common misconception when sacrificial language is applied to the death of Christ runs something like this: 'God was angry with sinners. The Jews had tried to placate his anger by symbolically offering the lives of animals to him in place of their guilty selves. But this was inadequate and so Jesus offered a perfect sacrifice. He died as our substitute to appease God's anger.' With certain degrees of sophistication, this is the general picture one gets from listening to sermons or reading the majority of easily available books. Yet it is far from doing justice to the real religious outlook of the Jews, or the early Christians who used sacrificial terminology to sense the depth of meaning in the death of Christ. Clearly, if we are going to be able to appreciate the language of the liturgy and the New Testament, of our hymns and prayers, we need to go back and try to understand what sacrifice meant in the ancient world and what the new use of sacrifice language in Christianity meant to the worshippers of that time."[5]

We will present here the conclusion of numerous scholars after their extensive research into the ancient Israelites' sacrificial system. Remember, the Israelites did not hold a 21st-century Western view of life. They held a world view totally different from our modern one, which has been strongly shaped by science. We cannot understand their ideas about sacrifices through the filter of our modern world view. Their sacrificial ideas corresponded with the way in which *they* understood the world, so we can only understand their sacrifices properly within their cultural context.

Israel's sacrifices

Cultures that sacrifice tend to perform a number of different rituals at different times for different purposes. Israel's sacrificial system fitted this general rule. It used *three* major concepts that many other cultures also used: gifts, meals, and purification.[6]

---

[5] Young, *Sacrifice and the Death of Christ*, p. 11.

[6] Stephen Finlan, *The Background and Content of Paul's Cultic Atonement Metaphors* (Atlanta, GA: Society of Biblical Literature, 2004), p. 31; Young, *Sacrifice and the Death of Christ*, p. 21, 25; Nigel B. Courtman, 'Sacrifice in the Psalms' in R. T. Beckwith and M. J. Selman (eds.), *Sacrifice in the Bible* (Carlisle: Paternoster; Grand Rapids: Baker, 1995), pp. 51 – 52; Gordon J. Wenham 'The Theol-

Gifts

People in the ancient world often sacrificed to give "gifts to the gods," as one ancient Greek writer noted.[7] We noted earlier that ancient cultures valued the giving and receiving of gifts highly. People could have many different motivations for giving gifts: to gain a person's favour; to appease an angry person; to thank someone; or to repay a debt. It was believed widely that the gods abided by the normal rules of social interactions, and so people thought it appropriate to give them gifts for any of these reasons. The notion that gods accepted sacrifices as gifts thus had tremendous flexibility, and seems to have appeared in all sacrificial cultures.[8]

Israelites gave the 'first fruits' offering to the priests of God as thanks for the harvest. In presenting this offering at the Temple, the offerer thanked God publicly for bringing his ancestors to the fertile land of Israel.[9] In a 'burnt offering' sacrifice, a whole animal would be burned as a gift to God. People would sometimes sacrifice a burnt offering in the hope that God would respond favourably to their prayers. We might call it 'bribery', but many ancient societies used this standard practice on a daily basis. They also gave gifts as a common customary way in which to appease those they had offended. So, if people believed they had angered God for some reason, they often attempted to appease him by giving him a gift.

Initially, ancient Israel had no prisons. No crimes resulted in imprisonment and punishments took instead the form of either death or a fine. The ancient Israelites had very little coinage – since the wealth of their agricultural society consisted in livestock and grain – and therefore had to pay fines in food products. In some cases, the monetary value of the sacrifice was downgraded for poorer people according to what they could afford – birds instead of livestock, or just flour.[10] They paid these fines to God, and burned the offerings whole as compulsory 'gifts.' Hence, the Israelite 'burnt offering' served several purposes: the motivation varied, but in all cases the giver sacrificed an animal or grain to God as a *gift*.

---

ogy of Old Testament Sacrifice' in Beckwith and Selman, *Sacrifice in the Bible*, pp. 82 – 83.

[7] Plato *Euthyphro* 14C-D.

[8] Jacob Milgrom, *Leviticus 1-16 – A New Translation with Introduction and Commentary* (New York, NY: Doubleday, 1991), p. 441.

[9] Deut 26.

[10] Lev 5:7-13.

Meals

Meat was far rarer and more expensive in ancient societies than it is in modern times. The ancient world had no refrigeration and very poor quality salt, so they also needed to eat killed animals quickly. Naturally, many people were required in order to consume an entire animal in a short time, and the killing of an animal for meat was generally reserved for special celebrations involving many people. The group dynamics at such meals mattered greatly. Who sat where, who got which cuts of the meat, and even the preparation of the meal itself had great significance.[11] Many cultures gave a portion of the meal to the gods, who they believed shared the meal in fellowship with the community.

Israel called such group banquets 'well-being', 'thanksgiving', and 'free-will' offerings. They performed sacrifices of this type most commonly. A modern reader may feel that these do not truly count as 'sacrifices' at all, but, as in many ancient cultures, the Hebrew word for 'sacrifice' also meant 'slaughter.'[12] They considered life sacred, and taking the life of an animal, even for eating, required an appropriate ritual. The Israelites held these community meal sacrifices in the presence of God and followed the relevant customs carefully.

Purification

Many pre-scientific cultures believed in the existence of magical forces of purity and impurity. As a useful analogy for these ideas, imagine this impurity as invisible dirt or bacteria. If people did not take care to keep things clean, they could become contaminated. If things became too dirty, and stayed dirty for a long time, then disease and suffering could result. People believed that demons thrived in an impure environment. An impure person or house could therefore become inhabited by demonic forces and powers. Purity had special importance around temples, in order to keep demons out of the homes of the gods. Hence, people performed rituals carefully in order to clean up any impurity quickly and keep things clean. Today, if parents saw that their children had failed to take off muddy shoes and trekked mud through the house, they would probably use some cleaning product to

---

[11] Stanley K. Stowers, 'Greeks Who Sacrifice and Those Who Do Not' in L. M. White & O. L. Yarbrough (eds.), *The Social World of the First Christians* (Minneapolis, MN: Augsburg Fortress, 1995), pp. 327 – 328. See also M. Detienne J.-P. Vernant (eds.), *The Cuisine of Sacrifice among the Greeks* (Chicago; London: University of Chicago Press, 1989, trans. Paula Wissing), pp. 132 – 145.

[12] Detienne and Vernant (eds.), *The Cuisine of Sacrifice among the Greeks*, p. 25.

remove the dirt. In the same way, cultures that believed in magical purity and impurity used cleansing agents to remove impurity. Such cultures had various sets of cleansing agents, rituals, and incantations that they used to purify people or places, and used various substances and rituals to purify items magically.

The Israelites used purification agents that included blood, ashes, coals, oil, water, cedarwood (a strongly scented red wood), red cows, red wool,[13] and hyssop (an aromatic herb). They believed that these substances acted in the way detergents do today. The detergent analogy even appears in the Bible.[14] As an example, one Israelite purification ritual after contact with dead bodies involved the following:

> Take some ashes of the burnt purification offering, and running water shall be added in a vessel; a clean person shall take hyssop, dip it in the water, and sprinkle it on the tent, on all the furnishings, on the persons who were there, and on whoever touched the bone, the slain, the corpse, or the grave.[15]

Obviously, cultures like that of the West would not perform such a ritual, as typically people do not believe in this kind of magical impurity today. The Israelites, however, believed that such rituals removed the magical contamination that resulted from contact with the dead. The Israelites believed that these magical impurities came from several sources, including corpses, some skin diseases, genital discharges, and moral wrongs.[16] Impurity could also arise if people made mistakes in rituals and did not follow proper procedure.

The Israelites cared especially about maintaining the purity of the Temple, God's dwelling. They believed that impurities elsewhere in Israel could spread into the Temple and contaminate it. The more impurity in Israel, the farther into the Temple the impurity would reach. They feared that God would abandon both the Temple and Israel if impurities contaminated the Holy of Holies.[17] Hence, they purified the Temple regularly. For serious contamination, they purified the inner sanctums of the Temple. Israel's neighbours had similar practices to

---

[13] Things that are red in colour are used widely in rituals among different cultures due to the association between the colour and blood (see Milgrom, *Leviticus (A Continental Commentary) – A Book of Ritual and Ethics* (Minneapolis, MN: Augsburg Fortress, 2004), p. 39.

[14] Rev 7:14.

[15] Num 19:17-18. See also for example: Lev 8:15, 14:4, Psa 51:7.

[16] Milgrom, *Leviticus (A Continental Commentary)*, p. 12.

[17] Milgrom, *Leviticus (A Continental Commentary)*, pp. 31 – 32.

keep their temples ritually pure because they thought that purity warded off demons. They maintained the purity of their temples to prevent demons from entering, for if they did the gods would leave.[18]

As we have already noted, one of the substances used in these purification rituals was blood. People thought that blood contained the life-force of the animal, and that they could use this pure life-force to wash away impurity. Israelites used blood regularly to purify the contaminated parts of their Temple, pouring or sprinkling the blood of animals on the outer altars to purify them. Once a year, on *Yom Kippur* (the Day of Purgation), the High Priest would use blood to purify the Holy of Holies. Consider this typical passage about a purification ritual being performed in God's dwelling:

> The anointed priest shall take some of the blood of the bull and bring it into the tent of meeting. The priest shall dip his finger in the blood and sprinkle some of the blood seven times before the Lord in front of the curtain of the sanctuary. The priest shall put some of the blood on the horns of the altar of fragrant incense that is in the tent of meeting before the Lord; and the rest of the blood of the bull he shall pour out at the base of the altar of burnt offering, which is at the entrance of the tent of meeting.[19]

All the important parts of the altar and Temple needed ritual purification using blood to prevent magical impurities from accumulating within the Temple.[20] Blood served as a magical detergent, not as a means of personal forgiveness. Personal forgiveness in Judaism came through repentance (as we saw in an earlier chapter). One scholar explains the function of blood in this way:

> Failure to keep the temple pure meant to risk God's anger and the loss of his presence. ...the blood of the animal was the purging agent that was applied to various parts of the temple and removed the *consequences* of sins and impurities (that is, the pollution of the temple). The person did not receive forgiveness for

---

[18] Milgrom, *Leviticus (A Continental Commentary)*, pp. 31 – 32.
[19] Lev 4:5-7.
[20] Milgrom, *Leviticus (A Continental Commentary)*, p. 15, 30f.

a sinful act itself but dealt only with the consequences of such acts on the temple.[21]

Another scholar has reached the same conclusion:

> Who or what is being purified? Surprisingly, it is not the person with the moral or physical impurity. According to Leviticus, if his or her impurity is physical, only bathing is required to purify the body; if the impurity is moral (the unintended breach of a prohibition), a remorseful conscience clears the impurity. In neither case does the offering purify the person bringing the offering. ... Blood is the ritual cleanser that purges the altar of the impurities inflicted on it by the offender.[22]

A third scholar agrees that the Israelites viewed the animal's blood "as a kind of spiritual disinfectant purifying the sanctuary of the pollution associated with sin and uncleanness."[23] Traditionally, translators have called the rituals to purify the Temple with blood 'sin-offerings', but these rituals are translated more accurately as 'purification offerings.'[24]

The Israelite Passover also functioned as a purification ritual.[25] In the original Passover, the Israelites had dabbed two purification agents (hyssop and blood) on their doors. The instructions were to "take a bunch of hyssop, dip it in the blood that is in the basin, and touch the lintel and the two doorposts with the blood in the basin."[26] Other references to the Passover in the Bible confirm that the Israelites considered it a time of ritual purity in which they performed a purification ritual on their doors. The ancient Babylonians performed a similar practice. Their ritual involved "smearing a door with a mixture including bats' blood and crushed spider."[27] The Babylonians did this to create a barrier of purity around the door to protect against evil spirits.

---

[21] Stowers, *A Rereading of Romans*, p. 208.

[22] Milgrom, *Leviticus (A Continental Commentary)*, pp. 30 – 31.

[23] Gordon J. Wenham, 'The Theology of Old Testament Sacrifice' in Beckwith and Selman, *Sacrifice in the Bible*, p. 83.

[24] J. Milgrom, 'Sin-Offering or Purification-Offering?' in *Vetus Testamentum*, Vol. 21, Fasc. 2 (Apr., 1971), pp. 237 – 239.

[25] T. D. Alexander, 'The Passover Sacrifice' in Beckwith and Selman, *Sacrifice In The Bible*, pp. 1-25; Leon Morris, *The Apostolic Preaching of the Cross* (London: Tyndale Press, 2000, 3rd. ed.), pp. 131 – 132.

[26] Ex 12:22.

[27] Martin J. Selman, 'Sacrifice in the Ancient Near East' in Beckwith and Selman, *Sacrifice in the Bible*, p. 94.

People in the ancient Near East performed similar rituals, daubing vulnerable parts of structures with blood to purify them and thereby ward off demonic forces.[28] In the original Passover, the Israelites purified the doorways of their dwellings to ward off the Angel of Death.

Ancient Israelites, like people of many other ancient cultures, also believed in the power of curses – magical forces invoked by rituals to bring harm. Curses differed from impurity in that people could not simply wash them away. Instead, people could transfer them ritually. The ancient Greeks performed a ceremony in which they transferred the curses from a city to a slave. They then drove that person out of the city to bear away the curses. The Israelites had a similar annual ritual in which the High Priest placed two hands on a goat and prayed over it all the curses, sins and wrongs of the nation. They then drove that animal off into the wilderness to carry the curses away.[29] Note that they saw the goat simply as a means of transport, and that it did not die as an offering or a sacrifice. It did not die nor suffer on behalf of others but simply carried the curses away, out into the wilderness.[30]

These purification rituals were not, strictly speaking, sacrifices to God. In rituals involving blood, the actual death of the animal had no relevance. In many purification rituals they did not use blood at all and instead used other substances as purification agents. These rituals may strike us as magical, ritualistic and primitive, yet the ancient Israelites took them very seriously. Professionals performed them in a formal and public setting, and people believed these rituals had great power.

Clarifying modern misunderstandings

The three concepts of *gift, meal,* and *purification* correspond to an-cient Israel's three types of sacrifice – the three reasons they killed animals. In Israel's sacrificial system, as in most other cultures, the actual death of the animal itself had no relevance. As one scholar notes: "In ancient Jewish and ancient Mediterranean animal sacrifices and in the rites of numerous other cultures the death of the animal was an incidental prelude to the ritual. Strange as it may seem to people steeped in the legacy of Christianity; these sacrificing cultures attach no special significance to the death of the animal itself."[31] Rather, they attached importance to what they did with the animal's blood and flesh,

---

[28] Milgrom, *Leviticus (A Continental Commentary),* p. 85, 137.
[29] Leviticus 16.
[30] Milgrom, *Leviticus (A Continental Commentary),* pp. 168 – 169.
[31] Stowers, *A Rereading of Romans,* p. 207.

which they would eat, burn, or use in rituals. Israel's sacrificial texts discuss these aspects at length, and hardly discuss the death of the animal itself at all. They mention the actual death of the animals only briefly, often to outline simply the most humane way in which to kill the animals.

In Israel, sacrifices could not cleanse deliberate moral sins; repentance and prayer provided the only solution.[32] Israel had a strong tradition of repentance, prayer and forgiveness.[33] In their view, a burnt offering gift might appease God and encourage him to accept a person's repentance and prayers for forgiveness. Their standing before God, though, depended on his kindness and their own prayer and repentance, not on any sacrifices they might perform.

If a transgression deserved the death penalty, no sacrifice could be given. Israel's legal code either fined people in the form of compulsory burnt offerings or applied the death penalty (or in some cases, exile). People could offer sacrificial fines if, and only if, their transgressions did *not* deserve the death penalty. Hence, if we remain consistent with the way their law worked, we see that the animal never died as a substitution for the offerer. This concept would have been totally foreign to the Ancient Israelites.

Many different cultures followed the custom that the person bringing the sacrifice identified the animal publicly as theirs by placing a hand on it.[34] Some Christians have thought mistakenly that the Israelites did this to transfer the sins of the sinner to the animal. Many scholars, therefore, take pains to reject this view explicitly and note that the evidence contradicts it.[35] The Israelites followed the hand-laying practice for all their sacrifices – gifts, meals, and purification rituals.[36] In all three of these types of sacrifice, transferring sin to the animal would not have made sense. It would have polluted the gift that the worshipper gave to God, contaminated the meat they ate, or spoiled the blood that they used to purify the Temple. For meal sacrifices, the holy offerer

---

[32] Milgrom, *Leviticus (A Continental Commentary)*, p. 42, 60, 171.

[33] Milgrom, *Leviticus (A Continental Commentary)*, p. 30, 60.

[34] Finlan, *The Background and Content of Paul's Cultic Atonement Metaphors*, pp. 86 – 93; Milgrom, *Leviticus (A Continental Commentary)*, p. 24.

[35] Finlan, *op. cit.*, pp. 86-93; Milgrom, *op. cit.*, p. 24; Brondos, *Paul on the Cross*, pp. 21-22; Frances M. Young, *The Use of Sacrificial Ideas in Greek Christian Writers from the New Testament to John Chrysostom* (Eugene, OR: Wipf & Stock Publishers, 2004), pp. 51 – 53; Wenham, 'The Theology of Old Testament Sacrifice' in Beckwith and Selman, *Sacrifice in the Bible*, p. 79, 83.

[36] *Gift offerings*: Lev 1:4. *Meals*: Lev 3:2, 8, 13. *Purification Offerings*: Lev 4:4, 24, 29, 33.

did not even have any sin to transfer. The Israelite practice of hand-laying more closely parallels the customs we see in other cultures, in which it publicly identified the person bringing the sacrifice. It had little to do with atonement. The only time in the Israelite rituals where such a transfer of sin took place was on *Yom Kippur*. On that day, the high priest laid *both* hands on the goat, rather than only one. After praying over it the curses and sins of the nation he did not sacrifice it, but instead sent it away into the wilderness.

Development of sacrificial ideas

Studies have found that it is common for the sacrificial ideas within different cultures to change over time, moving typically toward moral ideas and away from ritual and magical ones.[37] One scholar has observed: "In cultures from Asia to Europe to Africa there is a progressive and observable development away from violent sacrificial practices toward a concentration on ethics."[38] Sacrificial systems tend to focus initially only on ritual and magic. People see morality as unrelated and irrelevant. Yet, over time, morality becomes as important as ritual. Eventually, people reject ritual and magic and stop making sacrifices. They then start to use sacrificial language metaphorically to talk about morality. A similar progression of ideas occurred among the Israelites and early Christians.

The writings of the Psalms and Prophets in the Old Testament seem to have moved the Israelites some distance toward emphasising morality at the expense of ritual. Some of their comments include:

> I do not delight in the blood of bulls, or of lambs, or of goats... cease to do evil, learn to do good; seek justice, rescue the oppressed, defend the orphan, plead for the widow.[39]

> Even though you offer me your burnt offerings and grain offerings, I will not accept them; and the offerings of well-being of

---

[37] See Stephen Finlan, *Problems with Atonement* (Collegeville, MN: Liturgical Press, 2005), pp. 3-6, 20; Stephen Finlan, *Options on Atonement in Christian Thought* (Collegeville, MN: Liturgical Press, 2007), p. 8; Young, *Sacrifice and the Death of Christ*, pp. 31 – 36; Roger T. Beckwith, 'The Death of Christ as a Sacrifice in the Teaching of Paul and Hebrews' in Beckwith and Selman, *Sacrifice in the Bible*, p. 133.

[38] Finlan, *Options on Atonement in Christian Thought*, p. 14.

[39] Isa 1:11-17.

your fatted animals I will not look upon...But let justice roll down like waters, and righteousness like an ever-flowing stream.[40]

They also used the word 'sacrifice' metaphorically to refer to morality rather than to an animal on an altar. One Psalm reads, "The sacrifice acceptable to God is a broken spirit; a broken and contrite heart."[41]

The New Testament authors rejected sacrifices and replaced them completely with morality.[42] Within the Gospels we see some clear statements about the importance of morality compared to that of sacrifices:

Go and learn what this means, "I desire mercy, not sacrifice."[43]

"To love [God] with all the heart, and with all the understand-ing, and with all the strength," and "to love one's neighbor as oneself," – this is much more important than all whole burnt of-ferings and sacrifices.[44]

Paul and Peter wrote of 'spiritual' sacrifices, which consisted of moral living:

Present your bodies as a living sacrifice, holy and acceptable to God, which is your spiritual worship... [Act in a way that] is good and acceptable and perfect.[45]

Rid yourselves, therefore, of all malice, and all guile, insincerity, envy, and all slander... be a holy priesthood, to offer spiritual sacrifices acceptable to God[46]

Hebrews says that Jesus abolished the old sacrificial system in order to establish in its place obedience to God's will:

"You [God] have neither desired nor taken pleasure in sacrifices and offerings and burnt offerings and purification offerings"

---

[40] Amos 5:22-24.
[41] Psa 51:17.
[42] Finlan, *Options on Atonement in Christian Thought*, p. 82.
[43] Matt 9:13, 12:7.
[44] Mark 12:33.
[45] Rom 12:1-2.
[46] 1 Pet 2:1, 5.

(these are offered according to Torah), then he [Jesus] added, "See, I have come to do your will." He abolishes the first in order to establish the second.[47]

Hebrews also uses sacrificial language as a metaphor for doing good. It teaches: "Do not neglect to do good and to share what you have, for such sacrifices are pleasing to God."[48] This passage uses the term 'sacrifices' non-literally to talk about doing good, rather than the slaughter of animals.[49] We can see from the above passages that terms from the old sacrificial system became metaphors for moral ideas.

The concept of 'purification' also moved away from the original idea of applying purifying substances to cleanse an object magically. The New Testament authors used it to refer solely to moral transformation. Peter wrote, "You have purified your souls by your obedience to the truth so that you have genuine mutual love."[50] John wrote that followers of Jesus "purify themselves, just as he is pure." He explained that this means they do what is right rather than what is wrong, and are "righteous, just as he is righteous."[51] According to Titus, Jesus came to "purify for himself a people of his own who are zealous for good deeds."[52] Hebrews explains that Jesus can "purify our ethics from dead works to worship the living God!"[53] James too referred to correct conduct when he instructed: "Cleanse your hands, you sinners, and purify your hearts, you double-minded."[54] The significance of the term 'sanctification' changed in a similar way. The term sanctification had its roots in ritual purity, and yet most Christians know it relates to morality in the New Testament.[55] Likewise, originally yeast had implications of ritual impurity (which is why people made unleavened bread without it), but it became another moral metaphor for the early Christians. They

---

[47] Heb 10:8-9.

[48] Heb 13:6.

[49] For further non-literal 'sacrifices' in the New Testament, see: Phil 4:18; 2 Thess 2:13; Heb 13:15-16; Jas 1:18.

[50] 1 Pet 1:22.

[51] 1 John 3:3.

[52] Titus 2:14.

[53] Heb 9:14.

[54] Jas 4:8.

[55] Ben Witherington III & Darlene Hyatt, *Paul's Letter to the Romans: A Socio-Rhetorical Commentary* (Grand Rapids, MI: Eerdmans, 2004), p. 173.

used it as a metaphor for "malice and evil,"[56] and for the wrong teachings of the Pharisees and Sadducees.[57]

As sacrifice and purity became associated more with morality and less with the old rituals, the places where sacrifices took place also changed. Priests had performed literal sacrifices in the Temple in Jerusalem, yet followers of Jesus could perform moral sacrifices in their own bodies. Hence, they located their 'temple' not physically in Jerusalem, but metaphorically within them. Paul saw Christians as 'God's temple',[58] and Peter saw them as the new 'priesthood' who performed these new kinds of 'spiritual sacrifices'.[59]

In this way, the early Christians moved radically away from ideas of literal sacrifice, spiritualising and moralising the notion instead. They began to use sacrificial language to refer to correct conduct, rather than using literal animal slaughters. Christians became their own temple and their own priests, and gave God acceptable 'sacrifices' and 'offerings' by living morally 'pure' lives in obedience to his will. They rejected the value of performing the cultic and ritual laws, and emphasised the value of good works and faithfulness to the will of God. The cultic goal of purity thus was achieved through morality, and a moral life in obedience to God replaced the old sacrificial system. The New Testament authors used the sacrificial ideas familiar to their first-century readers as metaphors to describe this new state of affairs.

Jesus and purification

We have seen above that the New Testament authors used the common sacrificial ideas of their day often to explain ideas. Paul described his own suffering and impending death in sacrificial terms, for example.[60] The New Testament authors also used sacrificial language to explain what Jesus did. Out of the three types of sacrifices (gift, meal, and purification), they seldom wrote of him as a gift sacrifice.[61] They wrote of him as a meal sacrifice only occasionally in the context of the Eucharist. The vast majority of sacrificial references to Jesus relate to purification.

---

[56] 1 Cor 5:7-8.
[57] Matt 16:6-12; Mark 8:15; Luke 12:1.
[58] 1 Cor 3:16, 6:19; 2 Cor 6:16; Eph 2:21.
[59] 1 Peter 2:5, 2:9.
[60] Phil 2:17, 2 Tim 4:6.
[61] Arguably, Hebrews 9:14 and Eph 5:2 refer to Jesus as a gift-offering.

So in what way did the New Testament writers think Jesus brought purification? We saw in an earlier chapter that they spoke in many ways of the moral transformation brought by Jesus. They drew on ideas from many spheres of life to express vividly how Jesus had changed their lives. As we have just seen, they also referred to moral issues using sacrificial language – especially the idea of purification. We would therefore expect them to have used the language of the ancient sacrificial system to speak of the moral changes Jesus brought. We find exactly this in their writings. They used the ideas of purification sacrifices to speak about the moral changes in their lives, and also about Jesus himself, since obvious parallels existed. The ancient purification rituals took away the ritual impurity from people or places and brought ritual purity. Jesus, on the other hand, brought a way of life that took away immorality and replaced it with right living. Both cases have the concept of purification in common (either ritual or ethical). The two processes worked differently, but had similar effects. The Israelites had believed their rituals worked by magical principles, whereas the Christians believed that by following Jesus' teachings their lives could be transformed. They did not believe this transformation worked by the same magical principles of sacrifice rituals. Nobody among them thought that Jesus' blood literally dripped down onto people from the cross and cleansed magical impurities from them. Rather, the teachings and movement for which Jesus died brought moral transformation to the lives of Christians.

The writer of Hebrews regularly wrote of Jesus as both performing and embodying a purification sacrifice.[62] He used sacrificial language about Jesus consistently to discuss morality rather than ritual purity. This language referred to a transformed lifestyle and mindset, not a change in ritual state from impure to pure. Hebrews depicts Jesus abolishing the traditional concept of sacrifices. Instead of literal sacrifices, Jesus brought a kind of sacrifice that involved living in accordance with God's will.[63] The author argued that old purification sacrifices never cleansed sinfulness properly. In contrast, the actions of Jesus led to real changes in peoples' lives, which purified them from sinfulness.[64] The writer believed that Jesus' blood brought "a better message than the blood of Abel," and warned that if we ignore this message we will not escape judgment.[65] Note the concept that his blood

---

[62] Hebrews 1:3, 9:11-14, 26, 10:10-14, 13:11-12, etc.
[63] Heb 10:8-9.
[64] Heb 9:14, 10:24-27, etc.
[65] Heb 12:24-25.

had a message. It emphasises the message Jesus taught and died for, rather than the magical power of blood to purify what it touches.

John used the idea of Jesus as a purification sacrifice as a metaphor for moral purity in a similar way. He wrote that "the blood of Jesus cleanses us from all sin" only if we "walk in the light."[66] As we saw in the previous chapter, John used the idea of 'walking in the light' to refer to correct conduct. John taught that, in order to receive the purification Jesus offered, we must live according to his example and teachings.

Peter also saw Jesus as a purification sacrifice in moral terms. In the middle of a discourse on moral transformation he wrote:

> Do not be conformed to the desires you formerly had in igno-
> rance. Instead... be holy yourselves in all your conduct... You
> know that you were ransomed from the futile ways inherited
> from your ancestors... with the precious blood of Christ, like
> that of a lamb without defect or blemish... Now that you have
> purified your souls by your obedience to the truth so that you
> have genuine mutual love, love one another deeply from the
> heart.[67]

Here, the concept of ritual purification refers to morality. The passage concerns the 'purification' of people's souls through obedience to Jesus' message, linking that moral purification with Jesus' blood – a reminder of his martyrdom. His blood rescued people metaphorically from 'futile ways' of living and taught them to live with genuine love. Paul, too, referred to Jesus as a purification sacrifice in moral terms. He explained that the Torah could not free us from sinfulness,[68] yet God freed us though sending Jesus and transforming our lives so that we might fulfil his moral requirements.[69] In the middle of this discussion he called Jesus a 'purification sacrifice'.[70] The idea of Jesus cleansing people from moral impurity can also explain a much debated Pauline passage that may refer to Jesus as a purification sacrifice.[71] In that passage, Paul taught that Jesus acted for our sake so that we could gain godly righteousness.

---

[66] 1 John 1:7.

[67] 1 Pet 1:14-22.

[68] Rom 7.

[69] Rom 8:3-4.

[70] Rom 8:3. He speaks of Jesus as a *"peri hamartias"* ("concerning sin") which is the phrase the Septuagint uses for a purification sacrifice.

[71] 2 Cor 5:21.

According to Revelation, Jesus "freed us from our sinfulness by his blood, and made us to be... priests serving his God and Father."[72] Here, Revelation likens Jesus' martyrdom to a purification sacrifice, which purifies us of our sinfulness. It uses cultic language metaphorically not only of Jesus, but also of Jesus' followers, calling them 'priests of God'. In a similar passage, Revelation speaks later of people who have "washed their robes and made them white in the blood of the Lamb [Jesus]."[73] Literally speaking, no one uses blood as a detergent to wash his or her clothes. In the metaphorical language of Revelation, white robes represent good works.[74] Thus, the metaphor of washing them in Jesus' blood to whiten them suggests that these good works came through the purifying effect that Jesus had on his followers' lives.

As we saw earlier, the Passover involved a purification ritual. Paul used this metaphor to write about Jesus, once again in the context of our moral transformation: "For our paschal lamb, Christ, has been sacrificed. Therefore, let us celebrate the festival, not with the old yeast, the yeast of malice and evil, but with the unleavened bread of sincerity and truth."[75] Here, Paul used an analogy between the Passover lamb that brought ritual purification and Christ's sacrifice that brought moral change away from sinfulness (represented by the yeast). Paul again moved the concept of Christ's sacrifice from the realm of ritual purity to the area of moral transformation.

We must read all these references to Jesus and his purifying blood in the spirit in which the New Testament writers intended them. Magical purification through the smearing of blood interested them no longer; instead, they concerned themselves with spiritual sacrifices rather than literal ones, and moral purity rather than ritual purity. People once thought purification sacrifices performed by smearing blood on the altar brought magical purity. Now, however, Christians believed that Jesus could bring moral purity through his martyr's death and the subsequent spread of his teachings through the church.

People sometimes misinterpret the New Testament sacrificial language in reference to Yom Kippur. On that day, as we have already seen, the High Priest performed a purification ritual in the Holy of Holies to purify it, and then transferred the curses and sins of the nation to a goat which he sent into the wilderness. The New Testament likens Jesus to

---

[72] Rev 1:5-6.

[73] Rev 7:14.

[74] Rev 3:1-6.

[75] 1 Cor 5:7. John's Gospel also depicts Jesus' crucifixion taking place on the same day as the killing of the Passover lambs, and John 1:29 and 36 are possible references to this.

the High Priest on Yom Kippur who performed the purification ritual. Yet, contrary to what some Christians today believe, it never likens Jesus to the goat that carried the curses and sins into the wilderness. It seems the New Testament writers preferred to use the metaphor of a purification offering rather than concepts like the scapegoat.

Jesus and covenant sacrifice

The New Testament writers also explained what Jesus achieved using another idea. This idea related to sacrificial rituals, but focussed on covenants (agreements or contracts). The Jews divided their history into a series of separate covenants between God and their nation. Jesus aimed to bring the Kingdom of God, a radical social renewal. This heralded a new age, which would require a new covenant. The prophet Jeremiah had promised that a new covenant would supersede the Torah, bringing morality and forgiveness of sins.[76] Jesus introduced this covenant among his followers. At the Last Supper, he made clear to his disciples that he intended to bring such a new covenant.[77] Hebrews echoes this idea. The writer paralleled Jesus and Moses as mediators of the two covenants.[78] Jesus functioned as the new go-between between humanity and God, and had instituted this covenant with God on their behalf just as Moses did for the Sinai covenant. Hebrews emphasises heavily the concept of Jesus as the mediator of this new covenant in which people would live rightly. With regard to this function, Hebrews portrays Jesus regularly in a priestly role.[79] This idea that Jesus brought about a new covenant arose naturally from his mission of social reform. The early Christians saw him as inaugurating a radical new Kingdom of God on earth, since his movement transformed their society and their relationship with God.

Sacrifices often sealed covenants in the ancient world. The intended goal of such sacrifices varied widely and no standard meaning existed. In ancient Hittite agreements, cutting animals to seal a contract symbolised a ritual-curse which meant that the party who broke the agreement would be likewise cut into pieces.[80] A covenant between

---

[76] Jer 31:31-34.
[77] Matt 26:26-28; Mark 14:22-24; Luke 22:19-20; 1 Cor 11:23-26.
[78] Heb 8:6, 9:15, 12:24.
[79] Heb 2:17, 3:1, 4:14, 5:5, 6:20, 7:26, 8:1, 9:11; Rom 8:34.
[80] Meredith G. Kline, *By Oath Consigned: A reinterpretation of the Covenant Signs of Circumcision and Baptism* (Grand Rapids, MI: Eerdmans, 1975), pp. 16 – 17.

Abraham and God involved this kind of covenant sacrifice.[81] At Sinai, Moses threw blood over the people in a purification ritual and called it a covenant sacrifice.[82] People also saw sacrifices made to seal agreements and treaties as gifts to the gods, inclining the gods to look favorably upon the agreement and perhaps to take action against any who broke it.[83] Most commonly, though, such sacrifices functioned simply as a joint meal held to celebrate new unity and fellowship. For example, the parties in a peace treaty or a new alliance would mark and celebrate the occasion by eating together. At the last supper, Jesus instituted a shared meal in which he was eaten symbolically. The New Testament portrays this as a covenant sacrifice and it seems to fall into this 'joint meal' category.[84] Perhaps this helps to explain why Paul insisted so strongly that Jew and Gentile Christians could eat together.[85] Elsewhere, Paul likened Jesus to a peace sacrifice, since he removed the division between Jews and Gentiles created by the Torah of the old covenant.[86] Of course, since Jesus had died as a martyr because of his work to inaugurate a new covenant, Christians could speak of him as the metaphorical 'sacrifice' that accompanied this new covenant. Jesus had cast himself in this role at the Last Supper, and Hebrews also reinforces this idea.[87]

Conclusion

Morality had replaced sacrifice for the New Testament Christians, and they rejected the value of the ritual sacrifice system. They used the language of ritual purity not because Jesus' accomplishments worked through the same magical mechanism, but to express the moral transformation Jesus had brought to their lives. They saw themselves as a temple that Jesus had purified morally with his 'blood' in a way analogous to the way in which blood had purified temples ritually in the past. Christ's martyrdom lent itself naturally to the parallel of a purification sacrifice. His noble self-sacrifice brought purity to his followers through his movement that had transformed their lives. His

---

[81] Genesis 15.

[82] Ex 24:6-8; Heb 9:19-20.

[83] For example, before finalising the Sinai covenant, Moses sacrifices burnt offerings – Ex 24:5.

[84] Matt 26:26-28; Mark 14:22-24; Luke 22:19-20; 1 Cor 11:23-26.

[85] Gal 2.

[86] Eph 2:14.

[87] Heb 9:16-22, 10:29, 13:20.

followers used this language of a new covenant to describe these profound changes to their lives. Hence, they also cast Jesus in the role of Priest because he had catalysed this reconciliation between humanity and God. The early Christians found moral purity through Jesus in a way that the old sacrificial system could never have wrought.

Chapter 13

Martyrdom

The early Christians saw Jesus' death primarily as a martyrdom. The concept of martyrdom became very significant to the Christians of the first few centuries AD, as they faced martyrdom repeatedly themselves for their Christianity at the hands of Roman authorities. At the time, the Greek language had no word that meant 'martyr', so the early Christians invented one. They adopted the word for 'witness' (*martys* in Greek) and used it to mean 'martyr'. By 150 AD, the Greek word *martys* had come to mean in Christian writings what we mean by 'martyr' in English.[1] The modern English word 'martyr' originates from their use of the term.

As soon as the early Christians coined the term 'martyr', they applied it to Jesus. The concept of Jesus being a martyr pervades Christian literature right through to the 4th century AD, especially in writings about Christian martyrdom.[2] They did not consider him merely *a* martyr, but rather *the* martyr – the archetype for all subsequent Christian martyrs. An account from about 180 AD that describes Christian martyrdoms states: "They were so eager to imitate Christ... they gladly yielded the title of martyr to Christ, the true Martyr and Firstborn from the dead."[3] The early Christians saw Jesus as *the* martyr and their own martyrdoms as mere imitations. Several accounts describe Christian martyrdoms as imitations of Christ's martyrdom,[4] and this idea dominates their descriptions.[5] One scholar explains: "The Christian martyrs went to death with the example of Christ, the perfect martyr, before them."[6] Jesus was a martyr *by definition*, because the Christians who coined the word 'martyr' wrote of him as the greatest

---

[1] J. W. van Henten & Friedrich Avemarie, *Martyrdom and Noble Death: Selected Texts from Graeco-Roman, Jewish, and Christian Antiquity* (London; New York: Routledge, 2002), p. 2.

[2] Frances M. Young, *The Use of Sacrificial Ideas in Greek Christian Writers from the New Testament to John Chrysostom* (Eugene, OR: Wipf & Stock, 2004), pp. 107 – 237.

[3] The document is preserved in Eusebius, *Church History* 5.1.2.

[4] E.g. *Martyrdom of Polycarp* 19:1; Ignatius, *Romans* 6.3.

[5] Young, *The Use of Sacrificial Ideas*, p. 110.

[6] Young, *The Use of Sacrificial Ideas*, p. 107.

martyr and saw him as an archetype for martyrdom. Others were martyrs only insofar as they conformed to the pattern of Jesus' own martyrdom.

The post-Reformation tradition seldom presents Jesus as a martyr, instead emphasising other ideas about his death. Perhaps for this reason, Christians today often do not conceive of Jesus as being a martyr. Jesus, however, fits quite clearly with the dictionary definition of the English word 'martyr': (1) "One who chooses to suffer death rather than renounce religious principles." (2) "One who makes great sacrifices or suffers much in order to further a belief, cause, or principle."[7] In fact, Jesus meets not only these rather minimal dictionary definitions, but also can be thought of as a martyr in a much richer and fuller sense. After considering the ideas we commonly associate with martyrdom, we can list several features of archetypical martyrdoms:

1.	**A hero**	A person of some renown who is devoted to a good, just, or admirable cause.
2.	**Opposition**	People who oppose that cause.
3.	**Foreseeable risk**	The hero foresees action by opponents to harm him or her, because of his or her commitment to the cause.
4.	**Courage and Commitment**	The hero continues, despite knowing the risk, out of commitment to the cause.
5.	**Death**	The opponents kill the hero because of his or her commitment to the cause.
6.	**Audience response**	The hero's death is commemorated. People may label the hero explicitly as a martyr. Other people may in turn be inspired to pursue the same cause, even in the face of opposition.

The story of Jesus presented in the Gospels contains all these elements. The Gospels speak of Jesus along heroic lines as a charismatic leader, wholly devoted to the cause of transforming people's lives for the better and ushering in God's Kingdom on earth. The religious

---

[7] *The American Heritage Dictionary of the English Language*, Fourth Edition. (Houghton Mifflin Company, 2004), Definitions 1 & 2 of 'Martyr'.

leaders opposed him and his movement because it threatened them. According to the Gospels, Jesus knew the risks and foresaw his death at the hands of the authorities, yet continued his activity courageously despite knowing where it would lead. He encouraged his followers to remain committed and warned that they too might face persecution and even death for the cause. Ultimately, his opponents plotted against him and put him to death on a cross. His followers commemorated his death repeatedly with the ritual of the Eucharist. Once Christians had coined the term for 'martyr', they labelled him as a martyr. His martyrdom also inspired many Christian martyrs during the first four centuries AD. Therefore, Jesus conforms to this archetypical concept of martyrdom. He died a 'martyr' in a very rich, full, and strong sense of the term.

The segments of the Gospels dealing with the death of Jesus have notable similarities with ancient martyrdom accounts. The 'passion narratives', as they are called, are the continuous sections in each Gospel spanning the events from the decision by the authorities to arrest him, through the last supper, to Jesus' arrest, trial, execution and burial. Scholars have pointed out many similarities between the passion narratives and martyrdom accounts by Jewish and Greco-Roman writers.[8] Basic similarities include the decision by authorities to kill the martyr, a hostile trial scene, and a detailed account of the martyr's death. Some more detailed similarities include the use of preliminary physical abuse in an attempt to make the martyr behave in certain ways, and ridicule accompanying physical punishment. The martyrs often expect and accept their deaths and accounts sometimes depict them going to their deaths willingly, just as Jesus did. The dialogue recorded in the Gospel trial scenes also has several similarities with dialogue in martyrdom accounts. As in the passion narratives, martyrdom accounts often present both parties as entrenched in their views and unwilling to compromise, with no persuasive or reasoned dialogue. The accounts often highlight the true identity of the martyr and indicate their opponent's motivation. Typically, the martyrs deny the authority of the accusers, and instead highlight God's authority. They evade their accusers' questions, heap scorn on them, and often respond with deliberate silence or in ways their accusers do not understand. They contrast earthly authority and rule with heavenly

---

[8] J. W. van Henten "Jewish Martyrdom and Jesus' Death" in Jörg Frey & Jens Schröter (eds.), *Deutungen des Todes Jesu im Neuen Testament* (Tübingen: Mohr Siebeck, 2005), pp. 157 – 168; M. E. Vines, "The 'Trial Scene' Chronotype in Mark and the Jewish Novel," in G. van Oyen and T. Shepherd (eds.), *The Trial and Death of Jesus: Essays on the Passion Narrative in Mark* (Leuven: Peeters, 2006), pp. 194 – 201.

authority and rule. The idea that God sees the trial and will reward the martyrs and avenge their accusers appears commonly. The martyrs speak often of God's judgment on their opponents. The Gospel accounts of Jesus' trial contain all these features typical of other martyrdom accounts, and extensive similarities like these have led many scholars to conclude that the passion narratives *are* martyrdom accounts in terms of their genre and style.[9] The Gospel writers present their accounts of Jesus' death in ways typical of how Jewish and Greek writers presented their accounts of martyrs.

Since most New Testament writers wrote before the word 'martyr' had been coined by Christians, they did not generally apply that word to Jesus. One exception is the book of Revelation. Its author wrote it late enough that the word *martys* was beginning to mean 'martyr' among Christians. Most scholars consider *martys* to have a dual meaning in Revelation, about halfway between its original meaning of 'witness' and its later meaning of 'martyr'. Revelation speaks of "the blood of the witnesses/martyrs of Jesus."[10] Elsewhere it speaks of how "they have conquered [their accuser] by the blood of the Lamb and by the word of their witness/martyrdom, for they did not cling to life even in the face of death."[11] It praises another Christian group: "You are holding fast to my name, and you did not deny your faithfulness to me even in the days of Antipas, my faithful witness/martyr, who was killed among you."[12] These passages appear to use the *martys*-group words with the meaning of 'martyr', as do several other passages in Revelation.[13] In light of this usage, it is significant that Revelation labels Jesus explicitly as a *martys* at the very beginning of the book: "Jesus Christ, the faithful witness/martyr, the firstborn of the dead."[14] Here, it describes Jesus in exactly the same way that it describes other Christian martyrs. Hence,

---

[9] J. W. van Henten, "Jewish Martyrdom and Jesus' Death," pp. 157 – 168; J. W. van Henten, "Martyrdom, Jesus' Passion and Barbarism" in Ra'anan S. Boustan (ed.), *Violence, Scripture, and Textual Practice in Early Judaism and Christianity* (Leiden: Brill, 2010), pp. 237 – 251; Stephen J. Patterson, *Beyond the Passion: Rethinking the Life and Death of* Jesus (Minneapolis, MN: Augsburg Fortress, 2004), pp. 56 – 65; Donald W. Riddle, "The Martyr Motif in the Gospel According to Mark." *The Journal of Religion*, IV.4 (1924), pp. 397 – 410; M. E. Vines, "The 'Trial Scene' Chronotype in Mark and the Jewish Novel," pp. 189 – 203.

[10] Rev 17:6.

[11] Rev 12:11.

[12] Rev 2:10-13.

[13] E.g. Rev 6:9, 11:3, 20:4.

[14] Rev 1.5. See also Rev 3:14.

Revelation seems to provide an example of the Bible labelling Jesus explicitly as a martyr. Other New Testament writers, such as Paul, wrote before the Greek word had gained this meaning, so they could not use the word *martys* to directly label Jesus as martyr. However, these other New Testament writers could and did present Jesus as a martyr in other ways, as we shall see.

Death for a cause

The concept of martyrdom flourished in Greek and Jewish thinking long before the word 'martyr' was invented. The idea of dying in a praiseworthy and honourable manner pervades ancient Greek literature, and Greeks celebrated people who faced death unselfishly and bravely for the sake of helping others. They remembered heroes who died to defend, save, help, or rescue others, as these heroes had chosen to die honourably rather than compromise their values. People celebrated these heroic martyrs through monuments placed in city squares with inscriptions of praise. Stories and tales lauding these famous heroes developed. Greeks felt that such heroes gained a kind of 'immortality' in story and memory by dying in such a noble and memorable way.

This theme of noble death arose most often in the context of battles. When an invading army threatened a city, soldiers would gather to defend it. These brave soldiers would face death to defend their people, and many did die, yet their deaths had significance and purpose. People did not think that these selfless warriors had died in vain. Their deaths *meant* something because of their selfless intentions, their perseverance, and the ultimate triumph of their goals. People would raise monuments to brave soldiers who had "died to save their city" and "poured out their blood to save their homeland." The soldiers' willingness to fight and die for their city brought victory over their enemies and the salvation of their people. Even 500 years after one famous battle, Greeks still commemorated annually the brave soldiers who had died.[15]

In praising the martyrdoms of these brave and selfless heroes, the Greeks were not extolling death in and of itself. They did not want more people to die more often, nor did they wish that more of their soldiers had died in the battles. The reasons for their praise lay in the context of the heroes' deaths. People celebrated the heroes' virtues of courage,

---

[15] Plutarch, *Aristides* 21.1-4 in *Parallel Lives*.

selflessness, love, and commitment. They also celebrated the victory, freedom, and salvation that they had gained through these heroes' actions. People saw the deaths themselves as a sad part of the story. They died as heroes, and the people they had saved remembered their praiseworthy sacrifice for generations.

Greeks who wrote of these martyrdoms commonly used phrases like "X died for Y" or "X gave his life for Y." As one scholar notes, this was the "principle martyrological formula in Greek literature."[16] Another scholar has searched many surviving Greek texts and found that these phrases occur over a hundred times.[17] Studying these instances, he found that, when the writers told of the brave deaths of these heroes, the causes for which they died featured prominently. These writers almost always used the word 'salvation' to speak of the benefits that had come through the brave deaths of the heroes. For example, the deaths of the soldiers in battle would 'save' the city from destruction. In addition, authors wrote typically of how these heroes had defeated or destroyed the powers that had threatened their people (by defeating the enemy army in battle, for example). Virtually all surviving Greek writings that use these martyrdom phrases mention both these concepts of salvation and defeat of the enemy.[18] In some cases, Greek writers included sacrificial language in their descriptions of soldiers' noble deaths on the battlefield.[19]

The concept of martyrdom and dying for a cause had flourished in Roman society for several decades preceding Jesus' death and the New Testament writings. It appears that the great Roman orator Cicero sparked interest in this concept with his famous depiction of Cato's death. Discussion of this topic of noble death became widespread quickly among writers, orators and thinkers of the period.[20] One writer from the time commented that the topic was "droned to death in all the schools."[21] Greek writers wrote often of the famous martyrdom of

---

[16] Finlan, Cultic Atonement Metaphors, 193

[17] Jeffrey Gibson, 'Paul's "Dying Formula": Prolegomena to an Understanding of Its Import and Significance' in Sheila E. McGinn (ed.), *Celebrating Romans: Template for Pauline Theology* (Grand Rapids, MI: Eerdmans, 2004), p. 22.

[18] Gibson, p. 25.

[19] Henk Versnel, "Making Sense of Jesus' Death" in Jörg Frey, Jens Schröter (eds.), *Deutungen des Todes Jesu im Neuen Testament* (Tübingen: Mohr Siebeck, 2005), p. 232.

[20] Writers who discussed this theme include Philo, Plutarch, Epictetus, Seneca, Musonius Rufus, Maximus of Tyrus, Tacitus, and Stoic and Epicurean literature generally. See Versnel, pp. 228 – 229.

[21] Seneca, *Moral Epistles*, 24 ('On Despising Death')

Socrates as a great example of dying for one's beliefs and philosophy, and also praised the noble deaths of other philosophers.[22] One scholar comments: "In first-century Rome then, and far beyond, the noble death of philosophers was a favourite example for admiration and imitation."[23]

Jews also wrote of martyrdom. During the Maccabean Revolt of around 165 BC, many suffered torture and martyrdom for their commitment to Jewish customs. The Jewish book of 2 Maccabees records the history of this period and depicts the martyrs' bravery and courage. Various other Jewish religious texts written before or during the 1st century AD portray Jews willing to suffer or die for their religion favourably.[24] According to the 1st century AD Jewish writers Philo and Josephus, many Jews were prepared to die for their religion and traditions. Josephus emphasised repeatedly the strong Jewish tendency toward martyrdom in his writings on the history of Judaism.[25]

The concept of martyrdom was, therefore, extremely widespread in both Greco-Roman and Jewish thinking during the 1st century AD. Although the *word* for 'martyr' did not yet exist, the concept of martyrdom did, as did standard ways of discussing it. Writers described people who "died for others" or "gave their life for others." Descriptions like these usually went hand in hand with talk of 'salvation' and 'deliverance', and sometimes included sacrificial metaphors.

Jesus' death for a cause

The New Testament authors drew on the ways in which their culture wrote about martyrdoms to write of Jesus' death. The Apostle Paul used this kind of language most often, writing of Christ's death using the Greek martyrdom phrase "X died for Y." He used variations of this phrase, "Christ died for us," about a dozen times to speak of Christ's martyrdom.[26] As one scholar notes: "We are reading Hellenistic

---

[22] Versnel, p. 229.

[23] Versnel, p. 229.

[24] Eg the book of Daniel, the Prayer of Azariah, the Assumption of Moses, the Letter of Aristeas. Also, see 4 Maccabees – though the dating of this book is uncertain.

[25] Tessa Rajak, *The Jewish Dialogue with Greece & Rome: Studies in Cultural & Social Interaction* (Leiden, Brill: 2001), pp. 124 – 126.

[26] E.g. Rom 5:6-8; 1 Cor 8:11; 2 Cor 5:14-15; Gal 2:20, 3:13; 1 Thess 5:10, plus variations on this phrase.

martyrdom language when we read, in Paul, of Christ dying 'for us'."[27] Paul wrote most commonly of Jesus' death using such phrases, and they appear in nearly all of his letters. Paul also followed the standard Greek pattern of accompanying these phrases with talk of 'salvation' and 'deliverance'. In addition, he sometimes used sacrificial language metaphorically to speak of Jesus' death in ways similar to other Greek accounts of martyrdom. Paul could not say "Christ was a martyr" because no word meaning 'martyr' existed, but he used the standard Greek ways of talking about Jesus as a martyr. Paul's common use of these phrases would have communicated clearly to his Greek audience that he understood Christ's death as a martyrdom.

Paul's letters also reference Jesus' martyrdom in several additional ways. In Romans 5, Paul wrote: "rarely will anyone die for a righteous person, though perhaps for a good person someone might actually dare to die."[28] Paul alluded here to the question of who would be a worthy cause for martyrdom, which people in Roman society debated often at that time.[29] After establishing martyrdom in this way as the context of his discussion, Paul stated in the next verse: "while we still were sinners Christ died for us."[30] Here, Paul presented Christ as a martyr using the standard "X died for Y" phrase, and contrasted him with other martyrs. Paul emphasised Christ's unusually high level of selfless love, as he died for the sake of people usually deemed unworthy of such an act.

Paul's discussion of Jesus' death in Romans 3:24-25 also seems to portray Jesus as a martyr. The unusual words and grammar of this passage have long caused difficulties for translators. Many regard it, however, as arguably the most important passage in Paul's writings about the death of Christ. Importantly, then, this passage is markedly similar to a passage found in an account of Jewish martyrs. The passage that describes the Jewish martyrdoms[31] contains language almost identical to that which Paul used to write of Jesus' death in Romans 3:23-25. This striking similarity suggests that Paul used language typical of martyrdoms to present Jesus as a martyr here.[32]

---

[27] Stephen Finlan, *Problems with Atonement* (Collegeville, MN: Litergical Press, 2005), p. 55. See also Versnel p. 291.

[28] Rom 5:7.

[29] Martin Hengel, *The Atonement: a Study of the Origins of the Doctrine in the New Testament* (London : SCM, 1981), p. 13.

[30] Rom 5:8.

[31] 4 Maccabees 17:21-22.

[32] Stanley K. Stowers, *A Rereading of Romans* (Ann Arbor, MI: Edwards Brothers, 1994), p. 212.

Martyrs tend to exemplify a particularly strong commitment to their cause. Jewish martyrdom accounts like 2 and 4 Maccabees emphasise the commitment of the martyrs to remain faithful and obedient to God's will.[33] Similarly, Paul emphasised the extraordinary commitment, obedience and faithfulness that Jesus showed through his martyrdom. Paul's emphasis on these ideas is explained easily by his view of Jesus as a martyr.[34] For example, when writing of Jesus' death, Paul emphasised his obedience: "he humbled himself and became obedient to the point of death— even death on a cross."[35] Elsewhere, Paul seems to have summarised what Jesus did as 'obedience': "by the one man's obedience the many will be made righteous."[36] Arguably, Paul refers a great many times to Christ's faithfulness,[37] which corresponds well with his view of Christ as a martyr. As one scholar explains: "It seems entirely appropriate... to suggest that [Paul's] account of Jesus' death – an essentially martyrological story – could include the element of faithfulness."[38] Paul seems to have written of Christ's obedience and faithfulness as if it summarised his life and work.[39] When Paul wrote of Jesus' death, he often drew attention to the faithful obedience Jesus demonstrated rather than to the physical death

---

[33] E.g. 4 Macc 5:16, 7:21-22, 15:24, 16:22, 17:2, 17:10; 2 Macc 6:30, 7:40.

[34] Versnel, p. 278; van Henten, "Jewish Martyrdom and Jesus' Death," p. 150; Douglas A. Campbell, *Deliverance of God: An Apocalyptic Rereading of Justification in Paul* (Grand Rapids, MI: Eerdmans, 2009), pp. 611 – 612 and elsewhere; David Seeley, *The Noble Death* (Sheffield: JSOT Press, 1990), pp. 103 – 107; Patterson, p. 51.

[35] Phil 2:8.

[36] Rom 5:19

[37] This is a topic of great current controversy in scholarship. Douglas A. Campbell argues the case most strongly for why a number of Paul's references to *pistis* refer to Christ's own faithfulness in Rom. 3:22, 26; Gal. 2:16; 3:22; Eph. 3:12; Phil 3:9 and other passages. For a number of excellent arguments on the subject, see his paper, "The Faithfulness of Jesus Christ in Romans and Galatians" (SBL, 2007). In his book, *Deliverance of God*, he argues that many other verses also refer to Christ's own faithfulness, including Gal 3:2, 5 (pp. 853 – 856), Gal 3:23, 25 (pp. 866 – 886), and Rom 3:25 (p. 647). See also Seeley pp. 105 – 107 for a list of scholars who interpret *pistis* to refer to Christ's own faithfulness in some verses.

[38] Campbell, *Deliverance of God*, p. 611.

[39] See Richard B. Hays, *The Faith of Jesus Christ: The Narrative Substructure of Galatians 3:1-4:11* (Grand Rapids, MI: Eerdmans, 2002), for a discussion of how Paul used the concept of faithfulness to represent the narrative of Christ's entire life.

itself. These notable aspects of Paul's letters agree entirely with the idea that Jesus died as a martyr.

Writers sometimes use a martyr's death as a quick means of referring to the martyr's entire life and cause. We can understand this tendency because a martyr always dies *for a cause*, and so the martyr's death in some way represents that cause. Paul referred to Jesus' death as if it represented and encapsulated Jesus' entire life and cause. For example, he wrote: "I decided to know nothing among you except Jesus Christ, and him crucified."[40] In another place, he summarised his message like this: "We proclaim Christ crucified."[41] We could interpret these passages to imply that Paul wax fixated on the crucifixion, yet that interpretation does not seem most appropriate. Paul instructed his converts in the details of Jesus' life and did not focus solely on the crucifixion.[42] Thus, these short statements seem to be better understood as references to Christ's martyrdom, which represented his entire life and cause. For Paul, Jesus' death as a martyr could represent his entire life and cause, just as Jesus' obedience or faithfulness could.

In short, Paul wrote of Jesus' death in exactly the ways we would expect if he understood it as a martyrdom. Throughout his writings, Paul used standard Greek martyrdom phrases when talking of Christ's death, and compared that death explicitly with the deaths of other human martyrs. In one of Paul's most central passages, he described Jesus in terms that closely parallel those of Jewish martyrdom accounts. Furthermore, Paul often emphasised Christ's commitment, obedience, and faithfulness unto death, apparently seeing that death as representative of Christ's entire life and cause. In light of this evidence, many scholars have concluded that Paul understood Jesus' death as a martyrdom.[43] One scholar summarises it this way: "Paul and his audience share the belief that Jesus died as a martyr."[44]

---

[40] 1 Cor 2:2. See also Gal 3:1.

[41] 1 Cor 1:23.

[42] Accounts of Paul's preaching in Acts suggest a focus on the resurrection instead. Paul's own writings reference implicitly the events of Jesus' life and his teachings as depicted in the Gospel accounts. These suggest that Paul and his converts were familiar with at least the basic events of Jesus' life and the content of his teachings.

[43] For example: Stephen Finlan, *The Background and Content of Paul's Cultic Atonement Metaphors* (Atlanta, GA: SBL, 2004), pp. 193 – 210; Sam K. Williams, *Death as Saving Event: The Background and Origin of a Concept* (Missoula, MT: Scholars Press for Harvard Theological Review, 1975), pp. 38 – 41; Seeley, *The Noble Death*, pp. 83 – 112; Stowers, *A Rereading of Romans*, p. 212f; Jarvis J. Williams, *Maccabean Martyr Traditions in Paul's Theology of Atonement* (Eugene,

What Jesus died *for*

Martyrs always have a cause for which they are killed or persecuted. Let us turn to look at how the New Testament letter writers spoke of the cause for which Jesus died. What did they believe Jesus' goals to be? We can answer this question by looking at their passages that take the form "Christ died for Y in order that Z." Such phrases tell us for whom or for what the early Christians believed Jesus had died a martyr (the 'Y'). They also tell us something about the *purposes* for Jesus' activity (the 'Z').

When we look at these "Christ died for Y in order that Z" phrases, we find that a clear theme emerges. We can summarise it loosely in this way: 'Jesus transformed people's lives, teaching them to live rightly, and for this cause he died selflessly.' Many New Testament verses seem to convey this basic theme, although they do so in a variety of ways. Consider the following examples:

Titus. Jesus gave himself for us that he might redeem us from all iniquity and purify for himself a people of his own who are zealous for good deeds.[45]

Ephesians. Christ loved the church and gave himself up for her, in order to make her holy... so that she may be holy and without blemish.[46]

Galatians. Jesus gave himself for our sinfulness to set us free from the present evil age, according to the will of our God and Father.[47]

Colossians. You who were once estranged and hostile in mind, doing evil deeds, he has now reconciled through his fleshly body's death, so as to present you holy and blameless and irreproachable before him.[48]

OR: Wipf and Stock, 2010); S. A. Cummins, *Paul and the Crucified Christ in Antioch* (Cambridge: Cambridge University Press, 2001).

[44] Stephen Finlan, *Options on Atonement in Christian Thought* (Collegeville, MN: Liturgical Press, 2007), p. 2.

[45] Titus 2:14.

[46] Eph 5:25.

[47] Gal 1:4.

[48] Col 1:21-22.

2 Corinthians. He died for all, so that those who live might live no longer for themselves, but for him who died and was raised for them.[49]

Revelation. Jesus freed us from our sinfulness by his blood, and made us to be a kingdom, priests serving his God and Father.[50]

The above passages use Greek martyrdom language to present the basic idea that Jesus died as a martyr because of his mission to teach people how to live rightly. The goals they mention all fit with early Christian ideas of what Jesus accomplished through his activity: moral purification, new life, and freedom from sinfulness.

The theme of freedom from sinfulness helps us to understand better several shorter phrases about Jesus' martyrdom. Paul wrote of how "Christ died for our sinfulness"[51] and "was handed over to death for our trespasses."[52] Paul did not elaborate or clarify these phrases. Nevertheless, these verses parallel closely the passage in Galatians (above), in which Paul elaborated using the phrase "to free us from the present evil age." Paul's short statements are interpreted best in light of such longer statements, which clarify his meaning. The general theme of freedom from sinfulness also explains why Paul saw Christ's martyrdom as a "ransom for all."[53] As we saw in an earlier chapter, Paul used this metaphor of ransom from slavery to write about freedom from sinfulness. Other short statements in Hebrews describe this freedom using sacrificial language of sanctification.[54] Hebrews also states that Jesus died to remove sinfulness[55] and purify our ethics,[56] which again appears to refer to the same idea of freedom from sinfulness.

The early Christians associated Jesus' death with the concept of reconciliation with God. They believed his death as a martyr had resulted from his work to transform the character and conduct of unrighteous people, thus reconciling them to God. Peter wrote of this idea using martyrdom language: "Christ also suffered [crucifixion] for sinfulness once for all, the righteous for the unrighteous, in order to

---

[49] 2 Cor 5:14-15; see also Rom 14:7-9.
[50] Rev 1:5-6.
[51] 1 Cor 15:3.
[52] Rom 4:25.
[53] 1 Tim 2:5-6.
[54] Heb 13:12; see also 10:12.
[55] Heb 9:26.
[56] Heb 9:14.

bring you to God."[57] The above statement uses the martyrdom phrase "X died for Y in order that Z" to link Jesus' death with his goals and accomplishments. Paul sometimes reordered this martyrdom phrase. He wrote: "while we were enemies we [Y] were reconciled to God [Z] by the death of his son [X]."[58] This phrase appears to make the same point as Peter's statement above. Paul wrote elsewhere that we have been "made righteous by his blood."[59] In yet another place, he wrote that we have gained redemption and forgiveness "through his blood."[60]

In general, the New Testament Christians pointed to what Jesus had achieved as the reason for his martyrdom: salvation from sinfulness, moral purification, new life, forgiveness, and reconciliation. In addition to these general themes, Paul also associated Christ's martyrdom with his opposition to Torah purity regulations. We saw that the Gospels depict Jesus' opposition to Torah purity practices as a major reason for his death at the hands of the authorities. Paul argued that, if all Christians adopted Torah, Jesus would have died for no reason.[61] Paul also depicts Christ's martyrdom as a result of his teachings that removed the division between Jews and Gentiles caused by the ritual purity laws.[62] He wrote of this elsewhere, saying that the requirements of Torah died metaphorically with Jesus on the cross.[63]

The above verses show that the early Christians saw a significant purpose behind Jesus' death; the purpose towards which Jesus had directed his teachings and movement. Jesus had died as a martyr for that goal, and his followers continued to work towards it in his name. The goal was this: to save people from sinfulness so that they would live rightly and receive a favourable judgment from God.

Application of his death

Many of the New Testament verses that refer to Jesus' death are of a different kind. These verses do not discuss the purpose behind his death, but instead draw out practical applications from the events around it. The New Testament writers drew out three main applications. Firstly, Jesus' death showed his great love for them. Secondly, this

---

[57] 1 Pet 3:18. Jewish writings often present martyrs as the 'suffering righteous'.
[58] Rom 5:10; see also Rom 5:6 and Col 1:20.
[59] Rom 5:9.
[60] Eph 1:7. See also Col 1:12-14.
[61] Gal 2:21.
[62] Eph 2:13-16.
[63] Col 2:14.

great act of love meant they had an obligation to respond appropriately. Thirdly, they looked to imitate Jesus' example of selfless perseverance. These are exactly the kinds of applications people take from a martyr's death, and thus fit well with the early Christian view that Jesus died as a martyr. We will examine each in turn.

A demonstration of love

The early Christians saw Jesus' death as hugely significant in proving his love for them. Jesus had died for the sake of others, and, as Jesus had taught, such noble death represented the greatest act of love.[64] Of course, Jesus' physical death itself did not prove his love for them. He selflessly helped others even though he knew doing so would cost him his life, and in this way proved his great love for them. Jesus' martyrdom also proved that God loved the people to whom he sent Jesus, since he went to such lengths to save them from sinfulness. Paul mentioned this idea to the Romans: "God proves his love for us in that while we still were sinners Christ died for us."[65] The fact that God loved the early Christians enough to send Jesus even when they lived sinfully demonstrated that surely nothing could separate them from God's love.[66] In light of God sending Jesus, the greatest gift, Paul argued that God would surely give them other blessings also.[67]

Obligation to follow Jesus

We noted in an earlier chapter that people in the 1st century were obliged culturally to repay favours done for them. Jesus had done people a great favour by giving his life to help them, and so, in a sense they *owed* him. The New Testament authors sometimes mentioned this obligation that his selfless death placed upon his followers in order to motivate their readers to remain faithful. For example, Paul twice reminded the Corinthians that since Jesus had given his life for them, they should conduct themselves correctly[68] and obey his teachings.[69] Elsewhere, he argued that since Jesus had given his life for their sakes, they were obliged to live for him and his cause.[70] His death obliged

---

[64] John 15:13. See also Gal 2:20.
[65] Rom 5:8.
[66] Rom 8:31-39.
[67] Rom 8:32.
[68] 1 Cor 6:20.
[69] 1 Cor 7:23.
[70] 2 Cor 5:14-15.

them not to abandon his teachings on Torah, since otherwise they would make his death a waste and reject God's favour of sending Jesus.[71] Peter added weight to his moral exhortation in a similar way, reminding his readers of the obligation placed on them by Jesus, who had given his life to save them from their futile ways of life.[72] Paul reminded leaders of the church to lead diligently, so that they would not make Jesus' death in vain.[73] Jesus' selfless death for the sake of his followers obliged them to remain loyal to Jesus above everyone else.[74]

An example to imitate

The early Christians also applied Jesus' death to their lives as an example of endurance, selflessness and perseverance. The example of "Jesus Christ, the faithful martyr"[75] inspired many early Christians to endure through persecution. One scholar has noted that Mark's Gospel encourages its readers implicitly to follow the example of endurance Jesus set through his martyrdom.[76] On this same topic, Peter wrote that Jesus endured through suffering for the sake of his followers and left them an example to follow.[77] Jesus had suffered for doing good, and Peter used his example to encourage Christians to do likewise, despite the persecution that it might bring them.[78] He reiterated the point again one chapter later: "Christ suffered in the flesh, arm yourselves also with the same intention."[79]

The love Jesus demonstrated by giving his life for others also set an example for his followers. Paul taught: "live in love, as Christ loved us and gave himself up for us."[80] John wrote likewise: "We know love by this, that he laid down his life for us – and we ought to lay down our lives for one another."[81] Paul believed that Christians should love their brethren regardless of differences in customs, since Jesus loved them all and had given his life for all of them.[82] Specifically, regarding marriages,

---

[71] Gal 2:20-21.
[72] 1 Pet 1:14-20.
[73] Acts 20:28.
[74] 1 Cor 1:13.
[75] Rev 1:5.
[76] Patterson, pp. 56 – 60.
[77] 1 Pet 2:19-23.
[78] 1 Pet 3:18.
[79] 1 Pet 4:01.
[80] Eph 5:2.
[81] 1 John 3:16.
[82] Rom 14:9-15.

Paul taught that husbands should love their wives in the same way that Jesus had loved his followers and given his life for them.[83] In ways like these, the Christians took important lessons from the love that Jesus had demonstrated to them by dying for their sake.

Paul also saw the manner in which Jesus died as an example of humility, obedience, and faithfulness. He used this to inspire Christians to adopt the same virtues: "Let the same mind be in you that was in Christ Jesus... he humbled himself and became obedient to the point of death — even death on a cross."[84] Paul emphasised here not only the mere physical death of Jesus, but also the selfless love and virtue to which he remained committed even "to the point of death." Paul strived to imitate these virtues during his own hardship and martyrdom. He wrote, "I want to know Christ... and the sharing of his sufferings by becoming like him in his death."[85] Many early Christians seem to have shared such an attitude. Like Paul, the author of Hebrews exhorted readers to imitate the selfless service and love that Jesus exemplified through his martyrdom:

> Let us run with perseverance the race that is set before us, looking to Jesus the pioneer... who for the sake of the joy that was set before him endured the cross, disregarding its shame... Consider him who endured such hostility against himself from sinners, so that you may not grow weary or lose heart. In your struggle against sinfulness you have not yet resisted to the point of shedding your blood.[86]

Jesus' death set the standard of selfless courage among his followers, and the author of Hebrews saw his death as an appropriate one for a perfect role-model. Jesus pioneered their way of life, and that way of life involved a willingness to endure suffering. Yet God had crowned Jesus "with glory and honour because of the suffering of death" – and his followers expected also to receive this reward by following his example.[87] The example of endurance Jesus gave by continuing his activity even to the point of death provided powerful encouragement to the early Christians.[88]

---

[83] Eph 5:25.
[84] Phil 2:5-9.
[85] Phil 3:10-11.
[86] Heb 12:1-4. See also Heb 13:12-13.
[87] Heb 2:9-10. See also Phil 2:5-9.
[88] Rev 12:11 seems to refer to this idea.

Christ's death as a mechanism

At various times in history, some Christians have believed Christ's death achieved something in and of itself. Rather than seeing Jesus' death as a consequence of his activity, these Christians have viewed his death as a supernatural event that achieved certain cosmic changes. In such thinking, Christ's death functions as the mechanism that achieved those changes. The death itself has a *supernatural effect*, and thus scholars label this idea 'effective death'.

Greek accounts that portray human deaths as effective are generally stories of human sacrifice. A good proportion of Greek stories of human sacrifice occur in the 5th century BC plays of Euripides,[89] but others exist.[90] The Greek stories of human sacrifice tend to provide a clear 'set-up' – they lay out the need for a human sacrifice clearly. Typically, some obvious disaster is befalling the people – such as a drought. The people consult an oracle to determine the best way in which to avert the disaster. The oracle advises that a human sacrifice is necessary. The human chosen for sacrificing usually had some role in bringing about the disaster. Often, the accounts reference only vaguely any supernatural entities causing the disaster. Occasionally, the oracle reveals that fate, necessity, underworld spirits, demons, or the gods in general are the cause. Very rarely does the oracle mention a specific god as the one demanding a human sacrifice.[91] After the death takes place (if it does), the stories make it clear that the death fulfilled its purpose and averted the disaster. Overall, these accounts set up clearly a situation that demands a sacrificial death. They also indicate clearly that the death will bring about some effect, and then make it clear that the death achieved its purpose.

There also seems to have been a widely-held view among the general Roman populace that a person could offer their own life in exchange for the life of a sick relative. Evidently, they believed that when the spirits of the netherworld demanded a life, they did not mind which life they actually got. In this popular view, a person could therefore swap their own life for that of a sick relative, and many surviving inscriptions attest to the prevalence of this idea.[92]

---

[89] Versnel, pp. 234 – 235.
[90] All Greek accounts of human sacrifice are surveyed by Dennis D. Hughes, *Human Sacrifice in Ancient Greece* (London; New York: Routledge, 1991), pp. 73 – 81.
[91] Versnel, p. 235.
[92] Versnel, pp. 241 – 243.

Such Greek stories of human sacrifice and popular Roman ideas of effective death-healing are not really martyrdoms in anything approaching the rich, full sense of archetypical martyrdom. Martyrdom accounts do not present the deaths of martyrs as effective like those of human sacrifices, and thus these two types can be clearly distinguished.[93] The vast majority of Greek martyrdom stories concern the death of soldiers for others in battle.[94] Here, the deaths themselves did not provide the mechanism of victory. If the soldiers on the battlefield had simply killed themselves, rather than fought to the death, their army would not have won the battle. A soldier who 'died *for* his country' fought to the death for his cause and died in the process of doing so. The soldier intended to serve and protect the country, not to die. The death itself did not function as the mechanism that defeated the enemy. So when we ask *why* a soldier died for his city, we must distinguish between two different reasons for his death.[95] The first reason is the end *goal* the soldier had. In the case of the soldier, he died as a consequence of his goal to defend his city in battle. The second reason is the specific *mechanism* that caused the soldier to die. So in the same example, we could say that the soldier died because an enemy soldier thrust a sword through his body. These two reasons for his death are completely different. Obviously, the soldier's death was not the mechanism by which his army won the battle.

In answer to the question of "why did the martyr die?" the Greeks pointed to the goals for which that hero had strived and sacrificed. To do so, they wrote of what the martyr died 'for the sake of' and died 'in order to' achieve. Such phrases refer to the *goal or cause* for which the martyr died, and do not imply that the martyr's death itself was the mechanism to achieve some effect. Occasionally, some Greek writers employed metaphorical language to describe the soldier's deaths, speaking *as if* the deaths had some magical effects. Yet it is relatively straightforward to discern such metaphors and exaggerations.[96] Some examples of exaggerations include descriptions of "a sacred sacrificial death,"[97] or statements that "death in war is a sacrifice for the gods."[98] As one scholar has noted, such statements contain generally no notion

---

[93] Versnel, p. 232.

[94] Gibson, pp. 20 – 41.

[95] The ancient Greek philosopher Aristotle distinguished these two kinds of causes, labelling them 'final' and 'efficient' causes. See Physics II-3 and Metaphysics V-2.

[96] Versnel, p. 232.

[97] Pindar, Fragment 78 (Maehler).

[98] Plutarch, *Moralia* 192c.

of a magically effective death even though their language may suggest it to modern readers.[99] Jewish martyrdom writings prior to the New Testament also do not depict the deaths of martyrs as supernaturally effective.[100]

The New Testament's statements about Jesus dying for us (and similar constructions) fit very well with ancient ways of describing martyrdom. They do not correspond so well, however, with concepts of effective death. We noted earlier that Christians in the post-Reformation tradition have often downplayed or ignored the concept of Jesus as a martyr. These Christians thus tend to interpret Paul's phrases of "Christ died for us" not as martyrdom statements but as statements about a supernaturally effective death. Yet in Greek and Jewish martyrdom accounts, the deaths of the martyrs did not typically have magical effects. The presence of martyrdom language in the New Testament should not be taken as proof that Jesus' death had a supernatural effect. If anything, it should incline us away from that conclusion. To have reason to think that the early Christians saw his death as supernaturally effective, we would need to find other supporting evidence in the New Testament. In reality, when we survey the New Testament evidence, we find that it points us in the opposite direction; away from the concept of a supernaturally effective death.

Unlike the Greek accounts of human sacrifice, the Gospel accounts provide no 'set-up' for effective death. The Gospels present no problem for which Jesus' death provided the necessary solution. They do not outline any disaster facing humanity or Israel, or present the people trembling in fear for their immanent destruction. The people do not seek a divine oracle to tell them how to avert disaster. Nowhere do the Gospels indicate any need for a human sacrifice. Not one of the Gospels depicts any problem for which a supernaturally effective death would provide the solution. The post-Reformation tradition teaches that Jesus' effective death was required in order for God to forgive the guilt of past sins. The Gospel accounts, however, do not set this up as a 'problem' that needs a solution. Jews believed that God forgave sins through repentance, and the Gospel accounts endorse this view consistently and record it occurring. Israel already had ways to deal with sins: a sacrificial system which imposed fines for some sins and provided means of ritual purification for others, which worked alongside repentance and forgiveness. A first-century Jew reading the Gospel

---

[99] Versnel, p. 232.
[100] Versnel, pp. 255 – 278.

accounts, therefore, would never have understood them as depicting a problem with human sin that required a human sacrifice.

The Gospels provide lengthy and detailed accounts of the death of Jesus, and yet provide no clear description of any supernatural effects of his death. They describe the events leading up to his death, the death itself, miracles that occur,[101] and the events after his death. None of the Gospels, however, sets out any theory that Christ's death itself caused some supernatural effect. No Gospel writer mentioned the idea that the world's sin centred on Christ when he died on the cross, nor did they state that Christ suffered the punishment for all of humanity. Despite describing the whole course of Jesus' death at length, they failed completely to mention any concept of effective death. This omission by the Gospel writers thus challenges strongly the idea that they believed Jesus' death had an important and supernatural effect.

Since the Reformation, this idea of 'supernatural effect' has relied primarily on support from a small number of brief passages.[102] Paul wrote of Jesus "becoming a curse for us" and becoming 'sin' for our sake.[103] One verse in Hebrews states that Jesus died "to bear the sins of many."[104] Another similar verse by Peter states that Jesus "bore our sins in his body on the cross... by his wounds you have been healed."[105] A full analysis of these phrases and their various possible interpretations warrants a book in itself. David Brondos' excellent work *Paul on the Cross* discusses these verses and others. It concludes that the best interpretations of these verses do not imply effective death.[106] Here, let us simply make some general observations.

Scholars debate widely the meaning of these passages. In fact, scholars regard several of these passages as containing some of the most difficult phrases in the New Testament to translate and interpret. Some passages contain rare Greek words that have obscure meanings.[107] In other verses, the meaning of key terms is unclear.[108] Some verses

---

[101] In a sense, these miracles could be called a supernatural effect of his death, but not in the sense that we are discussing here. Their effects do not play any role in bringing about human salvation.

[102] E.g. Rom 3:25, Gal 3:13, 2 Cor 5:21, Heb 9:28, 1 Pet 2:24.

[103] Gal 3:13, 2 Cor 5:21.

[104] Heb 9:28.

[105] 1 Pet 2:24.

[106] David Brondos, Minneapolis, *Paul on the Cross: Reconstructing the Apostle's Story of Redemption* (MN: Fortress Press, 2006).

[107] E.g. *Hilasterion* in Romans 3:25.

[108] E.g. 'faith' and 'righteousness of God' in Rom 3:25, being 'made sin' in 2 Cor 5:21, 'bearing' sin in 1 Pet 2:24 and Heb 9:28.

present difficulties when it comes to piecing together the logic of the wider passage.[109] In others, it is unclear how the writer interpreted a quoted passage.[110] At different times in history, Christians who have thought Christ's death had some supernatural effect have held widely different views about what that effect was. Consequently, they have interpreted these ambiguous phrases in very different ways. Today, many different interpretations of these verses exist, and scholars do not agree about which interpretations are appropriate.

The contexts of these passages do not elaborate on any notion of effective death. They do not spell out a mechanism by which such a death might have worked. In fact, whenever passages elaborate on the cause for which Christ died or draw an application from his death, they always do so in terms of his cause of moral transformation. Paul seems to have never expanded on his brief allusions to Christ's death by expounding the idea that his death had supernatural effects. Conversely, whenever Paul did expand on these allusions, he always did so in terms of moral transformation. Thus, the contexts in which these statements occur do not support an interpretation of effective death. Looking to the works of Christian writers in the 2nd century also fails to support such an interpretation. Although the early Church Fathers echoed Paul's martyrdom language, they did not elaborate on these phrases in terms of a mechanism by which Christ's death 'worked'.

It is telling that people rely on such a small number of passages to prove the theory that Christ's death was 'effective'. If the early Christians had really believed that Christ's death had far-reaching supernatural and cosmic effects, we would expect them to have mentioned it often. Writings from the post-Reformation tradition spell out clearly and repeatedly that Jesus' death had such effects. They leave readers in no doubt, and do not trust such a central doctrine to a small number of short and ambiguous sentences. In the New Testament, however, we do not find unambiguous and widespread descriptions of Christ's effective death. Instead, we find only a few brief phrases that people could interpret in many ways. Neither the Gospels nor the rest of the New Testament provide any clear explanation of effective death. If the New Testament writers had believed that Christ's death had some important supernatural effect, we would expect them to have explained it clearly. We can therefore conclude that the early Christians probably

---

[109] E.g. the logic and flow of Paul's argument in Gal 3:10-14 is debated, as is his argument in Rom 3:24-25.

[110] E.g. 1 Pet 2:24 and possibly Heb 9:28 quote Isaiah 53, but Isaiah 53 is itself the subject of much scholarly discussion because of the large number of different interpretations that have been proposed for it.

did not believe that Christ's death was effective. If they did, the idea does not seem to have held a very important place within their theology, since they did not believe it warranted a clear explanation.

Conclusion

Jesus suffered a cruel and humiliating crucifixion, yet his death was far from meaningless to the early Christians. They saw purpose behind his death; the same purpose that drove his activity and movement. As one scholar concludes: "For the early followers of Jesus, his death was not simply the death of a victim. Jesus died as a martyr."[111] The authorities had killed him because of his movement to bring beneficial economic, social, religious, and social transformation in the lives of those around him. Another scholar puts it like this: "The real reason why the death of Jesus mattered is because of who Jesus was *before* he was martyred."[112] So his crucifixion was not simply a death, but a monument to his cause and to his selfless activity for humanity's sake. His martyrdom symbolised his cause, for which he ultimately died. The early Christians wrote of Jesus as a martyr, but in the early decades the word for 'martyr' had not come into use. Instead, they wrote of his death using the common Greek ways to describe martyrdom for a cause. Later, once a special word for 'martyr' developed, the early Christians applied the term readily to Jesus and his death. We find such language applied to Jesus in the book of Revelation. Later Christian writers recognized Jesus as *the* pre-eminent and archetypical Christian martyr.

The early Christians believed that Jesus had died a martyr as a consequence of his activity to free them from sinfulness into a new way of life. They linked his death repeatedly with this goal, which they believed he had accomplished. The early Christians also drew practical applications from his martyrdom, and many New Testament passages that mention his death have these applications in mind. They held up his martyrdom as a demonstration of his selfless love. Some passages remind Christians that Jesus had done them a favour which obliged them to respond and follow his message. Other passages exhort Christians to imitate the steadfast obedience of Jesus even to the point of death.

---

[111] Patterson, p. 65.
[112] Finlan, *Paul's Cultic Atonement Metaphors*, p. 209.

We have seen that the New Testament provides no 'set-up' for the notion of Jesus having a supernaturally 'effective' death. It presents no problem requiring his death as a solution. It provides no clear description of any supernatural effect of his death. It does not explain any mechanism of how his death worked, and neither do any other Christian writings from the early centuries. In addition, scholars have found that Greek martyrdom accounts that contain similar language did not imply effective death. Interpretations of his death as effective seem to rely overly on a small number of brief and ambiguous phrases, mostly in the writings of Paul. We looked at several reasons why it seems unlikely that these phrases refer to the idea of effective death. As one scholar notes: "There is simply no reason to attribute to Paul such ideas."[113] The contexts of these passages refer to the *goals* of Christ's life and ministry, and his commitment to them. So, it seems best to conclude simply that the authors saw Christ's death as a martyrdom, since the New Testament provides ample evidence for this view. This view also corresponds well with the wider early Christian message that we have been exploring in this book.

---

[113] Brondos, *Paul on the Cross*, p. 112.

Chapter 14

Resurrection

The resurrection of Jesus had great importance for the early Christians. The New Testament writers mention it frequently, and in ways that suggest that they held it as one of the central tenets of Christianity. Accounts of early Christian preaching from the book of Acts suggest a particularly strong focus on the resurrection. We read: "with great power the Apostles gave their testimony to the resurrection of the Lord Jesus."[1] Acts' account of Peter's initial preaching contains half a verse on Jesus' death but nine verses on the topic of his resurrection.[2] The same pattern appears in one of Paul's sermons in Acts, in which one verse alludes to Jesus' death while eight verses concern his resurrection.[3] Later, Acts depicts Paul preaching "the good news about Jesus and the resurrection.[4] In Acts' account of Paul's trial, he states, "It is about the resurrection of the dead that I am on trial before you today."[5]

The New Testament letters also stress the importance of the resurrection. Paul's own writings reference it often, and as if it had great importance. If not for the resurrection of Jesus, Paul believed Christianity would be worthless: "If Christ has not been raised, then our proclamation has been in vain and your faith has been in vain."[6] Paul reiterated a few verses later: "If Christ has not been raised, your faith is futile and you are still in your sins."[7] Paul seems to have seen the resurrection as a major event in salvation history: "We bring you the good news that what God promised to our ancestors he has fulfilled for us, their children, by raising Jesus."[8] Paul listed to the Corinthians the most important Christian teachings that he had received. Only half a verse concerns the death of Jesus here, but the resurrection and appearances fill up six verses.[9] In Hebrews, resurrection appears in the

---

[1] Acts 4:33. See also Act 4:2.
[2] Acts 2:23 vs. 2:24-32.
[3] Acts 13:29 vs. 13:30-37.
[4] Acts 17:18.
[5] Acts 24:21. See also Act 23:6.
[6] 1Co 15:14.
[7] 1Co 15:17.
[8] Acts 13:32-33.
[9] 1 Cor 15:3-7.

list of the most basic Christian teachings.[10] A statement in 2 Timothy also seems to name the resurrection of Jesus as a core teaching: "Remember Jesus Christ, raised from the dead, a descendant of David— that is my gospel, for which I suffer hardship, even to the point of being chained like a criminal."[11]

For the New Testament writers, the resurrection of Jesus certainly had great importance. They mentioned it roughly the same number of times as they mentioned his death. Many times, they mentioned the resurrection together with the death of Christ.[12] As we have seen above, they seem sometimes to have emphasised his resurrection more than his death, while in other passages the death takes precedence. It seems that in their view, these two events were of comparable importance.

The way the New Testament authors wrote of Christ's resurrection contrasts with post-Reformation teaching. The post-Reformation tradition has often emphasised the death of Christ at the expense of the resurrection. This teaching holds that his death plays a vital role in salvation, while his resurrection does not. This leads many post-Reformation Christians to speak and write extensively on the death of Christ but pay relatively little attention to the resurrection. As one observer notes, the post-Reformation view seems to treat the resurrection as "nothing more than the 'happy ever after' at the end of the story."[13] This post-Reformation tendency, however, does not fit well with the emphasis that the New Testament writers gave to the resurrection. This difference in emphasis indicates a mismatch between the post-Reformation view and that of the early Christians.

Hence, we will investigate why the New Testament writers felt that the resurrection of Jesus was important. On inspection, we find that they wrote about Jesus' resurrection in three main ways:

---

[10] Heb 6:1-2.

[11] 2 Tim 2:8-9.

[12] E.g. Acts 2:23-24, 3:15, 4:10, 5:30, 10:39-40, 13:28-31; Rom 4:25, 14:9; 2 Cor 5:15; 1 Thess 1:10, 4:14.

[13] Steve Chalke, *The Lost Message of Jesus* (Grand Rapids, MI: Zondervan, 2003), p. 172. See also Joel B. Green & Mark D. Baker, *Rediscovering the Scandal of the Cross: Atonement in New Testament & Contemporary Contexts* (Downers Grove, IL: InterVarsity Press, 2000), p. 148; Tom Smail, *Once and for All: A Confession of the Cross* (London: Darton, Longman & Todd, 1998), p. 96; Paul S. Fiddes, *Past Event and Present Salvation: the Christian idea of Atonement* (Louisville, KY: Westminster/John Knox Press, 1989), p. 100.

1. His resurrection proved that it was right to follow him.
2. It gave followers hope of receiving a resurrection also.
3. It gave them courage in persecutions.

We will look at each of these aspects of the resurrection in turn.

Proof that Jesus was right

The cruel and shameful death of Jesus posed a problem to the early Christians, making many of them question whether God had really endorsed him and his teachings. Over a hundred years after his death, Jews still objected to Christianity on the grounds that God would surely not have let his Messiah die in such a way.[14] As Paul explained, this idea of a crucified Messiah became "an offence to Jews, and foolishness to Greeks."[15] The resurrection of Jesus provided the key to overcoming this problem.

Many people had rejected Jesus and the authorities had killed him. Yet God had then raised him from the dead, thus putting a divine stamp of approval on his activity. Many statements in the New Testament mention this. They take the form: "people rejected and killed Jesus, but God raised him up." They contrast human rejection with divine approval. For example:

> You that are Israelites... you crucified and killed [Jesus] by the hands of those outside the Torah. But God raised him up, having freed him from death... God has made him both Lord and Messiah, this Jesus whom you crucified.[16]

Other verses focus on the resurrection as a stamp of God's approval. Paul, for example, wrote that Jesus was "declared to be Son of God with power according to the spirit of holiness by resurrection from the dead."[17] Moreover, the early Christians believed that, since God had resurrected Jesus, God had also appointed Jesus as his judge. Paul supported this idea: "They put him to death by hanging him on a tree; but God raised him on the third day... he is the one ordained by God as judge of the living and the dead."[18] This idea that God had appointed

---

[14] Justin Martyr, *Dialogue with Trypho*. Chapters 89 – 90.
[15] 1 Cor 1:23.
[16] Acts 2:23-36. See also: Acts 3:12-15, 4:8-10, 5:30, 7:52, 10:39-40, 13:27-30; 1 Thes 2:14-15.
[17] Rom 1:4.
[18] Acts 10:39-42. See also Rom 14:9-10, Act 17:31.

Jesus as judge appears in several other verses also, which we have covered in an earlier chapter. Since Jesus would be the ultimate judge, the early Christians believed that, if they followed his teachings and example, he would judge them favourably.

The hope of resurrection

Jesus' resurrection gave his followers hope for a similar resurrection. At the time, only some Jews believed in an afterlife. Some Jews thought that God would resurrect all humans to stand before his throne and receive judgment, honouring and rewarding some, while punishing others with shame and condemnation. Other Jews, like the Sadducees, did not believe in such an afterlife.[19] The resurrection of Jesus, however, proved to the early Christians that God had both the power and the will to resurrect humans. They saw it as definitive proof of an afterlife – proof that death was not the end.

That conviction had huge repercussions for the early Christians, since it gave them the hope that God would resurrect them after death.[20] Peter expressed it in this way: "By his great mercy [God] has given us a new birth into a living hope through the resurrection of Jesus Christ from the dead, and into an inheritance that is imperishable, undefiled, and unfading, kept in heaven for you."[21] Paul also expressed clearly this hope of resurrection: "I have a hope in God... that there will be a resurrection of both the righteous and the unrighteous."[22] He mentioned this hope in almost every one of his letters.[23] John's epistles, Jude and Revelation, also express the same hope of resurrection.[24] The emphasis this idea receives throughout the New Testament reflects the importance it had for the early Christians. At times, Paul defended the doctrine of the resurrection vigorously against those who denied it: "Why is it thought incredible by any of you that God raises the dead? ...the Messiah [was] the first to rise from the dead."[25] Paul warned Timothy to guard against people who claimed that the resurrection had

---

[19] Acts 4:2.

[20] 1 Cor 6:14.

[21] 1 Peter 1:3-4.

[22] Acts 24:15-16.

[23] Rom 6:2-8; 1 Cor 15; 2 Cor 4:14; Gal 6:8; Eph 2:4-6; Php 3:11; Col 3:4; 1 Thes 4:14; 2 Thes 2:14, 16; 1 Tim 6:19; 2 Tim 2:10-11; Titus 3:6-7.

[24] 1 John 2:25; Jud 1:21; Rev 1:5 and Rev 20.

[25] Acts 26:8, 23. See also 1 Cor 15:12-20.

already taken place, since it would deny the hope of it happening in the future.[26]

The existence of an afterlife meant that death was not the end and that final judgement mattered. This fact had huge implications; it meant that the way one lived would affect the judgement one received. As Paul noted, people needed to think about the afterlife and not this life only. Attitudes such as 'let us eat and drink, for tomorrow we die'[27] were no longer appropriate given the existence of an afterlife and a judgment. The resurrection of Jesus proved that living in the right way mattered. As we just discussed above, it also convinced the early Christians that Jesus had taught that right way. Combined, these two ideas provided key motivation for people to join Jesus' movement and follow his teachings.

A source of courage

Popular Greek philosophy held that the fear of death was the ultimate cause of all evil deeds as it led humans to act in selfish ways. The resurrection of Jesus was interpreted in this context as a great victory over death. Several New Testament verses take note of this victory, reminding the reader that the power of death could not hold Jesus,[28] and that death no longer had dominion over him.[29] He had conquered death[30] and had taken the metaphorical 'keys' of Death and Hades.[31] For the early Christians, Jesus' victory over death meant they too could have a similar victory over death through similar resurrections. They believed that Jesus had "abolished death and brought life and immortality to light through the gospel."[32] God had given them this victory over death through Jesus.[33]

This conviction removed the early Christians' fear of death. Hebrews explained that Jesus had destroyed the power of death, and freed those who "were held in slavery by the fear of death."[34] Christians

---

[26] 2 Tim 2:18.
[27] 1 Cor 15:32.
[28] Acts 2:24.
[29] Rom 6:9.
[30] Rev 5:5-6.
[31] Rev 1:18.
[32] 2 Tim 1:10.
[33] 1 Cor 15:52-57.
[34] Heb 2:14-15.

believed that they would overcome the great 'enemy' of death.[35] For this reason, death had lost its power, as Paul explained:

> When this perishable body puts on imperishability, and this mortal body puts on immortality, then the saying that is written will be fulfilled: "Death has been swallowed up in victory." "Where, O death, is your victory? Where, O death, is your sting?" The sting of death is sin, and the power of sin is the law. But thanks be to God, who gives us the victory through our Lord Jesus Christ.[36]

The early Christians "more than conquered" death because they feared it no longer.[37]

The hope of resurrection also made the early Christians lose their fear of martyrdom. It gave them courage to follow Jesus when doing so would lead often to persecution. It meant that Christians could meet death fearlessly and even willingly, since following Jesus was worth any price. Revelation provides an example of how they drew this kind of courage from the hope of resurrection:

> Do not fear what you are about to suffer. Beware, the devil is about to throw some of you into prison so that you may be tested, and for ten days you will have affliction. Be faithful until death, and I will give you the crown of life. Let anyone who has an ear listen to what the Spirit is saying to the churches. Whoever conquers will not be harmed by the second death.[38]

The resurrection gave the early Christians courage amid the suffering and persecution they endured for following Jesus. Paul explained: "We suffer with him so that we may also be glorified with him. I consider that the sufferings of this present time are not worth comparing with the glory about to be revealed to us."[39] The letters to Timothy express a similar sentiment.[40] The hope of resurrection gave Paul courage to continue his work despite having to endure suffering. He explained: "I want to know Christ and the power of his resurrection and the sharing of his sufferings by becoming like him in his death, if somehow I may

---

[35] 1 Cor 15:24-26.

[36] 1 Cor 15:54-57; see also Eph 4:8.

[37] Rom 8:36-37.

[38] Rev 2:10-11.

[39] Rom 8:17-18. See also 2 Cor 6:4-11.

[40] 1 Tim 1:16; 2 Tim 1:12.

attain the resurrection from the dead."[41] This hope enabled Paul to 'rejoice' in his sufferings[42] and even to say, "dying is gain."[43] The hardships the early Christians endured paled in significance compared to their hope of resurrection. This hope of the resurrection gave the early Christians striking resilience against persecution.

Conclusion

The early Christians saw Jesus' resurrection as hugely important. They spoke and wrote of it often, in ways that suggest they considered it to be a central part of their teachings. Their belief in his resurrection appears to have provided them with crucial motivation to follow Jesus and continue his movement. It formed a central part of their preaching because they believed it could motivate others in the same way, proving that Jesus was right, and that it was worth following him to obtain a resurrection despite any cost. His resurrection ignited the early Christians' desire to follow him, their hope for resurrection, and their fearless loyalty to Jesus in the face of persecution.

---

[41] Phil 3:10-11.
[42] Col 1:24.
[43] Phil 1:20.

Part 4

Ideas throughout history

We have investigated the New Testament in order to build up a picture of Jesus' life and activity, the early Christian doctrines about salvation and their view of Jesus. Taken as a whole, this picture represents the early Christian paradigm of salvation. In this section, we will see that the early Christians in the period from about 100 AD to 313 AD continued to hold these same ideas. Next, we will outline some key changes from 313 AD through to the Reformation which moved Christian tradition away from the earlier ideas. Finally, we will review the salvation doctrines in the modern post-Reformation tradition, and discuss some key differences between that view and the original Christian paradigm of salvation.

Chapter 15

The early centuries

The generation of Christians immediately following the Apostles learned Christianity first-hand from the people that Jesus himself had taught. They in turn passed it on to the next generation. Thus, these early Christians were very well placed to learn Christian doctrines accurately. We have no reason to presume that Christians worldwide forgot the heart of the Christian message after the completion of the New Testament. The first significant cause for change did not come until 313 AD, when Emperor Constantine legalised Christianity within the Roman Empire. This decree set the stage for massive changes within Christianity during the 4th century AD and beyond. We will investigate those changes in the next chapter, but here we will focus on the period prior, from around 100 AD to 313 AD. In this period, we would expect Christians to have held theology substantially in agreement with the ideas of the New Testament authors.

Over 7,000 pages' worth of Christian writings survive from this historical period.[1] This huge resource of literature thus provides a strong independent verification of the view of the earliest Christians presented in previous chapters. We can compare the ideas in this literature with the core New Testament ideas we have outlined. If the Christian doctrines from this period match the interpretation of the New Testament outlined in the previous chapters, then they provide strong support for that interpretation. If instead they match poorly, then they would bring that interpretation into question.

When we compare these writings, we find a great deal of agreement with the New Testament doctrines we discussed earlier. This chapter shows that the Christians in the 2nd and 3rd centuries believed these same doctrines. They saw Jesus as a teacher of morality and virtue, who showed people how to live and who freed them from wrong ways of life. They, too, shared the same views on final judgment. They emphasised moral conduct as the heart of the Christian message, and called people to choose the Christian way of life. To show that the Christians from this period shared these views, we will draw from the

---

[1] The 10 volumes of the *Ante-Nicene Fathers*, an English translation of most of the Christian writings from this period, run to 6,500 pages.

work of several scholars who have studied the doctrines of this period in detail.

The Apostolic Fathers

The earliest group of surviving post-New Testament Christian writings, the writings of the Apostolic Fathers, date from around 100 AD to around 150 AD. A variety of Christians from many different parts of the Roman Empire wrote these fifteen different letters, sermons and books. Yet, despite their diversity, the theology expressed in these works does not vary widely and testifies to a unity within early Christian doctrine. They "all represent the same general type of Christianity."[2]

These writers considered following the teachings of Jesus paramount and they believed that, if they followed his teachings, God would judge them positively.[3] These writers called Jesus' teachings the 'new law' or simply 'the law'. They held "that salvation is to be had only by obeying God and doing his will."[4] In other words, they understood Christianity as "a divine law by keeping which a man may win eternal reward and escape eternal punishment."[5] All the Apostolic Fathers agreed that "The keeping of the law was the indispensable and sufficient condition of salvation."[6] As one scholar explains: "He that obeys the law will inherit eternal life; he that disobeys will suffer eternal punishment. Upon this the greatest emphasis was laid."[7] For the Apostolic Fathers, Christianity involved principally living in accordance with the moral law given by Jesus. Christianity was "a moral system based on divine sanctions... It was as a law that these Christians chiefly thought of Christianity."[8] For this reason, the Apostolic Fathers focused primarily on the new knowledge of how to live that Jesus had given,

---

[2] Arthur C. McGiffert, *A History of Christian Thought: Volume 1, Early and Eastern* (New York; London: C. Scribner's sons, 1932), p. 68.

[3] E.g. Didache 9.3, 10.2; 1 Clement 36.1-2.

[4] McGiffert, p. 85.

[5] McGiffert, p. 95. See for example Ignatius Ephesians 17.1-2.

[6] McGiffert, p. 80. See also Justo L. Gonzalez, *A History of Christian Thought Volume 1: From the Beginning to the Council of Chalcedon* (Nashville: Abingdon, 3rd ed., 1993), pp. 87 – 88 regarding the Shepherd of Hermas for some examples.

[7] McGiffert, p. 69.

[8] McGiffert, p. 68. See also Gonzalez, p. 88, regarding the Shepherd of Hermas for an example.

and, by extension, on the benefits of living by this new law.[9] They viewed the gift that Jesus had given to people "principally as the revelation of a new law (*nova lex*). Christ was taken to be the new lawgiver."[10] Another scholar observes the same thing: they thought of Jesus "chiefly as lawgiver and judge, a conception quite in line with the interpretation of Christianity as a divine law."[11] This 'divine law' was the Christian way of living taught by Jesus, a way in accordance with God's moral commandments. Another scholar summarises concisely the Christianity of the Apostolic Fathers, which he labels 'moralism':

> The Gospel was presented as a new law that Christ taught and by which He showed the way to salvation. ... The Christian life was said to consist, above all, in the obedience to this new law. ... There was a strong tendency among the Apostolic Fathers to emphasize obedience to the Law, as well as the imitation of Christ, as the way to salvation and the essential content of the Christian life.[12]

The Apostolic Fathers believed that final judgment depended on conduct, and that Jesus thus saved people from a negative judgment by teaching them how to live rightly. Several scholars have noted that they viewed Jesus' role and work in this way:

> At times, in all these writers, the saving efficacy of Christ's work is made to consist mainly – sometimes wholly – in His teaching.[13]

> The interpretation of the Redemption which Christ brought primarily in terms of knowledge, and of Christ first and foremost a Teacher, is especially characteristic of the Apostolic Fa-

---

[9] J. N. D. Kelly, *Early Christian Doctrines* (San Francisco: Harper Collins, 1978), p. 163. See for example 1 Clement 59.2.

[10] Jeurgen Neve and Otto Heick, *A History of Christian Thought* (Philadelphia, PA: Fortress, 1965), Vol. 1, p. 49. See also for example The Shepherd of Hermas 5.5.3, 8.3.2f; and Gonzalez, p. 94, regarding 1 Clement and The Shepherd of Hermas.

[11] McGiffert, p. 92.

[12] Bengt Hägglund (trans Gene J. Lund), *History of Theology* (St. Louis: Concordia, 1968), p. 16.

[13] Hastings Rashdall, *The Idea of Atonement in Christian Theology* (London: Macmillan, 1919), p. 198.

thers[14]... We can hardly overstress the importance in their writings of the idea of Christ the Teacher.[15]

We would expect exactly these observations from our early investigation of the New Testament, which showed the same focus on final judgment and correct conduct in accordance with Jesus' teachings and example.

The Apostolic Fathers thought of righteousness as moral virtue obtained by acting in accordance with the commandments of God. They conceived of righteousness "as the actual newness of the Christian life: the righteousness which a Christian does rather than that which he believes."[16] Righteousness for them always meant "an active, actual righteousness."[17] They did not see it as an imputed gift of God. One scholar notes:

> *Righteousness,* as a general rule, was described not as a gift of God bestowed on men of faith... but rather in terms of proper Christian behaviour. ... It is not unmerited grace that stands at the center of this teaching but rather the new way of life that Christ taught and which He empowers.[18]

They saw God's grace not as unmerited pardon, but as coming through the teachings that God gave them graciously through Jesus. Through this gift of grace, they could "strive after righteousness and walk in the way of the new obedience,"[19] and thus obtain a positive final judgment. The Apostolic Fathers used *pistis* ('faithfulness') to refer to fidelity to the one God (as opposed to other gods) and faithfulness to obey his commandments. They saw it "as a motive leading men to obey God and do his will, or leading them specifically to accept Christianity and live the Christian life."[20] God's law which he gave through Jesus centred

---

[14] H. E. W. Turner, *The Patristic Doctrine of Redemption: A Study of the Development of Doctrine During the First Five Centuries* (Eugene, OR: Wipf & Stock Publishers, 2004), p. 33.

[15] Turner, p. 43. See for example Barnabas 14.5; 2 Clement 20.5, 1.4-7; Ignatius *Magnesians* 9.1; *Ephesians* 1.1, 10.3, 17.1-2; *Magnesians* 10.1-2. 13.1; *Trallians* 1.2; *Philadelphians* 7.2.

[16] Heick, p. 51.

[17] Reinhold Seeberg, *Textbook of the History of Doctrines, Volume 1: History of Doctrines in the Ancient Church* (Grand Rapids: Baker, 1964), p. 78.

[18] Hägglund, p. 17.

[19] Hägglund, p. 18.

[20] McGiffert, p. 84.

upon love, and so faithfulness to God and Jesus involved primarily loving others. For this reason, the Apostolic Fathers often connected the ideas of 'faithfulness' and 'love.'[21] In general, these writings give love central importance. "Love is emphasized over and over in the writings we are dealing with. It occurs in all the lists of virtues, and is often spoken of as if it were the characteristic Christian virtue."[22]

The extent to which the ideas of the Apostolic Fathers differ from modern post-Reformation views amazes some modern historians. Such historians do not understand the early Christians' focus on correct conduct and their view of Jesus as Teacher because they fail to appreciate the basic ideas of their Christianity, which we have outlined in this book. Instead, these scholars attempt in vain to understand early Christian ideas through the lens of post-Reformation ideas. For example, one scholar writes:

> By this point some readers may be wondering why these apostolic fathers – or at least some of them – are included in the story of Christian theology as heroes of orthodoxy. Why not consider them heretics? Certainly compared to the gospel of grace, their message seems severely moralistic, focusing on conduct rather than mercy, and on salvation as a struggle rather than a gift.[23]

Post-Reformation theology, in particular, misreads the writings of Paul. As a result, some post-Reformation scholars see a huge divide between what they see as Paul's teachings and the teachings of the Apostolic Fathers:

> [In the Apostolic Fathers there is] an emphasis laid up on right conduct, and upon works of obedience, which is somewhat in contrast with the manner of St. Paul when he is defining the method of justification... This peculiarity of the early Christian writers, it is worth while to reiterate, springs from no conscious dissatisfaction with the teaching of St. Paul."[24]

---

[21] G. P. Fisher, *History of Christian Doctrine* (Edinburgh-Clark, 2nd ed., 1949), p. 43.

[22] McGiffert, p. 80.

[23] Roger E. Olson, *The Story of Christian Theology: Twenty Centuries of Tradition & Reform* (Downers Grove, IL: InterVasity Press, 1999), p. 52; also p. 41.

[24] Fisher, pp. 42 – 43.

The Christian church in the 2ⁿᵈ century AD had nothing resembling the doctrine of original sin as many post-Reformation Christians know it today (a subject to which we will return later). The Apostolic Fathers had little to say on the subject. As one scholar notes: "their writings are characterized by an almost complete absence of preoccupation with the Fall and its consequences."[25] Only *Barnabas* of the Apostolic Fathers references the Fall,[26] and he believed that children were born sinless.[27] The authors of this early period believed universally that children are born innocent of the sin of Adam, that people incur guilt only for their own sins, and that every person has the God-given power of free will to do good or evil. Many modern scholars also express amazement at the lack of post-Reformation ideas about the significance of Jesus' death. For example, the works *Didache*, *2 Clement* and *Shepherd of Hermas* do not mention any connection whatsoever between Christ's death and salvation despite dealing with repentance, forgiveness and salvation at length.[28] *First Clement* presents instead both Christ's suffering and his death as examples.[29] After studying their writings, one scholar remarks: "The most astonishing feature [of all the Apostolic Fathers] was the failure to grasp the significance of the death of Christ."[30] Another scholar notes reluctantly that in *First Clement*, "It is difficult to see any place for Christ in the Christian salvation beyond that of a preacher of the 'grace of repentance.'"[31]

In our view, these early Christians actually understood the original Christian message well, but many modern scholars misunderstand it due to the widespread influence of post-Reformation theology. The Apostolic Fathers believed they followed the teachings of St Paul and the Apostles closely, as many of their writings explain. Furthermore, they had a much better prospect of correctly understanding the original Christian teaching, as they had been taught by the Apostles or by those that followed them, wrote in the same language and had a very similar culture. There is no reason to believe that the Apostolic Fathers failed to understand Christianity, and many reasons to think that they preserved faithfully the doctrines of the earliest Christians. Importantly, their

---

[25] Turner, p. 71.

[26] Barnabas 12.5.

[27] Barnabas 6.11.

[28] Rashdall, p. 190.

[29] 1 Clem 2.1, 16f. See also Kelly, p. 165, for discussion.

[30] Thomas F. Torrance, *The Doctrine of Grace in the Apostolic Fathers* (Grand Rapids, MI: Eerdmans, 1959), p. 137.

[31] Torrance, p. 46.

writings agree substantially with the key New Testament doctrines we have outlined previously in this book.

The Apologists

The next group of early Christian writers, known as 'the Apologists', wrote during the 2nd century AD. The name comes from the Greek word for 'defence speech'; *apologia*. These writers have this name because they published works in defence of Christianity. They directed their writings to the Emperor or the public to explain and defend Christian doctrines, so that the Roman Empire might accept Christians and their beliefs. Their writings provide important insights into the teachings of early Christianity. They wrote to non-Christian audiences, and thus explained Christianity more clearly and systematically than did those who wrote for Christian readers. Generally, their works dealt with doctrinal issues at much greater length than the Apostolic Fathers, and they explained, argued and defended their positions.

The dozen or so different Apologists all explained Christianity in very similar ways, so few scholars bother to distinguish individual Apologists when discussing their ideas. Justin Martyr authored the lengthiest surviving works in this group, so scholars commonly consider him representative of all the Apologists. The other Apologists "represent in the main the same general type of Christianity as Justin's."[32] Furthermore, the theology of the Apologists differed little from that of the Apostolic Fathers – a fact hardly surprising given that they wrote around the same time period. Like the Apostolic Fathers, the Apologists saw Christianity "as a way or code of conduct."[33] One scholar explains:

> The general conception of Christianity was the same with all the Apologists however much they differed in detail, and what is even more significant it was for the most part identical with that of the Apostolic Fathers with whom we have already studied.[34] ... [Their] conception of Christianity was in line with that of the [Apostolic] Fathers... To them Christianity was a divine

---

[32] McGiffert, p. 122.
[33] Turner, p. 115.
[34] McGiffert, p. 96.

law to which was attached the promise of salvation for those
observing the law.[35]

Like the earlier groups of Christians we have examined, the Apologists emphasised the final judgment heavily and stressed that God
would judge people based on their conduct. They gave this idea utmost
importance, and it formed the basis of their moral exhortations to
repent and follow Jesus.[36] Indeed, this doctrine provided the foundation
of their Christianity. One scholar explains it this way:

> Above all they wished to show that God demands virtue and
> that he will reward the good and punish the wicked. In this
> they found the essence and most of them the whole of Christi-
> anity.[37]

The Apologists understood Jesus' role and work in light of this final
judgment based on correct conduct. They viewed Jesus in a way
consistent with what we find in the New Testament and the Apostolic
Fathers. They saw him as a teacher of moral virtue, who taught them a
new code of conduct by which to live rightly. Several scholars have
noted that, in the writings of the Apologists:

> Christ was the revealer of the new law, obedience to which was
> necessary to salvation.[38]

> Christ is above all the teacher of a new morality or of the true
> philosophy...[39] [The Apologists] speak of Christ almost exclu-
> sively as a teacher and illuminator.[40]

> [Christ's] chief vocation as Savior was to teach men the truth
> about monotheism and the moral life.[41]

---

[35] McGiffert, p. 120.

[36] McGiffert, p. 124.

[37] McGiffert, p. 123. See also McGiffert, p. 101.

[38] McGiffert, p. 104.

[39] Justo L. Gonzalez, A History of Christian Thought Volume 1: From the
Beginning to the Council of Chalcedon (Nashville: Abingdon, 3rd ed., 1993), p.
119.

[40] Gonzalez, pp. 119 – 120 .

[41] Jaroslav Pelikan, The Christian Tradition: A history of the Development of Doctrine
(Chicago: University of Chicago Press, Vol. 1), p. 153. See also Seeberg, p. 115.

Another scholar explains that Justin Martyr understood Jesus' mission and role principally as that of a teacher. Jesus illuminated the moral law by which people should live, and imparted to them this saving knowledge.[42] The Apologists, like the Apostolic Fathers, viewed what Jesus achieved in terms of enlightenment.[43] They often called Jesus the *Logos* ('Word'), who through his moral teachings and example brought virtue to humanity. In Greek philosophy, the *Logos* functioned as an intermediary between God and humanity who communicated knowledge about God and morality to humanity. The Apologists drew on this term and applied it to Jesus to explain their ideas about him as God's appointed teacher.[44]

Since the Apologists believed firmly that final judgment depended on conduct, and that the Christian message concerned living correctly, they also stressed that people had a real choice about the way in which to live.[45] Like the Apostolic Fathers, the Apologists saw righteousness as correct conduct. They believed that people had a choice between improper conduct and the way of life Jesus had taught. They defended this Christian concept of free will vigorously against the Gnostic ideas of human depravity and original sin,[46] and also against the Roman ideas of fate and predestination.[47] They defended the idea of free will because if people had no free moral choice, the final judgment based on their moral conduct would be unjust. As one scholar explains:

> All men, Justin maintained, are endowed with free will and hence can live righteously if they choose to do so. Upon this he was very insistent... If a man's character is due to God it is not his own and deserves neither reward nor punishment.[48]

In emphasising people's choice between right and wrong conduct, the Apologists in no way undermined the necessity of Jesus' work. They believed that, first and foremost, salvation came through the teachings of righteousness that Jesus gave to humanity. Indeed, God's 'grace' towards them involved largely this revelation of his teaching.[49] They

---

[42] Kelly, pp. 168 – 169. See Justin, *Dialogue* 11.2, 18.3, 43.1, 51.3.

[43] Kelly, p. 169.

[44] Hägglund, p. 29.

[45] McGiffert, p. 125.

[46] Bernhard Lohse, *A Short History of Christian Doctrine* (Philadelphia, PA: Fortress Press, 1966), p. 104.

[47] Heick, p. 62; Fisher, p. 66.

[48] McGiffert, p. 101.

[49] Seeberg, p. 116.

emphasised confidently, however, the role of human effort in salvation, and did not shy away from stressing the role of the individual in living rightly and attaining a positive judgment. This emphasis led one scholar to over-exaggerate with the comment that "Justin thought of salvation as man's own achievement."[50] The Apologists emphasised both our need for Jesus' teaching and also our need to obey it as the means of salvation. As one scholar explained, they believed that God gave people the choice "to embrace Christ and live virtuously if they will and thus win eternal life."[51]

As a consequence of these ideas surrounding judgment, Jesus' role and free will, the Apologists emphasised repentance as the first step in becoming a Christian. One scholar summarises their idea of repentance in this way:

> The first thing needed is the conviction that God demands virtue and that he will reward and punish men according to their deserts. This conviction leads to repentance which is the beginning of the Christian life. Repentance is rewarded by divine forgiveness for all past sins. Thus the slate is wiped clean and a man is enabled to start on the Christian life with nothing against him. Repentance and forgiveness must be followed by a life of virtue or obedience to God.[52]

Once people repented of their old way of life, God forgave them, and they then lived virtuous lives as Christians. Baptism served to mark their repentance, their commitment to a new life, and the associated forgiveness. Thus, it cleared the way "to obtain the rewards of heaven through a course of obedience."[53]

In essence, we can summarise the Christianity presented by Justin Martyr and the other Apologists in four main doctrines:

1. Only one true God exists (monotheism).
2. Jesus came as God's teacher of correct conduct.
3. A final judgment based on conduct will occur.
4. People have the free will to choose their conduct.

---

[50] McGiffert, p. 105.
[51] McGiffert, p. 105.
[52] McGiffert, pp. 102 – 103.
[53] Fisher, p. 68.

The Apologists defended these doctrines, which together constitute largely what they saw as 'Christianity'. One scholar explains:

> The essential content of revealed philosophy is viewed by the Apologists... as comprised in three doctrines. First, there is one spiritual and inexpressibly exalted God, who is Lord and Father of the world. Secondly, he requires a holy life. Thirdly, he will at last sit in judgment, and will reward the good with immortality and punish the wicked with death. The teaching concerning God, virtue, and eternal reward is traced to the prophets and Christ; but the bringing about of a virtuous life (of righteousness) has been necessarily left by God to men themselves; for God has created man free, and virtue can only be acquired by man's own efforts. The prophets and Christ are therefore a source of righteousness in so far as they are teachers.[54]

The Apologists thus defended clearly the core Christian doctrines and paradigm that we have outlined throughout this book. They even died as willing martyrs because of their commitment to these ideas.

Theologians

In the period from 160 AD through to 313 AD, several Christians wrote theological works hundreds of pages in length. These writers covered a wide variety of issues, and the volume of their writings leaves us with few doubts about their general ideas. Some of these writers grew up within Christian families, while others converted to Christianity as adults. Some wrote in Latin and some wrote in Greek, reflecting the geographical diversity of these writers around the Roman Empire. These theologians all reaffirmed the basic ideas we have already outlined, as we shall see.

Irenaeus (~130 – 200 AD) came originally from Turkey, but seems to have spent much of his adult life in Rome, finally travelling to France as a missionary. Unfortunately, he used imaginative metaphors and difficult language frequently, which makes him the most difficult of the early church writers to understand.[55] Irenaeus presented a theological

---

[54] Adolf von Harnack (trans. Neil Buchanan), *History of Dogma* (New York: Dover Publications, 1961, Vol. 2), p. 203. Similar summaries are provided by Seeberg, p.115; McGiffert, p. 101; and McGiffert p. 131, c.f. p. 128.

[55] "It is difficult to discover from his writing where metaphor is supposed to end, and sober fact to begin." (Rashdall, p. 246)

paradigm that God originally created people as spiritually child-like, and desired them to grow and mature in Christ-likeness. Adam's sin was a step in the wrong direction.[56] Yet Irenaeus did not view the Fall as very serious for humanity. As one scholar put it, he held "a 'light' doctrine of the Fall and its effects."[57] Irenaeus believed that God required obedience to his instructions and saw Christ as an example of that obedience.[58] Jesus led people into godly obedience through his teaching and example. Irenaeus held that "God regards as righteous everyone who acknowledges Christ and is ready to follow his teaching."[59] In Irenaeus' writings, "there are traces of the 'moralism' of the Apologists, which exalts the teaching element in Christianity and makes everything depend on the free choice of the path of obedience."[60] Irenaeus held to the same concept of repentance, forgiveness and righteous living laid out by other Christians of this period.[61] Like the Christians writers before him, he emphasised strongly the concept of free will and stressed that humans controlled their own destiny.[62] According to Irenaeus, *pistis* (faithfulness) is about doing God's will.[63]

Clement of Alexandria (~150 – 215 AD) was one of the first leaders of a Christian seminary in Egypt. Clement held the same general theological views as the other writers we have discussed. He believed firmly in a final judgment according to people's conduct. Right living thus had paramount importance, and he saw Jesus as a teacher who instructed people in how to live rightly.[64] Jesus also provided an important role model, and by imitating him people could avoid sinning.[65] People became righteous in God's sight by following Jesus' teachings and example. Several scholars have noted this clear teaching by Clement:

> [Christ's] activity as the *Paidagogus* or Teacher of the human race is central to his thought.[66]

---

[56] Kelly, p. 171.
[57] Turner, p. 74.
[58] Kelly, p. 174.
[59] Seeberg, p. 132.
[60] Fisher, p. 88.
[61] McGiffert, p. 137.
[62] Heick, p. 110; McGiffert, p. 137.
[63] Heick, p. 110. See Irenaeus, *Against Heresies* 4.6.5.
[64] McGiffert, p. 179.
[65] Clement, *Paed* 1.3.7.
[66] Turner, p. 40, cf p. 45, 79. Emphasis added on the Greek term.

> Clement is equally fond of speaking of Christ as the Teacher and the Saviour. And the two words mean for him much the same thing, for it is mainly by His teaching and His influence that Christ saves.[67]

> His most frequent and characteristic thought is that Christ is the teacher Who endows men with true knowledge, leading them to [love and righteousness].[68]

> The Logos [Word] instructs men in the way of righteousness and so saves them. ... it is quite clear that he was really interested in Christ only as the Logos [Word], or as an instructor. The Logos took on flesh and appeared in Jesus Christ that he might influence them to choose the way of life instead of death. ... On earth the Logos simply continued the work he had always been doing, the work of a teacher or revealer.[69]

Clement insisted that people could choose freely how to live,[70] since this idea went hand in hand with his view of Jesus as a teacher. "Clement laid the greatest emphasis on the freedom of the will. ... If he [man] makes the right choice and lives as he should he will be saved, otherwise not."[71] Clement saw that for salvation people needed not only the teachings of Jesus but also the self-discipline with which to obey them. With regard to that self-discipline, Clement wrote, "God desires us to be saved by our own efforts."[72] He viewed this process of salvation as entirely possible, since "the doctrine of original sin played no part in Clement's thinking."[73] Like Irenaeus, Clement believed that people began life as spiritually child-like, so that they would gradually mature towards the ideal of Jesus.[74] From this perspective, he saw Adam as "the typical example of sin, rather than the foundation whence it is spread through the race."[75] He insisted that a new-born baby that

---

[67] Rashdall, p. 225. See also Kelly, p. 183.

[68] Kelly, p. 183.

[69] McGiffert , pp. 198-201. See also Seeberg, pp. 143-144.

[70] Gonzalez, p. 203.

[71] McGiffert, p. 197, 200.

[72] Clement, *Stromata* 6.12.96.

[73] McGiffert, p. 198.

[74] Kelly, p. 179.

[75] Fisher, p. 96.

has done nothing has not fallen under the curse of Adam,[76] and that children enter the world exempt from sin.[77]

Like the earlier Christian writers we have already examined, Clement interpreted Jesus' death as exemplary and not of core importance. Scholars have commented on this:

> When the sufferings of Christ are dwelt upon it is always either for the purpose of increasing our sense of Christ's goodness, or by way of example. … much more stress is laid upon the saving work of the Logos in guiding and healing souls by means of reward and punishment, and upon the life and characters, the teaching and example of the Logos in His incarnate life, than upon any effect of His death: he even explains the blood of Christ to mean knowledge.[78]

> He views the Cross, in connection with his general outlook, as the supreme martyrdom, making a moral appeal to the hearts of men and inspiring Christ's followers to suffer as he suffered.[79]

Tertullian (155 – 230 AD) worked as a lawyer and lived in North Africa. He wrote in Latin, unlike the authors we have studied previously, but despite this language difference he presented a theology very similar to those of the writers before him. Like them, he understood Jesus almost solely as a teacher of righteous living, whose instructions and example people could obey in order to obtain salvation. For Tertullian, "Christ is pre-eminently the bringer and interpreter of the new law."[80] Another scholar noted this:

> There is a distinct tendency in Tertullian to reduce Christ's achievement to 'the proclamation of a new law and a new promise of the kingdom of heaven', and to represent Him as 'the illuminator and instructor of mankind'.[81]

---

[76] Clement, *Stromata* 3.10.100.

[77] Clement, *Stromata* 4.25.160.

[78] Rashdall, pp. 222 – 223. On p. 230, Rashdall notes that Clement also did not suggest any link between Jesus' death and forgiveness.

[79] Laurence W. Grensted, *A Short History of the Doctrine of the Atonement* (Manchester University Press, 1962), p. 26.

[80] Heick, p. 128.

[81] Kelly, p. 177. Tertullian, *De praescr* 13; *Apol* 21.

For Tertullian, the gospel was about this new law.[82] He placed importance on it because by following this law a person could gain positive
judgment from God and eternal life. As one scholar explains:

> Tertullian... presented Christ as the teacher who proclaims a
> new law (*nova lex*), thereby strengthening man's free will so that
> he can live according to God's commands. ... Salvation, said
> Tertullian, is given as a reward for human merit. Good deeds as
> well as evil must be recompensed by God.[83]

Tertullian believed that repentance brought forgiveness. Baptism
marked this repentance and forgiveness, and also marked the start of a
new way of life lived according to Jesus' teachings.[84] Tertullian
emphasised "in the strongest manner the freedom of man's will."[85]
People had the freedom to choose either correct conduct or improper
conduct[86] – they possessed freedom to live in the way that Jesus taught.
This idea of free will mattered greatly to Tertullian because final
judgment depended on conduct and Jesus taught people how to live
rightly. "The Fall was not regarded as destroying human freedom of the
will."[87] Thus, people had the capacity to live in a way that God
considered righteous and attain positive judgement. Like the other
writers of this period, Tertullian held that we do not share in Adam's
guilt,[88] and that children begin their lives as innocent.[89] Tertullian
understood *pistis* (faithfulness) in a way similar to that of earlier
Christian writers. He used pistis to refer to a faithful commitment to
Christ and obedience of his teachings.[90]

Origen (~185 – 254 AD) spent much of his life in Egypt and probably taught at the seminary there. Origen authored a *huge* number of
works, including commentaries on most of the books of the Bible.

For Origen, a final judgment according to conduct formed a key
part of the apostolic teaching. For example, he wrote:

---

[82] Gonzalez, p. 174.

[83] Hägglund, p. 56.

[84] Heick, p. 129.

[85] Seeberg, p. 123. See also Lohse, p. 104.

[86] Fisher, p. 93; Heick, p. 128.

[87] J. F. Bethune-Baker, *An Introduction to the Early History of Christian Doctrine to
the Time of the Council of Chalcedon* (London: Methuen, 1958), pp. 305 – 306.

[88] Kelly, p. 175.

[89] Fisher, p. 93. E.g. Tertullian, *On Baptism* 18.

[90] Heick, p. 129.

The apostolic teaching is that the soul, having a substance and life of its own, shall, after its departure from the world, be rewarded according to its deserts, being destined to obtain either an inheritance of eternal life and blessedness, if its actions shall have procured this for it, or to be delivered up to eternal fire and punishments, if the guilt of its crimes shall have brought it down to this.[91]

Hence, Origen focussed on the way in which humans grow in godly virtue, and he saw Jesus as a teacher sent to help them mature in this way.[92] Jesus taught people how to direct their lives in order to be saved.[93] Origen saw Jesus primarily as a teacher, law-giver and role-model.[94] Several scholars have noted this in Origen's writings:

> In order to promote human salvation the Logos or Son of God became incarnate that he might be seen by men and might show them by example as well as precept the way of life. ... The saving work of Christ, the incarnate Logos, was commonly represented by Origen as a work of instruction. Christ showed men the will of God by teaching and example, telling them of the future rewards and punishments to follow on obedience or disobedience.[95]

> If we inquire for the work of Christ, we find the dominant thought to be, that Christ was physician, teacher, lawgiver, and example. ... We have here the conception of the work of Christ which was characteristic of the second and third centuries... Christ is, above all else, the teacher and lawgiver, the pattern, in whom begins the deification of humanity.[96]

Origen saw Jesus' death as part of his mission to teach humanity righteousness through his example. Origen explained, "by his endurance of death, he gave men an example which teaches us to resist sins even to the point of death."[97]

---

[91] Origen, *De Principiis*, preface 5.

[92] E.g. Origen, *De Principiis*, 3.1.15.

[93] Gonzalez, p. 223.

[94] Kelly, p. 184. Origen, *De Princ* 4.1.2, 4.2.12, 4.4.4; *C. Cels* 1.68, 2.52, 3.7,8.17.

[95] McGiffert, pp. 225-226.

[96] Seeberg, p. 153, 155.

[97] Origen, *Commentary on Romans* 4.12.4.

One of Origen's important works, *On First Principles,* is the oldest surviving work of systematic theology. In the preface he laid out what Christians at the time considered essential doctrines passed down from earlier Christians. He gave six doctrines:[98]

1. The Father, Son, and Spirit exist, and have certain characteristics.
2. A final judgment according to conduct will occur.
3. People have free will to act rightly or wrongly.
4. The Devil and his angels exist, as do good angels.
5. The world had a beginning and will have an ending.
6. Scripture is inspired by God.

In his first sentence of this book, he stated that Christians "derive the knowledge which incites men to a good and happy life from no other source than from the very words and teaching of Christ." Origen said that these six ideas above were the undisputed teachings of the church passed down by the Apostles. One scholar summarised these core ideas as follows:

> … The knowledge and worship of the One God, the Creator; faith in Jesus; the fulfilling of his commandments in a virtuous life; the promise of salvation and threatening of eternal ruin. To this is added the life of Christ as the "model of a virtuous life," particularly as a pattern in the endurance of suffering.[99]

Like earlier Christians, Origen understood righteousness as correct conduct and repentance as a true change in conduct. One scholar explains Origen's view:

> The only way in which a bad man can justly be freed from punishment by a good and just God is by his being induced to repent and so to become actually good. Justification to Origen means simply the being made actually righteous. The incarnation of the Word, the example and teaching of Christ, the life which is shown by His incarnation and His voluntary death, the influence which He continues to exercise over the hearts of men through His Church, help to produce this effect.[100]

---

[98] Origen, *De Principiis,* preface.
[99] Seeberg, p. 153.
[100] Rashdall, p. 273. See Origen, *Commentary on Romans* 2.1, 6.12.

Origen believed that humans had true free will and could become righteous by choosing to follow Jesus' teachings and example. For Origen, Clement and Irenaeus, "the chief premises of the doctrine of original sin... was largely absent from their thinking."[101] Origen recognised that habits and temptations meant that people needed to practise constant diligence in order to conduct themselves rightly.[102] He recognised that Christ-like virtue required effort from the individual[103] and encouraged his readers to make such an effort.

Hippolytus (d. 235 AD) lived in Rome. He defended and maintained traditional doctrines and practices as a conservative theologian, and his theology differed little from that of the writers we have already discussed. In his major work, he portrayed Jesus primarily as a teacher who gives people the 'knowledge of God.'[104] This knowledge did not mean mere information about God, but rather instruction in the correct way in which to live. Through this knowledge, people can escape judgment and gain immortality, since they can become more like Jesus by obeying his teachings and example.[105] Hippolytus reveals how much importance his contemporary Christians gave to correct conduct by describing the process they followed before accepting new converts. People who made an initial commitment to Christianity had their conduct carefully monitored for a three-year period, during which time they learned correct Christian living. They had to demonstrate over the course of this time that they had completely repented of their old way of life and had become completely faithful to Christ's teachings. Only if they did so would the leaders baptise and initiate them as full Christians.[106]

Cyprian (d. 258 AD) lived in modern-day Tunisia, North Africa, and was another conservative Christian leader. Around this time, the church had suffered sporadic outbreaks of persecution from the Romans. Many Christians avoided persecution by claiming they were not Christians when questioned by the authorities. They performed whatever actions the authorities demanded as proof of this, such as sacrificing to pagan gods. Cyprian, however, thought that Christians should remain honest and faithful despite persecution. He thought that the church should exclude those who claimed publicly not to be Christians.

---

[101] Kelly, pp. 178 – 179.
[102] McGiffert, p. 225. See Origen, *De Principiis*, Preface 5.
[103] Rashdall, pp. 269 – 271.
[104] Kelly, p. 178. See Hippolytus, *In Dan* 4.41.
[105] Hippolytus, *Refutation of All Heresies* 10.34.
[106] Hippolytus, *The Apostolic Tradition* 16-20.

A variety of his letters and books survive. One scholar explains that Cyprian "presents Christ as the teacher of truth Who bestows 'a new law' and reinforces it through His own example."[107] In Cyprian's view, "God now endeavours to deliver men from sin and death. This is first attempted through the [Jewish] law, but finally through Christ, who as teacher of the truth gives a 'new law' and makes it impressive by his example."[108] Cyprian's writings also clearly contain the key themes of a final judgment based on conduct, Jesus as a teacher, and the importance of correct conduct. One scholar summarises Cyprian's views:

> Baptism brings forgiveness of sins and blots out sin in a man; he is now equipped with the Spirit and fulfils the law of God, because he believes that God will reward this struggle to live virtuously and will bestow upon him eternal life. By good works, man really wins for himself a merit before God… He who performs the works of the law is righteous before God.[109]

Cyprian did express some views on baptism and forgiveness that departed from previous teaching, which we will investigate further in the next chapter. Yet, for the most part, his writings reaffirm the widespread Christian views on Jesus, final judgment, and correct conduct.

Methodius (d. 311 AD) worked as a Christian bishop in Turkey and wrote a small number of works. He opposed strongly some of Origen's more creative ideas, and criticised his views on the nature of the resurrection body. Methodius emphasised both the idea of Christ as an example and the importance of temperance and moral living.[110] In teaching these ideas, he maintained the earlier Christian tradition.

Lactantius (~240 – 320 AD) came originally from North Africa, but travelled around the Roman Empire teaching rhetoric. To defend against pagan critics, he wrote an important 200-page systematic theology of Christianity – the oldest surviving systematic theology written in Latin.[111] Lactantius wrote remarkably clearly, making his works very easy to read and understand. He also noted, justifiably, that several earlier Christian writers had not written very clearly. His systematic theology has much in common with the earlier Christian tradition. He dealt at length with the work of Christ, explaining the

---

[107] Kelly, p. 178. See Cyprian, *de op et eleem* 1, 7; *de laps* 21; *de dom or* 15, 28.
[108] Seeberg, p. 193.
[109] Seeberg, p. 195.
[110] Rashdall, p. 292.
[111] Lactantius, *Divine Institutes*.

nature of Jesus as a teacher of moral virtue who strengthened his teaching through his example.[112] He saw Jesus as a teacher and example, and saw these roles as the entire work of Christ. He dealt with Christ's death at length, and explained how the example of his death inspires us to remain steadfast and hold to our moral life when faced with persecution and death. In Lactantius' view, "Both the incarnation and the death upon the cross find their purpose completely attained in instruction and example."[113] The earliest Apostolic Fathers had written of Christians imitating the death of Christ, and Lactantius did likewise. He wrote that Christ died in a way "by which the humble and low usually suffer, that there might be no one at all who might not be able to imitate Him."[114] In discussing Jesus' lifestyle as an example to imitate, he rejected explicitly the claim that humans cannot live like Jesus. He even went so far as to cite himself as an example of someone who lived like Jesus.[115] Lactantius emphasised repeatedly that eternal salvation depends on whether we live morally virtuous lives, and wrote: "He has given us this present life, that we may either lose that true and eternal life by our vices, or win it by virtue."[116] We can summarise the doctrines that Lactantius presented at length in a few simple points:

1. Monotheism, one creator God.
2. Jesus, teacher of virtue, both human and divine.
3. The importance of humans living virtuously.
4. Eternal judgment based on conduct.

We have seen these points set forth time and again by all the various Christian writers throughout this period. All the Christian writers affirmed them, none denied them, and they repeatedly claimed that these represented the core content of Christianity.

Summary

All the orthodox Christian writers in the period 100 – 313 AD seem to have agreed on the core doctrines of Christianity. In this period, Christian doctrine revolved around the ideas of a final judgment based

---

[112] Kelly, p. 178. See Lactantius, *Divine Institutes* 4.10.1, 4.11.14, 4.15.1, 4.14.15, 4.24.1, 4.24.6.
[113] Seeberg, p. 193.
[114] Lactantius, *Divine Institutes* 4.26.
[115] Lactantius, *Divine Institutes* 4.24.10; cf. Turner, p. 35.
[116] Lactantius, *Divine Institutes* 7.5.

on conduct and the importance of that conduct. Christians saw Jesus as a teacher of moral virtue and as an example of moral living, and believed that these two roles encapsulated Jesus' work. By following his example and teachings, they expected a positive final judgment. As one scholar explains about the Christian ideas of this period:

> It is clear that meditation on the life and teachings of Jesus was a major preoccupation of the piety and doctrine of the Church [of the second century]... Christ as example and Christ as teacher were constant and closely related doctrinal themes... [A common teaching was] salvation through the obedience to the teachings of Christ and through imitation of his example. ... the work of Christ was represented as that of the exemplar and teacher who brought the true revelation of God's will for man.[117]

Another scholar agrees: "We are on firm ground in treating the concept of Christ the Example, Teacher, and Illuminator as the starting-point in our study of the patristic doctrine of Redemption."[118]

The Christian writers in the 100 – 313 AD period supported and defended these core ideas with several other teachings. They all emphasised that people have the freedom to choose their conduct as they wish, since otherwise God's judgments based on their conduct would not be warranted. They believed that the Fall did not remove human free will nor render everyone guilty before God. They stressed that people can indeed attain real righteousness before God through diligent effort to follow Jesus' teachings and example. Indeed, they saw this as a requirement for salvation. They saw Christ's martyrdom as an example to imitate figuratively or even literally in the face of opposition. Above all, they stressed love as the primary moral virtue taught by Christ and the primary characteristic of Christian life. Christians had the responsibility to grow in Christ-likeness, and the church had the responsibility to guide them in this. With the exception of Cyprian, these writers all believed that the repentance at conversion brought God's forgiveness, and that baptism signified this forgiveness. God would forgive further serious sins through repentance. If a Christian persisted in serious sin, however, then it would bring into question the sincerity of his or her repentance and thus salvation.

---

[117] Pelikan, pp. 142 – 152.
[118] Turner, p. 46.

The writings of Christian leaders from the close of the New Testament era to the legalisation of Christianity in 313 AD attest consistently and uniformly to these ideas, with only minor variations. We outlined earlier the teachings of Jesus and the New Testament writers. Now, we have seen that the entire orthodox church also taught these same ideas in the first two centuries after the writing of the New Testament. Furthermore, they believed that the Bible taught these ideas. These writers believed that they followed faithfully the teachings of Paul and the New Testament, and they quoted from these sources thousands of times. This agreement between the New Testament authors and Christian writers from the two centuries following supports strongly the New Testament paradigm that we have outlined throughout this book. Such a view appears to be an accurate interpretation of both the New Testament and the teaching of the early Christians.

Chapter 16

Changes through history

Anyone familiar with typical post-Reformation doctrines will notice that they differ strikingly from the early Christian paradigm outlined so far. This observation prompts the question: how did these differences come about? In this chapter, we seek to trace briefly some major developments in the doctrines of salvation that seem to have led to these differences. Let us begin by recalling four key ideas that had remained largely unchanged up to the beginning of the 4th century:

The role of Jesus	Jesus came as God's appointed teacher and example of correct conduct (righteousness), who saved people from sinfulness.
Human conduct	People have free will and can follow his teachings and example, leading God to consider them righteous.
God's forgiveness	God will freely forgive the former sins of the righteous because of their repentance.
God's judgment	God will base final judgment on conduct and judge the righteous positively.

Early extensions of Jesus' role

Theological study blossomed in the Eastern Roman (*Byzantine*) Empire during the 4th and 5th centuries AD. The major doctrines of salvation taught by earlier Christian writers remained universally taught. Some new ideas developed, however, and Christians added two additional key ideas to the existing concept of salvation – Christus Victor and Spiritual Union.

Christus Victor

It seems that, during the 4th century, theologians became interested in how, and in what ways, Christ had 'overcome Satan'. Earlier

Christian writers had discussed how Christ had overcome Satan when tempted, and had also seen the cross and resurrection as a defeat of Satan's rule. They had written of converts who followed Jesus' teachings, turned from sinfulness to lives of virtue, and thus became free from Satan's power over their lives. During the Byzantine period, interest in the role of Satan increased because theologians thought he had some kind of power over humanity. Many Christian writers of this era thought that Christ's victory had either defeated Satan or rescued people from his power. Two main perspectives of the Christus Victor theme emerged:

Conquest of Satan. Some people thought that Christ had overthrown Satan's power by conquering him in a great spiritual battle that occurred between Christ's death and resurrection. Writers portrayed him marching into Hades wielding a sword and destroying the armies of Satan. Eusebius for example, used vivid imagery to depict such events:

> He charged into the midst of the devil and his array of daemons, trod upon asp and basilisk, trampled on lion and dragon, and destroyed the thousands and ten thousands of enemies that had ruled so long, some fighting on His right hand, some on His left, rulers and powers, and those too who are called "World-rulers of this darkness," and spiritual powers of evil.[1]

Such vivid images of cosmic warfare against the demonic forces seem to have gained wide popularity, yet they did not detract from the concept of Christ as a teacher of righteousness. Eusebius began his work from which the above quote comes by speaking of Jesus as "a teacher of true knowledge of God" who called men to "hear His divine and perfect teaching about true holiness." Eusebius added that the Jewish prophets had looked forward to a time when "every nation and race of men would know God, escape from the daemons, cease from ignorance and deceit and enjoy the light of holiness." These Jewish prophets "could picture the disciples of Christ filling the whole world with their teaching, and the preaching of their gospel introducing among all men a fresh and unknown ideal of holiness."[2] These ideas of Eusebius reflect a concern about moral conduct consistent with the earlier Christian tradition.

---

[1] Eusebius, *Proof of the Gospel,* 9.7.
[2] Eusebius, *Proof of the Gospel,* 1.1.

Rescue from Satan's power. Some people thought that Satan had power over the souls of humanity in the afterlife. One popular idea emerged: that Jesus had rescued people from Satan's power, freeing them from his rule in the afterlife. People had different ideas about why Satan had such power in the first place. Some writers suggested that God would hand over sinful humans to Satan. Others suggested that, since Satan had sinned first, subsequent sinners naturally fell under his power. Still others thought that Satan had struck a bargain with God in which Satan gained control over the souls of sinners. In any case, these Christian writers considered Satan's control over human souls in the afterlife a serious problem. Their ideas about how Jesus freed people from Satan's power varied. Some suggested that after Jesus died on the cross, Satan reached out to take his soul, but in doing so over-extended his authority, since Jesus had not sinned. As a consequence, Satan lost his authority completely, and all humanity gained freedom. Other Christians suggested that God entered into a deal with Satan, offering to trade the soul of Jesus in exchange for all human souls, and Satan accepted greedily because he so valued Jesus. But then, after the trade, God raised Jesus from the dead and left Satan with nothing. In another version of this idea, the human form of Jesus masked his divinity, and Satan tried to take Jesus' soul without realizing his divinity. Jesus' divine nature destroyed Satan's power and left him with nothing. This idea portrayed Jesus as the metaphorical bait swallowed by the Devil.[3] These theories of how Jesus ransomed humanity from Satan made for popular stories and exciting sermons.

These two versions of the Christus Victor theme outlined above, conquest of Satan and rescue from Satan's power, only became popular after the 3rd century. One scholar notes that Christian writings in the 2nd century AD show "little trace of the idea of ransom from the devil as it unfolded in the writings of some later Fathers."[4] The Christus Victor themes likely grew out of earlier ideas. The semi-Christian sect of Marcionism which originated around 140 AD popularised one earlier idea, teaching that the Jewish creator-god was an evil demi-god who ruled unjustly over humanity. The higher, good God had sent Jesus secretly to free people from the satanic god of the Jews. Due to the popularity of Marcionism, orthodox Christians would likely have gained a working knowledge of this concept of "rescue from Satan,"

---

[3] Gregory of Nyssa, *The Great Catechism*, 24.

[4] H. E. W. Turner, *The Patristic Doctrine of Redemption: A Study of the Development of Doctrine During the First Five Centuries* (Eugene, OR: Wipf & Stock Publishers, 2004), p. 54.

even though they rejected Marcion's identification of the God of the Jews with Satan. In the 3rd century, Origen emphasised heavily the idea that Jesus saved humanity from the Devil. The biblical commentaries Origen wrote hint at how he may have formed his views. He looked at the passages in the Gospels that spoke of Jesus as a "ransom for many." He reflected on whom had received the ransom, and concluded that since it was obviously not paid to God it must have been paid to Satan.[5] Origen spoke of Christ's victory over Satan in a wide variety of ways, and suggested many of the forms of Christus Victor we listed above. He seemed unsure of exactly how Jesus had defeated Satan, suggesting at times that he had done so magically or mysteriously.[6] The concept of Christus Victor became widespread in the 4th century, probably as a result of the huge influence of Origen's writings during that period.

Theosis and Spiritual Union

Christians in the Byzantine period continued to hold to the teaching that people become more Christ-like by following Jesus' teachings and example. However, they united it with an idea from Plato. Recall Plato's idea that material objects were imperfect copies of ideal archetypes called 'Forms': material objects mimicked these spiritual Forms, and Plato saw this similarity as a kind of spiritual participation. For example, any blue objects would participate spiritually in the archetype of 'Blueness'. Plato's theory implied that people who imitated Christ participated in the archetype of Christ, and they also participated in the archetype of God along with Christ. The concept of Christ-likeness combined with the Platonic idea of spiritual union to form the single concept of *theosis*, which means literally the 'divine transformation' of humanity. In the process of theosis, humans grew more and more Christ-like and hence grew more and more united spiritually with God. This concept captured the imaginations of many Byzantine theologians. Many believed world history and creation itself had as its goal this growth in godliness and union with God. They believed that this process would continue into eternity, as humans in heaven continued to grow closer and closer toward the likeness of God and towards ever-greater spiritual union with him.

---

[5] Origen, *Commentary on Matthew* 12.28, 13.9, *Homilies on Exodus* 6.9.
[6] Frances M. Young, *The Use of Sacrificial Ideas in Greek Christian Writers From the New Testament to John Chrysostom* (Eugene, OR: Wipf & Stock Publishers, 2004), pp. 179 – 185.

Some Christian writers of this period drew on this concept of theosis and suggested another problem from which humanity needed saving. Using Plato's logic, they concluded that everything must derive its existence through participating in the archetype of existence: God's existence. Things separated from God could not continue to exist since they would be cut off from their source of existence. They believed that godliness unified people spiritually with God and that sinfulness separated them from God. Hence, they thought that if humans cut themselves off from God spiritually by sinning, then they cut themselves off from actual existence. The biblical link between sin and death proved this to them. They believed that humans not only died physically because of sin, but also that their actual souls could decay as well. They believed that sin had set all of creation on a path toward non-existence, and that therefore God had to reunite himself spiritually with the created order to save it. The logical way for God to do this required him to take on a human body and become part of the created world. Through the act of incarnating himself in human flesh, God could re-establish his spiritual connection with the created order and save the created universe from its decay into non-existence. They believed that God had achieved this act through Jesus, insisting that Jesus himself must have been both fully God and fully man in order to unite creation with divinity. The appearances of the resurrected Jesus became for them proof that this endeavour had succeeded. Jesus had destroyed spiritual death and averted the decay and eventual annihilation of the created order. People have also called this Spiritual Union view 'Recapitulation', the 'Incarnational theory', and the 'Physical theory' of atonement. While most people today would not hold this view, it flourished in 4th century culture.

The unchanged doctrines of salvation and final judgment

Most of the theologians of the Byzantine era taught *three* concepts about the work of Christ. To the traditional concept of Jesus as teacher of moral virtue, they added the ideas of Spiritual Union and Christus Victor. In these two additional ideas, they believed that Jesus had achieved something effective for all humankind. By adding these two theories, they saw Jesus as doing *more* to save people. He had not only saved people from sinfulness by teaching them correct conduct, but had also freed people from Satan's influence and reunited them spiritually with God. Yet, nothing had changed in terms of final judgment and the role of individuals. Christians still believed that God based final judgment on conduct and that, to attain a positive judgment, people still needed to repent from sinful ways and live moral lives in obedience to

Jesus' teachings. The theologians of this period made this point very clear. Neither Christus Victor nor Spiritual Union made a difference when it came to final judgment. Spiritual Union and Christus Victor made it *possible* for there to be an afterlife, and gave people the chance of freedom from Satan's influence and authority in that afterlife. Neither, however, affected the outcome or basis of God's final judgment of humans.

There remained only one belief about the connection between Jesus and individuals passing the final judgment. They saw Jesus as a teacher and example of correct conduct, and believed that, by following his teachings and example, they could obtain a positive judgment from God. They could maintain this idea alongside the newer ideas of Christus Victor and Spiritual Union, because the later two did not concern final judgment and human righteousness before God. These two self-contained ideas simply added to the traditional view of salvation and final judgment. The idea of Jesus as a teacher and example remained central during the Byzantine period. In the 8th century AD, the Byzantine theologian John Damascus wrote a book summarising the orthodox theology of the Byzantine period. He described their main view of Christ as follows: Christ "made himself a way and image and pattern that we also, following in his footsteps, might become by adoption what he is by nature, Sons and heirs of God and joint heirs with him."[7] A more recent historian summarised their main view of Christ in this way: "With them is intimately connected the thought, that Christ is the lawgiver, pattern and example. Christ restores again in and through himself the original nobility of the human nature together with immortality, but he imparts this to us by teaching us the knowledge of God and virtue."[8]

Doctrines regarding baptism and God's forgiveness

The first fundamental changes to the Christian concepts of salvation began to occur in the 2nd century AD. They concerned the link between repentance and forgiveness. The Jewish culture in which Christianity originated had always linked repentance with forgiveness, and the early Christians had seen forgiveness as a consequence of an inward commitment to follow Jesus' example and teachings. Repen-

---

[7] John Damascus, *An Exact Exposition of the Orthodox Faith* 4.13.
[8] Reinhold Seeberg, *Textbook of the History of Doctrines, Volume 1: History of Doctrines in the Ancient Church* (Grand Rapids: Baker, 1964), p. 297.

tance brought forgiveness. Unfortunately, this doctrine caused a problem during periods of persecution by the Romans. Many people renounced Christianity when threatened by the Romans, but later went straight back to the Christian community and claimed repentance and forgiveness. This behaviour horrified some Christian leaders. In an attempt to guard the need for commitment, they argued that Christians could obtain forgiveness for sins only with difficulty. Some even went so far as to say that Christians could never receive further forgiveness subsequent to baptism. The majority, however, felt that God could forgive even a major sin through sincere repentance. Such 'sincere repentance' was interpreted often to mean many years of prayer, repentance and good works.[9] These ideas developed further over time, however. By the end of the 2nd century, many Christians believed that they had to undertake a great deal of repentance, prayer and good works to offset even minor post-baptismal sins.

Traditionally, baptism and repentance had always gone hand in hand, and baptism functioned as an outward sign of inward repentance and commitment. God granted forgiveness because of the inward repentance, not because of the ritual itself. Indeed, one scholar has noted that the earliest Church Fathers saw no mystical significance in baptism beyond it presenting a symbol of inner repentance.[10] Christian views had now changed, however. They believed that God granted forgiveness at baptism easily, while post-baptismal forgiveness now came only with difficulty. Given this difference, it made sense to conclude that these two different kinds of forgiveness must work by different mechanisms. The link between baptism and repentance faded, and a new idea arose.

In the 3rd century AD, a small church council led by Cyprian expressed the view that a supernatural power of God operated during the ritual of baptism. This idea that baptism had supernatural significance became popular. People came to see baptism as a supernatural and mysterious ritual that washed away sin. Some even felt that small children should be baptised so that they might receive this supernatural blessing.[11] Consequently, they understood forgiveness differently. The means of forgiveness for past sins became not repentance, but God's supernatural power operating during baptism.[12] This change to the

---

[9] Shepherd of Hermas expounds such ideas at length. Possibly Hebrews 6:4-6 refers to this issue.

[10] Arthur C. McGiffert, *A History of Christian Thought: Volume 1, Early and Eastern* (New York; London: C. Scribner's sons, 1932), p. 83.

[11] Cyprian, *Epistle 108* (To Fidus, on the Baptism of Infants).

[12] Seeberg, *Textbook of the History of Doctrines*, p. 195.

doctrine of forgiveness that occurred in Cyprian's region stands out since, in general, the 3rd century Christians remained faithful to the earlier Christian tradition of repentance and forgiveness.[13] A person could only be baptised once, of course, so this new doctrine provided an important incentive to not fall away from the faith. Post-baptismal forgiveness was now separated completely from baptismal forgiveness, and the two were understood to work by entirely different mechanisms. Christians came to see post-baptismal forgiveness as even harder to receive. They could 'satisfy' God only through strenuous human effort and repentance, and thus only in this way could they keep secure their hope of positive judgment.[14] Eventually, this idea became known as Penance.

As post-baptismal forgiveness became harder to achieve, people saw baptism increasingly as the one great chance to obtain free forgiveness for sins. The Roman emperor Constantine took this idea to its logical extreme during the 4th century by waiting until he was about to die before being baptised. Many other people also used baptism in this way. Of course, the early Christians would have opposed such a practice, and some Christians at the time did. In the 4th century, the theologian John Chrysostom wrote a scathing parody opposing it.[15] The underlying changes to the doctrines of baptism and forgiveness, however, had already merged into tradition.

Doctrines regarding free will and human conduct

The Greek Christians in the first four centuries AD emphasised character and exhorted good conduct because they believed humans had free will. They believed that people had the willpower to follow the teachings and example of Jesus, and thus to live as God wanted. As one scholar notes, the "Greek Fathers strongly emphasized man's freedom and his accountability."[16] They did not see humanity as born sinful or corrupt. To explain evil desires, they pointed to the temptations of the Devil rather than to human nature.[17] Another scholar explains:

---

[13] Seeberg, *Textbook of the History of Doctrines*, p. 198.

[14] Seeberg, Textbook of the History of Doctrines, p. 198, c.f. p. 195.

[15] John Chrysostom, *Baptismal Instructions* 9.5-6 and 8

[16] Jeurgen Neve & Otto Heick, *A History of Christian Thought* (Philadelphia, PA: Fortress, 1965), Vol. 1, p. 191.

[17] Neve & Heick, *A History of Christian Thought*, p. 192.

A defining characteristic of the Greek Anthropology is the uniformity and emphasis with which the freedom of the will, and its continued liberty after the incoming of sin, is asserted... Cyril of Jerusalem says explicitly, "we come sinless into this world; we sin now voluntarily." Athanasius goes so far as to say that there have been many saints who have been free from all sin. Jeremiah and John the Baptist are mentioned as examples. Gregory of Nyssa, Gregory of Nazianzus, Basil and Chrysostom pronounce new-born children free from sin...[18]

The Latin Christians drifted apart from Eastern Christians who spoke Greek. When the Roman Empire split into the Western and Eastern Empires in the 4th century, the West spoke mainly Latin while the East spoke Greek. The Western Empire had fewer people and less wealth than the Eastern Empire, and would soon succumb to invasions from 'barbarians' and enter the Dark Ages. The barriers of language and politics hindered communication between Latin and Greek Christianity and the two developed nearly in isolation. The theology of the Latin Christians changed slowly into a grimmer and darker picture of humanity. They began to see people as inherently sinful, guilty before God, and lacking free will to do good.

Augustine of Hippo lived in this Latin West from 354 AD to 430 AD, and became perhaps the most influential theologian of all history. As a Christian bishop and philosopher-theologian, he wrote over 100 books, over 200 letters and almost 400 sermons. His writings have survived exceptionally well due to their popularity, with copies of over 96% of his works surviving today. He was an extremely original thinker, keen to speculate on theological and philosophical issues, and to debate biblical exegesis and doctrine. Since the beginning of the Dark Ages coincided with his death, he became almost the sole major Latin theologian of the first millennium AD. He towers above other writers through the sheer volume of his works and his classical education in logic and philosophy. Hence, his works influenced Christians of the Medieval period and the later Reformation greatly. As one scholar observes: "No theological writer has exercised so great an influence over the development of western Christian thought as Augustine of Hippo. ... *All* Medieval theology is 'Augustinian', to a greater or lesser extent."[19] That said, Greek-speaking Byzantine theologians of his time

---

[18] G. P. Fisher, *History of Christian Doctrine* (Edinburgh-Clark, 2nd ed., 1949), pp. 164 – 165.

[19] Alister E. McGrath, *Iustitia Dei: A History of the Christian Doctrine of Justification* (Cambridge University Press, 2005, 3rd ed.) p. 38, c.f. pp. 53 – 54, italics in original.

did not read Augustine's Latin writings, and his writings seem to have remained unknown to the Eastern Church until recently.

We have already seen that Christian doctrine up to the time of Augustine taught firmly the freedom of the will and the ability of humans to do good. As one scholar explains: "The pre-Augustinian theological tradition is practically of one voice in asserting the freedom of the human will."[20] Originally, Augustine held to this same tradition, as another scholar has observed:

> As is to be expected, when Augustine became a Christian he began to know and accept the concept of sin and grace which were current in the West at the time. Thus, in his early tract *On Free Will* Augustine... said that man's will is basically free and that sin is a motion of the will.[21]

It appears that Augustine's views changed after studying Paul's letter to the Romans.[22] In 396 AD Augustine published *To Simplician: On Various Questions,* putting forward his new views on the power of sin, the Fall and God's election. These ideas were "in the light of tradition somewhat new" and resulted from Augustine's interpretation of Paul's writings.[23] Augustine became the first teacher of the Church "to represent man as unable to even will what was good and right."[24] Unfortunately, Augustine relied on a Latin Bible translation which had inaccuracies in some places. One of those inaccuracies occurred in a key verse upon which he based his new ideas. In his Bible, Romans 5:12 said that all sinned *in* Adam. Augustine took this to mean that all humanity had somehow existed in Adam and that God saw everyone as guilty at birth because of Adam's sin. He relied heavily on this verse and "his defence of the doctrine of original sin turned upon it."[25] Scholars now recognise widely that the translation of this verse used by Augustine was inaccurate, and that the original Greek of the passage meant something very different:

---

[20] McGrath, *Iustitia Dei*, p. 34.

[21] Bernhard Lohse, *A Short History of Christian Doctrine* (Philadelphia, PA: Fortress Press, 1966), p. 111.

[22] McGrath, *Iustitia Dei*, pp. 39-40; Lohse, p. 111.

[23] Lohse, *A Short History of Christian Doctrine*, p. 112.

[24] J. F. Bethune-Baker, *An Introduction to the Early History of Christian Doctrine to the Time of the Council of Chalcedon* (London: Methuen, 1958), pp. 307.

[25] Fisher, *History of Christian Doctrine*, p. 186.

Augustine based his doctrine of original sin as a universal inherited guilt on a proof text in Paul's Epistle to the Romans. The Greek of Romans 5:12 says that death passed to all human beings "inasmuch as all sinned." But Augustine did not read Greek and used a very poor Latin translation of Romans that mistranslated the verse to read *in quo omnes peccaverunt*, or "in whom [that is, Adam] all sinned." In other words, when Augustine read Romans 5:12, he saw the message that death spread to all human beings inasmuch as all sinned in Adam. But this is not what the verse says in the original language.[26]

Perhaps because of the language barrier between Augustine and the Greek Christians, his error went uncorrected. Therefore, contrary to the theologians of the Eastern churches, "Augustine believed that all humans except Christ himself are born not only corrupt, so that sin is inevitable, but also guilty of Adam's sin and deserving of eternal damnation."[27] He came to believe that humans are born into the sinfulness of Adam, and that the Fall so marred human nature that humans now lack the ability to do true good. Such thinking posed a problem – for how could humans ever achieve a positive final judgment if they could not actually do good?

Augustine solved this problem by taking the view that God's Spirit could alter human psychology radically. The Spirit would alter humans supernaturally and empower them to do the good works required for salvation. So, although humans in their 'natural' state could not do good or please God, humans could do so when empowered supernaturally by the Spirit. The idea of the Holy Spirit empowering believers had always existed in Christianity, but Augustine took it further than ever before. Augustine named this supernatural intervention 'grace'. By doing so, he introduced a key change in the concept of grace. Previously, the word had referred to God's gracious favour in sending Jesus to teach us how to live rightly, and his favour toward those who followed Jesus. Yet Augustine made 'grace' an active supernatural power, equated closely with the workings of the Holy Spirit, which reached inside human minds to transform them.

---

[26] Roger E. Olson, *The Story of Christian Theology: Twenty Centuries of Tradition & Reform* (Downers Grove, IL: InterVasity Press, 1999), p. 272; similarly, Lohse, *A Short History of Christian Doctrine*, p. 113.

[27] Olson, *The Story of Christian Theology*, p. 272.

Augustine's view of human depravity and his concept of active supernatural grace had huge significance, both because of Augustine's influence and because of this radical departure from Christian tradition:

> It is clear that Augustine imparted to the traditional doctrine of sin a profundity which it had not had before. ... Similar to his radical definition of sin is Augustine's understanding of grace. He emphasized both the necessity and the work of grace as no one before him [had]. ...The importance of Augustine's doctrine of grace can hardly be overemphasized. Not only is this true with respect to the overarching influence of his thought upon the Middle Ages, upon the Reformers, and upon certain recurring tendencies within Catholicism. The accomplishments of Augustine assume their full dimension only when they are seen against the background of the ancient church and its [earlier contrasting beliefs].[28]

Augustine did not shy away from the logical consequence of these new doctrines – human free will could not play any role in salvation. Augustine believed that people in their fallen state cannot even will or desire to perform the good conduct that final judgment requires. On the other hand, people changed supernaturally by grace would desire inevitably to perform the required good deeds. In this way, Augustine's salvation did not depend on human will at all, but solely on whether God gave transforming grace to an individual. The decision to save an individual, therefore, lay solely in God's hands. Augustine accepted and taught this logical consequence, and it became known as the doctrine of Predestination. According to this view, at the beginning of time God decided on those to whom he would give grace and thus save, and those to whom he would not give grace and thus damn. Despite this idea's significant departure from more traditional doctrines, Augustine argued that scripture taught his view.

In this way, Augustine pioneered four major doctrinal innovations:

1. Newborns begin life as guilty of Adam's sin.
2. Humans have a sinful nature, which cannot do true good.
3. Our minds need supernatural regeneration by the Holy Spirit.
4. God predestines individuals to salvation and damnation.

---

[28] Lohse, *A Short History of Christian Doctrine*, p. 114, 117.

Over the course of his lifetime, Augustine's views had moved away from traditional Christian doctrine to embrace these new views. Hence, near the end of his life, he wrote a book called *Retractions*, which covered each of his previous works and pointed out the ideas with which he no longer agreed. Several scholars comment on how Augustine's views changed. Initially, Augustine viewed humanity optimistically, reaffirming that they had free will. Yet a far grimmer portrait emerged in his later works, in which the human will cannot achieve much at all. He came to think that God predestined most people justly to eternal punishment, but that he predestined a small minority for salvation through unmerited mercy. One scholar highlights the way in which Augustine changed his views:

> It is important to appreciate that Augustine's doctrine... underwent significant development. For example, prior to his elevation to the See of Hippo Regis in 395, Augustine appears to have held precisely the same opinion which he would later condemn – the Massilian attribution of the 'beginnings of faith' (*initium fidei*) to the human free will. Some thirty years after his consecration, Augustine conceded that his earlier works... should be corrected in the light of his later insights concerning the doctrine of grace.[29]

Augustine's innovations aroused immediate opposition from many theologians. They feared that his doctrines of predestination and human inability to do good denied the very essence of Christianity. They thought his views would inflame the problem of moral laxity in the state-run institutional churches. Before his conversion to Christianity, Augustine had participated in the Manichaean sect, and some saw in his doctrinal changes a strong Manichaean influence. One scholar has noted, "Augustine [could] even say that human nature has been corrupted by sin. Such assertions must have appeared... as being only a thinly veiled Manichaeism."[30] In an ongoing controversy, Augustine wrote and campaigned vigorously against those that opposed his new views. His opponents used his own older writings on human free will to argue against his new ideas.[31] Many of his contemporaries rejected his new ideas, as several scholars have noted:

---

[29] McGrath, *Iustitia Dei*, p. 39. See Augustine, *Retractions* 1.23.3-4.

[30] Lohse, *A Short History of Christian Doctrine*, p. 113.

[31] Mendelson, Michael, "Saint Augustine," *The Stanford Encyclopedia of Philosophy* (Fall 2009 Edition), Edward N. Zalta (ed.), online:

His views were not by any means generally accepted in all their details. Offence was taken, especially of his doctrines of man's absolute inability to do good and of predestination, however for the time being his illustrious name and the charm of his writings may have smothered opposition. But, even before his death, doubts were openly expressed upon these points.[32]

Not all… were ready to follow Augustine's daring ideas in all respects.[33]

Augustine, however, took the initiative against his opponents and attempted to get *them* condemned for heresy. Augustine enlisted his local North African bishops in aid of his cause. They condemned his opponents, and sent many letters and envoys to bishops throughout all parts of the Roman Empire. This behaviour annoyed Pope Zosimus, who sent letters to the North African bishops demanding an end to the trouble-making, and excommunicated some of those involved. The North Africans remained one step ahead of the Pope, however: they appealed to the Western Roman Emperor. The Emperor intervened and forced the Pope to condemn Augustine's opponents and to expel 17 of the Pope's own bishops who had refused to abandon their traditional views in order to support Augustine.[34]

Augustine did not succeed in wholly silencing his opposition, and disputes regarding his doctrine dragged on for centuries. During the Medieval period, however, Western theologians read Augustine far more than any other author. They embraced many of his new doctrinal ideas without appreciating how significantly they differed from the Christian doctrines before him. In the West, Augustine's theories of human sinfulness and supernatural grace became standard, and his doctrine of predestination had a large influence, although it never gained universal support. The Eastern churches developed separately and remained uninfluenced by Augustine's doctrines. They retain the pre-Augustinian views to this day.

---

http://plato.stanford.edu/archives/fall2009/entries/augustine/. See *Retractationes* I.9.3-6.

[32] Seeberg, *Textbook of the History of Doctrines*, p. 368.

[33] Lohse, *A Short History of Christian Doctrine*, p. 122.

[34] J. Patout Burns, "Augustine's Role in the Imperial Action Against Pelagius," *Journal of Theological Studies*, 30, 1979, pp. 67 – 83. Lionel Wickham, "Pelagianism in the East" in Rowan Williams (ed.), *The Making of Orthodoxy* (Cambridge: Cambridge University Press, 1989), pp. 200 – 213.

Augustine's teachings on the purpose and work of Christ were not novel, however. Augustine saw Christ primarily as a teacher of righteousness and an example of virtue.[35] He stressed the exemplary aspect of Christ's work particularly strongly.[36] One scholar notes: "Augustine can describe the whole life of the Son of God as a moral instruction… [at times he] assigns as the sole reason for the Incarnation the need to supply men with precepts and examples of virtue."[37] Augustine also expounded the concept of Ransom from Satan, which we examined earlier. Famously, Augustine described the cross as "the devil's mousetrap," speaking of Christ as 'bait' for the devil.[38] Augustine believed that, after reaching out to take Christ's soul upon his death, Satan lost his power over the dead.

Ideas about Christ's saving work

The doctrines concerning what Jesus achieved in order to bring about salvation began to change in the 4th century AD. These changes appear first in the works of the writer Athanasius, who analysed comprehensively the mechanisms by which Christ saved humans.[39] Like earlier Christians, Athanasius viewed Jesus as a teacher of righteousness and taught that salvation came through following his teachings and example. Athanasius was arguably the first Christian writer to set out the Spiritual Union view which we looked at earlier clearly and unambiguously.[40] The Spiritual Union view required that Christ unite divinity and humanity in himself. Athanasius' view would not work unless he understood Christ's divinity in a certain way. His commitment to this view led him to a life-long bitter struggle with the followers of Arius over the details of Christ's divinity.

Athanasius held that sin had introduced non-existence to the world in the form of death. He dwelt on the passage in Genesis in which God told Adam he would die if he ate forbidden fruit. Adam's sin intro- duced death (i.e. eternal non-existence), and created the problem from

[35] McGrath, *Iustitia Dei*, p. 44; c.f. Augustine, *On True Religion* xvi/32, *Letters* 11.4, *On Christian Doctrine* 1.11.

[36] J. N. D. Kelly, *Early Christian Doctrines* (San Francisco: Harper Collins, 1978), p. 393.

[37] Turner, *The Patristic Doctrine of* Redemption, p. 35.

[38] Augustine, *Sermon 261*.

[39] Athanasius, *On the Incarnation of the Word*, written in around 335 AD.

[40] Scholars debate the extent to which this view can be found in the writings of Irenaeus, who wrote earlier.

which Christ had to save humanity. The incarnation of Christ could then save the world by uniting humanity and divinity in one body. Yet, somewhat bizarrely, Athanasius read the passage in Genesis as a promise from God. He felt that God was obliged to keep his word and that, if Christ saved humanity from death, God had broken on his promise that sinning would lead to death.[41] Athanasius seems to have muddled through several attempts to absolve God on this account. In his favoured explanation, he saw Jesus' death as sufficient to satisfy the requirement that sin must lead to death. Jesus' death thus vindicated God's word[42] and, through his death, Jesus fulfilled God's promise.[43]

Athanasius still held that Jesus had given an example and teachings to humanity by which they could do good and gain a positive final judgment. In addition, he believed that Jesus had saved humanity from non-existence by his Spiritual Union, and that he had also vindicated God's word that sin would lead to death. These latter two ideas arose as new ideas to Christian theology. Many Greek theologians who held to Platonic ideas adopted the Spiritual Union view. Athanasius' idea of Christ's death fulfilling the promise of Genesis 3 was not so widely adopted. Traces of it can be found in a few subsequent fourth-century writings, such as the works of Ambrose of Milan and Cyril of Jerusalem. Yet the more general idea that Christ's death fulfilled a need for death would eventually take shape as one of the key tenets of Western Christianity.

Medieval views of Christ's work

The Greek Christians had focussed on the behavioural aspect of sinfulness and the harm that sinful behaviours did to people. They had no interest in talking of *guilt* in connection with sin.[44] One scholar notes:

> Among the Greeks, the guilt of sin was not felt with the same intensity as was its effect, which was seen in the corrupting influences of sin... Jesus, as Savior, was taken to be more the restorer of sin's injury than the remover of its guilt. ... The idea of Christ's death bringing the forgiveness of sin had no stress among the Greeks.[45]

---

[41] Athanasius, *On the Incarnation*, 6.3.
[42] Athanasius, *On the Incarnation*, 8.4.
[43] Athanasius, *On the Incarnation*, 9.2, 20.5.
[44] Fisher, *History of Christian* Doctrine, p. 161, italics in original.
[45] Neve & Heick, *A History of Christian Thought*, p. 232.

In the Medieval period in the Latin west, all this changed. Born in 1033 AD, Anselm of Canterbury was a monk and bishop in England. He became the first major philosopher-theologian of the Medieval period. Among other writings, he published a revolutionary work entitled *Why God Became Man*. In this work, he criticised Augustine's Ransom from Satan view. Anselm argued that it did not make sense for Christ to have rescued humanity from the Devil. Instead, Anselm formulated a new paradigm, expounding a fully comprehensive and stand-alone theory of atonement which explained human salvation in full. To do this, Anselm drew on feudal concepts of honour, and perhaps was also inspired by Athanasius' idea of Christ fulfilling God's promise of death. Anselm depicted God as an infinitely honourable feudal Lord, obliged to show wrath against those people who offended his honour by sinning. Anselm critiqued the doctrine of God's forgiveness, arguing that free forgiveness was dishonourable according to the standards of his day. He denied flatly that God could forgive sin freely and leave it unpunished.[46] This denial of the possibility of free forgiveness marked an important and major change in Christian doctrine. Anselm's view of Christ's work (and that of the Reformers after him) relied fundamentally on this premise that free forgiveness is impossible. Anselm wrote: "Consider it, then, an absolute certainty, that God cannot remit a sin unpunished, without recompense."[47] In Anselm's society, offences had either to be punished or to be compensated. Gifts functioned as the socially accepted way of resolving grievances and preventing feuds within Medieval society. Thus in Anselm's view, God needed to receive a suitable gift to 'satisfy' his wrath and avert his need to punish humanity.

Anselm argued that humans had no worthy gift to offer God – since he had created them, they owed him everything. He saw the incarnate Christ, who owed God nothing, as the solution to this problem. This sinless Christ had lived an obedient life in faithfulness to God. Christ could thus 'gift' his obedient life to God on behalf of humanity. According to the etiquette of feudal honour, this gift provided compensation for human sins and meant that God no longer needed to punish them. In this sense, Anselm wrote of Christ: "The life of this man was so sublime, so precious, that it can suffice to pay what is owing for the sins of the whole world – and infinitely more."[48] What satisfied God was that Jesus remained fully obedient to God's will to

---

[46] Anselm, *Why God Became Man*, Book 1, Ch 12.
[47] Anselm, *Why God Became Man*, Book 1, Ch 19.
[48] Anselm, *Why God Became Man*, Book 2, Ch 18.

the end, so much so that he was willing to die.[49] His death provided the opportunity for gifting his life faithfully to God. Yet Anselm did not see Christ as suffering a substitutionary punishment or enduring God's wrath on the cross.[50]

Anselm's satisfaction theory had a massive influence on subsequent Western Christianity. Adherents to the idea believed that Christ had offered his obedient life to God as a gift in compensation for human offences, to save them from his wrath. God accepted this gift as appropriate compensation and thus refrained from punishing anyone. Generally, however, Anselm retained the earlier Christian view that people needed repentance and correct conduct in order to attain a positive final judgment. He wrote: "There is but one thing which Thou will have, without which no sinner can be saved, namely, that we repent us of our sins, and, so far as we may, strive to amend our lives."[51] He also retained the view of Christ as a teacher and example:

> For who can set forth how necessarily, how wisely, it was done, when he, who was to redeem men and to lead them back by his teaching from the way of death and ruin to the way of life and blessedness, moved among men, and, in that very association, presented himself as an example, while by word he taught them how to live?[52]

Even so, Anselm's satisfaction theory marked a major new development in Western Christian doctrine. As one scholar notes, Anselm's understanding of Christ's work was distinctly different from that taught in Eastern Christianity:

> It is clear that in much of his argument in *Cur Deus Homo*, Anselm has gone far beyond anything found in Scripture. ... aspects of his argument are clearly grounded more in his own philosophical system than in Scripture. Finally, it is evident that, in many regards, Anselm is in discontinuity not only with the New Testament but also with the Eastern patristic tradition. This means that, to the extent that it followed Anselm, the un-

---

[49] Anselm, *Why God Became Man*, Book 1, Ch 9.

[50] David A. Brondos, *Fortress Introduction to Salvation and the Cross* (Minneapolis, MN: Augsburg Fortress, 2007), p. 83.

[51] Anselm, *Meditation 3*.

[52] Anselm, Why God Became Man, Book 2, Ch 11.

derstanding of salvation and Christ's work in Western Christianity increasingly distanced itself from that found in the East.[53]

Many Christians did not agree with Anselm's new ideas, and opposition developed immediately. Peter Abelard (1079 – 1142 AD), a famous
and controversial French philosopher and theologian, became his
greatest opponent. One theologian has noted: "More or less every
aspect of Anselm's position was subjected to a penetrating theological
critique by Peter Abelard."[54] Abelard rejected both Augustine's Christus
Victor view, and Anselm's Satisfaction view, and saw Christ primarily
as an example and teacher. Many of his statements about the work of
Christ followed the teachings of the early Christians closely. For
example:

> His Son took our nature, and in it took upon himself to instruct
> us alike by word and example even unto death.[55]

Such comments by Abelard echo closely Augustine's writings on the
subject, which reflected the standard Christian teaching of Augustine's
time. Numerous Medieval theologians and subsequent Popes also
shared this view of Christ as a moral instructor.[56] Abelard's view of the
atonement became known as the 'moral exemplar' or 'moral influence'
view, and it has become associated with Abelard's name. This,
unfortunately, has led many subsequent Christians to assume wrongly
that Abelard invented the view when, in fact, Abelard was reaffirming
the ideas of the earlier Christians. He drew on their writings, especially
those of Augustine, and reiterated the view of Christ as teacher and
example.

Penal Substitution

During the Reformation period (1517 – 1648 AD), massive changes
occurred within Western Christianity: a complete reassessment of both
theology and politics. The new Protestant movement broke off from the
Roman Catholic Church and attempted to align itself with the biblical
scholarship of the day. By this time, the Latin-speaking West used the
Vulgate of the 4th and 5th centuries as its standard Bible translation.

---

[53] Brondos, *Fortress Introduction to Salvation and the Cross*, p. 87.
[54] McGrath, *Iusutitia Dei*, p. 82.
[55] Peter Abelard, *Epist. ad Rom., Opera*, in Hastings Rashdall, *The Idea of
Atonement in Christian Theology* (London: Macmillan, 1919), pp. 371 – 372.
[56] Rashdall, *ibid.*

From the time of its writing until the Reformation, the original Greek New Testament could be read by very few in the West. Thus, Westerners relied largely on the Latin translation for their doctrine. Significantly, the Vulgate translated the Greek moral term for correct conduct, *dikaiosyne*, using the Latin legal term for justice, *iustitiam*. This Latin term prompted the Reformers to understand righteousness primarily as a judicial term. Such a reading fitted with the culture of the time, since academics esteemed legal thought most highly. Generally, Law was the only advanced degree at the Latin-speaking universities. Hence, many university-trained scholars who read Paul's letters had trained as lawyers and interpreted his writings through the filter of the legal concepts they had learned. This Latin legal reading of Paul influenced the doctrines of the Reformers heavily – even though it deviated significantly from the intent of Paul's original Greek writings.

The Reformers also interpreted Anselm's satisfaction model through this legal paradigm. They recast God as a judge rather than as a feudal Lord. In this view, God presided over a cosmic court in which humanity were the defendants, guilty of breaking his laws. For Anselm, a gift negated the need for punishment. Yet, in the judicial paradigm, gifts cannot negate this need for punishment, and indeed punishment is the only option. In the judicial theory, the innocent Christ did not merely offer his *life* of obedience as a gift to God, he instead suffered the penalty for our crimes – death – as our substitute. For this reason, the judicial atonement theory became known as 'penal substitution'. In both the satisfaction and penal substitution theories of atonement, Christ targeted his atoning work at God to save humanity from the wrath that threatened them with punishment for sin. Importantly, the assumption that sin *needs* retribution forms the foundation for the idea of penal substitution. The need for punishment sets the scene for the theory, which has Christ take the punishment of death in our place. This view of the Reformers represented a significant doctrinal change in at least two ways. First, it rejected completely the repentance-and-forgiveness paradigm of the early Christians, in which God could forgive and was not obliged punish sin. Second, Anselm, Athanasius and other Christians before the Reformation had not believed that God had punished Christ on the cross for humanity's sins.

Imputation, grace, and faith

Up until the Reformation, the idea of justification had always involved moral transformation away from sinfulness and toward correct conduct. As one scholar notes: "Throughout the entire Medieval period, justification continued to be understood as the process by which humans are made righteous, subsuming the concepts of 'sanctification' and 'regeneration.'"[57] The Reformation marked a dramatic break from this tradition.

The change pivoted around a phrase that the apostle Paul had written in one of his letters, stating that Abraham's faithfulness (*pistis*) "was reckoned to him as righteousness." The Greek word translated as 'reckoned' (*logizomai*) by many modern English translations means to consider, calculate, and conclude. The word relates to drawing accurate conclusions from evidence and determining truth. An all-knowing God would only 'conclude' that someone was righteous if their thoughts and behaviour were indeed righteous. This idea had continued as standard orthodoxy until the Reformation. Then, in 1516 AD, Erasmus produced a new Latin translation of the New Testament. He translated the phrase into Latin by writing that Abraham's faith "was imputed [*imputatum*] unto him for justice." In the comments he provided with his translation, he wrote that by 'imputation' he meant "to consider as accepted, what you have not accepted, which is called acceptilation among the lawyers." This reading represented a significant departure from the previous standard Latin translation of the New Testament (the Latin Vulgate) which used 'reputed' (*reputatum*) instead of 'imputed'. The previous translations implied that God recognised the actual righteousness of a person, yet this new reading implied that God declared an unrighteous person to be righteous. It disconnected righteousness from conduct completely in an unprecedented manner.

The Reformer Melanchthon used Erasmus' new translation, and the doctrine of imputed righteousness became influential in Protestantism swiftly.[58] Melanchthon argued that he had returned to Augustine's view of justification, but in fact the Catholic Church at the time followed Augustine's view and Melanchthon had departed from it.[59] This new doctrine suggested that God considered people as righteous not because of their repentance and correct conduct, but instead because Christ's righteousness had been imputed to them through his death on the cross. Penal substitution had become the means by which God could now deem people righteous even though they may not in fact live rightly. This new doctrine replaced the idea that people became righteous by following Jesus' example and teachings.

---

[57] McGrath, *Iustitia Dei*, p. 214.

[58] See Joseph A. Fitzmyer, *Romans: A New Translation with Introduction and Commentary* (New York: DoubleDay, 1993), pp. 373 – 374; and Ben Witherington III, *Paul's Letter to the Romans: A Socio-Rhetorical Commentary* (Grand Rapids, MI: Eerdmans, 2004), pp. 121 – 122 for a discussion of this history.

[59] McGrath, *Iustitia Dei*, p. 216.

The idea of imputation went hand in hand with a re-interpretation of God's grace (favour). In early Christianity, God's favour had been to send Jesus as a teacher and example, to save people from sinful ways as they repented. Augustine had developed a view of grace as a super-natural working of the Spirit that transformed the human mind so that people thought and lived rightly. However, the Reformers focussed on the *guilt* of sin before God rather than right living, so they had little use for Augustine's concept of sanctifying grace. Martin Luther struggled greatly with feelings of guilt even as a Christian. He drew heavily on Augustine's doctrine of original sin, but went even further. He denied that Christians could gain freedom from their sinful natures even with God's grace, instead believing that they always remained intrinsically sinful in God's sight. In dramatic contrast with the early Christian tradition, he believed that a person's correct conduct could never make them righteous. While Augustine had believed that 'justify' meant 'to make righteous',[60] Luther understood it instead to mean 'to impute righteousness'. This new doctrine heralded a significant doctrinal change: "Luther... introduced a decisive break with the Western theological tradition as a whole by insisting that, through their justification, humans are *intrinsically* sinful yet *extrinsically* righteous."[61] Thus, instead of grace referring to God's part in transforming people's minds and behaviour, Luther's 'grace' involved God declaring unrighteous people to be righteous. God pardoned past sins and imputed righteousness, and penal substitution made both of these acts possible. The means of salvation had, therefore, shifted from obeying Jesus' teachings and example to penal substitution and the grace of imputed righteousness. The Reformers separated justification and righteousness from a person's conduct – completely breaking from previous Christian tradition. One scholar explains:

> The essential distinguishing feature of the Reformation doc-
> trines of justification is that a deliberate and systematic distinc-
> tion is made between *justification* and *regeneration*... The
> essential point is that a notional distinction is made where none
> had been acknowledged before in the history of Christian doc-
> trine. A fundamental discontinuity was introduced into the

---

[60] McGrath, *Iustitia Dei*, pp. 46 – 47.
[61] McGrath, *Iustitia Dei*, p. 213.

Western theological tradition where none had ever existed, or even been contemplated, before.[62]

This doctrinal innovation of the Reformers cast a whole new light on final judgment. The Reformers believed that final judgment still hinged upon whether or not God deemed a person righteous, as the earlier Christians had. The Reformers, however, understood righteousness as imputed and not dependent upon conduct. Thus, they believed that final judgment did not depend upon a person's conduct, but upon whether or not God imputed righteousness to that person. Concerning final judgment, the early Christians had sought an answer to the question, "How should we live?" Yet the Reformers now asked, "How can we have Christ's righteousness imputed to us?" This fundamentally different question led them to a very different answer. Their answer: *sola fide* – faith alone. Faith alone made a person righteous. God imputed righteousness on the grounds of faith and it did not depend upon conduct. Their ideas drove a wedge between faith and conduct – between faith and faithfulness. Over time, the concept of saving faith became concerned with believing, trusting in and relying on Christ's atoning work on the cross, which made imputed righteousness possible.

The idea that final judgment hinged upon belief in, trust of and reliance on Christ's atoning work differed radically from early Christian doctrine. It would not have gained such acceptance without some background developments that paved the way for the idea. One significant development involved the idea of Purgatory. In the 3rd century, Origen had suggested that God sent sinners to hell to reform them morally. Once they had reformed sufficiently, he would allow them into heaven. Some objected to Origen's idea, since it implied that everyone would end up in heaven and that no one needed to follow Jesus before death. A novel solution came forward in the 4th century. This new idea stated that sinful pagans would dwell in hell forever, while sinful Christians would only spend a finite time there. Hence, conduct still determined whether one went to hell or not, but getting to heaven depended ultimately on whether or not one was a Christian. Good Christians would go straight to heaven, while wicked Christians would spend a finite period in hell before enjoying an eternity in heaven.[63] This notion that wicked Christians endured a finite amount of suffering in the afterlife before eventually gaining admittance to heaven became known as 'Purgatory'. This doctrinal change seems to have

---

[62] McGrath, *Iustitia Dei*, p. 217.
[63] Kelly, *Early Christian Doctrines*, p. 484.

taken place slowly over centuries, with Augustine and Gregory 'the Great' (d. 604 AD) influencing its development. It changed the essential concept of 'final judgment', and made it not-so-final. Conduct now only determined a person's duration in Purgatory rather than his or her eternal destiny. In the Medieval period, the church exploited this idea of Purgatory. Church leaders claimed that monetary payments could change a person's duration in Purgatory, or even free souls from there. The Reformers opposed this exploitation strongly. They used scripture to argue that eternal destiny could not be bought with money. People accepted readily their idea that eternal destiny instead rested on *sola fide*, faith alone – believing, trusting, and relying on Christ's work of penal substitution.

Reflections

It is hardly surprising that the Reformation caused such contro-versy, conflict, and ultimate division among the members of the Church. The gospel of the Reformers differed vastly from the early Christian message, hingeing as it did upon ideas of penal substitution and imputed righteousness. To the present day, the Eastern Greek Christian tradition has never adopted these ideas. These ideas are also absent from the writings of Western Christians from the earlier periods. One church historian has explained it like this:

> There is only the most slender support to be found in the earli-est centuries for some of the views that became current at a later time. It is at least clear that the sufferings of Christ were not re-garded as an exchange or substitution or penalty, or as punish-ment inflected on him by the Father for our sins. There is, that is to say, no idea of vicarious satisfaction, either in the sense that our sins are imputed to Christ and his obedience to us, or in the sense that God was angry with him for our sakes and inflicted on him punishment due to us.[64]

Protestant scholars of doctrinal history often express puzzlement at the absence of these Reformation ideas in the early Christian writings. One such scholar has noted that since Tertullian (d. 220 AD) had trained as a Latin lawyer and taught the idea of penance, he was in the perfect position to understand and explain penal substitution. It puzzled this

---

[64] Bethune-Baker, p. 321.

scholar that Tertullian never even mentioned the idea,[65] and instead saw Jesus as "the illuminator and instructor of mankind."[66] Such observations should hardly surprise us in light of the history we have now covered.

The changes in doctrine we have examined represent major changes in the way in which Christians understood the basic concepts of salvation and the gospel. Let us conclude this section by tabulating some of these changes as follows:

Early Christian Views	Post-Reformation Views
Focus on conduct and character	Focus on guilt and standing before God
Humans are born sinless	Humans are born sinful, depraved and guilty
Humans have free will, and can live rightly by following Jesus' example and teachings	Humans are severely inclined toward evil and cannot live rightly, even with God's help
Christ taught right living, and died as an example and martyr	Christ died a penal substitutionary death, suffering the punishment of God in our place
God considers righteous those who follow Jesus' teachings and example faithfully	God imputes righteousness to anyone who believes and trusts in Jesus' atoning death
Final judgment is according to conduct	Final judgment is based on belief, trust, and reliance alone and not conduct

---

[65] Kelly, *Early Christian Doctrines*, p. 177.
[66] Kelly, *Early Christian Doctrines*, p. 177.

Chapter 17

Modern ideas

Let us now look at the salvation doctrines common in the post-Reformation tradition today in light of the ground we have covered so far. Such a task presents many difficulties. Every gospel tract and every preacher presents the doctrines differently, sometimes very differently. We cannot look at all the many variations of post-Reformation salvation doctrine here. However, most of the variations share a set of core ideas. We wish to focus on these core ideas of modern post-Reformation Christianity, which we summarise broadly as follows:

1. **We need to be saved.**

    We are all sinners, and so, without Jesus, we would go to hell rather than heaven after we die physically. We cannot change the fact that we are sinners because we all do at least one thing wrong during our lives, and that is enough to make us sinful. Human nature is inherently sinful, and we cannot make up for it by trying to do good deeds. We can do nothing to save ourselves from hell, and we need a saviour to intervene so that we may go to heaven instead.

2. **God has made a way for us to gain salvation through Jesus dying on the cross.**

    God in his love did not want all humanity to suffer eternally in hell, so he sent Christ to save us. Christ's substitutionary death on the cross means that we can now gain salvation from hell and go to heaven. Christ suffered the punishment we deserved for our sins so that we would not have to. As a result of this atonement, God can now see us as righteous rather than sinful. What Christ did on the cross dealt with our guilt and gave us a way to go to heaven rather than to hell.

3.   Now, in order to receive salvation, we must believe in Jesus.

God will receive us into heaven if we believe in, trust in and
rely on what Christ has done for us. His atonement for sin becomes effective for us through our faith. God offers this gracious gift of salvation freely through his grace, and through
Christ he approves and accepts those who have faith. Therefore,
those who believe in Jesus and trust in what he achieved on the
cross will go to heaven.

4.   Once saved, there are corresponding changes in our lives.

Salvation also marks the beginning of a new relationship with
God. Because our sin has been dealt with through Christ, we
have a new level of connection to God – a personal relationship
with him. He guides us, leads us, and answers our prayers.
God's Spirit works in us to transform our character and behaviour gradually in order to make us more Christ-like. We should
love others, and one of the most important ways to do this is to
save them from hell by helping them to believe the gospel also.

We provide this list to illustrate the *sorts* of doctrines to which we
refer. We cannot include all the variations upon these central doctrines,
or the many different ways in which people explain them. Many
Christians would also add other ideas to those listed above. Nevertheless, many Christians today understand salvation in a way containing
these central themes.

Christians have not always taught these doctrines. We have shown
how several of the distinctive ideas outlined above took shape over
centuries, reaching the above form only after the Reformation of the 16th
century AD. A hundred years before the Reformation, Christians had
quite different ideas about the core ideas of the gospel, and, a thousand
years before it, quite different again. Furthermore, the doctrines held by
different Christian denominations today vary, and not all Christians
today hold to Protestant doctrines. There are around one billion Roman
Catholics, making them the largest Christian denomination today.
Eastern Orthodox churches predominate throughout Greece, Russia,
Egypt and other countries in-between. Their tradition descended
through the Greek-speaking Eastern Christians, so it has quite a
different history and set of doctrines. Even within Protestantism,
countless distinct groups hold a wide variety of ideas. This diversity
within modern Christianity warns against assuming simply that the
ideas with which we may have grown up are correct. We can now

comment on typical modern post-Reformation doctrines in light of the biblical analysis and historical evidence presented earlier in this book. This chapter will explore some of the problems with two of these modern ideas: salvation through Jesus dying on the cross; and the idea of saving faith.

Salvation though Jesus dying on the cross

Christians have always believed that Jesus brought salvation. Scholars call the various ideas about the way in which he did this 'theories of atonement'. Since the Reformation, many Christians have held to the doctrine of penal substitution and believed that Christ's death on the cross had a saving effect. In the words of recent defenders of this theory: "The doctrine of penal substitution states that God gave himself in the person of his Son to suffer instead of us the death, punishment and curse due to fallen humanity as the penalty for sin."[1] Without Christ's suffering for our punishment on the cross, we could not obtain salvation. For many people today, "this understanding of the cross of Christ stands at the very heart of the gospel."[2] We will outline here three compelling reasons to reconsider such a position.

The New Testament evidence

Many Christians in the post-Reformation tradition see penal substitution as "nothing less than the essence of Christianity."[3] They believe that Jesus' most significant accomplishment occurred in the few hours he spent dying on the cross. This very strong emphasis on his death makes the rest of his life and ministry seem comparatively unimportant.[4] His life becomes framed within the events of his death. Some believe that the significance of his life lay in "his perfect obedience to the law of God,"[5] and that the work of the cross required this obedience. This reduces the details of Jesus' life to simple 'obedience', and suggests that the *specific* acts Jesus did during his ministry had little importance.

---

[1] Steve Jeffery, Michael Ovey & Andrew Sach, *Pierced for Our Transgressions: Rediscovering the Glory of Penal Substitution* (Nottingham: Inter-Varsity Press, 2007), p. 21.

[2] Jeffery, Ovey & Sach, *Pierced for Our Transgressions*, p. 21.

[3] Mark Dever, 'Nothing but the Blood' in *Christianity Today*, 50.5, May 2006.

[4] Steve Chalke, *Redeeming the Cross: The Lost Message of Jesus & the Cross of Christ*, 2004, p. 3.

[5] Jeffery, Ovey & Sach, *Pierced for Our Transgressions*, pp. 212 – 213.

He could have lived a sinless and obedient life by living in the wilderness and never doing anything of note. A strong focus on penal substitution can make his resurrection also appear comparatively unimportant. As we noted earlier, many people have commented that his resurrection can seem like "nothing more than the 'happy ever after' at the end of the story."[6] After all, a substitutionary atonement to save us did not require his ministry or resurrection, only his death.

The New Testament reveals quite a different focus. It does not focus narrowly on the death of Christ, as if it had infinitely more importance than anything else. Instead, the Gospels use the majority of their accounts to describe what Jesus did and taught. They present his death as part of a larger story which also involved his birth, baptism, ministry and resurrection. Other New Testament writings emphasise his resurrection to a similar extent as his death, and sometimes even more so. A narrow focus on the death of Jesus has little support from the Gospels or from the other New Testament writings. Jesus' martyrdom gained its significance for the early Christians from the content of his teachings, his movement and his resurrection. Separating his death from his teachings and movement therefore strips his death of its original significance. It would be comparable to commemorating Martin Luther King Jr. by meditating solely upon his assassination and the weapon that killed him, without remembering the cause for which he lived. Doing so would ignore the very reasons that his death had such significance: his civil rights movement and his support of desegregation, peace and justice. One scholar has noted this very point: "To celebrate [King's] death apart from the cause for which he lived would be ridiculous and meaningless. Yet this is what we have done for the most part with Jesus."[7]

Did the message Jesus preach focus upon his death? Not according to the Gospel accounts. They present him preaching a message that looked remarkably different from post-Reformation doctrines. His message concerned correct conduct, fairness and loving kindness. They present him as a prophetic teacher, who corrected the errors in how people thought and lived, and who showed them a new way of life. His down-to-earth message has a very different flavour in comparison to the somewhat-mystical doctrines of his death preached today. Hence, a

---

[6] Steve Chalke & Alan Mann, *The Lost Message of Jesus* (Grand Rapids, MI: Zondervan, 2003), p. 172. See also the references given in the chapter on Resurrection in Part 3.

[7] Stephen J. Patterson, *Beyond the Passion: Rethinking the Death and Life of Jesus* (Minneapolis, MN: Augsburg Fortress, 2004), p. 3.

large discrepancy exists between modern post-Reformation doctrines and the content of the Gospels.

Similar problems arise when we consider the preaching of the disciples as depicted in the Gospels. Jesus trained his disciples to preach his message and sent them out to proclaim it.[8] After they had preached it and returned, Jesus then told them that he would die and come to life again. Yet the Gospels tell us: "They understood nothing about all these things; in fact, what he said was hidden from them, and they did not grasp what was said."[9] So what message had the disciples preached? Throughout the Gospel accounts, the disciples did not understand Jesus' cryptic warnings that he would die – or they refused to accept it. This fact implies that the message both they and Jesus preached to the masses said nothing at all about Jesus' death. The gospel they preached, therefore, could not have involved penal substitution. Nor did they exhort people to believe and trust in that atoning death of Christ for forgiveness. If we believe the Gospels, then we must conclude that the 'good news' preached by both Jesus and his disciples had very little, if anything, to do with penal substitution.

The historical evidence

Our assessment of the early Christian writings from after the New Testament period yielded a similar conclusion. A careful historical study shows that the early Church Fathers did not emphasise penal substitution at all. Over 7,000 pages of their writings survive from the 2nd and 3rd centuries AD, ranging from church letters to theological tomes, biblical commentaries to defences of Christianity against paganism. Many different writers explained the core doctrines of Christianity for many different reasons in these pages. Yet these writers completely failed to present the key post-Reformation doctrines. Scholars studying their writings have noted this lack consistently.[10] Hence, no one familiar with their writings could conclude that penal substitution formed a central part of their gospel, and the evidence suggests that it had little or no place in their theology. Of course, in such a large collection of old writings, some ambiguous paragraphs exist. A recent book in defence of

---

[8] Luke 9:6; also Mark 16:20.

[9] Luke 18:34.

[10] As Gustav Aulen argues in *Christus Victor: An Historical Study of the Three Main Types of the Idea of Atonement* (New York: Macmillan Publishing Co., 1978, trans. A. G. Hebert). See also the various works cited in the earlier chapter on early church doctrine.

penal substitution cited one such paragraph.[11] While we think this book misinterprets the passage concerned, it hardly matters. If even ardent defenders of penal substitution can find only *one paragraph* that supports their view out of *thousands of pages* of the early Christian writings, then it proves simply that the early Christians did not teach this doctrine widely. Clearly, penal substitution did not feature as a significant part of the early Church Fathers' teachings.

Most of these early Church Fathers spoke the same language as the Apostles and lived in the same culture. Irenaeus wrote that he had listened in person to the preaching of Polycarp, whom John the Apostle had taught.[12] These Christians suffered sporadic persecutions from the Roman authorities, and many of them died as martyrs for their faith. They gathered together the books of the New Testament into a single group, and cited them as scripture thousands of times in their writings. Of course they were not perfect, but we can have confidence in their great passion for Christianity. It seems very unlikely that they completely misunderstood the central doctrines taught to them. The historical evidence suggests that the Christians of the 2nd and 3rd centuries AD would have remained reasonably true to the teachings passed on to them. Indeed, we found no suggestion that any significant differences exist between the New Testament teachings and the ideas of these early Christians. Yet the evidence from their writings raises a great problem for those who support the view that the Bible teaches penal substitution: how could the church have so quickly forgotten the central doctrine of its faith? It seems highly unlikely that they would have. Instead, it seems most reasonable to conclude that both the early Christians and the biblical authors never held penal substitution as their core teaching, if indeed they taught it at all.

So from where did the doctrine of penal substitution originate? We have traced the history of some key doctrinal changes that led to the development of penal substitution. These changes appeared in the writings of Augustine of Hippo, Anselm of Canterbury, and the Reformers. Their novel theological views evoked strong opposition during their lifetime and for centuries afterward, as other theologians condemned them for altering Christian doctrines. Ultimately, however, their new ideas survived and became highly influential despite the controversy surrounding them. Today, such doctrinal innovations

---

[11] Jeffery, Ovey, Sach, *Pierced for Our Transgressions*, p. 161, citing Justin Martyr, *Dialogue with Trypho*, ch. 95.

[12] Irenaeus' letter discusses the subject, and is quoted in Eusebius', *Church History*, 5:20:5-6, (325 AD), and other references are made in Irenaeus, *Against Heresy*.

become clear when contrasted with Christian groups who have developed in isolation from them. The Eastern Orthodox Church provides one such example. Their tradition has developed fairly independently since around the 4th century AD due to separations in language and geography. Consequently, Eastern Orthodox Christians do not share the particular doctrines and concerns that have emerged within Western Christianity.[13] A study of doctrinal changes throughout history and the differences among Christian traditions today reveals that penal substitution originated several centuries after Jesus' life. It originated not from Jesus, nor from the early Christians, but from gradual changes that developed from small beginnings in the late 3rd century through to maturity in the 16th century Reformation. This conclusion raises a major problem for the doctrine of penal substitution. What place should it have in Christian doctrine if did not originate from Jesus nor from the early Christians?

God's forgiveness

Scripture gives ample evidence of God's forgiving nature. Jesus instructed people to forgive others just as God forgives.[14] In the book of Jonah, we read that God forgave Nineveh out of kindness.[15] The Old Testament contains many other examples of God refraining from punishment and forgiving the offenders instead.[16] We also read in the Gospels that Jesus told people regularly that God had forgiven them.[17] These all make sense given the proverbial concept of repentance and forgiveness within Judaism, which we investigated earlier. The Jews believed that God offered forgiveness freely out of love if the person repented. They believed that God could forgive out of loving kindness and choose to avoid punishing sinners. He would forgive people who changed their ways. Speaking on behalf of God, Ezekiel explained:

> Though I say to the wicked, "You shall surely die," yet if they turn from their sin and do what is lawful and right... they shall not die. None of the sins that they have committed shall be re-

---

[13] See, for example, Timothy Ware, *The Orthodox Church* (Penguin, 1997), p. 229; Vladimir Lossky, *In the Image and Likeness of God* (SVS Press, 1997), pp. 101 – 102.

[14] Matt 6:14; Mark 11:25.

[15] John 3:3-10.

[16] E.g. Num 14:19-20; 1 Kings 8:33-39; 2 Chr 7:14; Psa 86:5, 103:3; Jer 31:34, 36:3.

[17] E.g. Mark 2:5; Luke 7:48.

membered against them; they have done what is lawful and right, they shall surely live.[18]

Ezekiel taught that God prefers to forgive than to punish: "I have no pleasure in the death of the wicked, but that the wicked turn from their ways and live."[19] These words from God contradict the later inventive view of Athanasius: "It would, of course, have been unthinkable that God should go back upon His word and that man, having transgressed, should not die."[20] This incorrect view of forgiveness provided the incentive for him to suggest his 'satisfaction' theory. Anselm perpetuated this misunderstanding, arguing explicitly that God cannot forgive freely. He concluded: "Consider it, then, an absolute certainty, that God cannot remit a sin unpunished."[21] Anselm's entire argument for his satisfaction theory depended on this claim. The Reformers likewise denied flatly the possibility of God's free forgiveness when they adopted the satisfaction theory and developed it into penal substitution. Their ideas have persisted in their tradition right up to the present day.

Some would say that penal substitution *does* speak of forgiveness, in that God can forgive us because he punished Jesus. An analogy will help to explain why such an act does not represent true forgiveness. Imagine a letter from your bank saying, "your mortgage does not need to be repaid and is forgiven, so long as it is repaid in full by one of your relatives." Obviously the bank has not cancelled the debt graciously at all! The bank is allowing someone else to pay it. Likewise, penal substitution suggests that God will 'forgive' – so long as there is punishment in full.[22] Yet that is not free forgiveness. It is simply transferring punishment to an innocent person (which raises another set of ethical problems). Contrary to popular belief, such a transfer of punishment has no basis in Israel's sacrificial customs, which we investigated earlier. One could call this 'forgiveness' only in a very twisted sense of the word. The idea of penal substitution takes us far from the biblical picture of a loving God forgiving repentant sinners freely and graciously.

Penal substitution developed as the solution to the problem created by an incorrect view of God's forgiveness. The early Christians believed

---

[18] Ezekiel 33:10-19, cf. 18:21-28.
[19] Ezekiel 33:11, cf. 18:23.
[20] Athanasius, *On the Incarnation of the Word*, 6.3.
[21] Anselm, *Why God Became Man*, 19.
[22] As argued by Steven J. Porter, "Rethinking the Logic of Penal Substitution," in William Lane Craig, Michael Murray, and J. P. Moreland (eds.), *Philosophy of Religion*, (New Brunswick, NJ: Rutgers, 2002), p. 602.

that God forgives freely those who repent sincerely. The 'problem' of how to deal with sin only arose after this view was forgotten or rejected. Penal substitution presupposes that free forgiveness from God is impossible, or undesirable, and that he must punish sins rather than forgive them. It suggests that God faced a dilemma in which he wanted to forgive people's sins but was instead compelled to punish them. God 'solved' this problem by punishing Jesus instead of the sinners. Such a radical solution is only needed if we rule out God's free forgiveness. If God can freely forgive then he faces no dilemma, he has no need to punish, and he has no need of a substitute. Hence, if we adopt the biblical and early Christian understanding of God's forgiveness, no basis nor need for penal substitution remains. This observation explains why it took so many centuries for the concept of penal substitution to arise within Christianity. It could not develop until the church had lost its earlier understanding of repentance and forgiveness.

Saving faith

Let us now turn our attention to the idea of saving 'faith'. Post-Reformation presentations of the gospel often emphasise the need for this faith. We saw earlier that the Greek term translated as 'faith' often carries the meaning of 'faithfulness' rather than 'belief'. This is true particularly in statements directing *pistis* toward a person, such as Jesus. We showed that the New Testament authors used this word to write of commitment and loyalty in following Jesus, his message, and his way of life. Having faithfulness as a disciple of Jesus meant following his example and teachings and continuing his work to transform people's lives and communities. It was about living rightly.

This view of the early Christians contrasts sharply with the post-Reformation concept of saving faith, which concerns primarily the belief in, trust of, and reliance on propositions about what Jesus achieved. It is not about *behaving* rightly, but about *believing* rightly. For some Christians today, the very essence of 'faith' entails depending fully on the cross of Christ for our salvation and refraining from all attempts to gain a positive final judgment through living morally. This modern idea of 'faith' stands in contrast to the early Christian idea of faithfulness to Jesus. The key biblical term, pistis, has taken on a very different meaning. This redefinition has coincided with a move away from the early Christian views of final judgment, correct conduct, free will and the importance of following the example and teachings of Jesus.

Modern gospel presentations often connect the post-Reformation idea of faith with penal substitution. They teach that Christ's atonement becomes effective for us because we believe in, trust in, and rely on what Christ has done for us. The problem is that this connection makes little sense. To illustrate, consider another mortgage analogy:

> You are not making your mortgage repayments. The mortgage firm will no longer tolerate your lack of payment, and so they plan to repossess your house. I take pity on you, go to the firm, and pay off your mortgage. As a result they will no longer re-possess your house. Your house has been saved. I then go to you and say "Good news! I have paid your mortgage. They are not going to repossess your house."

You might believe me, or you might doubt my words. Yet, no matter what you believe, the firm will not repossess your house. I have *really* paid your mortgage – regardless of your beliefs about this act. The action of the firm does not depend on you believing, trusting or relying on me or my payment for you. Your faith is simply not necessary in order for me to save you from your debt.

Now consider penal substitution, for which people often use the paying off of a debt as an analogy. If Jesus has indeed saved us by paying our debt on the cross, it follows that our debt is now paid and that God will not judge us negatively. Jesus would have paid our debt regardless of whether or not we believed that he had paid it. Therefore, God would have no need to punish us even if we did not believe in, trust in, or rely upon what Jesus did on the cross. Consider this scene:

> A person who does not believe the theory of penal substitution dies and finds herself at the final judgment. God says, "You may enter heaven if you wish." She asks, "Why are you letting me into heaven? Don't I deserve punishment?" God could re-spond, "Yes, you did, but Jesus took your punishment, paid your debt, and satisfied the need for justice. So I can let you in, if you want to come."

The above scene seems quite plausible given the idea of penal substitution, without any need for 'saving faith'. It illustrates that penal substitution need not require any belief in it to be effective. Likewise, several of the other views in church history about Christ's work did not require faith in order to be effective. We saw earlier that, for the first millennium, Christians saw the moral transformation of humanity as Christ's main work. Yet some added extra ideas about what Christ had accomplished. We saw that Athanasius, for example, added the idea that Christ had satisfied the law of sin and death. In Genesis, God had warned that sin would lead to death, and Athanasius read this statement as a promise that *obliged* God to kill all who sinned. Athanasius believed that, because Christ's death had satisfied this law of sin and death, God was no longer obliged to kill sinners. Athanasius saw this satisfaction as effective automatically for everyone. It did not require belief or 'faith' in order to be effective, and *regardless* of what sinners believed, it removed the obligation God had to kill them. Athanasius did not alter the underlying paradigm of salvation current at that time. He believed that final judgment depended on conduct, and thus he believed that people needed to live godly lives. He had no notion of "resting in the finished work of Christ." His idea that Christ had satisfied the law of sin and death stood alone, and did not affect his other doctrines. It had no connection at all to notions of faith or belief, and its effectiveness did not depend on these. In exactly the same way, logically, penal substitution does not require faith or belief to become effective. 'Faith' has become tied to the theory of penal substitution over the centuries, but not because of any inherent or biblical connection between the ideas. This logical disconnection is a symptom of the key salvation doctrines changing slowly over time. If we return to the original Christian views of salvation, we find that the modern idea of 'saving faith' has little place.

Athanasius' perspective, however, provides an example of how ideas like penal substitution can be *added* to the paradigm of moral transformation outlined in this book. Although the doctrine of penal substitution seems to have little biblical or historical support, it has become a central doctrine of post-Reformation tradition. It is possible to hold the basic paradigm outlined in this book and *also* believe that Christ has taken the penalty for human sin through his death on the cross. In such a view, Christ's death could have been necessary for God to forgive those who repented. This idea can be held alongside the basic paradigm presented in this book. Similarly, the idea of needing 'faith', in the modern sense of the word, does not interfere with the paradigm we have outlined. Roman Catholic doctrine, for example, speaks of salvation by faith and works. It emphasises the necessity of both having saving faith in Christ *and* practising the moral conduct needed for a positive final judgment. So, it is possible to believe the early Christian paradigm of salvation through moral transformation and also to consider penal substitution and the modern kind of faith important.

One doctrine, however, cannot rest alongside the paradigm of salvation through moral transformation outlined in this book. The Reformers denied the saving value of human conduct and character. Such a denial is fundamentally incompatible with the moral transformation paradigm. Post-Reformation ideas like "resting in the finished work of Christ" or "refraining from striving and relying on Christ alone" are completely incompatible with the early Christian paradigm we have outlined. Claiming that final judgment does *not* depend in any way on character and conduct directly contradicts it. Such a claim makes the teaching and example of Christ valueless for salvation. It nullifies the significance of imitating Christ for final judgment. Any moral teachings of Christianity would play no part in saving us from negative judgment. Moral conduct might still be desirable, and God might still command it. We could still learn from the teachings and example of Christ. Moral transformation might even be an inevitable consequence of working of the Holy Spirit. Yet claiming that final judgment does not depend on character makes all these of secondary importance. Whatever is needed to gain a positive final judgment becomes the most important focus, and the early Christian message of moral transformation becomes a message we need not actually follow. Quite simply, to deny that moral transformation matters for final judgment is to reject the early Christian message we have outlined here. In this respect, the post-Reformation paradigm of 'faith alone' is fundamentally incompatible with the paradigm of moral transformation. This incompatibility forces us to choose one view or the other on this matter. Either final judgment does *not* depend on our conduct and character, or it *does* depend on these. If it does *not*, then we must not overlook the real criteria for final judgment mistakenly. If it *does*, however, then our conduct and character are extremely important.

Conclusion

We have seen that the doctrine of penal substitution has serious biblical, historical, and theological problems. The idea is conspicuously absent from the New Testament writings, and they provide little basis for emphasising Jesus' death at the expense of his teachings and movement. Despite lengthy discussions of what Jesus achieved, the early Christian writers never mentioned the idea of penal substitution. Historical studies indicate that the theory arose gradually over centuries. At its core, penal substitution is based on a misunderstanding of God's forgiveness. Likewise, the modern doctrine of saving faith grew from a misunderstanding of the early Christian term for faithfulness, and it has no logical connection with penal substitution. We can no longer ignore the glaring inconsistency between these modern doctrines and the early Christian ideas.

Summary and Conclusion

How the Gospels present Jesus

Let us summarise briefly what we have covered. In Part 1, we explored the way in which the Gospels present Jesus and his activity in order to lay the groundwork for understanding the early Christian paradigm of salvation. We began by investigating the historical context of the Gospel accounts. We examined what it meant to live as an Israelite following the Jewish Torah in the 1st century. English translations often render the frequent New Testament references to the Torah as 'the Law'. This translation, however, fails to capture the real meaning of Torah. It referred to the entire Israelite way of life – their culture and customs, which they treasured as God-given. Israelites believed that, through following Torah, their nation maintained God's covenant with them and they lived in his favour. Variations of the Jewish ancestral traditions also existed, however, with different groups following slightly different sets of traditions. The spread of Greek culture (known as 'Hellenisation') influenced Israel deeply. When Israel came under foreign rule, the introduction of Greek culture challenged the Israelite way of life and led to conflict. It meant that many Israelites had to choose between continuing to follow the customs of their ancestors, or turning from their traditions and joining the 'modern' world. People used the labels 'Jew' and 'Greek' to distinguish the Israelites who lived by each set of customs. Many Jews resisted Greek influence and felt that they had to retain their traditions by all means possible in order to remain loyal to God. King Herod's massive spending on projects like a multi-decade renovation of the Jerusalem Temple had bankrupted the country. He revamped it in Greek style, making it the largest temple in the world. The Temple, once a symbol of the Jewish religion and God's reign, became a symbol of foreign influence and wealth in the eyes of the populace. The introduction of a monetary economy during this period replaced the previous barter systems gradually, causing serious hardship for the farming communities. Rich noblemen owned increasingly more land by taking it from families who defaulted on loans. A number of groups formed with different views about the appropriate response to these social changes. The Israelite response to foreign influence spanned the spectrum from welcoming 'progress' through to military resistance. It appears that the rich nobility tended to welcome the wealth and prestige that foreign dealings and influences brought, while the masses tended to resist the change. The majority of Jews longed for a return to an idealised past in which they had prospered as one people under God. The phrase 'God's reign', or 'the Kingdom of God', described this Utopian vision.

With this background in mind, we looked at the common themes in the four Gospel accounts in order to build an accurate view of Jesus' life and activity. The Gospels record Jesus engaging in conflicts with various groups, and these conflicts provide a useful way to understand Jesus' activity to address the intertwined social, political, and religious issues that confronted Israel. Much of the content of all four Gospels concerns these conflicts:

1. Economics and wealth

We saw that many passages concern issues of wealth and poverty. Economic issues appear repeatedly within Jesus' ministry and form one of its central themes. Jesus encouraged people to share their possessions. He emphasised the importance of valuing other people rather than material wealth. Many of his teachings on kindness and love related to how the rich should care for the poor. Jesus wanted a society in which the rich did not exploit those struggling in poverty, but instead shared their wealth out of love. To this end, he gave clear instructions on these matters to his disciples, tax collectors, rich rulers and the crowds.

2. Ritual and moral purity

The Gospels make it clear that Jesus objected to the views and goals of certain groups within Israel. In particular, he objected to the view held by the Pharisees that greater ritual purity would solve Israel's problems. Jesus did not value ritual purity very highly, and warned that an increased emphasis on ritual purity would cause even greater suffering for many of those who suffered already. Ritual purity codes excluded people deemed 'impure,' and often these people were the social outcasts who most needed assistance from others. Jesus tried to shift the emphasis from ritual purity (excluding others) to moral purity (helping others). He taught that God did not want ritual purity, but wanted people to care for others and help those in need. Jesus taught people to care also for cultural enemies. He challenged the ritual purity laws often when they stood in the way of what was morally right, such as helping those in need on the Sabbath. Many Gospel passages reflect the importance Jesus placed on helping others and caring for those in need.

3. Social equality

Jesus showed little regard for the accepted social hierarchy. He taught instead that people should treat one another equally. Jesus encouraged a community that honoured serving others more than being served, contradicting the accepted notions of status entirely. He taught that, in God's coming Kingdom, all would have equal status. No longer would some people be 'first' and others 'last' in the social order. He also appears to have treated the women around him on par with the men, ignoring the culture's traditional gender roles and the supposed subservient status of women.

4. The Temple system

The Gospels record Jesus' conflict with the Temple authorities. Jesus criticised the exploitation for which the Temple system had become a vehicle. He pronounced God's judgment against this system and taught that true purity before God involved caring for others rather than following Temple ritual.

5. Physical and spiritual affliction

Much of the Gospels tell of how Jesus cared especially for the sick and treated their physical and spiritual afflictions. At that time, sick people who could not work risked starvation, or else imposed a large burden on their families. Concepts of ritual purity excluded many sick people from society entirely, worsening their suffering. The care Jesus showed for the sick fitted with his compassion for those in need. At the time, many people thought that demonic forces caused sickness, and they saw Jesus' cures as victories over those demonic forces. The Gospel writers depicted Satan opposing Jesus' ministry as Jesus attended to people's physical and spiritual afflictions.

These themes together paint a picture of Jesus as the leader of a revolutionary movement for social and personal reform. We saw that Jesus did not work alone toward this cause. He recruited followers who joined in his cause to usher in God's Kingdom – a better way of life. He trained them to continue his work towards that end. Under Jesus' charismatic leadership, his movement grew quickly. For this reason, the religious leaders opposed him and his movement. These leaders challenged his authority, denying that he had any mandate from God to act as he did. Jesus, in turn, criticised the religious leaders, and argued publicly against their views. He became renowned widely as a popular prophet who claimed divine authority for his teachings. Gospel accounts indicate that many people saw him as a prophetic teacher, like Elijah of old, sent by God to guide Israel through hard times. His miracles confirmed to them his divine mandate. Jesus apparently tried to keep his movement secret at first – wise at a time when both the Romans and Jewish authorities used military force against revolutionaries and dissent movements – but knew that his movement could not remain hidden from the authorities forever. He knew that they would also oppose his followers, and so he warned his followers of future persecution and encouraged them to remain strong. He instructed them to remain faithful to his teachings, and promised great rewards to those who did so.

We saw how eventually the authorities put Jesus to death because they felt threatened by him and his movement. The Gospel writers present his death as a martyrdom. Before his death, Jesus encouraged his disciples to persevere in the face of persecution. After his death, his followers continued his movement courageously despite the risk to themselves because of their conviction that God had resurrected Jesus from death. Their belief in his resurrection convinced them that God had endorsed Jesus and his movement, and that he would reward them after death. Hence, they saw it as worthwhile to follow Jesus.

The Gospels accounts seem to have been written in order to tell of Jesus' ministry and teachings and thus encourage readers to follow him. They recount Jesus' way of life, his teachings and his commitment to the cause to show what it means to follow him. They also tell of how he encouraged his disciples and his resurrection by God. In these ways, the Gospels themselves motivated the early Christians to follow Jesus.

Doctrines of the early Christians

In Part 2, we turned to explore some central early Christian doctrines that together formed their paradigm of salvation. We devoted particular attention to those ideas that differed from modern post-Reformation views. We began by looking at the topic of final judgment, finding that the early Christians believed that God would judge people based on how they lived their lives. This belief had flourished within Jewish thinking in the Inter-Testamental period. In times of persecution, Jewish writers looked forward to God's justice in the afterlife to balance the injustice of the present. They expressed strong confidence that God would judge them favourably and judge their enemies negatively. The doctrine of final judgment was to them a hope of salvation rather than a reason for fear. This reflected their belief that God did not require complete perfection. They thought they could and did meet the standards that God required. We looked at many clear passages throughout the New Testament demonstrating that the early Christians adopted fully this Jewish idea of a final judgment in the afterlife. Many passages in the Gospels and in the writings of Paul, Peter and John show that the early Christians taught this idea of a final judgment based on character and conduct. The Christians only changed this Jewish doctrine by denying that Jewish ancestry or adherence to the Torah influenced final judgment. Instead, the Christians emphasised that final judgment depends solely on moral character and conduct, not on ancestry or customs. Paul used this idea to argue that God will judge both Jews and Greeks without partiality. We also looked at Christian writings from the first few centuries after the New Testament. These, too, showed that early Christians held a conduct-based final judgment as one of their core doctrines. This belief motivated them powerfully to pursue moral behaviour.

The early Christians, therefore, wanted to know what correct moral conduct really looked like, since people disagreed on the kinds of conduct that were correct. The resurrection of Jesus proved to them that God approved of the way of life Jesus had taught and exemplified. Jesus' message had been controversial during his lifetime, but his followers saw his resurrection as the once-and-for-all proof that Jesus' teachings did have divine approval. The early Christians also took Jesus' resurrection as an indication that God had appointed him to be the judge at the final judgment. In light of both these ideas, the resurrection of Jesus convinced the early Christians that Jesus had revealed true correct conduct. They reasoned that, by living according to his example and teachings, they could therefore attain a positive final judgment and resurrection. This conviction inspired them to imitate his example and obey his teachings. We saw that this theme of imitating Jesus by following his example and obeying his teachings features prominently throughout the New Testament. The early Christians used a variety of synonymous phrases, including 'in Christ', to speak of imitating and following Jesus. This concept also lay behind their language of shared kinship with Christ, sharing his life and death, and 'abiding' with him. In examining quotes from several early Christian writers, we saw that the concept of imitating Jesus continued to have a major role in the early Christian tradition.

The early Christians emphasised greatly the moral way of life that Jesus had taught, since the reward was a positive final judgment and resurrection. We saw that most of the New Testament books exhort moral behaviour and present positive final judgment as the ultimate reward and incentive. They encourage their readers to live rightly and warn them that failure to do so may bring a negative final judgment. Sometimes these writings encourage their readers to look forward to the hope of a glorious resurrection and rewards from God for doing good. Other passages warn readers of God's wrath and fury to come if they do not repent. They teach Christians to work to obtain a positive final judgment with great effort and striving, rather than taking this task lightly. New Testament writers like Paul called for a wholehearted effort by using analogies of athletes striving for a prize or warriors arming for battle. These writers also expressed concern that Christians might not continue steadfastly in their new way of life and thus not attain a positive final judgment. Hence, the New Testament writers exhorted Christians repeatedly to persevere in order to obtain a positive judgment. Their firm belief in a final judgment based on character and conduct seems to have motivated these moral exhortations. The New Testament writers always pointed to love for others as the central principle behind moral Christian teachings, and Christian disciples learned to care for the marginalised, poor, sick and disadvantaged. In following Jesus, they learned to value social equality and reject hierarchical social categories just as Jesus had done. The New Testament presents love for others repeatedly as the characteristic teaching of Christianity and the most important doctrine of all.

From there, we looked at how some of the other New Testament concepts fit into this basic framework. The first of these concepts was 'faith'. Post-Reformation teaching has misconstrued 'faith' (*pistis*) as being primarily about belief, and contrasted it to effort or conduct. To the early Christians, pistis instead meant *faithfulness* and included the ideas of effort and conduct. They understood this faithfulness to mean following Jesus' example and teachings and working towards his same vision of the Kingdom of God. We saw how Greek writings from around the 1st century used pistis to speak of faithfulness in the sense of steadfast loyalty, allegiance, commitment and perseverance. We argued that, in the New Testament passages about having 'faith' towards Jesus, this word refers to faithfulness to Jesus and his cause. A number of recent scholarly studies support this conclusion. We gathered further evidence that pistis towards Jesus meant faithfulness, obedience, perseverance, and loyalty by looking at New Testament passages that use synonyms or antonyms for the word. The early Christians did not seem to think of 'faith' as belief, trust and reliance on Jesus to save them. Rather they saw faithfulness as a steadfast commitment and obedience to Christ and his teachings. This faithfulness involved great effort. They did not contrast 'faith' with human effort and conduct.

Instead, the two went hand in hand. In a more detailed analysis of the word pistis, we outlined a framework to help us understand when and why pistis can take on different meanings. We argued that, when it expresses a relationship between one person and another, it indicates faithfulness. All the theologically important New Testament passages seem to involve people directing pistis toward Jesus or God. So in these passages, therefore, we should interpret the word with its normal and very heavily attested meaning of faithfulness. The evidence does not support a post-Reformation view that pistis refers to 'belief, trust or reliance' in ideas about what Jesus achieved for people. As the modern scholarly findings on the meaning of pistis become more well-established, we can expect new English Bible versions to translate pistis as the word 'faithfulness' more often, rather than as 'faith' or 'belief'.

We went on to study Paul's writings about 'righteousness' and to address some of the prevalent misunderstandings about these writings. Many of his writings on this topic address the conflict within the early church over the importance of following the Jewish Torah. Paul's own life story reflected this conflict well. Paul grew up as a Pharisee, trained to follow Torah carefully rather than to follow Greek customs. The Pharisees believed that God had chosen the nation of Israel, set it apart, and given it the rules of Torah for holiness and purity. They felt that God would make Israel prosper only if all Israelites followed the Torah zealously. Jesus had angered the Pharisees by dismissing the purity rituals of the Torah. He taught that these rules created social exclusion, which harmed rather than helped people. Hence, these angered Pharisees sought the execution of Jesus. After Jesus' death, Paul began arresting Jesus' followers, convinced that their teaching and cause opposed God's will. Yet Paul was struck down by a vision of the resurrected Jesus. This vision convinced Paul that God had resurrected Jesus, and thus endorsed Jesus and his teachings. It was *Jesus*, not the Pharisees, who had correctly taught what God wanted, and Jesus taught that Israel need not follow the Torah zealously. This conviction led Paul into heated controversies with Jews and other Christians on this issue for the remainder of his life. In Paul's view, Jesus' ministry had demonstrated that the purity laws of the Torah had little importance in God's eyes. Rather, God wanted people to follow Jesus' example and teachings. Consequently, Paul taught that even those people who followed Greek customs could follow Jesus and thus become part of God's people.

Differences in customs caused friction between Paul's Greek converts and Jewish Christians. Paul had learned a vital principle from Jesus' teachings: followers of Jesus should love and care for one another as a cohesive community. To enable such complete fellowship, Paul argued that Jewish Christians should bend those regulations of Torah that prevented fellowship with the Greek Christians. Jews believed, however, that righteous people should follow Torah. Hence, Paul stressed throughout his writings that righteousness comes through following Jesus faithfully rather than through following the Torah. We saw that, in order to interpret his arguments accurately, we must understand the Greek term for righteousness, *dikaiosyne*, correctly. This ethical term means 'correct conduct', and it relates to the way in which we live. Studies of its usage in the Old Testament and other ancient texts have established this meaning firmly. Paul used this ethical term to explain how correct and loving conduct comes through imitating Jesus faithfully and following his teachings. People become 'righteous' through their faithfulness in the sense that they learn to live rightly by following the teachings and example of Jesus. In contrast, the particular customs and rituals of the Israelite traditions (the 'works of the Torah') do not in and of themselves lead to the behaviour that God desires. Thus, Paul wrote that righteousness comes through faithfulness and not through following Torah (the 'Law').

Some Christians today believe that people cannot attain such righteousness. They think that people cannot live up to God's behavioural standards even with the empowering of the Spirit and Jesus' teachings and example. We explained how such a view misinterprets some passages by Paul and the view of the early Christians in general. We saw that Paul borrowed the language of 'sinful flesh' from Greek popular philosophy, adopting such language to speak of how the message of Jesus leads people to live righteously through moral transformation. He did not teach that Christians are unable to live in a way that God considers righteousness. Rather, we showed how Paul held views that matched well with Jesus' message and the teachings of the other early Christians.

We outlined how the New Testament teachings regarding forgiveness fitted within the early Christian paradigm of salvation. Jesus and his followers maintained the Jewish idea of repentance and forgiveness. In this view, God forgives people if they repent from living wrongly and begin to live rightly. People's behaviour testifies to their moral character, and their current character matters to God. God does not hold past actions or behaviour against those people who truly repent. When people make major changes to their lives through the process of repentance, their previous behaviour no longer matches their current character. God therefore forgives without punishment the wrongs they did prior to their sincere repentance. Jews used the phrase 'repentance and forgiveness' to speak of this concept, and the early Christians adopted it in full. The New Testament authors endorsed this view in various ways throughout their writings.

On a related topic, we looked at the New Testament term often translated as 'grace', *charis*, and we showed how it corresponded with the other doctrines of the early Christians. Translating charis as 'grace' can be somewhat misleading, since scholars have shown that people in first-century society used charis to mean 'favour'. It could refer both to *having* someone's favour and to *doing* someone a favour. In the minds of the early Christians, God had done them a huge favour by sending Jesus to teach them and lead them into the right way to live. Jesus saved them from living in wrong ways, and consequently from a potentially negative final judgment. Thus, the favour God did in sending them Jesus led to their salvation. God did this favour for them while they were living wrongly, and they had not deserved such a favour. This gave them great confidence that, once they repented and followed Jesus, they truly had God's favour. Post-Reformation tradition has often understood 'grace' in a way that contrasts it to human effort. For the New Testament writers, however, God's favour involved sending Jesus to lead people into a right way of living. The appropriate response is therefore to make an effort to follow his example and teachings faithfully. Failing to make such an effort would be rejecting the favour God did by sending Jesus. Understood in this way, God's favour and human effort are entirely compatible, not opposed. People require both God's favour of sending Jesus and also their own effort in order to learn how to live as Jesus taught. The New Testament writers viewed God as gracious and loving. They believed his graciousness and love had motivated him to send Jesus to free people from the power of sinfulness and lead them into a righteous way of life. Understandably, the early Christians treasured this favour, yet it did not conflict with their other doctrines regarding final judgement and the importance of correct conduct and effort.

The importance of Jesus

Part 3 focussed on understanding the importance of Jesus for the early Christians. We looked first at the various ways in which the early Christians spoke of what Jesus had accomplished for them. The New Testament writers expressed the same basic ideas using a variety of terms and metaphors. We studied each of these in turn, and found that they described salvation in ways that all reflect a concern for moral transformation. Jesus saved people from sinfulness, transforming their lives morally. The New Testament writers drew on the metaphor of freedom from slavery to convey this salvation. They also used the phrase 'new life' to discuss the new pattern of conduct Jesus taught them. Metaphors of ritual purity provided another way in which to describe the morality taught by Jesus. In addition, they spoke of the moral transformation that Jesus brought as being a conquest and defeat of evil. All these ideas describe the reality of what Jesus achieved for his followers through the moral transformation he brought about in their lives.

The New Testament authors also used sacrificial language to write about Jesus and what he accomplished. Modern societies have long since ceased practising animal sacrifice and therefore many people today do not know how to interpret this kind of language, missing its connection with the moral transformation that Jesus had brought. In the last fifty years, however, scholars have gained a comprehensive understanding of sacrificial systems by studying sacrificial cultures throughout history and from around the world. We drew on this research to outline first the three main types of sacrifices in the ancient Israelite system: gifts, meals and purification rituals. Like many other cultures around the world, the way Israel understood its sacrificial system changed over time, moving away from magical ideas and towards moral ones. They increasingly used sacrificial language metaphorically to discuss ethical concepts of moral purity rather than ritual purity. The New Testament writers seem to have used sacrificial language almost exclusively to discuss morality rather than literal animal sacrifice. They used language of purification sacrifices to speak of the moral behaviour and transformation that following Jesus brought. They also used this language to describe what Jesus had accomplished. This language does not mean that their moral purification worked in the same way as ritual sacrifices. They did not believe that Christ's death functioned in the same manner as ancient purification rituals. Rather, their moral purification came through following the teachings and example of Jesus, who taught them how to live rightly.

The early Christians saw Jesus as a martyr. They coined the term 'martyr' to speak of Christian martyrdoms in the first few centuries AD, labelled Jesus as a martyr, and saw him as the supreme example of Christian martyrdom. The post-Reformation tradition seldom sees Jesus' death as a martyrdom; yet, as we showed, his death fits the definition of martyrdom in a very full and rich sense. The New Testament writers depicted Jesus' death as a martyrdom, and several scholars have noted the strong parallels between the Gospels and other ancient martyrdom accounts. The book of Revelation, written after the term 'martyr' had come into use, labels Jesus explicitly as a martyr. Most New Testament authors wrote prior to the common use of this term, however, so they used instead the traditional Greek and Jewish martyrdom language. Many scholars have observed that the "Christ died for us" phrases used by Paul to discuss Jesus' death are Greek martyrdom phrases. In addition, Paul compared Jesus directly to other martyrs, and used language very similar to other descriptions of martyrs by other writers in his culture. This evidence has led many scholars to conclude that Paul saw Jesus as a martyr. We examined the way in which the New Testament authors expounded on Jesus' death, and found that they linked it invariably to the goal of his life and ministry: moral transformation. When they discussed the meaning of Jesus' death, they pointed invariably to the freedom from sinfulness and moral transformation that Christ had brought them. The early Christians also looked back on Jesus' selfless obedience and faithfulness to God in the face of death as an example to imitate. As Jesus had loved others even though it cost him his life, so should they love others. Not only that; they saw his martyrdom for their sake as indicative of God's great love for them. God had sent Christ to help them at a great cost, and this great favour obliged the early Christians to respond appropriately by following Jesus' example and teachings, so that his martyrdom for their sakes would not be in vain. We investigated the idea that Jesus' death had a supernatural effect, but found little evidence that the early Christians believed such an idea.

The early Christians were convinced that the story of Jesus' life had not ended with his death. They believed that God had resurrected him, and they held his resurrection as one of the most important parts of their message. It seems to have provided them with crucial motivation to follow Jesus. The early Christians saw the resurrection of Jesus as proof that Jesus had divine mandate, and it convinced them his teachings were true and that following those teachings was right. The early Christians also saw Christ's resurrection as proof that they, too, could receive a resurrection through following him. The New Testament authors encouraged their readers often with this hope, especially when they warned of possible hardship and persecution. Early Christians believed that they too would attain a resurrection, and that following Jesus was therefore worth any cost.

In general, it seems that when the New Testament authors discussed what Jesus accomplished, they had in mind the moral transformation that he had brought to people's lives. They expressed the idea that he had freed them from sinfulness and lead them into righteousness in many ways. Their metaphors of slavery, adoption, new life and purification all express various aspects of this salvation from sinfulness that Jesus had brought. They saw Jesus' death as a martyrdom. Hence, they found its primary significance in the cause for which he had been killed, and in the people for whom he had given his life. To the early Christians, Jesus was many things: teacher, miracle-worker, prophet of God, leader, master, example, martyr, hero and saviour. They saw him as a God-sent leader of personal and social change, who led people together into a new way of life. His resurrection convinced them of his divine authority and message, and gave them hope of a resurrection if they followed him. Through his ministry, martyrdom, and resurrection, Jesus established a revolutionary new way of life. Jesus founded the Christian movement, and through it he transformed and continues to transform the lives of millions.

Ideas throughout history

Part 4 examined Christian ideas regarding salvation throughout history. Christian writings of the first few centuries provide strong additional evidence that the view we have outlined here captures the essence of the early Christian teachings on salvation. As we saw, many modern scholars have concluded that the Christians in the 2nd and 3rd centuries believed essentially the same doctrines that we have outlined above. These doctrines formed the teachings of the Apostolic Fathers, the Apologists and other theologians in these early centuries. Some scholars have noted that their beliefs do not agree with the post-Reformation teachings. We have shown, however, that these teachings match very closely both the message of Jesus as depicted in the Gospels and that of the early Christians.

We also outlined the way in which Christian doctrines began to change in the 3rd century and beyond. These doctrinal changes affected Christian thinking increasingly. We outlined how Augustine's own views changed significantly throughout the course of his life, and saw the ultimate influence of his new ideas. We traced the development of the idea that would become known eventually as 'penal substitution'. We showed how new ideas began to emerge after the doctrine of repentance and forgiveness was replaced by other views. We saw that, in the 11th century, the thinking of the time reshaped these ideas into a complete account of the work of Christ. The Reformers reworked that theory to fit with their judicial ideas in the 16th century, introducing the penal and substitutionary elements. The doctrines of imputed right-eousness and a modern idea of 'faith' also gained full expression in their thinking. Their theory of penal substitution has now become the most important doctrine for many Christians in the post-Reformation tradition.

The way in which the post-Reformation doctrines developed over centuries has left them riddled with inconsistencies and problems. The most central doctrine, penal substitution, is especially problematic. If we trust the Gospel accounts, the message preached by Jesus and his disciples contained no mention of Christ's death or any such atonement theory. Not only that, but history also indicates that doctrines such as penal substitution originated not with Jesus and the early Christians, but through a gradual process that only began centuries later. We showed that penal substitution was developed to solve the problems created through misunderstanding God's forgiveness, as penal substitution is inconsistent with the biblical view of God's forgiveness. The modern ideas surrounding the post-Reformation idea of 'faith' also present problems. In general, the post-Reformation tradition seems to have lost the biblical meaning of faith – faithfulness. 'Saving faith' now focusses on believing in, trusting in and relying on the idea that Christ made atonement on our behalf. The logic connecting 'faith' with penal substitution is tenuous. Post-Reformation teachings seem to have sandwiched 'faith' together with penal substitution without solid biblical or logical reasons. The historical, biblical, and logical considerations we reviewed thus challenge us strongly to reconsider the post-Reformation view. Nevertheless, we explored how it is possible to hold the view of penal substitution *in addition* to the moral transformation paradigm of the early Christians. In contrast, we outlined why the doctrine of a final judgment based on 'faith' rather than on character and conduct is incompatible with the message of the early Christians.

Salvation through moral transformation

We have covered a diverse range of topics in this book. Let us tie these ideas together to summarise briefly the early Christian view of salvation. For the early Christians, salvation centred on the moral transformation of individuals, communities and societies that Jesus brought. We can summarise their idea of salvation as follows:

Jesus lived in a time and place of cultural and political unrest. Laws and customs often disadvantaged the common people, and society marginalised and neglected many. Families and communities were losing the bonds of solidarity, and those who fell through the cracks of the social network had little support. Meanwhile, the people in power prospered by exploiting the less fortunate. They wedged the social classes further apart at the expense of those who had no way in which to escape the trap of their society.

Jesus wanted to change all that. He envisioned a new way to live that would mend many of the most pressing issues in their society – a way in which God wanted people to live. He saw that people needed to cross the social, religious, and cultural boundaries of the day in order to truly love each other. Therefore, he challenged the rich to share their wealth with the poor, to value the people in need, and to take seriously God's instructions to love others. He taught that love for others rather than rituals determined true purity, and he called people to avoid allowing purity customs to prevent them from caring for those in need. In a society where everyone had their place in the social hierarchy, Jesus advocated equal status. He criticised the way in which the Temple system exploited people and circumvented it by teaching people to live according to a code of moral purity, not ritual purity. Jesus spent his time teaching this new way of life and exemplifying it among the socially disadvantaged, healing their diseases and changing their ways of thinking. Consequently, the public saw him as a divinely appointed prophetic teacher who brought a message of personal and social reform.

For this cause, Jesus brought together a group of followers who would help this movement to gain more momentum. Jesus became the public leader of a controversial movement. Those whom Jesus helped welcomed him as a prophet and a revolutionary; but those who stood to lose from his teachings and movement considered him a dangerous rebel. Jesus' activities threatened the authority and privilege of those in power. He knew the dangers that he and his disciples faced because of this conflict, and he encouraged his disciples to remain committed and to persevere with his cause in the face of opposition or even death. He foresaw that the Pharisees, Scribes, High Priests, Elders, and finally the Roman procurators would view him as a threat requiring elimination. Their interests conflicted with Jesus' vision of a reformed society without oppression, in which people would live in a way characterised by love, kindness and community solidarity. Because of this conflict, they killed him.

After Jesus' death, however, his followers claimed that God had resurrected him from the dead, and that they had seen him alive. In the minds of the early Christians, Jesus' resurrection vindicated him, his message and his movement. It proved to followers of Jesus that his message was correct and convinced them that God would judge them favourably and reward them with resurrection. The cross that symbolised Jesus' martyrdom became a powerful reminder that his vision was indeed worth living and dying for. Spurred on by his martyrdom and resurrection, the early Christians fully embraced Jesus' vision and way of life. They worked towards creating the kind of society he had envisioned. Their challenge to join Jesus' movement lies at the heart of both the Gospel accounts and the early Christian message.

Imitating Jesus' example and following his teachings formed the core of the Christian practice. Those 'in Christ' (Christians) lived by the same moral principles that he had taught and exemplified. Their central principles included love, care for the disadvantaged, fairness, equality and the sharing of wealth. Jesus had focussed on these same issues in his teachings. His followers continued his focus on living a morally virtuous life, free of the moral vices that would threaten their own good and the good of their communities. Early Christians also exhorted and encouraged each other frequently toward the moral behaviour taught by Jesus. Because they lived in this way, they had confidence that God would judge them positively and reward them with a resurrection after death. This hope gave them strength to persevere in the face of sometimes fierce opposition.

The early Christians stressed frequently the idea of remaining faithful to Jesus' message and cause. For them, this is what it meant to have 'faith' toward Jesus. Remaining faithful to Jesus involved more than simply believing things about what he did and taught. Instead, it meant following his teachings and example loyally and faithfully, and persevering with that commitment. Faithful disciples lived in the way in which Jesus taught and exemplified, sharing his goal of renewing society to become one characterised by love and godliness.

Not all people who heard Jesus' message agreed that it represented the right way in which to live. Many Jews felt that God's measure of righteousness was the Torah, and to live rightly meant to live by a certain interpretation of the Torah. Paul and the other early Christians sought to persuade them otherwise. They argued that Jesus exemplified and taught the way of life that God considers righteous, and pointed to Jesus' resurrection as proof. According to their argument, if people faithfully follow Jesus, God will consider them righteous also. Therefore, the early Christians argued that righteousness comes not through following the Torah but through following Jesus and his teachings faithfully.

Those in the early Christian communities who had experienced massive positive changes in their lives as a result of joining the community gave thanks to God. They celebrated and praised the favour that God had done for them by revealing this way of life through Jesus. These early Christians thanked God regularly for leading them into a righteous way of life that had tangible benefits for them and for their community during their lives, especially for those who had been poor or social outcasts. It also provided the hope of a resurrection. These Christians thanked God for his readiness to forgive them for their former errant ways of life. He would not judge them according to how they used to live. Forgiven of their past wrongs, they had confidence that God would judge them favourably, and, ultimately, reward them with resurrection, because they lived according to Jesus' teachings and example.

In teaching and showing the early Christians the right way in which to live, Jesus had saved them from all the harmful behaviours and attitudes of their past, leading them instead into a way of life that united them in communities of loving support. Jesus' followers received salvation from living in ways of which God disapproved, and gained the confidence of a positive final judgement and the reward of resurrection. Jesus had saved them from the captivity of their wrong ways of living, and had given them a new way in which to live righteously in God's sight. In this way, Jesus led Christians to triumph over evil and wrongdoing, so that they could again live as people worthy to be called children of God.

In this book, we have worked through a large amount of evidence in support of the view we present above. Yet more evidence comes from considering the view in its entirety. It joins together a wide variety of conclusions by modern scholars and finds them to be in harmony with the Gospels, Paul's letters, and the rest of the New Testament. This view is consistent and explains the New Testament content well. If the early Christians believed this view, then we would expect them to write about the very topics we find in the New Testament. It explains why the Gospel writers, Paul and the other New Testament authors wrote the things they did. Lastly, but most importantly, it paints a simple and powerful picture of a message that people in the early centuries would have really heard as good news: "We have discovered the way God wants you to live, and it brings great rewards. It is the way Jesus taught and exemplified – and we can help you to live it."

Made in the USA
Middletown, DE
18 December 2018